Ethnicity and Human Rights in Canada

SECOND EDITION

Ethnicity and Human Rights in Canada

SECOND EDITION

Evelyn Kallen

Toronto   Oxford   New York
OXFORD UNIVERSITY PRESS
1995

Oxford University Press
70 Wynford Drive, Don Mills, Ontario M3C 1J9

Oxford New York
Athens Auckland Bangkok Bombay
Calcutta Cape Town Dar es Salaam Delhi
Florence Hong Kong Istanbul Karachi
Kuala Lumpur Madras Madrid Melbourne
Mexico City Nairobi Paris Singapore
Taipei Tokyo Toronto

and associated companies in
Berlin Ibadan

Oxford is a trademark of Oxford University Press

Canadian Cataloguing in Publication Data

Kallen, Evelyn, 1929–
    Ethnicity and human rights in Canada

2nd ed.
Includes bibliographical references and index.
ISBN 0–19–541079–3

1. Civil rights – Canada.   2. Minorities – Canada.
I. Title.

JC599.C2K34 1995   323.1′71   C94–932210–5

TABLE OF CONTENTS

DIAGRAMS

ACKNOWLEDGEMENTS

I wish to acknowledge the understanding support provided to me in the preparatory stage of revising this book by my colleagues at the Human Rights Research & Education Centre, Faculty of Law, University of Ottawa. During my tenure as Chair in Human Rights (1989-90) at the Centre, I was afforded the opportunity to interact with and to learn from a variety of scholars and practitioners dedicated to the pursuit of human rights.

I also want to express my appreciation for the access granted me to the invaluable resources of Human Rights Library at the Centre and to the aid of a graduate research assistant. Many thanks to Magda Seydegart, Bill Black, Doug Williams, Iva Caccia, Richard Cholewinski and all the others.

And, most importantly, I wish to express my profound gratitude to my husband, David Hughes, for providing his many valuable insights on issues of race and racism, and for honouring my right to privacy for so many hours, over the last four years, when I cloistered myself in my study, with only my computer for company, in the process of revising this book.

EVELYN KALLEN
January 1994.

PREFACE

At the time of writing the 1982 version of this book Canadians were struggling to cope with the exigencies of an embattled economy, increased threats of separation by Quebec and the Western provinces, a visible expanding population of non-white immigrants, and pressing demands by aboriginal peoples for sovereignty and a just share of Canada's natural resources at a time when the nation's energy crisis cried out for large scale northern development. All of these and other factors converged to create a backlash in public opinion, marked, in its most extreme form, by racist clamour for a return to a 'White Canada'.

It was within the context of this volatile social climate that the human rights message of the book assumed a sense of urgency.

As I thought about writing this second edition of the book, some ten years later, I was struck with a sense of *déjà vu*. What has really changed?

Our economy is experiencing a recession, Quebec is still deliberating on the sovereignty option, aboriginal peoples are intensifying their still unmet demands for self-government, organized hate groups have stepped up their racist hate propagandizing activities, and the backlash against non-white immigrants and refugees has taken a most insidious turn in the escalation of racist demonstrations by members of increasing numbers of White Power (and anti-Semitic) groups such as the Ku Klux Klan and the Aryan Nations Church.

Despite vastly increased legal protection for human rights across Canada in the post-Charter decade, and, perhaps, as a backlash against increased recognition and protection of the human rights of minorities in this country, racism continues to ravage the multicultural fabric of Canadian society. This unsettling observation persuaded me that the human rights message of the original book needed to be forcefully restated and explicitly updated.

In briefest terms, the message is this: humankind is one. In biological terms, all members of humankind belong to the same biological species, *Homo sapiens*. Racial divisions in themselves present no barriers to human reproductive success, hence racial variations on the human theme are irrelevant for the ultimate question of the survival of the human species. Moreover, among the most salient features shared by all members of humankind is a high degree of adaptability. Throughout the ages, this particular characteristic has enabled humankind to successfully spread out and adapt to virtually all of the disparate environments in the world. Indeed, through vast developments in culture, another uniquely human feature, humankind has ventured beyond earthly frontiers, utilizing scientific and technological advances to explore the moon and outer space. Paradoxically, this very adaptability, the hallmark of the human species, has led to the creation of diverse (and sometimes mutually antagonistic) ethnocultures whose ethnocentric biases render salient the racial divisions of humankind.

When invidious distinctions based on assumed or perceived racial or ethnocultural differences are used to justify the denial of human rights of members of particular human groups, racism rears its ugly head.

From a human rights perspective, the challenge for humankind posed by ethnocultural diversity is, first, to recognize and celebrate the affinities among all human beings as members of the same human species and, second, to foster a global climate of respect and tolerance for ethnocultural differences, in order to enable human beings, as such, to interact amicably across group boundaries.

In order to protect both the individual human rights of all persons as members of humankind, and the collective, cultural rights of all ethnocultural communities as distinct collectivities, international human rights instruments have been developed by the United Nations to serve as moral guidelines for human rights legislation within states. Following international guidelines, Canada has enacted human rights statutes in virtually every jurisdiction across the country. At the time of writing the original version of this book, the Canadian Charter of Rights and Freedoms (Constitution Act 1982) had not yet been enacted. In the following decade, under the national, constitutional standard provided by the Charter, protection for human rights under statutory codes across Canada has been expanded and strengthened. Yet racism continues to flourish and thus to debase the very essence of human rights in Canada.

The question of central concern to me is: How do we account for the persistence of racism in the face of increasing legal protection for human rights? Clearly, one set of factors to be examined is the nature and effectiveness of human rights legislation in Canada. Here, we may ask: To what degree does the practice of human rights in Canada accord with the international principles which have informed Canadian human rights legislation?

This book adopts the principles of the International Bill of Human Rights and related UN covenants as the level of ideology for human rights issues. This is not to say that these principles are absolute or that they leave nothing further to be desired. Indeed, international human rights principles are continuously evolving as nations reconsider them and develop ever newer covenants to more explicitly protect the human rights of persons and groups throughout the globe. What we are adopting as the level of ideology, then, is the currently agreed-upon human rights principles of member states of the United Nations. Within this normative frame of reference, the current state of ethnic relations, racism, and human rights in Canada will be analysed.

Outline of Chapters

In the Introduction, we will draw upon the provisions of international human rights instruments in order to develop a comprehensive, human-rights oriented conceptual framework for the analysis of ethnicity and human rights throughout the book. In Chapter One, we will critically assess the biological concept of race and we will demonstrate that it is in the *unity* of the human species—over and above arbitrary racial divisions—that the biological roots of human rights are grounded. We then will examine the way in which the *socially constructed* concept of race (as opposed to its scientific counterpart) is used by dominant authorities to vindicate racist ideologies. In Chapter Two, we will analyse the conceptual foundations of racism and we will demonstrate the ways in which racist ideologies are employed by dominant authorities to justify violations of the human rights of members of racial and ethnic minorities. In Chapters Three and Four, we will delineate the key variables affecting patterns of intra-ethnic and inter-ethnic relations and processes of ethnic identity formation. Here, we will show how racist-motivated violations of ethnic minority rights impact upon dominant/subordinate ethnic relationships and ethnic identities. In Chapter Five, we will examine the key dimensions of systems of social stratification. We then will demonstrate how human rights violations, predicated on unequal power relations between dominant and subordinate populations, lead to the social construction of ethnic and other minorities. In Chapter Six, we will analyse the vertical Canadian mosaic, Canada's ethnic stratification system, and we will consider the part played by violations of ethnic minority rights in creating and sustaining the subordinate and inferiorized status of racial and ethnic minorities within the established system. In Chapter Seven, we will show how racist policies, leading to violations of minority rights, impede the processes of ethnic integration of various racial and ethnic minorities in Canada. In Chapter Eight, we will consider the evolution of ethnic minority protest in Canada and we will examine current minority rights movements among aboriginal peoples (toward aboriginal nationhood), immigrant (multicultural) minorities (toward a truly multicultural and anti-racist Canada) and Franco-Québécois (toward independence). Finally, in Chapters Nine and Ten, we will examine the development of the legal framework of (statutory and constitutional) human rights protection in Canada and we will consider current minority rights claims, through an examination of cases brought before various human rights commissions, and before the Courts. In Chapter Ten, we also will trace the developments in legal protection for ethnic minority rights in Canada within the context of the continuing Constitutional debates. We will explicate the conflicting positions of representatives of aboriginal, immigrant (multicultural) and Franco-Québécois ethnic constituencies within the Constitutional amendment process. In conclusion, we will offer suggestions for changes in law and public policy designed to afford full recognition and protection for the fundamental individual and collective rights of all of Canada's racial and ethnic minorities.

Caveat

This book addresses human rights issues from a social scientific rather than a legal perspective. The concept of 'rights' is employed throughout this book to refer to 'just' or 'justifiable' claims for specified kinds of treatment made by or on behalf of individuals or social collectivities against other individuals, social groups, or the state. This concept should not be confused with the legal concept of rights, i.e., rights recognized as such in law.

E.K.
1994.

INTRODUCTION

Conceptualizing the Human Rights Approach: Guidelines from International Instruments

The human rights approach applied in the analysis throughout this book is based upon cardinal human rights principles informing the myriad provisions of international human rights instruments. The key international declarations drawn upon in the formulation of the author's theoretical design are addressed in the section to follow.

International Human Rights Instruments: Key Provisions of the International Bill of Human Rights and Special Covenants

On 9 December 1948, in response to the world's outrage when the full chronicle of Nazi atrocities during World War II became public knowledge, the United Nations General Assembly approved the Convention on the Prevention and Punishment of the Crime of Genocide (Entry into Force: 12 January 1951). On the very next day, 10 December 1948, the United Nations General Assembly adopted and proclaimed the Universal Declaration of Human Rights (UDHR), a declaration which represents a statement of principles or moral guidelines for the recognition and protection of fundamental human rights throughout the globe.

Articles 1 and 2 of the UDHR (see Appendix A) endorse the global principle of the unity of humankind. They set out the three cardinal principles of human rights—freedom, equality, and dignity—as rights and freedoms everyone is entitled to without distinction of any kind. The twenty-eight articles to follow delineate particular rights and freedoms exemplifying the three central principles.

Since its proclamation, the Universal Declaration has had international impact, influencing national constitutions and laws, as well as international declarations such as the United Nations Declaration on the Elimination of All Forms of Racial Discrimination (1963) and the International Convention on the Elimination of All Forms of Racial Discrimination (1965). This impact notwithstanding, the UDHR represents only a general statement of ideals. It is morally but not legally binding on member states of the United Nations. Some countries sought a more forceful declaration which would establish binding obligations on the part of member states. As a result, two additional Covenants were drawn up and came into force in 1976. Their provisions, however, apply only to those member states that have decided to ratify them. Less than half of the member states, including the United States, have not ratified either covenant. Canada, however, has ratified both.

The first covenant, the International Covenant on Economic, Social and Cultural Rights (ICESCR) deals primarily with collective *societal* rights—defined as rights which are due to all people of a society and which are the responsibility of governments to provide. The second Covenant, the International Covenant on Civil and Political Rights (ICCPR), deals with individual rights—freedoms and responsibilities which all individual citizens must be allowed to exercise.

The International Covenant on Economic, Social and Cultural Rights adopts a collective societal or nation-wide perspective, which puts the onus on governments to provide adequate living conditions for all persons. The Covenant recognizes that all persons have a right to work, to fair wages, to social security, to freedom from hunger, to health and education, and to the formation of and membership in trade unions. While considerable time may be required, especially for developing countries, to implement all of these rights, nations choosing to ratify the Covenant are expected to initiate appropriate legal measures following ratification.

The International Covenant on Civil and Political Rights adopts an individual perspective, which places the onus on nations and judiciaries to protect all individual citizens against cruel, inhuman, and degrading treatment. This Covenant recognizes the right of every person to life, liberty, security, and privacy. It prohibits slavery, guarantees the right to a fair trial, and protects against arbitrary arrest or detention. It recognizes freedom of expression, freedom of association, and the rights to peaceful assembly and emigration.

These rights and freedoms guaranteeing protection to the individual include protection from abuses by governments. The burden of responsibility to uphold individual freedoms therefore lies not with governments but with the judicial system.

Nations that ratify this Covenant are expected to introduce laws which will reflect its provisions. Canada has taken measures to fulfil its commitment by enacting human rights legislation at both provincial and federal levels of jurisdiction and by entrenching a Charter of Rights and Freedoms in the Canadian Constitution (1982).

The Optional Protocol to the ICCPR provides individual citizens with direct recourse to the United Nations (UN). Persons who believe that their rights as specified in the Covenant have been violated can state their case before the UN Human Rights Committee. Such persons must first have exhausted all legal avenues within their own country. To date, Canada is one of only a small number of the nations signing the Covenant which has ratified the Optional Protocol.

In 1978, the UDHR and the two later covenants (ICCPR and ICESCR) were incorporated into the International Bill of Human Rights (IBHR).

The major thrust of international human rights instruments has been to endorse the principle of the global *unity* of humankind and to afford protection for the fundamental rights and freedoms of individuals.

Notwithstanding this observation, there are a number of important provisions which can be seen to endorse the global principle of group *diversity* and to afford protection for collective cultural rights and for categorical rights.

Collective Cultural Rights

Unique among international instruments (Magnet 1989: 746) is the provision for *minority rights* found under article 27 of the ICCPR. This article states that:

> In those states in which ethnic, religious or linguistic minorities exist, persons belonging to such minorities shall not be denied the right, in community with the other members of the group, to enjoy their own culture, to profess and practice their own religion, or to use their own language.

Magnet points out that legal interpretation of this article has recently shifted from a restrictive stance which limited its application to *individual* members of historically *well-established* minorities and imposed only *negative* obligations (non-interference) on ratifying states, to a broader stance which extends its application to *old* and *new* minorities *as collectivities* and which imposes *affirmative* obligations on ratifying states.

The latter interpretation of article 27 has gained considerable support with the recent adoption by the General Assembly of the United Nations, in plenary 18 December 1992, of the *Declaration on the Rights of Persons Belonging to National or Ethnic, Religious and Linguistic Minorities* (see Appendix D). In particular, Articles 4 through 7 of this declaration specify the obligations on ratifying States to take appropriate measures to protect the collective, cultural rights of minorities specified in the Declaration.

Collective Right to Self-Determination of Peoples

The collective right of self-determination of *peoples* is protected under the provisions of article 1 of both the ICESCR and the ICCPR. This article states:

> All peoples have the right of self-determination. By virtue of that right they freely determine their political status and freely pursue their economic, social and cultural development. (IBHR, 1978: 10)

Until quite recently, legal interpretation of this article has been based on a very narrow concept of 'people' which, in essence, equates 'people' with 'nation'. That is to say, the collective rights of peoples apply only to peoples (ethnic groups) whose cultural/territorial boundaries coincide with or have the potential to coincide with the boundaries of a state unit. Indeed, in its application under international law, the concept of peoples has been interpreted even more narrowly, so as to support the right to self-determination only in cases of non-self-governing territories formerly under Colonial rule by overseas states. This restrictive interpretation affords no support for the nationhood claims of peoples/nations living *inside* the territorial boundaries of recognized, sovereign states.

Over the last decade, however, largely in response to resolute lobbying by organizations and coalitions representing the world's 'internally colonized' aboriginal (indigenous) peoples, there has been increasing support for a broader interpretation of article 1 among international legal scholars.

A draft proposal for an International Covenant on the Rights of Indigenous Peoples was adopted in principle by the Third General Assembly of the World Council of Indigenous Peoples in May, 1981. This draft proposal incorporated the right to self-determination of peoples (under article 1) as a cardinal principle of the rights of aboriginal (indigenous) peoples. In response to this and other, parallel, declarations submitted by aboriginal organizations, in 1982, a United Nations working group on indigenous populations was established by the Sub-Commission on Prevention of Discrimination and Protection of Minorities. The mandate of the UN working group was to produce an international declaration on the rights of indigenous peoples for consideration by the General Assembly (Sanders 1989: 407). A preliminary document, the Draft Universal Declaration On Indigenous Rights, was introduced in August, 1988. While this draft recognizes the collective cultural and aboriginal rights of indigenous peoples as well as their 'collective right to autonomy in matters relating to their own internal and local affairs . . .' (Article 23, quoted in Sanders: 429) within the institutional structures of recognized states, it falls short of an explicit recognition of the right of self-determination. In response, aboriginal representatives are continuing to press for unambiguous recognition of the right to self-determination of aboriginal peoples in the declaration.

Ethnic Group Right to Freedom from Racial Discrimination and Group Defamation

The right of members of all racial and ethnic groups to freedom from the promotion of racial hatred is protected under article 20.2 of the ICCPR. This article states that 'Any advocacy of national, racial or religious hatred that constitutes incitement to discrimination, hostility or violence shall be prohibited by law' (UN, 1978: 11).

Under the provisions of international human rights instruments explicitly designed to prevent racial discrimination, namely, the United Nations Declaration on the Elimination of All Forms of Racial Discrimination (UNDEAFRD) and the

International Convention on the Elimination of All Forms of Racial Discrimination (ICEAFRD), two articles afford protection for the categorical right to freedom from racial discrimination and racial hatred. Article 2.3 (UNDEAFRD) and article 1.4 (ICEAFRD) allow special measures of affirmative action designed to redress past systemic discrimination for the sole purpose of securing adequate advancement of disadvantaged racial and ethnic minorities (UN 1978: 24-5). Article 4 (ICEAFRD) prohibits hate propaganda and enjoins states parties to declare illegal and an offence punishable by law all dissemination of ideas based on racial superiority or racial hatred and to declare illegal and prohibit all organizations promoting such ideas. This article protects the right of members of every racial or ethnic group to be free from racial discrimination and group defamation.

Canada has ratified the international human rights instruments containing these protections against racial discrimination and has enacted laws which endorse some of the provisions.[1]

The Legal Framework of Human Rights in Canada: Implications for Racial and Ethnic Minorities

The importance of human rights instruments, both at the international and the national levels, is that they provide standards upon which those who perceive that their rights have been violated can base claims. In Canada, the legal framework of human rights protection is based on a three-tiered system of standards governing human relations within the state.

International human rights instruments (IBHR and related covenants) apply to relations between states and provide the global standards to which all state legislation should conform. In keeping with the principles endorsed by international human rights instruments, Canada has enacted human rights legislation which prohibits discrimination on the grounds of race and ethnicity at all jurisdictional levels—provincial, federal and constitutional.

Constitutional rules apply to relations between governments within the state and provide the national standard to which all statutory laws should conform. In order to provide a national, constitutionally endorsed standard for human rights legislation throughout the country, Canada has enacted a Charter of Rights and Freedoms in its amended (1982) Constitution. In keeping with the non-discriminatory provisions of articles 1 and 2 of the UDHR, Canada has enacted the equality rights provisions of section 15 of the Charter under which discrimination on the specified grounds of race and ethnicity is prohibited. Moreover, in keeping with the international principle of collective cultural rights under the provisions of article 27 of the ICCPR, Canada has enacted section 27 of the Charter affording ethnic minorities constitutional protection for their 'multicultural' rights.

Statutory human rights legislation applies to relations between individuals and organizations within the state and should conform to the guarantees for human rights in the Charter and related constitutional provisions. Since the enactment of the Charter, Canada's provincial and federal human rights laws have been undergoing a process of amendment so as to bring their provisions into conformity with the Charter standard. For example, the constitutional provision for affirmative action under section 15(2) of the Charter has provided the catalyst for parallel, statutory legislation allowing affirmative remedies against the collective adverse impact of systemic discrimination for disadvantaged racial and ethnic minorities.

The Human Rights Approach: Conceptual Framework for Analysis

Fundamental human rights derive from the distinctive attributes shared by all members of humankind as a single species (*Homo sapiens*). Individual human rights represent the principle of biological unity, the oneness of all human beings as members of the same biological species. Collective human rights represent the principle of cultural diversity, the differentness of the unique ethnocultures developed by the various ethnic groups which, collectively, comprise the human species. Together, individual and collective human rights represent the twin global principles of human unity and cultural diversity.

As specified in the 1978 International Bill of Human Rights (IBHR) and related covenants, protections for individual and collective human rights essentially represent universal, *moral guidelines*, the global standards to which the laws of ratifying states should conform. What this means is that human rights principles are *prior to law*: laws themselves may violate or may endorse human rights principles.

When laws *endorse* human rights principles, then human rights become *legal* rights which can be claimed by individuals or groups who can provide evidence to show that their human rights have been violated. In other words, a legal framework of human rights protection allows those whose rights have been violated to bring forward claims for legal redress and recompense.

Individual human rights are rooted in the premise that all human beings are full and equal persons. All human beings, as such, have a fundamental right to life and to freedom, equality, and dignity in all life pursuits. Freedom to decide (self-determination), equality/equivalence of opportunity, and dignity of person can be conceptualized as 'natural rights' which accrue to every human being simply by virtue of belonging to the human species. Insofar as human rights are natural rights, they do not have to be earned; they can be claimed equally by all human beings regardless of differences among individuals in their particular abilities, skills, resources or other personal attributes, and regardless of differences in group status or class membership.

Individual human rights can be said to be inalienable human rights, but in their exercise, they are not absolute. For the exercise of each person's individual human rights is conditional upon non-violation of the rights of others. Human rights thus entail social responsibilities: each human being must respect the human rights of others.

Insofar as the human rights principles of freedom, equality, and dignity are conceived of as 'natural' rights, it may be argued that these principles have both an individual and a group-level dimension. As 'natural' rights, fundamental human rights principles apply not only to individual human beings but also to ethnocultural groups—for human (ethnocultural) diversity is as 'natural' a feature of humankind as is human (biological) unity. No human being is born or raised in a culture-free environment; all persons on this planet are moulded into human beings within a particular cultural context. From birth, they learn culturally specific and distinct ways of thinking and behaving—eating, talking, dressing, worshipping, and relating to others. As they grow up, their ethnocultural identity forms an integral component of their self-identity. As adults, some ethnic group members may shift their allegiance and affiliation to another cultural group, but, for most, self and ethnic group identities remain closely linked, even if only in a 'symbolic' sense.

From a human rights view, what this means is that offences against the ethnic community as a whole can be and often are experienced as offences against individual members. Accordingly, denial of ethnic group autonomy (the group's right to determine its collective cultural destiny) is experienced as a restriction on individual freedom of choice (oppression); denial of group-level equality of opportunity is experienced as a limitation on individual equality rights (neglect); and an affront to the ethnic group (group defamation) is experienced as a denial of the individual right to dignity of person (diminution). The argument, here, is that insofar as human unity and diversity are twin features of humankind, then the principles of 'natural' human rights apply not only to individual human beings but also to human groups.

The basic principle behind *collective cultural rights* is the right of ethnic communities *as collectivities* to legitimately and freely express their cultural distinctiveness. The distinctive elements of ethnocultures may be expressed in language, religion, politico-economic design, territorial links or any combination of these and/or other defining group attributes. Regardless of the specific cultural attributes emphasized at any given time, insofar as a people's ethnoculture is in itself consistent with human rights principles, every ethnic group has the collective right to develop, express and transmit through time its distinctive design for living (Kallen 1982: 14-17).

The one component of ethnicity which differentiates the kinds of collective claims that may be put forward by particular ethnic groups is that of territoriality. Internationally, a 'people' whose territorial/ethnocultural boundaries potentially or actually coincide with the geo-political boundaries of a state unit can be conceptualized as a 'nation'. As applied to ethnic groups within the boundaries of a given state unit, this interpretation is more problematic. Nevertheless, there is growing support among legal scholars not only for the view that all ethnic communities can claim collective cultural rights, but also for the argument that all ethnic communities which can demonstrate a continuing, integral association between its people, its ancestral territory, and its distinctive ethnoculture within the boundaries of a given state unit can claim *collective national rights* (nationhood claims).

Territoriality has an unique dimension in connection with the collective claims of aboriginal ethnic groups. From the aboriginal perspective, aboriginal right and title to land derive from occupancy and use (usufruct) by their ancestors 'from time immemorial'—as far back as any member of a particular aboriginal group can remember. Moreover, aboriginal rights are seen as derived from a collective form of land occupancy and use; they are collective rights: rights of aboriginal collectivities, not rights of individuals (Boldt and Long 1985: 17). Those aboriginal peoples whose ancestors never signed land cession treaties with State authorities whereby their aboriginal right and title were deemed, by the State, to be 'extinguished', can make claims based on *aboriginal rights*. Aboriginal peoples represented by living communities whose members continue to occupy and use their aboriginal lands and whose distinctive culture continues to be, at least in part, land-based, not only can claim *aboriginal* rights, but also can make *nationhood* claims.[2]

Categorical rights claims represent claims for redress against the collective adverse impact of past discrimination against members of a particular social category on the arbitrary basis of their (assumed) membership in that category. Insofar as group disadvantage has resulted from past discrimination against members of a social category *as a whole*, then individual or group-level claims for redress can be put forward. Such claims can be conceptualized as *categorical rights claims*. Because categorical claims do not address violations of collective, cultural rights, they may be put forward by representatives of social collectivities with or without distinctive cultures/subcultures.

Categorical rights claims may represent claims for redress against past categorical discrimination on the basis of ethnicity, nationality, race, religion, age, sex, sexual orientation, mental or physical disability, or other grounds. Any member of a specified social group or category who perceives that she or he or the group as a whole has experienced violations of the right/s to freedom, equal opportunity, or dignity on the arbitrary basis of (assumed) membership in the group, and, has as a result suffered unfair disadvantage, can make *categorical rights claims*. By way of contrast, *collective cultural claims* seek redress against cultural discrimination at the group level; hence they can only, justifiably, be put forward by representatives of minorities with distinctive ethnocultures or subcultures.

Human Rights as Legal Rights: Individual, Categorical, and Collective Claims

Under statutory human rights legislation at the provincial and federal levels, all Canadians, as individual persons, can put forward claims for redress against perceived violations of their *individual human rights* by other individuals or by organizations. Additionally, under the Charter and related constitutional provisions, individuals can put forward claims which challenge governments when their laws, policies or practices do not conform with constitutional guarantees for human rights. Under the equality rights provisions of the Charter, section 15(2) permits members of disadvantaged minorities to put forward *categorical rights* claims, individually or collectively, against governments for redress against the adverse impact of systemic discrimination upon the minority as a whole. Parallel legislation has been enacted by federal and provincial governments, allowing categorical rights claims to be put forward under statutory human rights laws.

As groups, ethnic minorities who perceive that their *collective right* to freely express their distinctive religion, language, or other ethnocultural attribute has been denied, can bring forward claims against governments under the combined provisions of s.15 (equality rights) and s.27 (multicultural rights) of the Charter. These collective rights claims essentially represent claims for recognition and protection of minority ethnocultures.

Collective Ethnic Claims: Cultural, National, and Aboriginal Rights

For purposes of analysis, I propose a threefold division among Canadian ethnic groups, on the basis of the differential nature of their collective claims: founding (English/French), multicultural (immigrant), and aboriginal (Indian, Inuit, and Métis) peoples. While all ethnic groups are able to put forward *cultural* rights claims, not all ethnic groups can legitimately make *national* rights claims. Insofar as immigrant/multicultural ethnic groups cannot provide evidence for ancestral/territorial links to a particular geographical area within Canada, they cannot, justifiably, make nationhood claims. The collective nationhood claims put forward by founding/charter and some aboriginal peoples derive their legitimacy from a demonstrable continuing link between ethnicity and territoriality.

The constitutionally recognized and historically grounded link between Franco-Québécois and Quebec—their ancestral homeland—underscores their claim to nationhood. Aboriginal peoples can make two kinds of claims: claims based on aboriginal rights and claims based on national rights. The latter (nationhood) claims rest on the demonstrable link between particular aboriginal peoples, their traditional aboriginal territories and their living, *land-based* ethnocultures.

Human Rights Claims Differentiated in Terms of Goals Sought

A critical distinction between human rights claims alleging violations of individual and/or categorical rights and claims alleging violations of collective rights lies in the goals sought by claimants.

Individual and categorical rights claims are *equality-seeking* claims. That is to say, the ultimate goal of claimants is to secure *equal status* of individuals and *equality/equity* of opportunity and treatment (e.g., equal pay for the same work/equal pay for work of equal value). Collective rights claims, alternatively, are predicated on the *collective right to be different*. The ultimate goal of claimants is 'distinct group survival' (Sanders 1989: 406).

Chart 1 A Typology of Human Rights Principles, Violations and Claims

Principles	Violations	Claims
Fundamental Human Rights		
Individual		individual claims
Right to life	homicide	
Freedom (self-determination)	oppression	
Equal opportunity	neglect	
Dignity of person	diminution	
Group or Category		categorical claims
Right to life	genocide	
Freedom (group autonomy)	group oppression	
Equal opportunity	group inequity	
Group dignity	group defamation	
Collective Cultural Rights		collective claims
Distinctive ethnocultural design for living (language, religion, institutions, customs)	cultural discrimination (deculturation/ cultural genocide)	
Collective National Rights		nationhood claims
Self-determination as a distinctive nation within own ancestral/territorial bounds	national discrimination (denial of nationhood status)	
Collective Aboriginal Rights		aboriginal rights claims
Right and title to aboriginal lands based on collective use and occupancy by aboriginal ethnic group 'from time immemorial'	land entitlement discrimination	

Collective rights claims can be divided into two categories, those based on *special status* and those based on *equivalent status*. Claims based on equivalent status seek a goal of *equality/equivalence* of group status and the right to equal/equivalent expression of unique ethnocultures (e.g., multicultural group status). Claims based on special status seek a goal of *distinctive group status* and the right to *special* treatment (e.g., founding/charter group status, aboriginal group status).

The human rights approach presented in the foregoing pages will inform the analysis throughout this book. The theoretical framework for the analysis of ethnicity and human rights in Canada conceptualizes human rights issues in terms of moral principles, violations and claims. A schematic representation of this framework is found in the typology of human rights, violations and claims shown in Chart 1.

Chart 1 suggests that, in Canada, individuals or groups who perceive that they have been subject to human rights violations may put forward the following types of claims:

1) *Individual Rights Claims* can be put forward by individuals who perceive that they have been personally subject to acts of individual or institutional discrimination (e.g., Chinese, Sikh, or Inuit applicants denied jobs on the grounds of race, religion, and aboriginal status, respectively, can make complaints for redress [job opportunities]).

2) *Categorical Rights Claims* can be put forward, individually or collectively, by members of minorities who perceive that the minority as a whole has been defamed and/or disadvantaged as a result of past discrimination (e.g., aboriginal or black minorities, collectively disadvantaged by a lack of adequate job qualifications as a consequence of deficient educational opportunities in Canada, can make claims for redress [special education and training programs]; Japanese-Canadians, incarcerated in internment camps in Canada during World War II, can make claims for redress against group defamation and disadvantage [public apology and monetary reparation from the Canadian government]).

3) *Collective Rights Claims*
   a) *Collective cultural rights* claims can be put forward by minorities whose members perceive that the minority as a whole has been subject to cultural discrimination (e.g., aboriginal, ethnocultural, or sub-cultural minorities such as Cree Indian, Ukrainian, or Rastafarian) whose distinctive language, religion, customs, or lifestyles have been denigrated, suppressed, or destroyed can make claims for recognition and protection of their distinctive cultural practices.

   b) *Collective national rights* (nationhood) claims can be put forward by minority ethnic groups with demonstrable links to an ancestral-territorial base or 'homeland' within Canada, whose members perceive that the minority as a whole has been subject to national discrimination, i.e., denial of their collective right to self-determination as internal nations within their own territorial bounds (e.g., Inuit of Nunavut and Franco-Québécois [cultural sovereignty and self-government]).

c) *Collective aboriginal rights claims* can be put forward by aboriginal ethnic groups (Indian, Inuit, or Métis peoples) whose aboriginal right and title to lands used and occupied 'from time immemorial' have not been 'extinguished' through land cession treaties with governments or by other lawfully recognized means [claims for monetary recompense and/or claims to occupancy and use of designated aboriginal lands].

The human rights framework elaborated in this introductory chapter will inform the analysis of ethnicity and human rights throughout this book. In Chapters Nine and Ten the analysis will focus on the legal implications of this framework for the protection of ethnic minority rights in Canada.

Notes

1 An analysis of the issues in the current debate concerning anti-hate propaganda legislation in Canada, which have come to the fore in the public trials of known hate propagandists, will be undertaken in the last part of Chapter Ten, in our presentation of Supreme Court cases involving Charter challenges.
2 The position on *nationhood rights* currently put forward by various aboriginal leaders throughout Canada holds that, before contact with European colonizers, aboriginal peoples were independent, self-governing nations with distinctive cultures. With colonization, their right to sovereignty was unjustly abrogated, their political institutions dismantled and their cultures systematically decimated. Aboriginal representatives argue that Canada's 'first nations' have an *inherent* right to self-government: it is a gift from their creator which has never been and can never be surrendered. As in the past, they assert their right to sovereignty and the right to create and administer their own, culturally distinctive political, economic and social institutions (Frideres 1993: 416).

CHAPTER ONE

Human Unity and Cultural Diversity: The Janus-Faced Underpinnings Of Human Rights And Racism

The Biological Roots of Human Rights[1]

This book offers an original, social-scientific perspective for the analysis of ethnicity and human rights in Canada. The key concepts behind this approach—race, ethnicity, human rights, and racism—are themselves widely misunderstood. Ethnicity has long been confused with race, and race continues to be erroneously equated with racism. The latter concept implies the restriction or denial of human rights—but upon what scientific premises are human rights based?

To understand the nature of the scientific evidence behind the concept of human rights, one must first grasp some of the facts concerning humankind as a biological species. The first thing we must do is to stress the biological unity of humankind today within one human species, i.e., *Homo sapiens*. What do we mean here by unity? Our human species is a closed genetic system; that is to say, our species is unable to hybridize with any other. This is because no other species of the genus *Homo* now exists; in fact, none has existed for probably a quarter of a million years. For reproductive purposes, therefore, our species is restricted to its own members. That there is no biological barrier to reproduction between any of the world's peoples is abundantly clear from our history, and from the many crossbred members of the human species. Mating between members of different human groups has led to the creation of new populations such as the Canadian Métis and American blacks. This process of miscegenation involves a biological overlap of gene pools: introducing through reproduction, genes, perhaps numerous in one population, into another population where they may be rare or even absent. The overall effect, then, is to broaden the spectrum of human variability. It is important to recognize this process not as one of blending characteristics, but as bringing forward new combinations or permutations of genes. Thus, a new gene pool, such as that possessed by Canada's Métis, includes genes characteristic of Canadian Indian peoples as well as those derived from Canada's British and French settlers. The test of whether such miscegenation is viable or not is simple: reproductive success. The answer is clear and positive.

We must not lose sight of the fact that, despite there being no convincing biological argument against miscegenation within our species, its occurrence is more likely to be dependent on sociocultural reasons such as religious prohibitions or language barriers. Looking at what is commonly called our Canadian ethnic mosaic, there is a tendency, all too often, to think in terms of stereotypes, and to misconceive of particular ethnic groups as virtually discrete and homogeneous racial units. This all-too-human tendency to emphasize and exaggerate observable differences among human populations obscures the range of individual variation within each of these groups. It also deflects attention from the very real similarities among all groups belonging to the same human species.

One of the contemporary tasks of the physical anthropologist is to attempt to demonstrate the biological *affinities* among human populations. Before we undertake this task, we will attempt to clarify some of the common misconceptions and misunderstandings associated with the concept of race. For it is these misunderstandings that have often influenced the kinds of prejudicial attitudes and discriminatory practices toward particular human populations which we refer to as racism.

Defining the Term 'Race'

The word race first occurs in the English language about AD 1500. A study of its etymology shows that it was adopted from the French word *race*, which is connected to the Italian word *razza* and the Spanish word *raza*. Beyond this, its origin is obscure.

The initial English usage of the word was apparently to indicate a class or set of persons (or even plants and animals) possessing some common feature or features, which might be of common descent or origin. In the sixteenth century the term race was used more widely, and could mean the people of a house, or a family, as well as a tribe, nation or people regarded as being of common stock. It was not until the eighteenth century, however, that the term was used to indicate major divisions of humankind by stressing certain common physical characteristics such as skin colour. While in earlier usage the term had generally been used to mean 'the human race', 'the race of men', or 'the race of mankind', its later meaning grew more narrow, particularly as the voyages of explorers and the journals of travellers revealed more and more physical varieties of humankind.

By the middle of the nineteenth century English usage of the term had come to include behavioural or temperamental qualities resulting from belonging to a particular people or ethnic origin group. Groups of several tribes or peoples were considered as making up these culturally distinct ethnic stocks or races. This *erroneous* connecting of physical attributes with behavioural and other cultural traits has persisted into modern times, and, unfortunately, continues to be used in the social construction of psuedo-scientific racist ideologies.

We should remember, of course, that earlier scholars had no knowledge of the science of human genetics that so importantly influences the scientific concept of race today. Beginning with the discoveries of Gregor Mendel (1822-1884), Abbot of Brunn, and subsequently elaborated by innumerable other scholars, the science of genetics revolutionized scientific thinking about the relationships among all human populations. Most importantly, the focus of study was to shift from the old preoccupation with racial *differences* to a new interest in the biological *affinities* among human populations.

Evidence from the study of human genetics demonstrates unequivocally that there is no such thing as *pure race*. Rather, racial differences are relative phenomena, indicated by greater or lesser frequencies of particular genes, rather than their absolute presence or absence. Indeed, the study of human genetics indicates that there is a greater range of variation *within* any given human population than exists *among* human groups.

Let us consider, then, evidence based on some commonly used genetic markers such as the frequencies of certain blood group substances. What kinds of primary racial divisions can be made using this kind of information alone, disregarding the physical appearance of the population samples being tested?

It is clear from these genetic data that primary divisions of humankind are distinguishable from one another. The evidence of physical features, skeletal features, and many genetic markers combine to indicate clearly that there are differences among populations of the same human species that are drawn from the three major geographical breeding grounds of human populations: Africa, Asia, and Europe. These broad biogeographical divisions (races) are commonly identified as Negroid ('Black'), Mongoloid ('Yellow'), and Caucasoid ('White'), respectively.

Evolving Races of Humankind

Virtually new races of humankind have been evolving as the species has become increasingly mobile and interchanging genetic material through repeated miscegenation. The gene pools originally characteristic of certain human populations have been modified accordingly. This brings not only variation in the frequencies of certain genetic markers, but also variation in external physical features. Such comparatively new populations are numerous on the world scene. The American black is one example. Historic and genetic evidence indicates that the American black is the product mainly of African (black) and European (white) miscegenation.

In the past these new populations were commonly considered below the levels of fertility, intelligence, and achievement of the two parental stocks. Such racist myths about 'halfbreeds' are now clearly held to be scientifically erroneous, and the viability of many of these new races is proof of this

Race and Intelligence

Can racial differences in intelligence be demonstrated to exist? Obviously differences between individuals, whatever their racial affinities might be, are going to exist. But what about means for intelligence quotient tests derived from large population samples of different racial affinities?

Intelligence tests have been conducted on a world-wide basis for many years in an effort to elucidate any connection between race and intelligence. The results seem to point to certain very general conclusions. The culture of the population being studied appears greatly to affect average scores. Tests found useful in one culture are often completely inappropriate in another. A test devised for, say, English Canadians is unlikely to be as appropriate for testing Canadian Inuit, American blacks, or Australian aborigines. Intelligence tests can never be culture free; they inevitably reflect the background of experience and skills considered important by the testers. Again, different peoples will approach tests with different degrees of sophistication and will expend different amounts of mental energy and perseverance on them. Social custom may affect motivation in tests, so that in one culture individuals may strive for personal success, while in others they may have been taught to avoid it. Survival may have been facilitated in some communities by a pretence of stupidity in the presence of superiors. Nutritional status and health status will affect test results. It is difficult, if not impossible, then, to weigh the many imponderable variables, and attempts to objectively relate human genetics and intelligence in situations of this kind are clearly premature. They may well remain so.

Today, many social scientists, human geneticists and educators have virtually abandoned the proposition that intelligence, however defined, can be accurately and objectively tested. Such tests as are now administered are usually given with restricted goals in mind and designed in accordance with the population sample being studied.

The problems of objectively measuring intelligence notwithstanding, it is worth noting at this juncture one of the key findings of an extensive review of the evidence on racial differences in intelligence in the United States by Loehlin, Lindsey and Spuhler (1975). These three social scientists found that: 'The majority of the variation in either patterns or levels of ability lies within U.S. racial-ethnic and socio-economic groups, not between them. Race and social class are not very powerful predictors of an individual's performance on tests of intellectual abilities' (ibid.: 235).

These observers attribute differences in the average scores of members of different racial-ethnic groups on intelligence tests in part to one or another of three factors: (1) the biases and inadequacies of the tests themselves, (2) differences in environmental conditions among the racial-ethnic groups, and (3) genetic differences among the groups (ibid.: 238). They conclude that: 'Regardless of the position taken on the relative importance of these three factors, it seems clear that differences among individuals within racial-ethnic (and socio-economic) groups greatly exceed in magnitude the average differences between such groups' (ibid.: 239).

A recent report by four Canadian psychologists (Weizmann *et al.* 1990) indicates strong continuing support for this position. This report serves to debunk the highly publicized racist theories of Professor Phillipe Rushton (University of Western Ontario), which will be analysed in some detail later in this chapter.

The Oneness of Humankind: Biological Roots of Human Rights

The foregoing conclusions about race and intelligence bring our discussion of human unity and diversity full circle. We began by pointing out that, today, there is a general scientific acceptance that all members of contemporary humankind belong to the same biological species: *Homo sapiens.* We showed that one important criterion in defining a species is that it has reproductive or genetic unity. Members of a species are interfertile. They may mate with one another without hindrance if given the opportunity. In some cases, of course, geographical barriers or distance may preclude such mating opportunities; thus there are no recorded instances, for example, of Canadian Inuit mating with Australian Aborigines or with Kalahari Bushmen. On the other hand, there are numerous examples of inter-ethnic matings within the human species (for instance, between Chinese or Japanese and American blacks or Europeans) that, in biological terms, have resulted in no deleterious effects. We may confidently assert that there is no basic biological or genetical difference between the various populations making up our contemporary species. Differences such as skin, hair, and eye colour have no bearing upon human reproductive abilities. Such superficially obvious physical racial characteristics do not display discrete boundaries between populations. The tendency, rather, is for them to grade imperceptibly from one category to another across a continent.

Biological Unity, Cultural Diversity and Human Rights

It is the essential biological oneness of humankind which provides the scientific underpinnings for the concept of fundamental and universal human rights. For fundamental human rights are natural rights which accrue to every human being simply by virtue of belonging to the human species.

Yet every human being is born not only into the human species, but also into a particular ethnocultural collectivity. Like human unity, cultural diversity is a characteristic feature of humankind. It is this feature of humankind which provides the basis for collective cultural rights. However, as this book will demonstrate, the potential for antagonism between individual human rights (unity principle) and collective cultural rights (diversity principle) is what can and frequently does manifest itself in racism.

Human Rights and Human Rights Violations: The Ethnocultural Roots of Racism

The concept of fundamental human rights has its roots in the principle of biological unity of the human species. In the very first paragraph of the preamble to the Universal Declaration of Human Rights (UDHR) recognition is given to the 'inherent dignity' and the 'equal and inalienable rights of all members of the human family' as 'the foundations of freedom, justice and peace in the world'. Thus, a primary assumption behind the UDHR is that of the fundamental unity and kinship among all members of humankind.

Like human unity, cultural diversity is recognized under international human rights instruments as a characteristic feature of humankind. However, as this book will demonstrate, ethnocentric biases of different ethnocultural communities can render arbitrary racial/ethnic differences salient and can lead to ethnic antagonisms. When invidious distinctions based on assumed or perceived racial or ethnocultural differences are used to justify the denial of human rights of members of particular human groups, racism rears its ugly head.

In order to comprehend the complex social processes through which racism is generated, justified, and perpetuated, attention must be paid to the *social construction* of race and ethnicity within human societies.

Race and Ethnicity as Social Constructs

Within any human society, in any historical era, the social construction of the concepts of race and ethnicity reflect the ideological, political, economic and cultural biases of the ruling authorities of the society. Those with the power to rule inevitably have the power to define. Populations defined in terms of the social constructs of race and ethnicity are not merely categorized or classified in a statistical sense; they also are evaluated in terms of the values and standards established by majority authorities as the norms for all members of the society. It follows, then, that the social constructs of race and ethnicity are not in any way neutral or scientific classifications. Their social relevance, however, lies not in themselves, but in the use to which they can be put in the hands of majority authorities. When social constructs of race and/or ethnicity are used by majority authorities to rationalize differential treatment of populations so classified, socially-created 'race' becomes translated into the social reality of *racism.*

Troper (1993) has argued that race was always the key concept used to discriminate against ethnic minorities in Canada. Prior to the changes in immigration laws which opened the doors to 'visible minorities' (defined in terms of skin colour and assumedly related 'racial' attributes), immigrants whose ethnocultural characteristics (religion, language, customs) were perceived to differ in undesirable ways from dominant British-Canadian norms were perceived and treated as 'races' distinct from and inferior to Canada's two 'founding races' (English and French). Like today's visible minorities, they were socially constructed as people of colour, on the basis of various combinations of physical, cultural, and behavioural criteria.

Today, Troper suggests, with the immigration to Canada of substantial numbers of racially visible minorities, the earlier immigrant 'races' have become 'whitened'. I would also suggest that they have become ethnicized. Majority authorities in Canada now make clear distinctions between visible minorities (now defined in terms of the social construct of race) and ethnocultural minorities (now defined in terms of the social construct of ethnicity).

Notwithstanding the critical importance of these social constructions, which will be analysed in some detail throughout this book, the fact remains that, as a scientific concept, race (like sex) has biological referents, and ethnicity (unlike race) has both biological and cultural referents. In the following section, I will briefly distinguish between these two concepts.

What is 'race'?

The concept 'race' refers to any arbitrary classification of human populations using biological criteria such as observable physical traits and/or genetic indicators (gene frequencies for particular traits).

This scientific definition of race includes two important points: first, race refers to an arbitrary social category (*not* a social group) and second, racial classifications are based solely on biological differences between human populations (*not* on cultural differences).

The three most commonly used racial categories today are Caucasoid ('White'), Mongoloid ('Yellow'), and Negroid ('Black'). These categories are *not* based on cultural criteria. There is no White Culture or Black Culture or Yellow Culture, based solely on race. However, each of these broad racial categories can be sub-divided along lines of ethnic origin, national origin, religion and many other variables. Once we begin to differentiate among various populations within the broad racial categories, we introduce the component of culture. For example, within the 'White' category, we find Italians, Irish, Jews, English, Spanish and many other national, ethnic, and religious collectivities. Within the 'Yellow' category, we find such diverse populations as Chinese, Inuit, Japanese, Vietnamese. Within the 'Black' racial category we find a similar range of variation: Jamaican, Nigerian, Afro-American, and so forth. All of these diverse populations within each of the three broad racial categories can be distinguished, at least in part, by cultural differences. Some of these differences pertain to ethnicity.

What is ethnicity?[2]

The concept of ethnicity refers to any arbitrary classification of human populations based on the biological criterion of common ancestry in conjunction with cultural criteria such as language or religion.

The most important criterion behind the concept of ethnicity is common ancestry or ancestral origin. Common ancestry has three main components: peoplehood (biological descent from common ancestors), nationhood (attachment to a real or mythical ancestral territory), and ethnoculture (maintenance of a common ancestral cultural heritage).

Ethnicity may be expressed in a wide variety of forms, ranging from denial (disassociation from one's ethnic category), symbolic ethnicity (voluntary psychological identification with selected aspects of the cultural tradition of one's ethnic category), to some degree of commitment to the preservation of aspects of one's cultural heritage and some degree of participation in the living institutions of one's ethnic community.

When ethnicity is expressed in the form of living ethnic communities whose members maintain distinctive ethnocultures over time, then an ethnic category becomes transformed into an ethnic group. For members of ethnic groups, in addition to common ancestry which links members through time, bonds of common kinship and ethnoculture link together living members of existing ethnic communities. What this means, then, is that members of the same ethnic group are linked together through time and space by common bonds of kinship and culture.

In order to fully comprehend the meaning of ethnocultural diversity, it is important to clarify the concept of culture underlying it. In its anthropological sense, culture is synonymous with ethnoculture, and both terms refer to the distinctive ways of viewing and doing things shared by members of a particular ethnic collectivity and transmitted by them from one generation to the next through the process of enculturation (distinctive ethnic socialization). More specifically, the culture/ethnoculture concept refers to the total configuration of patterned and institutionalized ideas, beliefs, values, standards, skills, and behaviours that characterize the distinctive world view, ancestral heritage, and life ways of a particular ethnic group. The most important point about culture, from a social scientific perspective, is that it is a learned phenomenon; it is acquired, for the most part, through the ordinary processes of growing up and participating in the daily life of a particular ethnic collectivity.

Anthropologists generally agree that for a cultural life style to be categorized as a culture in the sense of ethnoculture, it must have both a spatial (synchronic) and a historical (diachronic) dimension. When a given cultural life style has been transmitted over at least three generations, it can be regarded as a genuine ethnoculture rather than a subculture (an alternate life style within a given culture).[3] This distinction has important implications for the question of collective cultural rights, for legal precedent reveals that under international human rights instruments, cultural rights accrue only to members of genuine ethnocultures.

Insofar as culture is part of the condition of being human, then all individuals must learn to be human. But culture is not learned in the abstract. Every member of the species *Homo sapiens* learns to be human by learning the language, religion, and customs of a particular culture. As a direct consequence of the particularistic nature of learning to become human through cultural acquisition, human beings tend to identify themselves, firstly, as members of their own ethnocultural collectivity, and only secondly as members of humankind in general.

Members of ethnic communities committed to the continuance of their distinctive ethnocultures are constrained to adopt boundary-maintaining mechanisms, designed to keep ethnic insiders in, and to keep ethnic outsiders out. Ethnocultural boundaries provide artificial barriers to human intercourse between insiders and outsiders and, the more ossified the ethnic bounds, the greater the tendency to deny human rights to outsiders on arbitrary racially or culturally defined grounds. This observation may be taken as a starting point in our attempt to understand and address the roots of racism.

Racism and Human Rights

Racism, in its most general sense, contains both ideological and behavioural assumptions. Racism can be defined as a set of beliefs, policies, and/or practices predicated on the erroneous assumption that some human populations are inherently superior to others and that human groups can be ranked in terms of their members' innate (biological) superiority/inferiority. A second erroneous assumption behind racism is that biology determines culture, temperament and morality. Following from these premises, the diverse populations of humankind are ranked in accordance with the presumed superiority/inferiority of their members' physical, cultural, and behavioural characteristics.

From a human rights view, it is important to distinguish between the ideological and the behavioural dimensions of racism. Racist ideologies do not, in themselves, violate human rights; racist behaviours invariably do. When racist ideologies are used to justify policies or acts of discrimination against members of particular human populations, then racism becomes the instrument for human rights violations.

International Protection for Human Rights: Anti-Racist Declarations

The United Nations pronouncements most specifically addressed to the relationship between ethnocultural diversity, racism, and human rights are the Convention on the Prevention and Punishment of the Crime of Genocide (1948) and the International Convention on the Elimination of All Forms of Racial Discrimination (1965). In the latter covenant, racial discrimination is defined, under Article 1, as:

any distinction, exclusion, restriction or preference based on race, colour, descent, or national or ethnic origin which has the purpose of nullifying or impairing the recognition, enjoyment or exercise, on equal footing, of human rights and fundamental freedoms in the political, economic, social, cultural or any other field of public life.

The most extreme form of racial discrimination against a human group is undoubtedly the act of genocide. Article 1 of the United Nations Convention on the Prevention and Punishment of the Crime of Genocide declares genocide, whether committed in time of peace or time of war, to be a crime under international law. In the process of drafting this covenant, genocide was defined as a criminal act directed against national, ethnic, racial or religious groups of human beings, with the purpose of destroying a human population in whole or part, or of preventing its preservation or development. Phrased succinctly, the crime of genocide refers to discriminatory measures for the extermination of any national, ethnic, racial, or religious group.

Genocide represents racism carried to its extreme. However, as a prelude to the analysis of racism and human rights in this chapter, it is important to point out that any human being who violates the human rights of another human being on the arbitrary grounds of assumed racial or cultural differences is committing an act of racism.

The following pages draw upon the social scientific literature on racism to develop a conceptual framework for our analysis of racism and human rights in Canada.

Invalidation Myths and Ideologies: The Paradigm of Racism

Dominant groups, whose members are over-represented among the governing authorities in a society, have the power to use *invalidation myths and ideologies* to rationalize categorical discrimination against less powerful minorities and, thereby, to violate their human rights.

Invalidation *myths* are falsified statements which allege that identified human populations are innately inferior or invalid (defective) with regard to particular human attributes.

Invalidation *ideologies* are unsubstantiated theories which are designed to give credibility to invalidation myths by providing purported 'evidence' for them.

Invalidation ideologies contain both prejudicial and discriminatory assumptions. That is to say, they can be expressed in negatively prejudiced attitudes towards particular populations and in discriminatory acts against particular populations.

In general, invalidation ideologies—like racism, sexism, and ageism—can be conceptualized as a set of beliefs, policies, and/or practices designed to justify and legitimate invalidation myths by fabricating theories which purport to offer pseudo-scientific or religious evidence for them. From the erroneous assumption that some human populations are innately inferior to others with regard to particular human attributes, follows a second assumption, that human populations can be ranked by their members' inherent superiority and inferiority. This false assumption regarding a 'natural' hierarchy of human populations provides a *platform for discriminatory action against inferiorized populations*. It affords the rationale for alleged superior populations to claim that they are the 'natural' rulers of society and that they should control the life destinies of alleged inferior populations. In this way, *invalidation ideologies* provide the justification for categorical discrimination—involving human rights violations—against alleged inferior populations.

The role of invalidation myths and ideologies in legitimizing categorical discrimination against minorities is of critical importance for the understanding of majority/minority relations in Canada, for Canada is a democratic country with an international reputation and a constitutional mandate for the equal protection of the human rights of all its citizens. In order to *legitimize* the enactment or the continuation of discriminatory laws, policies, and/or practices against any particular minority, majority authorities in Canada must be able to provide a persuasive rationale in order to gain public support for their proposals. However, as has been convincingly argued in the Introduction to this chapter, *no scientific evidence exists to support any ideology based on notions about the superiority or inferiority of any human population*. Majority authorities determined to promote such ideologies must, therefore, rely on invalidation myths which have become deeply imbedded in the public psyche and thus can be counted upon to generate public support.

For the purposes of this book, with its focus on racial and ethnic minorities, the particular kind of invalidation myths and ideologies to be considered are those which underscore racism. We have previously defined racism as follows:

> Racism, in its most general sense, contains both ideological and behavioural assumptions. Racism can be defined as a set of beliefs, policies and/or practices predicated on the erroneous assumption that some human populations are inherently superior to others and that human groups can be ranked in terms of their members' innate (biological) superiority/inferiority. A second erroneous assumption behind racism is that biology determines culture, temperament and morality. Following from these premises, the diverse populations of humankind are ranked in accordance with the presumed superiority/inferiority of their members' physical, cultural and behavioural characteristics.

In the following pages we will illustrate this definition of racism by providing concrete examples of racist myths and ideologies used by dominant powers to deny the human rights of racial and ethnic minorities.

The Socially-Constructed Races of Humankind: Mythical Models

Prior to the twentieth century, EuroWestern anthropologists seem to have been preoccupied with the process of classification of humankind into various arbitrary subdivisions or 'races' on the basis of observable biological criteria. Differences between Europeans and visibly different peoples from other parts of the world were assumed, at this time, to be preordained by some Divine Maker. Accordingly, 'races' initially were mistakenly assumed to represent discrete and immutable divisions within humankind (the fallacy of 'racial purity'). A second fallacy, predicated on the first, was that race determined culture. Observable cultural differences were thus mistakenly attributed to innate racial differences among the peoples of the world. These two invalidation myths—the 'pure race' myth and the 'race determines culture' myth—formed the basis of racist invalidation ideologies which were used to justify the subordination of non-White, non-European peoples by EuroWestern powers.

Ideologies of White Supremacy arose from an evaluation of non-European peoples from an ethnocentric Euro-Christian perspective which equated 'civilization' with material and technological developments. This was closely linked with a theological ethnocentrism that invariably ranked Christianity far and above 'uncivilized' religious forms, lumped together as 'primitive' under the derogatory label of 'paganism'. Using these Eurocentric criteria, scientists proceeded to rank the 'races' of the world in a hierarchical order of innate inferiority and superiority ranging from primitive to highly civilized. It followed, of course, that at the pinnacle of the hierarchy, the 'White' EuroChristian 'races' reigned supreme.

Racism: Early Religious Ideologies

In the era of Colonial expansion, EuroWestern governments sent administrators to 'undeveloped' overseas countries in order to ensure that the Colonial powers gained access to the valued resources in the area. In order to facilitate their control over the 'savages' residing in the newly administered territories, Colonial governments encouraged Christian missionaries from the so-called 'mother' country to undertake the task of civilizing (Christianizing and westernizing) the aboriginal inhabitants of the administered countries. This civilizing mission was 'justified' by Biblical invalidation myths such as the myth of 'manifest destiny' and the 'hamlite rationalization' (Anderson and Frideres 1981: 211-12). Passages in the Christian bible were interpreted so as to lend support for the contention that white peoples are destined to rule the world (manifest destiny) and that non-white peoples are destined to be the servants of white masters (hamlite rationalization).

The manifest destiny postulate included two related ideas, that of the 'white man's burden' and that of 'noblesse oblige'. The white man's burden was the task of civilizing the savages. Noblesse oblige referred to the idea that privilege entails responsibility, i.e., the white man, privileged with the power to rule, had the responsibility to care for and protect the non-white savages under his control. The hamlite rationalization postulate provided an invalidation myth designed to justify the subordinate and even servile position (as slaves) of non-white peoples.

While the idea of manifest destiny has been supported through reference to various passages in Biblical texts, the hamlite rationalization refers specifically to the Biblical story of Ham. The main points of this myth may be summarized as follows:

Ham and his brother came home late one evening and found their father drunk and lying naked on the floor. The room was in disarray and looked as though a wild party had taken place. Ham stood and stared at his father but his brother did not. His brother fetched a blanket and covered his father's body. The story concluded with the decree of God that Ham and all of his descendants should have a mark placed upon them and that they should occupy the status of servants forever. Over the years, the 'mark' has been interpreted as non-white skin, and the 'servants' decree has been used to justify the subordination of non-whites by whites.

Racism: Current Religious Ideologies

Among the many and varied hate groups in North America, some of the most virulent racists are found in a number of fundamentalist Christian groups. Generally speaking, these religious groups share with other fundamentalists a rejection of the values of modern society which they perceive as atheistic, secular, materialistic, and immoral. Where they differ is in their explanation for the perceived ills of modern society: they hold that specified 'inferior' groups, in particular, Jews, who are portrayed as synonymous with Satan, are responsible for all of the world's social ills.

In 1985, *The Globe and Mail* published a series of articles on a racist religious organization called the Church of Jesus Christ Christian-Aryan Nations. At the time, this hate group, headquartered at Hayden Lake, Idaho was the subject of extensive media coverage because 23 of its members were on trial, charged with crimes that included machine-gunning to death a Jewish radio talk host, bombing a synagogue, robbing banks, killing a state trooper, and a variety of other crimes (*Globe and Mail*, 8 Oct. 1985). The organization has since expanded and now has at least one active branch group operating in Canada, near Calgary.

The religiously legitimated invalidation ideology of the Aryan Nations church preaches that the white race is God's Chosen People, the good 'seed' of Adam and Eve, while Jews are the evil 'seed' of Eve and the Serpent or Satan (*Globe and Mail*, 5 Oct. 1985). Jews (Satan's people) are the source of all evil. The Aryan Nations church further preaches that Jews have enslaved the world. The United States government has fallen under Jewish power, bringing about decadence and blinding white people to their fallen state. It is the religious duty of the 'Aryans' (the superior white race) to join in a race war to overthrow the (Jewish-controlled) government of the United States, referred to by the church as the 'Zionist Occupation Government' or zog.

The aim of the Aryan Nations Church is to establish an all-white, all-Christian, Aryan-governed nation-state in the territory of North America. In Canada, Terry Long, a church leader who operates out of Alberta's Aryan Nations group, holds the position of 'High Aryan Nation Warrior Priest' (Canadian Jewish Congress, 1990).

Modern Racism: Pseudo-Scientific Racist Ideologies

Like religious racism, pseudo-scientific racism is predicated on the twin invalidation myths of racial purity and racial determination of culture. The difference between the two forms of racism is in their grounds of legitimation: religious ideologies versus pseudo-scientific ideologies.

Prior to the publication in 1859 of Charles Darwin's path-breaking treatise *Origin of Species*, anthropologists and naturalists who classified human beings into racial categories on the basis of observable physical characteristics tended erroneously to equate these biological traits with social and cultural attributes. Moreover, many of those involved in classification also tended to evaluate and rank the different racial categories. Samuel Morton (in *Crania America*, 1839), for example, suggested that the Caucasian race was superior to the Ethiopian race because the Caucasian skull was nine cubic centimetres greater in internal capacity than that of the Ethiopian (Rose 1968: 35).

With the publication of Darwin's theory of biological evolution of species, a new, (pseudo-scientific) rationale for ranking of 'races' came into being. Popularized in the phrase 'survival of the fittest',[4] Darwin's theory of natural selection was erroneously applied by nineteenth-century anthropologists and other 'Social Darwinists' to lend scientific legitimacy to their racist theories.

While Darwin's own concern was largely with the biological evolution of species, early Social Darwinists like R. Knox (1850), W. Bagehot (1873), and B. Kidd (1894) used his theories to link together biological and social evolution of sub-specific groupings, i.e., human societies and cultures. Despite the fact that some of these scholars later retracted their earlier racist theories, their thinking, generally, had an important and lasting influence on the development of modern racism as exemplified in the writings of such diverse scholars as J.A. de Gobineau (1854), H.S. Chamberlain (1899), M. Grant (1916), C. Putnam (1961), C. Coon (1962, 1965), D. Collins (1979), and many others.[5]

Historically, one of the most insidious political uses of Social Darwinist invalidation ideologies lay in their provision of a pseudo-scientific basis for Colonialism. Indeed, the pejorative connotation which has come to be attached to the term Colonialism derives from the racist consequences of invalidation ideologies of White Supremacy, used to legitimate the subordination and exploitation of colonized non-White peoples by White colonizers.

Invalidation ideologies of White Supremacy, developed by European Whites in the grand era of empires and colonial expansion in which they reigned supreme, depict the White races, variously defined, as the 'fittest', i.e., as culturally and biologically superior to all other so-called races. At the bottom of this purported scale are the dark-skinned 'savages'. Their supposed inferior or uncivilized culture and technology is attributed to an assumed evolutionary lag by virtue of which they are deemed biologically incapable of achieving the fullest human and cultural development. Such invalidation ideologies have served to endow the words 'primitive' and 'native' with a connotation of innate inferiority, and have served, at the same time, to legitimize paternalistic Colonial government policies toward aboriginal peoples so defined.

Similarly, the racist ranking order spelled out in the invalidation ideology of anti-Semitism, an anti-Jewish political movement that surfaced in Germany in 1873, classified the Germans as the élite of the supreme Aryan or Nordic category; all other races were accordingly superseded. Specifically, the Jews were singled out as an inferior, vile, and depraved Semitic race; their very presence in Germany was considered to present a threat of contamination and degeneration of the 'superior' civilization. This ideology was clearly manifested in the writings of Houston Stewart Chamberlain (1899), who argued that the Jews were waging a permanent war for the destruction of Aryan civilization; he advocated 'expelling this alien and noxious element from the body of European society'. The ideology of anti-Semitism was used to justify repeated acts of hostility toward and persecution of Jews in the nineteenth century, and in the twentieth century, by Adolph Hitler, to justify the racist policy of genocide that culminated in the death of millions of Jews during World War II. Like the thinking that underscored colonial suppression of the world's 'primitives', the Nazi theory of Aryan apotheosis was an extreme variation of the common invalidation ideology of White Supremacy.

Critique

Let me address two key fallacies behind pseudo-scientific racial myths and behind the racist ideologies predicated upon them.

First: the fallacy of 'pure', discrete races. This myth is based on the erroneous assumption that there are absolute biological differences between discrete populations which are responsible for qualitative differences in culture, personality, temperament, morality, etc. Associated with this view is the myth that inter-breeding between superior and inferior races interferes with the natural order, corrupts the pure stock of the superior race, and results in degeneration and decay. Inter-breeding, the myth holds, will eventuate in a 'race' of sub-human creatures (idiots and monsters).

To illustrate the kind of racist propositions that derive from these fallacies, a few quotes, taken from a pamphlet distributed by a White Power group centred in Australia, will be presented. (Source: T. Graham, 'BE TRUE TO YOUR RACE', Sydney, Australia: undated.)

Choose an Aryan mate of the same or Nordic blood. When like meets like, you get harmony. When breeds mix that do not harmonize, the result is degeneration and decay. (p. 4)

MIXED BLOOD IS THE CAUSE OF ALL OUR TROUBLES, SPIRITUAL, PHYSICAL AND ECONOMIC, as we always find that people of bad blood are of low moral standards and practices, and this reacts on the social position and conditions.

We can all see the tragic state of affairs in America, who threw her gates open to all and sundry to solve a labour problem. By this tragic error she sold her birthright. DO NOT LET THIS HAPPEN HERE: UNITE TO KEEP AUSTRALIA WHITE. (p. 6)

As the prime example of the dangers of inter-racial breeding, the pamphlet describes the Jews as a mongrelized people, made up of a mixture of races, mostly all bad, including mediterranean, oriental and negroid strains. The pamphlet goes on to point out a few basic characteristics by which Jews can be readily identified:

Feet pointed outwards, feet pointed inwards, this is Jew or Jew strain. If one waddles like a duck when walking, this is also Jew or Jew strain. If body is bird-shaped, . . . chest out, stomach in and behind out—this is Jew . . . Jewish humour is always sexual perversity. Jews have no creative ability . . . only low cunning . . . Fish eyes (bulging out)—this is Jew . . . After a man finishes shaving, one sees a steely bluish tint on his face. This is Jew or Nigger. (p.16)

Pseudo-Scientific Racism Today: The Phillipe Rushton Controversy

For some time during 1989, media attention in Canada was focused on the newly reported findings of research studies conducted by Phillipe Rushton, a Psychology professor at the University of Western Ontario. Rushton's findings reportedly reveal an evolutionary hierarchy of races of mankind in which Orientals rank highest, closely followed by Whites, who far outdistance Blacks, ranked at the bottom of the scale.

During February and March of 1989, the *Toronto Star* published a series of reports which revealed that Rushton's research was based on the premise that the different races of mankind (Oriental, White, and Black) can be ranked for superiority and inferiority on the basis of three sets of criteria: physical attributes (brain size, penis size), mental attributes (intelligence, measured in IQ tests), and behavioural attributes (sexual restraint and law-abidingness). Rushton's propositions in regard to these criteria were: the larger the brain, the more advanced the race; the larger the penis, the less advanced the race; the greater the ability to restrain sexual impulses (and thus to control family size), the more advanced the race, and the more law-abiding (measured in criminal statistics), the more advanced the race. On the basis of these criteria, Rushton claimed that Orientals rank highest on the evolutionary scale, Whites rank second (close behind), and Blacks rank lowest (far behind).

Rushton claims that his findings confirm his Darwinian-based, evolutionary theory which holds that the more recently 'emerged' the race, the more superior its members' attributes: the criteria of brain size, penis size, intelligence, sexual restraint and law-abidingness. Rushton claims that Orientals 'emerged' most recently (some 40,000 years ago); Whites emerged earlier (some 100,000 years ago); and Blacks emerged earliest (some 200,000 years ago).

In light of scientific observations on race, and the social scientific paradigm of racism presented earlier in this chapter, Rushton's theories clearly constitute invalidation ideologies which fall within the parameters of pseudo-scientific racism. Submitted to the scrutiny of academic authorities in his own field (Psychology) his works have been found not only to be based on outdated and discredited theories and methodologies but also to be replete with errors of fact and interpretation. Weizmann *et al.* (1990: 22) comment that 'the repeated acceptance of his work in reputable publications raises some disturbing questions. These questions go beyond Rushton himself to the performance of those institutions through which science regulates itself.'[6]

From a human rights perspective, the fact that Rushton is able to continue to publish his questionable 'findings' in established academic journals which lend an aura of legitimacy to his theories raises a human rights issue of serious dimensions. The issue concerns the conflict between Rushton's freedom of speech and the right of members of his target 'races' to be free from insidious racial stereotyping and group defamation. This issue will be explored in depth in connection with the analysis of the current hate propaganda debate presented in Chapter Ten.

Summary: Racism as the Debasement of Human Rights

Racist myths and ideologies, and the policies, programs and practices predicated on them, tend to follow a fallacious, unscientific or pseudo-scientific line of reasoning whereby a human population's distinctive biological endowment is held to determine the equally distinctive culture, personality, mentality, and morality of its members. The logic of the argument which ensues from the erroneous initial assumption of racial purity is that the higher the race in the natural hierarchy of humankind, the more advanced is the culture and the more civilized and human is the person. The political implication of this line of reasoning is that the highest human race(s) should naturally dominate if not exterminate the lower ones. The human rights implication is that only 'full' human beings (the highest human races) have inalienable human rights: races defined as less-than-human (the lowest races) can thus, 'justifiably', be denied human rights.

Racism and human rights are diametrically opposed concepts. Every human being, simply by belonging to the human species, has the same inalienable human rights. Racism debases the very premise of inalienable human rights by violating the human rights of those human beings whom racists define as members of inferior, less-than-human 'races'. The various UN human rights instruments that currently prohibit racial discrimination against any human population represent a modern attempt to combat and eliminate racism in all of its insidious manifestations.

The 'New Racism'

Among the most pernicious expressions of racism in contemporary democratic societies is a subtle form of ideological deflection which serves to deny the social reality of racism. This 'new racism' has been conceptualized as an 'ideological gambit' (Baker 1981), employed by majority authorities in a democratic society to maintain the *status quo* of racial and ethnic inequality in the face of espoused democratic ideals of anti-racism and egalitarianism.

In Canada the constitutional protection for equality rights, under s.15 (1) and (2) of the Charter, is impugned by the systemic inequality of visible minorities. In order to maintain the *status quo* of racial/ethnic inequality in face of an anti-racist/egalitarian national ideology, majority authorities have shifted their ideological stance from a focus on inherent (biological) racial inferiority to a focus on 'natural' cultural difference. This shift, however, does not alter the fundamental premise of 'White racism', that of blaming the victim for social and economic problems perceived as a 'natural' consequence of group differences.

Baker (1981) argues that the new racism is expressed in a language of innocence which disguises its insidious intent by framing its messages in a way that endorses 'folk' values of egalitarianism, social justice, and common sense. Racism, in effect, is ideologically transformed in ways that disavow, diminish or distract from its actuality in a democratic society.

In the context of the British political debate over the issue of immigration of visible minorities, Baker demonstrates that one ideological gambit frequently used is the argument based on 'genuine fears'. The case is presented that we (British) are normally fair and tolerant, but that these good qualities are overstrained. The (folk) ordinary people's fears and resentments concerning immigration are genuine ('there is no smoke without fire'). A tough stand on immigration is not racist; it is not based on irrational fears or racial prejudice. Rather, it is a rational, realistic (common-sense) response based on facts about real economic and social problems which may arise from immigration.

The 'genuine fears' idea, Baker suggests, is a 'bridge concept' between the idea of protection of a distinctive national culture or way of life and the avoidance or elimination of a perceived threat to that way of life. The 'genuine fears' idea is used to justify policies taken to remove the perceived threat (repatriation, restrictions on immigration).

In contrast to traditional, pseudo-scientific racism which posits a hierarchy of human superiority and inferiority based on immutable racial differences, the new racism is expounded in theories of ethnic absolutism based on 'human nature'. This approach posits the existence of 'natural' boundaries between human populations (nations) rooted in immutable *cultural* differences.

The theory of human nature behind the new racism proposes that human beings have a natural 'instinct' to form a bonded community, a *nation*, aware of its differences from other nations. Each national community, it is argued, has a natural home and its members share a natural instinct to preserve their common national identity and to defend their territory (homeland). The language of this theory is race-free, but its covert agenda links together race/ethnicity/culture and nation, based on 'legitimate', 'natural' human instincts.

As Baker so astutely observes, the language of innocence in which the new racism is couched leaves racists free of any imputation of racial superiority/inferiority, or even of dislike or blame against those who pose the threat of 'cultural alienness'. The theory of 'pseudo-biological culturalism' holds that nations are built on human nature. Our biological instincts predispose us to defend our way of life, traditions and institutions against outsiders, *not because they are inferior, but because they are naturally different.*

Gilroy (1987) suggests that the 'novelty' of the new racism lies in its capacity to link discourses of patriotism, nationalism, xenophobia, militarism, and sexism (patriarchy is 'natural') to provide a definition of race framed in terms of culture and identity. The theory of ethnic absolutism, Gilroy argues, views nations as culturally homogeneous 'communities of sentiment'. National cultures are seen as fixed, mutually impermeable expressions of ethnic and national identity. The new racism denies that race is a meaningful *biological* category; instead, race is displayed as a cultural issue.

Gilroy uses the example of 'black criminality' to illustrate his point. While Gilroy's data are based on the British experience, a parallel case can be made for Canada; later sections of this chapter deal with relations between blacks and the police.

Gilroy argues that the new racism endorses the view that law represents the cultural ideals of national unity and equality of citizens in a democratic nation. Identification of racially distinct crimes and criminals is attributed to the economically disadvantaged and politically marginalized status of blacks, which, in turn, is attributed to 'residual ethnic factors' in their inner-city culture ('deviant', single-parent, female-headed families; lack of work ethic, street-gangs bent on revenge against the white oppressor, drug sub-culture and so forth). Legality, the ultimate symbol of national culture is held to be threatened by the entry of the 'alien wedge'. Cultural aliens (blacks) are seen as hedonistic (non-productive) and dangerous (criminals). Deviant black culture, it is argued, is expressed in particular forms of crime—drugs, street-violence, and robbery ('mugging')—which have resulted in national chaos, a crisis in law and order, and a real threat to the distinctive, national way of life cherished by loyal and law-abiding citizens.

Another form of the new racism is found in sociobiological theories of 'social nationalism' (see, for example, Pierre van den Berghe, 1978). This school of xenophobia holds that the source of racism, ethnocentrism, and nationalism is genetic. The argument holds that, in the struggle for existence, evolutionary processes have genetically and therefore immutably programmed humans to forge powerful in-group bonds ('kin altruism') within one's own genetic community (breeding population) and nation (cultural community characterized by organic social unity). At the same time, it is argued, human nature has been programmed with the opposite instincts of selfishness, hostility, and aggression towards competitive outsiders. The theory holds that xenophobia is an evolutionary trait bred into human beings over millions of years because of its genetic advantage. It is, therefore, 'natural' for nations to isolate themselves behind cultural and genetic barriers.

Baker (1981) observes that, like the 'genuine fears' form of the new racism, the sociobiological form leaves racists free of any imputation of racial superiority or inferiority. The theory appears 'neutral' and, like earlier pseudo-scientific theories of racism, it appears 'scientific' in the context of its time. Baker suggests that this form of the new racism is particularly insidious in its implications for ethnic relations because it has a powerful selling image in contemporary democratic societies.

In Canada, as in Britain, the professed ideals of egalitarianism and anti-racism have become incorporated into law; thus the contemporary constraints against overtly racist acts or words are formidable. Canada's constitutional commitment to the values of multiculturalism and social harmony provide further constraints against overtly racist commentary. In consequence, the old racism has 'gone into the closet' where it has become transformed, in cultural guise, into the new racism. As in Britain, in Canada the cultural differences (real or assumed) and the empowerment demands of visible minorities have been perceived as a threat to national unity and identity and to national values of equal opportunity and justice for all citizens. In the Canadian context, two current examples come to mind: the continuing controversy over Sikhs wearing turbans, and the escalating opposition to affirmative action measures designed to provide visible minorities with redress against the adverse (disadvantaging) impact of systemic discrimination.

The turban controversy illustrates the position of the new racism on irreconcilable cultural differences/threat to national culture. The current controversy over whether Sikh veterans can wear turbans inside Royal Canadian Legion branches emerged several years ago but resurfaced in November of 1993 when five Sikh veterans were refused entry to a Legion branch in Surrey, B.C. (*Toronto Star*, 2 Dec. 1993). Several Legion branches, in defiance of an order from national headquarters, insisted that all head covers must be removed inside Legion branches as a sign of respect for the Queen, for fallen comrades, and for any women who might be present. (The Queen has refused to become involved in the controversy.) The Sikhs argue that the ban on turbans is a form of religious discrimination that undermines the (multicultural) values and freedoms veterans fought for. Clearly, the two sides in this debate endorse conflicting views on exactly what constitute '*Canadian* cultural values' today.

The opposition to affirmative action for visible minorities, framed in the language of reverse discrimination, decries such programs as unfair to white Canadians. This form of the new racism prioritizes individualistic principles of equality and meritocracy and condemns as inegalitarian any measure of affirmative action designed to remedy group-level disadvantage of visible minorities (Henry 1993). This covert expression of the new racism represents a strategy designed to maintain racial inequality in the face of the constitutional provisions of equality rights, particularly s.15 (2) which allows programs of affirmative action. Given the economic climate of recession, unemployment and overwhelming national debt in Canada, this argument has gained considerable public support.

An editorial comment in the *Toronto Star* (25 July 1993) criticized Ontario's NDP government for providing grants, out of public funds, for a credit union and a legal clinic that would serve black people only. The editorial argued that this policy initiative creates a sub-class of 'black' services which undermines 'everyone's battle for and right to equality'. This form of reverse discrimination, the editorial suggested, negates attempts to eradicate barriers to racial discrimination in mainstream Canadian society.

Following this editorial comment, under the headline 'Other Views', was an excerpt from an editorial in *The Ottawa Citizen*. This editorial comment criticized then Prime Minister Kim Campbell's reorganized government for moving Immigration to the new Department of Public Security. The editorial argued that the move gave currency to a 'contemptible claim that immigration has become a threat to public safety'. The editorial went on to say that to the Campbell government, immigration is a 'policing problem' which will have to address growing public concern (read 'genuine fears') over law and order issues, including the smuggling of goods and the entry into Canada of illegal immigrants.

As regards more general public ('folk') attitudes, a recent survey carried out under the auspices of the Canadian Council of Christians and Jews (*Toronto Star*, 14 Dec. 1993) indicated that nearly three quarters of Canadians interviewed reject the notion of this country as a multicultural nation. Sixty-two per cent of respondents expressed the opinion that people should 'adapt to the value system and the way of life of the majority (read: White Anglo-Christian) in Canadian society'. Forty-one per cent of respondents believed that Canada's immigration policy 'allows too many people of different cultures and races to come to Canada'. Almost 50 per cent agreed with the statement: 'I am sick and tired of some groups complaining about racism being directed at them', while 41 per cent agreed that they are 'tired of ethnic minorities being given special treatment'.

Similar attitudes were expressed in the findings of a recent Gallup poll which indicated that three out of four respondents oppose government employment equity plans (*Toronto Star*, 23 Dec. 1993). The survey found that 74 per cent of respondents believe that governments should hire employees for management positions solely on their qualifications.

Caveat

While there is considerable evidence to support the view that the new racism has gained a foothold in Canada today, from a human rights view I am compelled to introduce a cautionary note. I believe that a careful distinction should be made between legitimate, informed criticism of social policy and racist commentary.

Alan Borovoy, general counsel to the Canadian Civil Liberties Association, has criticized Ontario's proposed employment equity law (Bill 79) for attempting to 'right yesterday's wrongs' against minorities by discrimination against majority members (*Toronto Star*, 2 Sept. 1993). He has argued that a legitimate plan of compensation for the disadvantaging effects of past discrimination would be to give hiring preference to the actual individual who suffered in the past, not to someone else who just happens to share the same minority status.

This line of argument is supported by many well-respected scholars who have criticized programs of affirmative action on this and on other grounds (see Chapter Nine). Can we, in all fairness, label all of these critics as 'new racists'? I think not. Indeed, I hope not.

The Old and the New Racism: Canada 1994

In Canada today, the old and the new racism flourish side by side. Dyed-in-the-wool bigots (Aryan Nations, Ku Klux Klan, Heritage Front, and other organized racist groups) continue to promote the religious and pseudo-scientific theories behind the established models of racism, while polite racists, as well as many self-professed anti-racists, cloak their parallel views in the discourse of culture promoted by exponents of the new racism. Yet, the source of both forms of racist discourse is the same: xenophobia—'an unreasonable fear or hatred of anyone or anything foreign or strange' (Hendrickson 1987: 571).

From a human rights perspective, what appears to distinguish the two forms of xenophobia is this: the established models of racism 'racialize' culture (e.g., Jews as a vile and depraved 'race'); the new models of racism 'culturalize' race (e.g., Blacks as a dangerous and deviant 'subculture'). But the end result is the same: blaming the victim for the disadvantaging consequences of institutionalized and systemic racism.

Racism and Social Reality in Canada

Canadian concern for human rights is largely a post-World War II phenomenon. Appalled by the revelations of Nazi atrocities representing the most extreme forms of human rights violation, member states of the United Nations drafted human rights instruments designed to prevent the recurrence of cruel and inhumane forms of treatment, culminating in acts of genocide. State signatories to these UN instruments, like Canada, followed suit and began to develop human rights legislation within their own countries. Over the last four decades, human rights legislation has been enacted and amended so as to provide expanded statutory protection for the human rights of Canadians all across this country. However, as Macdonald and Humphrey (1979: xvi) have pointed out, there is no necessary connection between the existence of human rights legislation and the empirical facts of respect for or denial of human rights in a given country. Glaser and Possony (1979: 228-9) present cross-national evidence which indicates that many countries, a number of whom were enthusiastic signatories of the UDHR, have constitutional provisions against discrimination and inequality; yet both of these phenomena are rife in practice. Paradoxically, concern for human rights, and even human rights legislation, may be symptomatic of long-term racism and denial of human rights.

The latter statement is particularly relevant in the case of Canada. Although Canadians long sought to deny the fact, racism in Canada has always been a serious problem. Within the last two decades, a series of violent racial incidents have shocked Canadians out of their long-term complacency and have forced them to consider the mounting evidence of racism throughout Canada. Hill (1977: 4-11) documented a number of incidents of racially motivated discrimination, ranging from name-calling or racial slurs through brawls, beatings, boycotts, and even killings. In former times, aboriginal Indian populations were the prime targets of racial attacks. The slaughter of the Beothuk Indians of Newfoundland in the eighteenth century was one of the earliest recorded acts of wilful racism in Canada. Today, other non-white minorities such as Chinese, East Indians (South Asians) and blacks have also become prime targets of racial violence. A 1970s report cited by Hill (ibid.: 5) indicated, for example, that 'Paki-busting' was a widespread sport among teenagers in Ontario. During this decade, racism directed against East Indians exploded into violence in Toronto, Vancouver, and Calgary, the three large urban centres that had received most of Canada's then more than 200,000 East Indian immigrants. A feature article in *Maclean's* magazine (2 July 1977) entitled 'Racism? You Can't Argue with the Facts' shocked the Canadian public with incontrovertible evidence of Canada's mounting 'anti-Paki' racism. The first reported incidents occurred in Vancouver in 1974, in the form of widespread vandalism and attacks against members of the Sikh community. In Calgary, during a six week period in the fall of 1976, there were more than a dozen incidents reported of assault causing bodily harm, property damage, and disruption of religious ceremonies. Cars carried bumper stickers with the admonition: 'Keep Canada Green: Paint a Paki.' The most serious incident reported from Alberta occurred on a CP work train station some distance south of Edmonton. Here, an obscenity painted on a sleeping car occupied by East Indian workers led to a four-hour battle between Euro-Canadians and East Indians, the hospitalization of two participants, and the charging of two others with trespass and assault. On New Year's Day 1977 there were two separate assaults on East Indians in the Toronto subway system followed by another attack a few days later. These two widely publicized incidents marked the culmination of some two years of racial violence against East Indians in Toronto, during which time homes had been vandalized, temples desecrated, and children beaten on school grounds.

In the 1980s, mounting evidence of racism against blacks, particularly in Toronto and in Montreal, captured continuing media attention. In 1982, violence between Haitian-born, black taxi drivers and their white counterparts followed the firing of 20 black drivers from one firm. Testimony at a Quebec Human Rights Commission inquiry revealed that customers often asked for white drivers and that taxi companies readily complied. Many companies, in fact, were refusing to hire blacks (Hill and Schiff 1988).

In 1985, evidence from two research studies conducted in Toronto indicated that whites were three times as likely to be hired for jobs for which black applicants were equally qualified and also that more than half of 199 major employers interviewed openly expressed negative attitudes toward visible minorities (Hill and Schiff 1988).

In 1992, a report of the Law Reform Commission of Canada revealed that politicians have for almost 20 years refused to deal with racism in the criminal justice system (*Toronto Star*, 27 May 1992). Given predictions that over the next two decades the populations of Canada's major cities will be 20 per cent non-white, this finding is alarming. The report notes that between 1974 and 1979 nine commissions investigated allegations involving racial and ethnic discrimination and made 229 recommendations. Yet virtually nothing has been done to remedy the situation. The report suggests that there is merit to the contention of racial and ethnic minorities that the justice system is racist. There is ample documentation of incidents, complaints, scandals, court judgments, and reform proposals which confirm the allegations about racism made by these groups.

In May of 1992, Metro Toronto's Action Committee to Combat Racism held hearings at which dozens of black parents and educators alleged that the public school system has failed black youth (*Toronto Star*, 14 May 1992). Speaker after speaker recited a litany of complaints of discrimination against black students. Among the most common allegations were: no teaching of black history and culture, with the result that black students feel marginalized/outside the mainstream; lower expectations for black than for other students; disproportionate 'streaming' of black students into general and basic-level programs; hostile climate between white teachers and black students; higher drop-out rate among black students.

In confirmation of these findings, Toronto's black teens complained that they continued to feel the sting of racism in classrooms and on the streets, despite thirteen years of anti-racist school board policies (*Toronto Star*, 13 May 1992). Young black males said that they were painfully aware of their stereotyped image as 'a gang of good-for-nothings' . . . 'useless' . . . 'sitting at home drinking or doing drugs'. That such negative stereotypes of black youth persist clearly does not augur well for their treatment by police. Many students complained of being harassed by police as they walked through their neighbourhoods.

Among the most volatile allegations of racism made by non-white minorities are those which have been put forward by representatives of the black community against Canada's police. At a 1988 rally condemning the police shooting of Lester Donaldson, a Toronto black man, Dudley Laws, a founding member of the Black Action Defence Committee, is reported to have said: 'Canada is a racist state' . . . 'If you have a racist state, then you have racist police' (*Toronto Star*, 8 May 1992). The defence committee, formed three days after Donaldson's death, has since organized a number of rallies to protest against police racism, particularly in the form of anti-black shootings. In May of 1992, a rally was called to protest the acquittal of two

Peel Region officers in the 1988 shooting death of a black seventeen-year-old, Wade Lawson of Mississauga. In the same month, the defence committee organized a demonstration to condemn the recent acquittal of four Los Angeles police officers in the videotaped beating of black motorist Rodney King as well as the killing by Metro Toronto police of Raymond Lawrence, a black suspected crack dealer. The 4 May demonstration was followed by a nighttime riot in downtown Toronto in which store windows were broken and shops vandalized. The police, reportedly swinging big billy clubs, arrested twelve rioters and charged them with breach of the peace. Following the riot, the defence committee organized another demonstration at Queen's Park, to outline demands it insisted were necessary to defuse tensions in the black community.

The Black Action Defence Committee prefaced its demands with the assertion that Metro blacks cannot trust police, government, or the justice system until meaningful steps are taken to restore their confidence. Among the committee's key demands were the following: racism must become a criminal offence; a government commission should investigate the racist actions of police; police should be retrained to use means other than deadly force to apprehend suspects; a new trial must be ordered for the two police officers acquitted in the shooting death of Wade Lawson; elected officials must acknowledge that black shootings are a manifestation of institutional racism in Canada (*Toronto Star*, 8 May 1992).

Soon after the anti-racism rally and the violence in downtown Toronto, Ontario's Premier, Bob Rae, appointed Stephen Lewis (a former Canadian ambassador to the United Nations) as a special advisor on race relations (*Toronto Star*, 10 June 1992). Lewis held more than 70 meetings with police, minority leaders, academics, politicians, civil servants, and counsellors across the province. On 10 June 1992, Lewis released his 37-page report on race relations in Ontario in which he warned that anti-black racism in the province is deeply rooted. Many of his 14 recommendations to government echoed those proposed earlier by the Black Action Defence Committee. Among his key suggestions were: police training in race relations as an integral part of cadet training programs; careful community monitoring of police policies and actions; employment equity legislation geared to visible minorities; revamping the educational system so that the curriculum, textbooks and teachers all reflect the racial and cultural diversity of the province, and a public inquiry into racism in the criminal justice system.

The 1980s and early 1990s also witnessed the spread of organized and institutionalized racism in Canada through the stepped-up membership drives and campaigns of violence promoted by White Power groups like the Ku Klux Klan and the Aryan Nations church. In January of 1981, at a time when the Ku Klux Klan had been actively promoting membership drives in British Columbia, the fire-bombing of the home of an East Indian family in a suburb of Vancouver sparked an upsurge of anti-racist demonstrations. Demonstrators carried placards urging the public to 'Unite in Action Against Racist and Fascist Violence' (*Globe and Mail*, 10 Jan. 1981). The KKK provided the most visible target for the Vancouver demonstrators, because of the high profile it had attained through its open membership campaigns and distribution of KKK propaganda in the city's schools. In March of 1981, a Metro Toronto teacher's decision to allow members to address a high-school history class gave rise to heated public controversy, culminating in a unanimous motion of condemnation of the KKK by the House of Commons (*Globe and Mail*, 12 March 1981).

In June of 1981, in the face of the stepped-up campaign activities of White supremacy organizations and in response to the fervent anti-racist demonstrations directed against them, the House of Commons unanimously endorsed a decision to conduct an investigation of the activities of the National States Rights Party. This group, an Alabama-based White Supremacy organization, had established a post office box in East Toronto and had gained visibility through their activities in this area. The organization in question had already been banned from using the Canadian mails in 1965 because of the potentially harmful nature of the racist propaganda it was disseminating. At the same time that the Commons agreed to hold an investigation of this White Power group, they also agreed to condemn 'in the strongest terms the race hatred and intimidation used by organizations such as the National States Rights Party and the Ku Klux Klan' (*Toronto Sun*, 3 June 1981).

Yet, almost a decade later, in October of 1990, Canadians were to be exposed to media coverage of a rally and cross-burning at Provost, Alberta, organized by White Power groups, including the KKK and the Aryan Nations church, in which about 30 White Supremacists clothed in white KKK robes and pseudo-Nazi uniforms danced around a burning cross chanting 'Sieg Heil', 'White Power', and 'Death to the Jews' (*Toronto Star*, 28 Jan. 1991).

The Self-Fulfilling Prophecy of White Racism

While the manifestations of institutionalized racism against blacks and other visible minorities in Canada highlight discrimination on the basis of non-white skin colour, the continuing anti-Semitic tirade of White Supremacists makes it clear that skin colour is not the only criterion behind racist acts. Assumptions of racial inferiority are imputed to a wide range of minorities whose cultural and/or behavioural characteristics are assumed to deviate from the norms of those *who define themselves as White*.[7] The reader should note that it is this socially constructed self-definition of *White* which is employed in the discussion of White racism to follow.

We may summarily define White Racism as the adoption of ideologies, policies, and practices predicated on the erroneous assumption that Whites are naturally superior to non-Whites. Because non-Whites are assumed to be innately inferior, and somewhat less than human, their political, economic and social rights are violated through denial of equal opportunities; and because they are accorded inferior opportunities, they become in fact 'inferior', not as human beings, but in terms of their *inferiorized* and disadvantaged societal status as stigmatized minorities.

Over time, non-White minorities in a White racist society become locked into their *inferiorized* and subordinate social position. This social fact is then used by Whites to justify differential and unequal treatment of non-White minorities by pointing to their inability to get ahead in White society. This vicious cycle of events constitutes the self-fulfilling prophecy of White Racism.

The important point is that in a White racist society the inferior position/minority status of non-Whites has nothing to do with their alleged racial inferiority. The disadvantaged social position of non-Whites is the virtually inevitable outcome of long-term oppression (denial of political rights), neglect (denial of economic rights), and diminution (denial of social rights/human dignity). Racism is not a function of racial differences *per se;* rather it is a function of the way in which alleged or perceived racial or cultural differences are manipulated by members of one human population so as to deny fundamental human rights to members of other populations. The example of White Racism is particularly instructive here, in that it demonstrates the way in which more powerful, 'White' ethnic groups are able to utilize racist myths and ideologies to their own advantage—to justify their own superior social position in a given society and to rationalize the disabilities to which non-White minorities are subject.

But Whites do not have a monopoly on racism. Any member of any social collectivity who denies outsiders equal societal opportunities, human rights, and fundamental freedoms on the arbitrary basis of ethnic differences is indulging in racism. Because much of the current evidence on racism in Canada documents acts of discrimination by Whites against visible minorities, there has been a notable increase in public references to White racism. The latter term, while not entirely inappropriate, is nevertheless misleading, because White racism suggests that so-called Whites have a virtual monopoly on racism. While this notion is hard to refute in a White/Euro-dominated society like Canada, it is far from the truth of the matter. Racism (like sexism and ageism) is not the prerogative of any particular ethnic group. The cross-national evidence indicates beyond a doubt that it is endemic to humankind (Glaser and Possony 1979: 208-11).

In the next chapter, in order to further a comprehensive understanding of the multi-dimensional concept of racism, we will undertake a detailed analysis of the key conceptual components of racism as expressed in racist ideologies, policies, and practices.

Notes

1 This introduction is a revised and abridged version of the Introduction to the first (1982) edition of this book, written by Dr David R. Hughes.

2 For a detailed analysis of the old and the new ethnicity the reader is referred to Chapter Three.

3 This point will be elaborated in Chapter Three in connection with our analysis of the differences between *sui generis* ethnocultural minorities and other kinds of minorities within human societies.

4 In fact, some scholars attribute this phrase to the earlier writings of H. Spencer (Banton 1967: 37).

5 Modern racism refers to the political use of racist ideologies to justify group discrimination through exclusion, subordination, exploitation, and genocide.

6 It should also be noted that Rushton has reportedly received $240,000 in funding for his research from the Pioneer Group, an openly racist organization dedicated to 'racial betterment' through such techniques as selective genetic breeding (eugenics). His research findings have been published in *Mankind quarterly*, a magazine known to promote racial superiority and Neo-Nazi propaganda (*Toronto Star*, 9 March 1989).

7 The capitalized designations 'White' and 'Black' are used throughout this book to refer to self-identified groups or organizations within the broader population categories, differentiated in common parlance as whites and blacks, on the presumptive basis of skin colour.

CHAPTER TWO

The Anatomy of Racism: Key Concepts

For a better understanding of the nature and social implications of racism, the inclusive concept of racism may be broken down into key components: ethnocentrism, prejudice, stereotypes, social distance, and forms of discrimination.

Ethnocentrism

The concept *ethnocentrism* refers to the ubiquitous tendency to view all the peoples and cultures of the world from the central vantage point of one's own particular ethnic group and, consequently, to evaluate and rank all outsiders in terms of one's own particular cultural standards and values. From an ethnocentric perspective, the traditions, customs, beliefs, and practices which make up the culture of one's own ethnic group are exalted as highest and most natural. An inevitable consequence of ethnocentrism is the making of invidious 'we' versus 'they' comparisons. Whether actual or assumed, the greater the differences between the insiders and the outsiders, the lower the evaluation and ranking of outsiders by insiders.

Ethnocentrism is as old as recorded history. Although commonly attributed to the ancient Hebrews, the idea of a 'chosen people' is neither original with them nor unique to them. Anthropological research has revealed the extent to which preliterate peoples referred to their own ethnic groupings as 'the people'. The English translation for many of the names in common use among aboriginal peoples, for example Inuit and Dene, is 'the people' or 'human beings', distinguishing members of the ethnic group from outsiders.

Inuit mythology depicts the first man to be created by the 'Great Being' as a failure, that is, imperfect, and accordingly to have been cast aside and called Qallunaat. The second, a perfect human being, was called Inuk (the singular of Inuit). The contemporary designation of Euro-Canadians as Qallunaat (Whites, Southerners) contains a further differential assumption, one of economic abundance: Qallunaat signifies not only White people, but 'the people who always have plenty'. Records of early fur traders and missionaries indicate their surprise to find that the 'poor barbarians' (aboriginal peoples) arrogantly regarded themselves as superior to the White intruders.[1] Evidently, each ethnic group regarded itself as superior and the outsiders as barbarians.

Ethnocentrism and Social Differentiation

Ethnocentric evaluations of members of one's own ethnic group and of outsiders are based on shared assumptions as to differences among peoples. Not all kinds of differences are, however, accorded the same social significance. Assumed differences among ethnic groups or categories may be physical, cultural, or behavioural. Since the members of an ethnic group presumably share a common ancestry, hereditary physical attributes such as skin and eye colour, hair colour and texture, the shape of the nose, and the thickness of the lips, traits which visibly differentiate human populations on a global scale, often become important social indicators of ethnicity. But their importance lies solely in the purpose they serve: that is, the extent to which they facilitate ethnic labelling. Because they often increase the visibility of particular categories of people, these physical characteristics enable outsiders to identify persons sharing these attributes as alike by virtue of common ancestry. However, the particular physical traits used as social indicators of ethnicity by outsiders are often not the characteristics used by insiders to socially differentiate and ethnically define themselves.

Perceived physical differences are only one potential source for ethnic labelling. Many cultural and behavioural traits, such as style of dress, food habits, language, religion, and even certain occupations may be predominantly associated with a particular ethnic group, by outsiders.

The parka and mukluks, attire which has traditionally been associated with the Canadian Inuit, are probably more reliable social indicators of ethnicity to outsiders than are the particular physical features of the Inuit. Southern Canadians who have had little or no contact with aboriginal peoples might find it difficult to differentiate between some Indian and Inuit populations, particularly in the regions of the western Arctic and Labrador, were it not for the traditional differences in dress, type of dwelling, and food habits. The unreliability of physical indicators in pinpointing ethnic group membership is well demonstrated in the common use by outsiders of the derogatory term Paki in reference to a wide variety of people. In reality, few visible Canadians labelled Paki by outsiders come from Pakistan. They originate from a variety of countries—India, Pakistan, Sri Lanka, Fiji, Tanzania, Kenya, Singapore, Guyana, and elsewhere—and represent an even wider variety of cultural, religious and linguistic groupings (Buchignani 1971).

Ethnocentrism and Prejudice

While ethnocentrism and prejudice are closely related concepts, one does not necessarily follow from the other. Ethnocentrism may be expressed, at least theoretically, in a *laissez-faire* mode of ethnic relations, whereby members of different ethnic collectivities, committed to different but not highly incompatible values, can co-exist symbiotically or even co-operatively, because they are willing to tolerate each other's differences and to accord one another mutual respect.

Ethnocentrism turns into prejudice when it leads to intolerance of ethnocultural differences and to the stigmatization of one human population by another. Glaser and Possony (1979: 84-8) make an important behavioural distinction between *enlightened* and *pernicious* forms of ethnocentrism. Enlightened ethnocentrism seeks the self-interest of the in-group, but does so with due regard for the rights and interests of the out-group. Pernicious ethnocentrism, on the other hand, seeks the self-interest of the in-group at the expense of the rights and interests of outsiders.

In the Canadian context, the strategies and goals of the Canadian Jewish Congress, the national Jewish organization instrumental in mobilizing pressure groups and in bringing about human rights legislation in Canada, represents a prime example of enlightened ethnocentrism. While the primary goal of the CJC in these efforts has been to combat anti-Semitism, in practice the issues have been universalized and the scope of its activities has extended to combat discrimination against minorities in general. By way of contrast, the activities of the Western Guard—a self-professed White racist organization, instrumental in provoking hatred and violence against Jews, Blacks, and all non-Whites—represents a prime example of pernicious ethnocentrism. Western Guard tactics are designed to create an all-White Canada by trampling on the rights of ethnic minorities.

Prejudice

In contrast to ethnocentrism, which focuses on the in-group, distinguishing it from outsiders in general, prejudice focuses on and is directed toward a specific out-group. Simpson and Yinger (1972: 24) define prejudice as an emotional, rigid attitude, rooted in prejudgement, toward a particular group or category of people.

Ethnic prejudice[2] refers to biased beliefs about and attitudes toward members of particular ethnic collectivities based on unsubstantiated assumptions about their shared physical, cultural, and/or behavioural characteristics.

With specific reference to the concept of racism, ethnic prejudice represents the ideological/affective component, while ethnic discrimination represents the behavioural/action component.

Probably the most insidious feature of prejudice is the fact that it is based on unsubstantiated opinion. Because prejudice, for the most part, is learned through the normal process of enculturation, that is, by the examples, exhortations, and actions of persons whom the growing child trusts and respects, the unsubstantiated racist assumptions behind the prejudice remain unquestioned and untested. Thus, for example, when Euro-Canadian children experience vicious Paki jokes as part of the family conversation; when media reports of 'race' violence involving Pakis are applauded; where obscene anti-Paki graffiti line the walls of public buildings; it is not surprising to find that prejudice against so-called Pakis is widespread. Similarly, when the only images of visible minorities presented to Euro-Canadian schoolchildren are negative ones, and when by way of contrast Euro-Canadian values and achievements are apotheosized, ethnic prejudice becomes an integral aspect of 'the forces which shaped them' (Ashworth 1979).

Another aspect of prejudice that reinforces the unsubstantiated racist prejudgement, even in the face of scientific facts to the contrary, is its emotional or affective underpinnings. Attitudes of prejudice may be expressed in diverse forms, from a relatively unconscious attraction or aversion to members of particular ethnic collectivities, to a comprehensive ideology of racism, such as a theory of White Supremacy. When the emotional component of ethnic prejudice is strong, unsubstantiated ideas increase in salience and resistance to change. Because of the strength of the emotional component in prejudice in general, confronting the prejudiced person or group with facts that invalidate racist assumptions is a tactic which is likely to prove ineffective in reducing or eliminating the prejudice (Glaser and Possony 1979: 86). Indeed, this kind of tactic may have the opposite effect.

In the 1930s the results of a psychological study of attitudes toward Jews in Toronto revealed that anti-Jewish prejudice sometimes bordered on hysteria (Betcherman 1975: 49). At that time, the myth of an international Jewish conspiracy for world domination, codified in the so-called 'Protocols of the Elders of Zion', was providing a racist rationale for widespread anti-Semitism in Canada. Betcherman reports that the Protocols were used by anti-Semitic politicians like Adrien Arcand and Joseph Ménard as 'proof' that Jews were the enemy of the Christian people. Indeed, evidence that the documents were forged did not deter Arcand and Ménard from using them to spread their defamation of Jews through the press, as a 'campaign of national defence' (Betcherman 1975: 22).

Positive and Negative Prejudice: The Two Faces of Racism

By its very nature, any general discussion of the concept of racism tends to emphasize the negative aspects of prejudice, stereotypes and discrimination. The reader should always keep in mind the fact that for each negative notion associated with the out-group, there is a corresponding, positive notion associated with the in-group. For example, negative traits, such as moral and intellectual inferiority, attributed to non-Whites by White Supremicists have their positive counterparts in the glorified images of the pure White supreme race, represented by the members of White Supremicist organizations themselves. Racist ideas and images tend, as the foregoing suggests, to be strongly biased in favour of the in-group. When such images become entrenched as mental 'stereotypes', they become highly resistant to change, and are extremely difficult to eradicate.

Stereotypes

Stereotypes are overgeneralized, rigid, cognitive maps or pictures in our heads based on unsubstantiated and usually sloganized beliefs about members of a given social category (Glaser and Possony 1979: 91). Ethnic stereotypes are associated with the cognitive or ideological component of prejudice. An ethnic stereotype is an over-generalized, standardized ethnic group image that amplifies selected physical, cultural, and/or behavioural characteristics and disregards others. Outsiders employing ethnic stereotypes as a component of ethnic distinction emphasize those ethnic diacritica considered the most dissimilar from characteristics attributed to the in-group.

While ethnic stereotypes are not entirely false—they generally contain a 'kernel of truth' (Mackie 1974)—they invariably represent distorted images or caricatures which exaggerate some group attributes and disregard others. Not only do ethnic group stereotypes ignore the natural range of individual variation within all human populations, they overlook the strong natural affinities in human attributes between populations. Group stereotypes, therefore, are rendered invalid by scientific evidence which clearly demonstrates that differences *within* human groups are far greater than differences *between* them. Because ethnic stereotypes frequently highlight and thereby increase the salience of unsubstantiated racial prejudgements, they often reinforce existing prejudices toward the ethnic collectivities they purport to represent.

While ethnic stereotypes and prejudices represent related components of the more inclusive concept of racism, they are not invariably co-existent phenomena. The degree of association between them, in any given instance, must be taken as problematic. Mackie's survey findings (1974) on the relationship between prejudice (measured in terms of social distance) and degree of stereotypy (measured in terms of somatic differential) based on public perceptions of Canadian Indians, Ukrainians, Hutterites, and Jews in Edmonton, Alberta indicated that greater social distance was not associated with either more frequent or more extreme attribution of negative traits. Mackie's data also revealed that prevailing ethnic stereotypes reflected reality more accurately than the 'kernel of truth' suggested by the literature. The most unfavourable ethnic stereotype was found to be that of the Indian, who was generally perceived as unambitious, dirty, poor, uneducated, oppressed, and in trouble with the law.

What the stereotypic skid-row image of the Indian represents, in stark actuality, is the disastrous consequences of the self-fulfilling prophecy of racism. Defined by

Euro-Canadians as lazy, uneducable, subhuman savages and, accordingly, denied the fundamental human rights and opportunities granted 'full' human beings, Canadian Indians have come, in fact, to constitute a stigmatized, lowly ethnoclass with many of the stereotypical attributes accorded them at the outset by the alleged White superiors. Thus, we would suggest that the Indian stereotype revealed in Mackie's findings mirrors White Racism more accurately than it reflects or resembles the reality of Indianness, in Edmonton or elsewhere in Canada.

In a national survey on public attitudes toward Canadian Indians, Ponting and Gibbins (1980: III) found that the negative 'skid row' Indian stereotype—which roughly paralleled Mackie's findings—was not the norm. Most respondents perceived Indians more realistically as victims of White Racism, beset by problems not of their own making.

In the aftermath of the 1990 'Oka crisis', the prevailing stereotype of Canada's Indians appears to have changed in some important respects. The 'Oka crisis' in the summer of 1990—the culmination of a lengthy dispute over some wooded land, claimed by Mohawk Indians and wanted by non-Indian residents of Oka in order to expand a golf course—focused media attention on a violent confrontation between police and Mohawk Indians. When Mohawks from the Kanesatake reserve set up roadblocks as a form of protest, Quebec police moved in and attempted to dismantle the barriers. Their efforts were openly resisted by Indians and their supporters, and the confrontation turned violent. On 11 July 1990, a Quebec police officer was killed during a failed police attempt to dismantle one of the barricades. The incident sparked a 78-day stand-off, sensationalized by graphic media coverage, that gripped the country and activated Indian politics. It ended after federal troops were called in (*Toronto Star*, 12 July 1990).

A national poll on attitudes towards 'natives', conducted by the *Toronto Star* in the aftermath of the Oka crisis, revealed that more respondents had lost, as opposed to gained, sympathy for aboriginal peoples (31 per cent vs 23 per cent). However, 56 per cent of respondents in the survey agreed with the statement that the problems of Canada's native peoples have been caused by the attitudes of other Canadians and the policies of governments, while only 27 per cent of respondents agreed with the statement that Canada's native peoples largely have caused their own problems (*Toronto Star*, 27 Nov. 1990).

In July of 1991, one year after Oka, a poll by Gallup Canada revealed that 39 per cent of respondents believe that 'native Indians' are well treated by governments in Canada. This figure was the *highest* registered by Gallup in the five times, since 1968, that the question had been put to the public. Only 14 per cent of respondents, the lowest figure registered since 1968, were found to believe that native Indians are badly treated (*Toronto Star*, 15 July 1991). These findings suggest that public empathy with the problems of Canada's aboriginal peoples has diminished since the 1980 survey conducted by Ponting and Gibbins. What they may also imply is that, in the wake of Oka, a new and more insidious stereotype of aboriginal peoples as 'violent and threatening' has taken hold among increasing numbers of Canadians.

In 1986, Ponting again surveyed Canadians on their attitudes toward Canadian Indians and Indian issues (Ponting 1990: 19-27). The survey findings, like those of the 1980 Ponting and Gibbins survey, revealed that most respondents lacked both familiarity with and interest in Indian affairs. Moreover, respondents who were relatively well informed about Indians generally were not any more sympathetic toward Indians and Indian issues than were those who were relatively uninformed. Ponting maintains that these findings, like those of the earlier (1980) study, suggest strongly that, contrary to public belief, knowledge *per se* does not induce sympathy or generate a more positive image. Accordingly, public relations campaigns designed to inform the Canadian public about the social realities of contemporary Indian life may have little or no effect on public opinion.

The educational implications of these observations, particularly in the uneasy political climate of post-Oka Canada, are manifold. Ponting's and Gibbins' findings should alert educators to the fruitlessness of textbook-focused teaching designed to correct stereotypes and to reduce prejudice. The teaching of ethnic relations in a vacuum without the active participation of members of living ethnocultures, and by educators who have never had first-hand contact with the peoples about whom they are teaching, may have the unanticipated consequence of reinforcing existing prejudices rather than eradicating them. Educational programs designed to reduce ethnic prejudice must be aimed at reducing the degree of social distance between members of different ethnic collectivities by promoting inter-ethnic encounters in which their human similarities can be mutually revealed. If such face-to-face interaction is not encouraged, then negative ethnic stereotypes (Indians as 'armed warriors'), fed by deceptive media coverage of events (the Oka incident), are likely to take root in the public psyche.

Social Distance

Among the key components in the definition of racism is the notion of social distance. This concept refers to the quantity and quality of social interaction among individuals or groups. Social distance between members of different ethnic collectivities can be measured in terms of the number and variety of social relationships, as well as the degree of intimacy and personal involvement which characterizes the social relationships between insiders and outsiders. Since people tend to act in terms of their ethnocentric evaluations of themselves and others, social distance in relationships between insiders (intra-ethnic relations) tends to be minimized, whereas social distance in relationships between insiders and outsiders (inter-ethnic relations) tends to be maximized. When social distance is high, social relationships among members of different ethnic collectivities tend to be of a categorical or impersonal nature, based on mutual utility. In this context, insiders relate to outsiders in terms of ethnic stereotypes rather than as individual personalities, because most people do not get close enough to outsiders to test the accuracy of their preconceived, unsubstantiated assumptions. On the other hand, when social distance is reduced and members of different ethnic collectivities interact more frequently and more informally, social relationships tend to become more intimate and more individualized. In this context, people become increasingly aware of the similarities, rather than the differences, between insiders and outsiders, while at the same time they become more conscious of individual differences among people categorized as outsiders. When this happens, members of different ethnic collectivities may come to relate to each other on a personal level without reference to ethnic stereotypes, but as social equals and as individual human personalities.

For example, given the increasingly multi-ethnic composition of the population of the urban-Canadian educational institution, students from many different ethnic collectivities are being increasingly exposed to daily interactions. To the extent that these young people evaluate students from different ethnic collectivities, not as individual human beings, but in terms of preconceived ethnic stereotypes, they tend to limit their social relationships with ethnically different students to the formal, educationally defined activities and pursuits of the school. Thus social distance between students from the various ethnic collectivities remains high. If, however, students begin to perceive fellow students from different ethnic collectivities as contemporaries, sharing common educational, social, and recreational interests and problems, the perceived similarities may come to override previously held notions of ethnic differences, and social distance will accordingly be reduced. When this happens, students may begin to form personal friendships with some students from other ethnic collectivities, in much the same way as they choose friends from within their own ethnic collectivities. That is, they will perceive not only the similarities between themselves and others, but the individual differences, and they will predicate their friendships on the bases of perceived common interests and individual personality preferences without reference to ethnic stereotypes.

Problems in the Measurement of Social Distance

Social distance scales, following the seminal work of Bogardus (1925), have long been used by social scientists to measure prejudice by inferring attitudes from statements about hypothetical behaviour. A basic assumption behind the early scales was that prejudice and discrimination are inextricably linked phenomena and that in any given situation the extent of either can be inferred or predicted by accounting for the extent of the other.

Thus, for example, a Euro-Canadian respondent might be presented with a number of questions relating to hypothetical degrees of social intimacy toward members of various ethnic collectivities. If blacks were ranked lowest on the scale of peoples the respondent would marry, bring home to dinner, socialize with, and so forth, this response would be taken to represent a high level of prejudice toward blacks as well as a strong likelihood (predictor) that the respondent would exclude blacks from intimate, personal relationships.

Banton (1967: x), in an excellent critique of cross-cultural social distance studies, questions the rarely tested assumptions behind these researches. He points out that social distance is a compound of a wide range of sometimes conflicting psychological and non-psychological variables. Particularly important, and often ignored in social distance studies, are the roles of cultural norms, environmental and situational contexts, and demographic and structural constraints. In support of Banton's critique, evidence cited by Glaser and Possony (1979: 91) suggests, for example, that there is a demographic tipping point where the proportion of outsiders, and especially racially visible minorities, is perceived by parents as a threat to their children and to their lifestyles. Banton contends that, because of the multifaceted nature of social distance, it is probably more fruitful to analyse the various factors independently and try to devise scales for each of them, rather than attempt to employ an inclusive definition and a scale of social distance (Banton 1967: 318).

The Problematic Relationship Between Prejudice and Discrimination

Banton's contention, that the various elements of social distance can and should be isolated as measures, is instructive for our discussion of the relationship between prejudice and discrimination.

Ethnic prejudice (as defined earlier) refers to biased beliefs about and attitudes toward members of particular ethnic collectivities based on unsubstantiated assumptions about their shared physical, cultural, and/or behavioural characteristics.

Ethnic discrimination refers to biased acts or practices towards members of particular ethnic collectivities which afford categorical advantage or disadvantage on the basis of unsubstantiated assumptions about their shared physical, cultural and/or behavioural characteristics.

While prejudice and discrimination—as two of the key components of the phenomenon of racism—are related concepts, in any given empirical situation their relationship must be taken as problematic. A racist belief or doctrine essentially represents a form of prejudice; a racist act or practice represents a form of discrimination.

Simpson and Yinger (1972) argue convincingly that to say that prejudice and discrimination are conceptually distinct phenomena is not to say that they are empirically separate. Prejudice and discrimination, they argue, can be found separately or together, and each may or may not be among the causal determinants of the other. Probably the most frequent empirical situation is the one in which prejudice and discrimination are found to be mutually reinforcing (Simpson and Yinger 1972: 29). In any given instance, the need is to specify the personal and structural conditions under which a given relationship between prejudice and discrimination prevails.

To return, by way of example, to our hypothetical case of the Euro-Canadian respondent who ranks blacks lowest on a social distance scale: Does this response indicate a high degree of anti-black prejudice, discrimination, or both? Insofar as the response represents an opinion about what the respondent might or might not do in a given situation it represents an attitudinal referent which may be taken as an indicator of prejudice. If however, the respondent is asked about actual behaviour with regard to degree of social intimacy toward members of different ethnic collectivities, the response represents a behavioural referent which may be taken as an indicator of discrimination.

The point is that prejudice does not *necessarily* or *invariably* lead to discrimination. The distinction between prejudice and discrimination lies in the difference between what one thinks, feels, and believes as against what one does.

From a human rights view, a critical distinction between prejudice and discrimination is that prejudice, in and of itself, does *not* violate human rights; discrimination (whether positive or negative) *invariably* violates human rights principles. A person may be highly prejudiced for or against any number of categories of people, but, unless that person *acts upon* one of these prejudiced beliefs or feelings, the prejudice, in itself, violates no other person's human rights. On the other hand, if a person performs acts or carries out practices which categorically advantage or disadvantage particular categories of people politically, economically, socially, or culturally, then the discriminatory acts themselves violate the human rights of members of the target population.

For example, if a black woman wants to pursue a career as a constitutional lawyer, it is quite conceivable that she might apply to an élite law school staffed by highly racist and sexist white male professors. Unless one of these professors discriminates against her on the grounds of race or sex, the racist and/or sexist prejudices and stereotypes held by the professors do not violate her human rights. However, if one of the professors tries to exclude the black female applicant from entering the law school on the grounds of race or sex, or if the applicant succeeds in becoming a law student and one of the professors makes racist or sexist remarks to her in class, or gives her low grades, or refuses to give her job references, on the grounds of race or sex, then the human rights of the black woman are unquestionably violated. She is being denied the fundamental human rights to equality of opportunity and dignity of person.

Forms of Ethnic Discrimination

Ethnic discrimination can be manifested in a wide variety of forms. At the level of the individual, an act of discrimination may stem from conscious, personal prejudice. This form of discrimination may be termed *individual discrimination.*

For example, an employer who is prejudiced in favour of English Canadians and against French Canadians acts upon his or her personal prejudice to exclude *equally qualified* or *more highly qualified* French Canadian applicants for positions with his or her firm. This case provides an example of individual discrimination based on ethnic prejudice.

Often, however, an act of discrimination does not derive from the personal prejudice of the actor, but from the carrying out by the actor of the dictates of others who are prejudiced or of a prejudiced social institution. This form of discrimination may be termed *institutional discrimination.*

For example, a Jewish high school teacher applies for a position at an exclusive private school. The school principal is not anti-Semitic (prejudiced against Jews); indeed, he happens to be married to a Jewish woman. However, the principal refuses to hire the Jewish teacher, despite his excellent credentials, because of a 'gentlemen's agreement' between the school board and the students' parents excluding Jewish persons from staff positions. This case provides an example of institutional discrimination based on ethnic prejudice. In this case, the person who performed the discriminatory act was not prejudiced against Jews; however, the discriminator acted in accordance with the prejudiced (anti-Semitic) policy of the (educational) institution.

To illustrate a different point, let us change the foregoing scenario by just one variable. Let us suppose that the school principal in the case *is* prejudiced against Jews. He harbours negative stereotypes of Jews as unscrupulous, money-hungry cheats. (He regards his own Jewish wife as a clear 'exception'.) Moreover, the principal fears that if a Jewish teacher should be hired, the carefully hidden fact that his own wife is Jewish might be discovered, and he might lose his own job. The principal, then, is predisposed to discriminate against Jewish applicants, and his own ethnic prejudice is supported by the anti-Semitic policy of the institution (private school) he represents. This case is an example of *both* individual and institutional discrimination.

Both individual and institutional forms of discrimination can ultimately be attributed to prejudicial attitudes: either the actor is prejudiced, or the actor conforms to the sanctions of a prejudiced reference group. Yet discrimination can occur even in the *absence* of conscious prejudice.

Unlike individual and institutional forms of ethnic discrimination, the *structural* or *systemic* form of ethnic discrimination cannot be attributed to prevailing prejudices (except, perhaps, with reference to their historical origins). Established, system-wide policies and practices in a society can have *unintended* yet pervasive discriminatory effects on disadvantaged ethnic minorities, by sustaining long-term, group-level ethnic inequalities.

The concept of *structural* or *systemic discrimination* refers to the collective, adverse impact upon disadvantaged ethnic minorities of group-level inequalities which have become rooted in the system-wide operation of society as a long-term consequence of past forms of ethnic discrimination. The collective adverse impact of systemic discrimination upon disadvantaged ethnic minorities operates, in the absence of conscious prejudice, to exclude substantial numbers of their members from significant participation in the major institutions of the society.

When members of ethnic minorities have been categorically denied opportunities to acquire or to use political, economic, educational and/or social skills and qualifications, as a long-term result, the minority category *as a whole* becomes collectively disadvantaged. The collective, adverse impact of group disadvantage can become compounded through the self-fulfilling prophecy of racism through which minority members come to internalize inferiorizing, majority-imposed labels, to blame themselves for their disadvantaged status, and to give up hope of status improvement. Members of ethnic minorities can thus become locked into their increasingly disadvantaged minority status and excluded from large areas of significant political, economic and social participation.

In the area of economic rights (equality/equivalence of educational and work opportunities), one way of looking at the difference between institutional and systemic forms of discrimination is this: Institutional discrimination denies equal opportunities for majority and minority members *with equal qualifications*; systemic discrimination *prevents minority members from acquiring or utilizing qualifications* which are equal/equivalent to those held by majority members.

To illustrate, consider an earlier example, that of the hypothetical black woman who wants to become a constitutional lawyer. Let us suppose that the woman succeeds in obtaining a law degree and then applies for a position with a prestigious law firm. Her credentials are superior to those of a white male applicant for the same position, but the male applicant is hired because the all-white, all-male law firm wants to keep it that way: the firm's policy is white males only. This is an example of institutional discrimination.

Suppose, however, that the black woman applicant had never succeeded in acquiring a law degree because, as a rule, law schools did not admit blacks or women. In this case, the black female applicant clearly would not have the qualifications for the position in the law firm, not because of her race or her sex, but because of the collective adverse impact upon blacks and women of past discrimination, i.e., denial of the human right to equality of educational opportunity. In this case, even if the law firm in question removed its racist and sexist hiring policy, the black female applicant could not compete for the position as she would still lack the necessary qualifications.

Forms of Discrimination in the Canadian Context

The most blatant form of racist behaviour, and one which most Canadians today would probably vehemently disclaim, is individual discrimination. Over the years, the various Human Rights Commissions in Canada have handled a host of cases of negative discrimination, but rarely has the discriminator admitted that the act in question was motivated by personal prejudice. In many cases of discrimination against ethnic minorities, in the areas of employment and housing, for example, the personnel manager or realtor typically disclaims personal prejudice as the reason for having refused the member of the ethnic minority. In fact, the grounds for the racist action may not have been personal prejudice. An employee may have been carrying out the unwritten policy or 'gentlemen's agreement' of the employer or client against hiring or selling to members of particular ethnic minorities. In such cases, the discriminatory act would be an example of institutional discrimination. In both cases, (individual and institutional discrimination), the *effects* of the action would be the same: equal opportunities for societal participation would be arbitrarily denied to members of ethnic minorities whose qualifications are equal to those of the ethnic majority members.

The most powerful and pernicious form of institutional discrimination is legislative or legal discrimination. For the most part, overtly racist legislation has been gradually phased out in Canada since World War II (Hill 1977: 16). Hill points out, however, that until the 1960s Canadian immigration laws were decidedly racist, at first overtly excluding particular ethnic collectivities from immigration to Canada, then covertly instituting criteria which militated for the most part against non-white immigration.

Historically, in Canada, racism toward aboriginal peoples has taken the form of paternalistic policies and treatment. The Indian Acts passed by Parliament nearly a century ago provide the chief legal source for paternalism toward Canadian Indians. These Acts, dating from 1876 to the present, in practice continue a policy of wardship initiated by the British to protect a supposedly childlike people considered incapable of managing their own affairs. An additional and even more paternalistic tendency toward protecting Indians against themselves is readily discerned in reading such legal documents as the Indian Act, Office Consolidation (1965).

Prior to the Emancipation Act passed by the British Parliament in 1833, racism toward blacks in Canada was overtly expressed in the institution of slavery. As slaves, black men and women were advertised and sold on the open market in much the same manner as cattle or home furnishings. They were evaluated and treated as things rather than as human beings (Winks 1971: 26).

The foregoing examples provide only an initial glance at the historical picture of legal forms of institutional racism in Canada. A more detailed analysis of this phenomenon and its contemporary implications will be presented in later sections of this book.

Individual and institutional forms of ethnic discrimination arise from either overt or covert prejudicial attitudes. If, however, existing prejudices could be suddenly and totally eliminated, the structural or systemic inequalities rooted in the daily impersonal (i.e., non-intentional) operation of the Canadian social system would continue to exclude substantial numbers of members of some ethnic minorities from full participation in public life. Because of the existing unequal distribution of opportunities and rewards, blacks, as well as Indians, Inuit and most members of visible ethnic minorities—victims of the self-fulfilling prophecy of racism—are less likely to possess the qualifications required for skilled jobs or the economic resources necessary for the purchase of a home.

The crucial human rights issue here is not that of providing equal chances for those with equal qualifications, but that of redressing the unequal access of different ethnic collectivities to the opportunities to acquire the necessary qualifications, skills, and resources for full participation in the public life of the society.

In such cases, it can be argued that some form of intervention (affirmative action measures) is necessary in order to ensure that (1) members of visible minorities are given an opportunity to acquire the education and training necessary in order for them to compete for jobs, at all levels, on an equitable basis with other Canadians and (2) members of visible minorities are proportionately represented throughout the ranks of the job market (i.e., proportionate to their numbers in the population).

Under the equality rights provisions of s.15 of Canada's constitutional Charter, s.15(1) protects all Canadians against individual and institutional discrimination. Section 15(2), however, allows special measures of redress against the collective, adverse impact of systemic discrimination for disadvantaged Canadians. This sub-section of section 15 of the Charter was inserted in order to guarantee that programs of affirmative action would be allowed. These programs are designed to provide disadvantaged minorities with some form of remedy for the adverse impact (disadvantaging effects) of systemic discrimination upon the minority as a whole. Canada's affirmative action mandate will be discussed in some detail in Chapter Nine.

Cultural Discrimination: Subtle Racism by Commission and Omission

Cultural discrimination is a function of ethnic diversity in a socially stratified society (Yetman and Steele 1975: 371). In a hierarchical, multi-ethnic society, only representatives of the dominant ethnic collectivity have the power to transform their ethnocentrism into cultural discrimination by imposing their cultural attributes, values, standards, and definitions of reality on all peoples in the society. For it is the normative imperatives of the dominant ethnic group, sanctioned in law and incorporated into public institutional policies, that provide the moral and cultural guidelines for the whole society.

Cultural discrimination occurs when alternative ethnocultural moral imperatives are denied expression in public life. Cultural discrimination is thus built into the dominant group requirement of minority acculturation, for this automatically denies the validity of minority ethnocultural alternatives.

Cultural discrimination may be expressed in the form of individual, institutional, and/or structural discrimination. At the individual and institutional levels, it may consist of discrimination against members of a particular ethnocultural community on the grounds of language, religion, or any other distinctive *cultural* characteristic. At the systemic level, cultural discrimination may be expressed in the fact that opportunities for participation in society are imbued with the cultural assumptions of the dominant ethnic collectivities. To the degree that members of all ethnic collectivities are expected and often required to conform to dominant norms and life ways in order to fully participate in public life, cultural discrimination is built into the institutional framework of society.

In Canada, cultural discrimination—institutionalized, for example, through the Official Languages Act—reflects Anglo-Canadian dominance outside the province of Quebec and Franco-Canadian dominance within Quebec. In a multi-ethnic society like Canada, where cultural discrimination operates through expectations of dominant cultural conformity in public life, those ethnic collectivities whose cultural attributes deviate most markedly from dominant norms are most severely culturally discriminated against. Alternatively, the more closely an ethnic collectivity approximates the dominant ethnocultural model in its language, religion, life style, symbolic diacritica and so forth, the more open and more easily accessible the public institutions of the society.

Cultural Discrimination in Education

Nowhere is cultural discrimination more evident than in the 'hidden' cultural curriculum of the Canadian educational system. Whether in its Anglo or Franco manifestation, the Canadian educational institution is a cultural monolith. Education in Canada, as in other modern industrialized societies, represents a formalized and extended aspect of the more general process of enculturation through which the growing and developing human individual acquires the skills and life ways appropriate to and necessary for adult participation in the society.

In Canada, primary and secondary school teachers in their role as delegate parents act as primary agents of enculturation. Not only are they responsible for imparting facts and honing skills, but they also are responsible for controlling student conduct and for developing Canadian citizens of good character (Magsino 1978: 90-1). D'Oyley (1978: 138) points out that, in the past century, governments have increasingly stressed compulsory school attendance and have enacted successive regulations to lengthen the school year. These moves have been designed to ensure that all Canadians, regardless of ethnic classification, achieve at least the minimum educational level necessary for participation in Canadian public life. Yet, D'Oyley argues, because school textbooks, teacher instruction, and trusteeship are subject to central control, ethnic minorities continue to encounter significant cultural and political obstacles to the achievement of an education that does not systematically negate their particular ethnocultural backgrounds. Hill (1977: 15) similarly contends that education in Canada is based on the cultural norms of the dominant white, urban, middle class. The ethnocultural models that Canadian teachers—including, perhaps, some non-white teachers—present to their students are seldom ones with which students from the lower ethnoclasses can easily identify (Case 1977: 59).

Cultural discrimination in Canadian education is manifested in acts of commission and omission. Ashworth (1979), in a study of the educational history of children from five ethnic minorities in British Columbia, clearly demonstrates that there is a strong tendency for the teacher, the curriculum and the environment of the classroom to apotheosize the achievements of the dominant ethnic group and to ignore the equally important contributions to Canadian society made by members of ethnic minorities. Through these and other subtle and not so subtle educational techniques the hidden curriculum shines through and the view of Canada as a cultural monolith (Anglo or Franco, as the case may be) is preserved.

In a multi-ethnic society like Canada, failure to accurately represent Canada's ethnic diversity throughout the educational process violates the human rights of minority ethnic students during every school day of their formative years.

Hill and Schiff (1988: 54) contend that, until recently, Canadian school boards and teachers generally manifested what could be called a 'race relations avoidance syndrome'. Despite the increased numbers of members of visible minorities in their classrooms, they chose to avoid discussion of race. In recent years, a number of school boards—in Toronto, Vancouver and Ottawa, for example—have developed anti-racism policies and strategies designed to ameliorate racial tensions in their schools. But, Hill points out, for all the newly aroused interest among educators, and for all the sophistication of newly developed anti-racism and multicultural curricular units, the educational initiative to combat racism is still tentative. Comparatively few of the multitude of available curricular programs have been adopted by Canadian school boards or teachers (1988: 55).

Discrimination of Silence

An important form of institutional and systemic discrimination which has only recently begun to receive the attention of scholars is the discrimination of silence, whereby educators and other Euro-Canadians in powerful positions say nothing and do nothing about racism in Canada. Case (1977: 37) contends that silence can be a form of complicity in an act of violence. The fear of denouncing the racist, the fear of discussing (let alone teaching) ethnic relations, and the fear of engaging in racially mixed encounters constitute expressions of covert racism that violate the fundamental principles of human rights. The 'race relations avoidance syndrome' whereby Canadian teachers, until very recently, chose to avoid any discussion of race despite the increased numbers of members of visible minorities in their classrooms, provides a glaring example of the discrimination of silence.

Even the victims of racist slurs can contribute to the conspiracy of silence by sitting back and letting their attackers repeat discriminatory practice with impunity.[3]

A national study of 'Multiculturalism and Ethnic Attitudes in Canada', Berry *et al.* (1977), found little evidence for overt racism. However, a certain level of covert concern and unwillingness to accept ethnocultural differences was revealed. Also, while overt racism was not high, race remained an important means of social classification and racially visible populations were ranked lowest among Canadian ethnic collectivities.

The subtle, covert racism, evidenced in the Berry *et al.* study, exemplifies the 'new racism' addressed in Chapter One of this book. The new racism infringes subtly but seriously on the human rights of ethnic minorities. Cultural discrimination and the discrimination of silence serve to perpetuate the ethnic *status quo* and to prolong the racist tendency to blame the victims, if not for their innate, biologically determined racial disadvantages, then certainly for their *culturally determined* ones. Instead of making structural changes in policy so as to equally or equitably accommodate the needs of different ethnic collectivities, Canadian bureaucrats and ideologues, like their American counterparts (Glaser and Possony 1979: 232), tend to provide forms of 'compensation' for cultural minorities, especially for those of the lowest ethno-classes. Grant and Anderson (1975) revealed a discriminatory pattern of school streaming for West Indian children in Toronto secondary schools. Hill and Schiff (1988: 55) point out that ethnoculturally influenced streaming persists in Canadian schools today. Further, evidence abounds on the long-term pattern of inadequate school facilities and resources, school drop-outs, and subsequent welfare hand-outs characterizing the 'compensatory' treatment of Canada's aboriginal peoples (Frideres 1993: 159-208).

As Glaser and Possony (1979: 95-6) so astutely point out, were all the international anti-discrimination conventions to be applied literally, not only Canada and the United States but virtually all of the countries of the world would be found to be discriminatory. Because of the subtle forms of systemic and cultural discrimination built into the social system as a whole, measures taken in the name of ethnic equality but not tuned to the specific needs of individuals and collectivities may serve to produce new inequalities and human indignities rather than to resolve old ones.

For a realistic assessment of the relative efficacy of legislation and other public policies and strategies designed to eradicate ethnic discrimination, we must first come to understand the nature of the social forces underlying racism. What kinds of social conditions are most conducive to the development of racism? What kinds of social environmental contexts lead to its cultural legitimation, and to its persistence, florescence, and decline? Is racism inevitable in a multi-ethnic society? Is it a cause or a consequence of strongly held ethnic identities and alignments? In the following chapters of this book we will attempt to shed some light on the nature of these processes in the Canadian context.

Notes

1 The above statement notwithstanding, Price (1950), Wade (1970), and Patterson (1972), among others, have pointed out significant differences in the early patterns of French-aboriginal and English-aboriginal relations in the context of European overseas

expansion. Firstly, these authors contend that the French were far less racist than were the British in outlook and in practice toward aboriginal peoples. Secondly, in the Canadian context, the French were not primarily colonizers, as were the British. They were traders, and, in the fur-trade, their relations with aboriginal peoples were essentially co-operative. Thirdly, French government policy towards aboriginal peoples was far more assimilationist than was the British. Their ultimate goal was absorption rather than subordination or extermination. In the Canadian context, to the degree that aboriginal peoples embraced French-Catholic values, standards, and life ways, they were deemed acceptable as both trading partners and marital partners. The latter attitude was responsible for the eventual creation of the Métis population, the reproductive product of early unions between European fur-traders and aboriginal women.

2 In this book, my general usage of the terms 'ethnic prejudice' and 'ethnic discrimination', subsumes the 'racial' referent. However, when prejudice and discrimination are predicated on *racial visibility*, the racial referent will be employed.

3 This phenomenon is described in the now classic novel *Gentlemen's Agreement* by Laura Hobson. Written in the 1940s, this book mirrors the social reality in the United States at that time. A newspaper reporter, posing as a Jew to research a series of true-to-life articles on anti-Semitism, discovers, much to his surprise, that Jews, as well as non-Jews, contribute to the perpetuation of anti-Semitism through fearful silence in the face of social exclusion and anti-Jewish verbal abuse.

CHAPTER THREE

The Anatomy of Ethnicity

In Chapter One, we introduced our discussion of racism with the thesis that racism is rooted in ethnocultural differences and not race in the biological sense. Ethnocentrism, prejudice, stereotypes, and discrimination—the key components of racism, elaborated in Chapter Two—all reflect the seeming inability of members of humankind to respect fully and equally the fundamental human rights and freedoms of peoples they consider inherently different from themselves because of their (presumed) ancestral origins.

Scientific evidence demonstrates that racial boundaries do not, in themselves, present barriers to human intercourse. Members of all human populations belong to the same species, *Homo sapiens*; males and females from different racial groups are thus capable of mating to propagate the human species. Moreover, many of the commonly held racist assumptions as to the natural, innate differences among human populations in intelligence, morality, capacity for cultural development, and so forth have never been scientifically proven. Why, then, in an age of scientific enlightenment, do members of humankind continue to place so much emphasis on ethnocultural distinctiveness and to make invidious comparisons between one human population and another? The answer to this question is anything but simple: a full explanation would necessitate drawing from the pooled resources of theologians, philosophers, historians, and many other scholars, as well as social scientists. Nevertheless, an examination of the ways in which the concepts of race, culture, and ethnicity have been utilized by social scientists can shed some light on this enigmatic phenomenon.

Race, Culture and Ethnicity

Scholars and laypersons alike have long used the terms 'racial' and 'ethnic' interchangeably with reference to biological and cultural differences between various human populations. For late nineteenth- and early twentieth-century anthropologists whose evolutionary interests focused on the study of prehistoric and aboriginal human populations, the original meaning of the term 'ethnic' pertained to the so-called primitive races and cultures of humankind. Bennett (1975: 5) points out that the 'ethnic' concept connoted the 'exotic, less than civilized, and probably less than human creatures out there for the taking, and for the ethnologist [social and cultural anthropologist], there for studying and preserving like wild species'. Anthropologists, despite their understanding and empathy, were outsiders. Accordingly, as Bennett (1975) suggests, concepts employed by early anthropologists reflected their ethnocentric, EuroWestern, cultural assumptions.

The old notion of ethnicity, variously defined, equated race, culture, geography, and human identity. Ethnic groups were conceived as 'natural' populations born, living, and dying in a known geographical range. This perspective associated the long-term geographical and social isolation of involuntary human groups with their distinctive biological and cultural attributes. Conceptualized in this way, ethnic groups were seen as corporate entities, highly adapted to particular geographical environments, and uniquely capable of maintaining group membership and cultural continuity through time.

To recapitulate, as typically employed by anthropologists and, later, sociologists (Isajiw 1970), ethnicity was conceived as an attribute of an organized and cohesive ethnic group whose members shared distinctive bio-cultural attributes which they transmitted from generation to generation through the processes of inbreeding (intra-ethnic mating) and enculturation (distinctive ethnic socialization). Based on these assumptions, ethnicity could be measured objectively in terms of the distinctive features—physiognomy, language, religion, art and artifacts, technology, and modes of social organization—characteristic of members of a given ethnic group.

The New Ethnicity

The contemporary social scientific usage of the concept of ethnicity reflects a shift in theoretical perspective among anthropologists, sociologists, and others, to a more subjective frame of reference (Bennett 1975; Glazer and Moynihan 1975). In part, this shift in orientation reflects radical changes in world conditions which have markedly altered the old ethnic/geographical balance and have brought formerly isolated human populations into face-to-face contact and confrontation. As a consequence of human breakthroughs in science and technology, particularly in the areas of transportation and telecommunications, geographical boundaries and distances no longer present barriers to human intercourse.

In the decades following World War II, massive cross-national migrations of human populations, together with the development of instant satellite communications, have led to and indeed necessitated the growth of an international technological culture, and have concomitantly greatly increased the potential for the creation of a global village of humankind. Paradoxically, while these developments have increasingly muted or eroded former cultural differences between human populations and have generated a certain degree of cultural uniformity at the international level, at the same time they appear to have heightened the salience of ethnic differentiation both within and among modern states.

At the level of the ethnic collectivity, exposure to compelling new options in ideas, values, and life ways has led to the fragmentation of former ethnocultures and communities, as well as to the creation of new ones. Consequently, today's ethnic collectivities do not represent cultural wholes. One of the most typical and most salient lines of internal division within contemporary ethnic collectivities is found between traditionalists—those members most committed to preservation of the ethnic heritage, ethos, and life ways—and transitionalists—those most eager to learn and adopt new ways of viewing and doing things. Members not strongly bound by tradition may seek marital partners from outside the ethnic collectivity. When this happens on a relatively large scale, it leads to the creation of a new ethnic strain, whose members may, over time, come to constitute a new ethnic collectivity. (The Cape Coloured in South Africa, the Métis in Canada, and the Eurasians in Southeast Asia are examples.)

Shifts in political boundaries, resulting from wars and treaties between states, as well as from the creation of new geopolitical units by Colonial powers, have led to the fracturing of former ethnocultural units, and to the creation of new ethnic minorities within state boundaries. With the demise of the Colonial era, the withdrawal of Colonial administrations from former territories, and the subsequent rise of newly created nation-states, many of the old ethnic antagonisms, forcibly contained under Colonial rule, have re-emerged in politicized form. Ethnic minorities throughout the post-Colonial world are demanding a reassessment of their other-imposed minority status and some are asserting demands for self-determination within existing state boundaries (for example, Canada's aboriginal peoples, Israeli dominated Palestinians, Iraq's Kurds). Where minority demands for self-determination within the state have been pushed aside or blocked by formidable governmental opposition, more radical demands for political secession have been voiced by some sectors within ethnic minorities (Quebec Separatists; Baltic and other minorities in the former USSR).

Other political shifts—in ideologies, power bases, national boundaries, and cross-national alliances—have also split peoples apart. New ethnic categories are emerging, for example, among political refugees—Palestinians in Israel, Indochinese refugees in Canada, Cubans in Florida, and many others.

As a result of these macro-level phenomena, the populations studied by anthropologists and other social scientists can no longer be conceptualized in terms of their old racial or ethnic group labels; nor can they be meaningfully analysed holistically, in the manner of traditional structural/functional analysis. Ethnicity is no longer coterminous with national and geopolitical boundaries. Indeed, the multi-ethnic state, as in the case of Canada, has become the global norm. Moreover, ethnic categories now crosscut state boundaries. This phenomenon is very evident in the Canadian context. Consider the ties between immigrants and their homelands; the ties between members of aboriginal ethnic collectivities artificially split by the Canadian/American border; and the ties between members of widely dispersed ethnic minorities such as Jews, resident outside of Israel. All of these vital inter-state bonds between members of cross-national ethnic collectivities demonstrate, unequivocally, that the age of ethnic isolation is over, thereby rendering static concepts of ethnicity obsolete.

New Theoretical Directions: Situational and Symbolic Manifestations of Ethnicity in Multi-Ethnic Societies

The shift from the old to the new ethnicity owes much to the seminal work of the anthropologist Fredrik Barth, who argued that the old biocultural/territorial-isolate frame of reference could not account for the persistence of viable ethnic collectivities, despite continuing contact across ethnic boundaries (Barth 1969: Introduction). According to Barth, in order to explain ethnic group persistence in the face of the loss of territorial distinctiveness through migration, loss of cultural distinctiveness through culture contact, and loss of physical distinctiveness through changes in ethnic strain, we must shift our attention from the morphological characteristics of the internal cultures of ethnic groups to the dynamics of inter-ethnic relations and of ethnic boundary maintenance. For Barth, the critical feature of ethnicity is the ethnic boundary, rather than the cultural *gestalt* (content) within it. Barth does not imply that cultural differences are irrelevant; the point he emphasizes is that we cannot assume a simple, one-to-one correspondence between ethnic collectivities and cultural similarities. Alternatively, we must focus our attention only on those physical and cultural diacritica (bodily mutilations and decorations, names, songs, religious icons, military medallions, and the like) singled out by in-group members as paramount symbols of ethnicity. Barth also stressed the crucial importance, for boundary maintenance, of behavioural norms (such as endogamy) that restrict interaction with outsiders and serve to maintain a high level of social distance between insiders and outsiders. Essentially, he argued, it is these key symbolic and behavioural attributes, and not culture as a whole, that help explain ethnic boundary maintenance in the face of extensive inter-ethnic contacts and intra-ethnic sociocultural changes.

For Barth and many of his followers, the most critical features of ethnic boundary maintenance are the characteristics of self-ascription and ascription by others. Thus, while selective objective criteria (key symbolic and behavioural attributes) are important, the critical variables underlying processes of boundary maintenance are subjective in nature. Put another way: ethnicity can be socially constructed by both insiders and outsiders, and the two social constructs may or may not correspond.

Adopting this perspective, we can explain ethnic continuity by examining how interacting ethnic collectivities define and maintain their dichotomous relationship, despite their increasing cultural similarities in response to the shared societal and global environmental contexts in which they find themselves.

In arguing that ethnicity needs to be defined with reference to some outside group, Barth highlighted the idea that the new ethnicity is contingent upon the prevailing social environment. Building upon this notion, social scientists have increasingly come to conceptualize ethnicity as a symbolic system which can be manipulated situationally by members. In this view, ethnicity is seen as an organizational strategy whereby members seek to satisfy their expressive and symbolic needs for group continuity and belongingness in those social environmental contexts where such emotive needs come to the fore, and/or to satisfy their instrumental needs for economic, political, and social power in those social environmental contexts where such individual and corporate group interests come to the fore.

In some societal contexts ethnicity may be unimportant or irrelevant, while in others it may be in the forefront of individual/group consciousness. In those situations where ethnicity is not highly salient, where other group affiliations and interests take precedence over ethnic ones, members may choose to maintain a low ethnic profile, to remain ethnically invisible. Thus, for example, within political pressure groups mobilized around minority issues like women's liberation, gay and lesbian rights, promotion of the rights of persons with physical or mental disabilities—ethnic differences between members may become muted in the pursuit of other common interests and corporate goals. Alternatively, in those situations where members believe that the very existence of the ethnic collectivity is threatened (e.g., the Métis in Canada, prior to the Riel Rebellion; the Canadian Jews, during the Arab-Israeli wars; and the Franco-Québécois, following the failure of the Meech Lake Accord) the salience of ethnicity becomes heightened, and the group is perceived both as a refuge and as a vehicle for concerted action in pursuit of corporate interests and goals.

In social environmental contexts where ethnicity is recognized by outsiders as a legitimate basis for group differentiation, ethnic diacritica can provide paramount symbols of ethnicity which serve as rallying points for group mobilization in pursuit of instrumental goals. In the emotionally charged atmosphere of the campaign period preceding the Quebec Referendum on 20 May 1980, ethnic diacritica were utilized to their fullest to symbolize the dichotomous relationship between *Yes* and *No* supporters. The Canadian ensign, with its maple leaf symbol of Canadian national unity, was fervently waved by the *No*—federalist—supporters; the flag of Quebec, with its fleur-de-lis, symbol of Québécois independence, was just as eagerly brandished by the *Yes* supporters of sovereignty-association.

The foregoing lends credence to the position of Bell (1975) and others who argue (against the neo-Marxists) that ethnicity has become more salient than economic class in advancing corporate interests because it involves more than interests; it can combine interests with affective ties. We can view the new ethnicity as an ethnic organizational strategy uniquely designed to resolve an inherent human conflict of modern times, between the expressive need for a sense of rootedness and group belongingness which can best be satisfied within an involuntary *gemeinschaft* community, and the instrumental desire for material gratification and political power which can best be satisfied by participation in the *gesellschaft* institutions of post-technological society.

Key Components of Ethnicity

Before we proceed to examine, in some detail, the nature of ethnicity and the relationship between ethnicity and ethnic identity, we must first clarify the conceptual distinction between the concepts of race and ethnicity adopted throughout this book.

In Chapter One, we distinguished between the concepts of race and ethnicity, as currently employed by physical and social anthropologists. To briefly reiterate:

The concept *race* refers to any arbitrary classification of human populations utilizing such biological criteria as physiological and/or genetic differences.

The concept of *ethnicity* refers to any arbitrary classification of human populations utilizing the biogeographical criterion of ancestry in conjunction with such sociocultural criteria as nationality, language, and religion.

The most important criterion underlying the concept of ethnicity is that of common ancestry or ancestral origin. Common ancestry, in turn, is a multifaceted concept implying at least three criteria: biological descent from common ancestors; maintenance of a shared ancestral heritage (culture and social institutions); and attachment to an actual or mythical ancestral territory or homeland. These criteria provide the foundation for the (actual or assumed) distinctiveness of an ethnic category—a people classified as alike on the basis of ethnicity.[1]

The criterion of biological descent from common ancestors underlies physical distinctiveness. When this criterion of ethnicity is emphasized in classification, we may speak of a *racially defined* ethnic category. The criterion of attachment to an ancestral territory or homeland underlies distinctiveness deriving from national origin. When this criterion of ethnicity is emphasized we may speak of a *nationally defined* ethnic category. The criterion of maintenance of an ancestral heritage underlies sociocultural distinctiveness. When this criterion is emphasized we may speak of a *culturally defined* ethnic category. Frequently, the criterion of ancestral heritage emphasizes one sociocultural phenomenon such as language or religion. Thus, we may speak of a linguistically defined or religiously defined ethnic category.

Although these distinctions are analytically useful, it is important to note that, in reality, a given ethnic category may be *socially constructed* on the basis of any one or any combination of these criteria in a given societal context. Moreover, because ethnicity is contingent on the prevailing social environment, criteria used for ethnic classification will vary with changing social conditions.

For example, the public preoccupation with race during the early years of Canada's development, when White Supremacy was a salient feature of public life and policy, led to the classification of Canada's so-called charter groups—the English and French—as the 'two founding races'. This scientifically invalid conception was found in government policy statements as recently as the 1960s, when the terms of reference of the Royal Commission on Bilingualism and Biculturalism were publicly announced (Privy Council 1963: 1106). Yet the salient feature of ethnicity underscoring the historical boundary between English and French was religion. Indeed, it was the Protestant/Catholic division between English and French, respectively, that became constitutionally recognized in s.93 of the BNA Act protecting minority—Protestant and Catholic—denominational schools.[2]

With the growth of the Franco-Québécois independence movement, language is increasingly the most prominent ethnic criterion behind French/English relations in Canada. The Official Languages Act (1969) accorded legal recognition to this distinction at the national level and the 1982 Charter constitutionally enshrined it.

Another example of changes in criteria for ethnic classification over time is provided in the case of the Jewish people. From the time of their dispersion from Palestine (*circa* seventy AD) to the late nineteenth century, the bulk of the world's Jews lived within various countries of Europe where the Jewish minority was classified by insiders and outsiders as ethnically distinctive, primarily in terms of religion. It was not until 1873, when the racist ideology of anti-Semitism took root in Germany, that the Jews were classified by outsiders (Germans and, later, other Europeans) primarily in terms of biological criteria, as a distinct and inferior race.

The foregoing illustrations demonstrate that the particular components of ethnicity selected as criteria for the social construction of ethnicity, at the level of public policy and practice, may be highly arbitrary and thus may vary with changing social conditions. Moreover, it is important to note that the defining ethnic criteria selected by outsiders in any given instance may or may not correspond with the criteria selected by insiders for purposes of ethnic self-identification.

To return briefly to examples previously cited; in the case of the Franco-Québécois, the negative results of the 1980 Quebec Referendum, together with the results of several public opinion polls conducted prior to and following the Referendum, made it clear that the majority of Canadians, both within and outside the Province of Quebec, did not accept the Franco-Québécois ethnic self-definition as a nation with the right to political independence. Alternatively, most Canadians continued to emphasize the language criterion of ethnicity and to define the French-identified population within and outside Quebec as Francophones. A similar example is provided in the case of contemporary Canadian Jews. Since the formation of the State of Israel in 1948, increasing numbers of Jews have come to identify themselves as Jews primarily in terms of ancestral territory—Israeli nationality. The Canadian public, on the other hand, continues to ethnically classify Jews primarily in terms of religion (except for self-professed White Supremicists like the Ku Klux Klan and the Western Guard who employ pernicious racial criteria).

Ethnicity and Nationality

With regard to the concept of *nationality*, both ethnicity and citizenship can provide bases for nationally defined sentiments and loyalties. As a criterion of ethnicity, the concept of nationality refers to the national, ancestral, and cultural origins associated with a particular ancestral territory or homeland. This multifaceted criterion of ethnicity underscores the political concept of nationhood. But ethnically defined nationality may or may not correspond to nationality based on actual country of birth or citizenship. Where the two concepts of nationality correspond, i.e., where the ancestral homeland is coterminous with the territorial enclave occupied by the ethnic collectivity—as in the case of Quebec for the Franco-Québécois—the criterion of nationality may provide the ethnic rallying point for political mobilization geared toward national independence. On the other hand, where the two concepts provide separate and distinct national frames of reference—as in the case of Canada and Israel for Canadian Jews—each may serve as an important yet different criterion for self-identification. Torontonian Jews, for example, have been reported to be highly ethnically identified with Israel as their national ancestral homeland and highly nationally identified with Canada as their country of birth or citizenship (Richmond 1973; Kallen 1977; Taras and Weinfeld 1993).

Ethnicity and Collective Rights in Canada

The distinction between Canadian ethnocultural collectivities, with and without territorial bases for ethnic claims to nationhood within the state, has important human rights implications. While all Canadian ethnocultural collectivities can justifiably seek recognition of their collective linguistic, religious, and/or broader cultural group rights, only those collectivities with territorial bases for their ethnic claims, i.e., charter groups and aboriginal peoples, can justifiably seek recognition of their collective national group rights.

Another conceptual distinction which differentiates between Canadian ethnic collectivities with regard to potential human rights claims is the distinction between ethnic category and ethnic group. Here, the relevant distinction is between arbitrary, artificial categories of classification, designed for analytic purposes (conceptual constructs) or statistical ends (numerical constructs), on the one hand, and actual *sui generis* social collectivities organized on an ethnic basis (ethnic groups), on the other. Ethnic categories may be represented empirically by loosely connected, dispersed social aggregates (such as Indians and blacks, in Canada) or by highly cohesive, closely-knit ethnic groups such as Hutterites and Sikhs.

The Canadian 'Indian', as a socially constructed racial/ethnic category, did not exist prior to contact with Europeans. Members of various aboriginal peoples, such as Cree, Ojibway, and Iroquois, identified themselves and were categorized by other groups as Cree, Ojibway, and Iroquois, respectively. But to the European, and later the Euro-Canadian, anyone who 'looked Indian' was believed to be of common ancestry. On this basis, the category 'Indian' was socially constructed in racially defined terms, and all peoples lumped together in this category were treated as 'Indians'. For a long time, the Cree, Ojibway, and Iroquois peoples continued to ethnically identify themselves as such, in spite of the fact that they were increasingly categorized by outsiders as Indians.

In the early days of the aboriginal independence movement, various aboriginal peoples subsumed under the arbitrary category 'Indian' began to rally around the Indian concept in order to mobilize significant numbers of members for political purposes. More recently, the constitutionalization of aboriginal issues and the burning question of defining aboriginal rights has led to a re-definition of members of the Indian, Inuit and Métis groupings as aboriginal peoples.

The foregoing lends credence to Barth's (1969: 14-15) contention that, for purposes of self-ascription and ascription by others, it makes little or no difference whether ethnic criteria selected as the foci for one's ethnic identity are real or artificial; if one feels and says that one is Dene or Indian or First Nation or aboriginal, in contrast to Euro-Canadian,[3] one is aligning oneself with one category of people, and, simultaneously, setting oneself apart from others.

Ethnic Group and Ethnic Category: Implications for Group-Based Human Rights Claims

The foregoing observations notwithstanding, the empirical distinction between ethnic group and ethnic category has important implications for the kinds of group-based human rights claims that can be made. (See the typology of rights outlined in the Introduction, page 10).

Ethnic categories defined arbitrarily on the basis of race (Caucasoid/Negroid/ Mongoloid or White/Black/Yellow) do not represent *sui generis* ethnocultural collectivities. Thus, members of these racial categories cannot make *collective rights* claims based on cultural group rights. There is no Caucasoid or White ethnoculture. White culture is an essentially racist concept historically employed to refer to the allegedly superior characteristics of modern, Western, civilized, industrialized societies and cultures in contradistinction to the allegedly inferior characteristics of primitive, non-Western, uncivilized, non-industrialized (or underdeveloped) societies and cultures, racially categorized as Negroid and Mongoloid.

While these arbitrary racial categories should not be confused with *sui generis* ethnocultures, they do have important human rights implications. Members of such categories who have been disadvantaged by racial discrimination can make individual or group-based claims to redress against the adverse impact of systemic discrimination on the category as a whole. We have conceptualized such claims as *categorical* human rights claims.[4] To exemplify: blacks and Indians in Canada—victims of the self-fulfilling prophecy of White racism—can make categorical human rights claims for redress against the adverse economic impact upon their racial category of systemic discrimination. They cannot, however, use 'Blackness' and 'Indianness' as the basis for collective rights claims based on cultural or national group rights. Here, their claims must be ethnically specific, e.g., Inuit of Nunavut claims to nationhood (national group rights) and Black Rastafarian claims to freedom of collective religious expression (cultural group rights).

A final conceptual distinction that has implications for the kinds of human rights claims which can be made by different Canadian ethnocultural collectivities is the distinction between those ethnic territorial claims based on charter group status and those based on aboriginal status. Territorial claims based on charter group status, i.e., the English outside Quebec and the French in Quebec, essentially represent constitutionally based claims to nationhood within Canada by its founding peoples, on the basis of their national group rights.

Territorial claims based on aboriginal status, i.e., the Indians, Inuit, and Métis peoples in Canada, represent as yet constitutionally unrecognized claims to nationhood within Canada on the basis of pre-Colonial nationhood status and aboriginal rights.

Aboriginal Group Status: Aboriginal Rights and Nationhood Claims

A brief historical sketch of the relationship between aboriginal peoples and Euro-Canadian government agents in Canada will provide a background for understanding the kinds of collective human rights claims currently being put forward by spokespersons for various aboriginal organizations.

At the heart of the conflicting positions of aboriginal spokespersons and government authorities with regard to aboriginal peoples' land claims and demands for self-government are different and seemingly incompatible concepts of land. As currently articulated by aboriginal spokespersons, the integral link between people, land, and culture which informs the aboriginal world view has provided one of the pivotal points of misunderstanding between Europeans and aborigines since they first came into contact.

The land and its resources, in the aboriginal view, are the sustainers of human life: people must, therefore, respect them and they must attempt to live in balance and harmony with their natural surroundings. From this view, one could no more own the land than one could own the rain clouds or the sunshine. Each people, that is each tribe, band, or community, is intimately associated with the land and resources within its own territorial boundaries; each people recognizes and respects the other's right to occupy and use their ancestral lands, and to transfer this right to their descendants. This view does not include the notion of permanent alienation of aboriginal lands through market sale or exchange. From the perspective of human rights, this means that as long as members of an aboriginal ethnic collectivity occupy, use, and respect their ancestral lands, the lands their people have been intimately associated with 'from time immemorial', they have a collective, aboriginal right to the lands and their resources.

The aboriginal view of sovereignty is closely linked with their view of land. Advocates of the aboriginal view maintain that sovereignty is a gift of the Creator which has never been and can never be surrendered (Frideres 1993: 416). As the concept 'First Nations' implies, prior to the arrival of European agents aboriginal peoples were independent, self-governing nations whose members lived and sought their livelihoods within clearly delineated territories. With colonization, they claim, their right to sovereignty was unjustly abrogated and their institutions of self-government systematically dismantled. But, as nations, they assert their sovereignty and their right to create and administer their own forms of self-government. From this aboriginal view, treaties made between aboriginal peoples and Governments should be regarded as treaties between sovereign nations, in the sense of public international law (Frideres 1993: 417).

The European view of land ownership differs markedly from the aboriginal view of land occupancy and use articulated by aboriginal spokespersons today. For Europeans, land is a form of property which can be alienated through the market processes of purchase and sale. An individual or a collectivity can buy, own, and sell land in the same way as one can buy, own, and sell other material goods available in the open market. To the European settler, Indian lands were desirable properties which could be purchased and cultivated. From the European view, the land and its resources were things quite distinct from the people occupying and using them; yet racist ideas about the primitiveness of aboriginal peoples enabled Europeans to view both land and people as things to be exploited and controlled rather than respected.

The European view of nationhood is consistent with their view of land and their view of aboriginal peoples. There is no question that, prior to the arrival of Europeans, aboriginal peoples occupied and governed the land now called Canada. However, the Government of Canada has taken the position that aboriginal peoples were never nations *in the legal sense*, and have no right to be treated as such (Frideres 1993). In refutation of claims based on Court decisions which support the aboriginal view, the Government has cited the doctrine of continuity. This racist doctrine holds that, in the case of conquest or cession, the rights of 'civilized' indigenous peoples and their laws remain intact until the Colonial government changes them through an Act of Parliament. If, however, the aboriginal inhabitants of the land are deemed 'uncivilized' at the time of European entry, the laws of the colonizers take immediate effect. The racist assumptions behind this doctrine have underscored Court decisions used by Governments to support their view that while agreements with aboriginal peoples (presumed to be 'uncivilized' at the time of contact) have been called treaties, they are not treaties between sovereign nations, in the sense of international law.

The Historical Background: Alienation of Aboriginal Lands / Extinguishment of Aboriginal Rights

Jackson (1979: 269-71) suggests that the numerical superiority of the Canadian Indians in the early period of European-Indian contact encouraged Europeans for practical rather than for moral reasons to recognize the right of these aboriginal peoples to their lands. Yet the fact that aboriginal lands were acquired by negotiation and purchase for European settlement and cultivation clearly indicates European recognition that the lands belonged to the Indian peoples. In 1763, this recognition was legally entrenched in a Royal Proclamation which has since been referred to as the 'Magna Carta' of aboriginal rights.

Under this Proclamation, a large area of lands lying west of the Allegheny Mountains (excluding the Hudson Bay region) was reserved to Indians as their hunting grounds. The Proclamation set out procedures for the acquisition of Indian lands, specifying public negotiation and sale between Indians and representatives of the British Crown; private sales of Indian lands were disallowed.

Since then, a series of court cases involving Indian claims based on aboriginal rights has led to an elaboration by EuroCanadian legal authorities of a theory of aboriginal rights. In support of this view, Jackson asserts that (up to 1979) court decisions have held that the right of political sovereignty and legal ownership of land by the discovering country is subject to the aboriginal right of the aboriginal peoples to use and occupy those lands which have been theirs 'from time immemorial'. Secondly, these cases have confirmed the validity of the collective basis of aboriginal title by asserting that the interest of the aboriginal peoples is a communal one: it is an interest of the tribe or band and not of the individual member, and that interest can only be alienated to the Crown (i.e., the Canadian Parliament, today), not to private persons. Finally, the qualifications of aboriginal title have been specified. Aboriginal title can be extinguished by conquest, by purchase, or by acts of Parliament that are inconsistent with the continuation of aboriginal rights.

Jackson goes on to argue that the Royal Proclamation of 1763 provided the legal foundation for the land cession treaties between Indian ethnic collectivities and the British Crown, which extinguished Indian interest to the largest and most resource-plentiful parts of Canada in the nineteenth and early twentieth centuries.[5] By means of these treaties, various Indian peoples exchanged their lands for monies, reserves, and other privileges.

Since the enactment in 1982 of the Constitution Act, according recognition and protection, under s.35, for the existing aboriginal and treaty rights of the aboriginal peoples of Canada, there has been an increasing rejection by aboriginal spokespersons and their EuroCanadian supporters of some of the key propositions in the foregoing theory of aboriginal right. In particular, opposition has been expressed to the idea that such rights can be extinguished or limited *without* the consent of aboriginal people. Sanders (1990: 128), in his analysis of the pathbreaking Supreme Court decision in *Sparrow v. The Queen* (June 1990), argues that the Court, in this recent case, adopted essential elements of the aboriginal position on s.35 (1) by saying that laws passed by governments do not extinguish aboriginal rights unless the Sovereign's intention to do so by way of the legislation has been made clear and plain, or unless the consent of the aboriginal people has been given. Sanders points out that there are almost no examples of legislation explicitly extinguishing aboriginal or treaty rights. The Supreme Court, then, has taken a position consistent with the aboriginal view that s.35 is a positive affirmation of aboriginal peoples' rights, not a confirmation of the legal *status quo*. The result, Sanders states, is that s.35 has rendered obsolete previous court decisions which upheld casual and unilateral extinguishment of aboriginal rights.

Current Status and Rights of Aboriginal Peoples

Jackson (1979: 269) points out that the question of who is an Indian is a complicated legal issue in Canada. Under the BNA Act s.91(24), the federal government has jurisdiction over Indians and lands reserved for Indians. However, the Supreme Court of Canada has ruled that the term Indian, as used under the BNA Act, includes 'Eskimos' (Inuit). Thus, aboriginal peoples, Inuit and Indians alike, are classified as Indians for the purposes of federal responsibility. (See: Re: Eskimos, 1939, S.C.R. 104.)

Within this jurisdictional frame of reference, Parliament has enacted the Indian Act, which provides the legal basis for administration of Indian affairs. But the Indian Act applies to only one subcategory of aboriginal peoples: Status or Registered Indians is the sole category of aboriginal peoples legally defined as Indians under this Act. The Indian Act (s.4:1) specifically excludes 'Eskimos' from the broader, racially defined Indian category, and it also excludes those persons of Indian or part Indian ancestry who have lost their legal Indian status, i.e., non-Status Indians and Métis.

Under the Indian Act (s.2:1g) 'Indian means a person who pursuant to this Act is registered as an Indian or is entitled to be registered as an Indian.' What these complex and confusing distinctions imply is that, for legal purposes, the constitutional category of 'Indian', i.e., aboriginal peoples, is broken down, first, by so-called 'race', into the two racially distinct categories of Indian and Inuit; secondly, the racial category Indian is divided into two subcategories: Status or Registered Indians with legal Indian Status, and non-Status Indians (including Métis) without legal Indian Status.

In Canada, today, there are approximately 1,604,000 constitutionally defined aboriginal persons (Frideres 1993: 31, Figure 2.1). Some 435,000 of these persons are Status Indians, legally defined as Indians under the Indian Act. Another 1,030,000 persons of Indian Ancestry do not have legal Indian Status, but, since changes made in 1985 to the provisions of the Indian Act some 10,000 non-registered Indians now have band membership. Some 104,000 persons of mixed

(Indian/non-Indian) ancestry are categorized as Métis, and some 35,000 are categorized as Inuit.

Status or Registered Indians

Historically, legal Indian Status was acquired in two ways: through land cession treaty or through voluntary registration. These processes gave rise to a division within the legal category of Status Indians into two subcategories: Treaty and non-Treaty Indians.

Treaty (Status) Indians are those Indians, and their descendants, who signed land cession treaties with the Crown, thereby surrendering huge tracts of aboriginal lands in return for reserves, gifts, and the promise of services. Non-Treaty (Status) Indians are those Indians, and their descendants, who chose legal Indian Status under the Indian Act, by having their names registered on Indian band lists.

A third means of acquiring legal Indian Status is through marriage. By marrying a Status Indian, a non-Indian female acquires legal Indian Status under the Indian Act; moreover, this legal Status is passed on to all descendants. However, until 1985, when the Indian Act was amended, the marriage provision did not apply equally to female Indians. Indeed, the converse was true: a Status Indian female who married a non-Indian lost her legal Indian Status and she, as well as her descendants, became non-Status Indians.

To digress briefly, this aspect of the Indian Act formed the basis for legal contests in which Indian women, who had lost their Status by marrying out, argued that the section of the Indian Act in question discriminated against women. However, the Supreme Court found the Indian Act to be lawful, and ruled against the complainants. (See: *Attorney General of Canada v. Lavelle* and *Isaac v. Bedard*. Judgment of 1973 08 22, reported in Dominion Law Report 38 (3d) 1973.) Conversely, a decision in 1981 by the United Nations Human Rights Commission (in the Sandra Lovelace case) found that the Indian Act negatively discriminated against Indian women who marry out by denying them and their children access to their ethnic community and its culture. This persuaded the federal government to change the Act. In 1985, Bill C-31 (*An Act to Amend the Indian Act*) was introduced, and as a consequence of the removal of the Act's discriminatory provisions against women, thousands of Indian women have been reinstated as Status Indians. The repercussions of these changes on Indian reserve communities are discussed later in this chapter.

Every Status Indian is a Registered Indian, i.e., a legally defined Indian whose name (with some exceptions) is registered on a particular band list and on the 'roll' in Ottawa (Frideres 1993). Until 1985, only these registered Status Indians were entitled to live on the Indian reserve on whose band list their name appeared.

In 1985, Bill C-31 (*An Act to Amend the Indian Act*) created new legislation which added new complexities to the definition of Indian status.[6] The bill also made changes in the rules regarding transmission of legal Indian status. Sexist provisions of the Indian Act denying Indian status to women who married out, and their children, were struck down and the concept of enfranchisement was abolished. In addition, under the provisions of Bill C-31, some persons who have lost their Indian status through marriage or enfranchisement may now reapply for legal Indian status. However, persons whose ancestors, more than one generation removed, lost their status are not eligible to reapply.

The new Act has introduced four types of Indian: 1) Status with band membership, 2) Status with no band membership, 3) Non-Status with band membership and 4) Non-Status, non-band. Applications for Indian Status are reviewed by the Department of Indian and Northern Affairs and government authorities determine whether the applicant has a legal right to claim Indian status. Band membership, on the other hand, is determined by the band council. The one exception to this rule is that the approximately 20,000 women who lost their legal Indian status through intermarriage automatically become band members if they are reinstated as Indians by federal authorities.

By 1989, nearly 67,000 Indians who had lost their legal Indian status had been reinstated (Frideres 1993: 36). However, because acceptance into a band means that ofttimes scarce resources (such as housing) must be shared, many band councils have refused to accept reinstated Indians into their band membership lists.

Indian Ancestry: Non-Status Indians and Métis

Non-Status Indians are persons of Indian or part-Indian ancestry who do not have and are not entitled to acquire legal Indian status.[7] Métis are persons of mixed ancestry who may ethnically identify as Métis, but who do not have and are not entitled to acquire legal Indian status. The Non-Status (Indian Ancestry) and Métis subcategories comprise those Indians and their descendants who have renounced or lost their legal Indian status in one of several ways.

Until 1960, the only way Status Indians could assume the full individual human rights of Canadian citizens was through the process of enfranchisement. The particulars of this process were fairly specific in their intent: Indians gave up their special legal Indian Status and acquired the right to vote in federal elections, the right to purchase and consume alcohol, and other benefits accorded individual citizens. As legal Status Indians, they had been denied these privileges because they were not defined as persons before the law. Indeed, as stated in the original version of the Indian Act (1876), 'the term person means an individual other than an Indian.'

With the introduction of the Canadian Bill of Rights in 1960, the human rights notion of equality of all persons before the law was invoked by Indian leaders and, under pressure exerted by Indian organizations and sympathetic citizens' groups, the right to vote in federal elections (federal enfranchisement) was extended to Status Indians.

Historically, another way that Indian Status was lost was through the loss of the right to live on a reserve. Prior to 1985, under the terms of the Indian Act, a Status

Indian was required to live on or maintain a residence on a reserve, to which he or she had to return for a specified period every three years. Legal Indian Status was forfeited if these conditions were not met.

For many Indian women, loss of legal Indian status occurred through *intermarriage*. Until 1985, a Status Indian woman who married someone other than another Status Indian, lost both her own legal Indian status and that of her progeny.

Historically, *hereditary* loss of legal Indian Status also occurred under the provisions of various Indian Acts. Before 1985, under the provisions of the 1951 Act, persons twenty-one years of age or older, who were the descendants of non-Status Indian parents, were not entitled to be legally registered as Indians.

Another way in which Indians could lose their legal Indian status was through formal *renunciation*. A Status Indian who renounced his or her legal Indian status received a share of the collective assets of the band to which he or she belonged and gave up the right to maintain a residence on a reserve. In this way, a Status Indian became a non-Status Indian and an ordinary Canadian citizen before the law. The descendants of these non-Status Indians were not entitled to claim legal Indian status.

Historically, some of the Métis people lost legal Indian status through 'taking scrip' or 'taking treaty'. This loss of entitlement applied specifically to the then legally-defined category of Métis, who were the descendants of European fur traders, mainly French, and Indian women, mainly Cree.

The Métis people developed distinctive ethnocultural communities in Canada's West, and their demands for the recognition of their aboriginal rights, in the face of European expansion, sparked the famous Riel Rebellion of 1869. From 1870-1875, following the defeat of Riel, the federal government recognized the treaty and aboriginal rights of the Métis in order to facilitate settler expansion. The Métis were pressured to relinquish their aboriginal rights in one of two ways: they could take scrip, i.e., cede their lands to the Crown in exchange for sums of money or land allocations, together with medical and educational subsidies, in which case they would retain their Métis identity and Status; or they could take treaty and, through much the same process, acquire the legal Status of Treaty Indians. In 1940, the Indian Affairs Bureau of the federal government officially abandoned the concept of the special legal Status of the Métis people, and, since that time, the Métis have been administratively classified as non-Status Indians. As a consequence of this arbitrary classification, the term Métis now refers to a particular category of persons of mixed Indian/European ancestry, rather than to a distinctive people with special legal Status.

However, Frideres (1993: 42) points out that some of the Métis currently are re-defining themselves as a distinct aboriginal ethnic group in Canada. (It also should be noted, here, that the Métis have gained constitutional recognition as a distinct category of aboriginal peoples, such under s.35 of the Constitution Act, 1982.) Frideres (42-3) suggests that the term Métis has two different meanings today. Written with a small 'm', métis refers to the Government-defined category discussed in the preceding paragraph (Pan-Métis). Written with a capital 'M', Métis refers to the self-defined Métis ethnic group, descendants of the historic Métis in Western Canada, whose members share a common cultural identity (Historical Métis). However defined, at present members of the Métis category share one common denominator: loss of legal Indian Status.

Aboriginal Status, Aboriginal Rights and Nationhood Claims

From the Indian view, the renunciation of legal Indian Status does not affect any potential claims that can be made on the basis of aboriginal rights. As long as the aboriginal title of the band or tribe from which an Indian is descended has not been recognized and extinguished, the collective aboriginal rights of the group have not been abrogated.

Within the legal category of Status or Registered Indians, the difference between the subcategories of Treaty and non-Treaty (Status or Registered) Indians has important implications for the question of claims based on aboriginal rights. In the case of Treaty Indians, the Crown has held that their aboriginal title has been recognized and extinguished through the process of signing land cession treaties. In the case of non-Treaty Indians, whose ancestors did not sign land cession treaties, their aboriginal title has not been recognized or extinguished.

Those non-Status Indians, Inuit, and Métis, whose ancestors did not sign land cession treaties or engage in other transactions with the Crown (e.g., taking scrip) that would abrogate their aboriginal rights, can, like non-Treaty Indians, make collective land claims based on their aboriginal rights.

With regard to nationhood claims, the human rights perspective which informs this book clearly supports aboriginal claims to sovereignty based on aboriginal peoples' inherent right to government as Canada's 'first nations'. To date, however, Canadian Governments have refused to recognize this position. While the Government of Canada recently has accepted the principle of an inherent aboriginal right to self-government, policy statements support only controlled forms of self-government and implicitly favour the delegated-municipal model, which ensures that ultimate decision-making remains a federal government prerogative (Frideres 1990: 5). To retain Government control over aboriginal affairs, and to safeguard aboriginal acceptance of Euro-Canadian values aboriginal proposals for alternate forms of government, rooted in aboriginal values and embodied in political forms consistent with these values, have invariably been rejected by Government.

The Relationship Between Ethnicity and Human Rights Claims

Analysis of the relationship between ethnicity and human rights in Canada demonstrates that differences in ethnic status, as well as differences between arbitrary cat-

Table 1 Human Diversity and Human Rights

Classification				Basis of Human Rights Claims
Species	*Homo sapiens*			Universal/Individual
Race (Category)	Mongoloid	Caucasoid	Negroid	Individual and/or Categorical
Ethnic Origin Group	e.g. Inuit/ Chinese	e.g. German/ Spanish	e.g. Jamaican/ Kenyan	Cultural and/or National Group
Subethnic Social Category	Children Aged	Mentally/ Physically Disabled	Women Homosexuals	Individual and/or Categorical

egories of ethnic classification and *sui generis* ethnocultural groups, have important implications for the kinds of human rights which can be claimed by different ethnocultural collectivities. What are the basic assumptions behind the various categories of human rights and human rights claims pertinent in the Canadian context?

Collective Rights and Ethnic Identity

The concept of collective rights has both instrumental and affective components. That is to say, collective rights claims may involve corporate, political, and economic goals, and/or they may focus on retention of distinctive ethnocultural identity. The latter aspect of collective rights is closely associated with a particular group's ethnic status in Canadian society.

In the case of Canada's Indian peoples, the ambiguities of aboriginal status and the divisive impact of the arbitrary administrative lines created between the various categories and subcategories of aboriginal persons render the question 'Who is an Indian?' highly problematic. And, as our previous discussion has shown, this question is intimately connected with the kinds of collective human rights claims which can be raised by different categories of aboriginal peoples. The question is a matter of (1) legal definition, (2) political classification, and (3) ethnic identity.

With regard to the first consideration, we must take into account the differential legal definitions of the concept Indian with regard to its constitutional (BNA Act/1867 and Constitution Act/1982) versus its statutory (Indian Acts) referents in Canadian society. With regard to the second consideration, we must take into account the arbitrariness and the mutability of the concept as a political definition based on racial and/or cultural criteria. With regard to the third consideration, we

Table 2 Categories of Human Rights Claims

Ethnic Classification	Individual	Categorical	Cultural	Collective National	Aboriginal
Racial category	x	x			
Immigrant ethnic group	x	x	x		
Charter ethnic group	x	x	x	x	
Aboriginal ethnic group	x	x	x	x	x
Subethnic social category	x	x			

must take into account the views and feelings of people who ethnically identify themselves as Indians, regardless of their legal status or their political/racial/cultural classification by dominant authorities within Canadian society.

Probably the most salient point of confusion in the public mind concerning the question 'Who is an Indian?' derives from the fact that Indian legal Status is not coterminous with Indian ethnic or racial status in Canada. The legal definition of Indian status has nothing to do with the amount of Indian 'blood' one is alleged to possess, despite the persistence of a powerful racist mythology to the contrary. There are many non-Status Indians with a far greater proportion of Indian ancestry than many Status Indians. Some non-Status Indians are more visibly Indian, i.e., they are more likely to be racially identified as Indian by outsiders than are their less visible Status Indian counterparts. Indeed, a great many Status Indians do not look 'Indian': many have so-called White (Caucasian) features like blond or red hair and blue eyes. Further, although non-Status Indians are not legally defined as Indians, they may identify themselves very strongly as Indians in ethnic terms. Clearly, contemporary Indian self-identity is a complex phenomenon, and one which must be understood as the outcome of a number of interacting, political, legal, and cultural variables.

In the next chapter, we will provide a conceptual scheme designed to aid the reader in understanding and analysing the multifaceted phenomenon of ethnic identity, for aboriginal peoples as well as for members of other ethnic collectivities in Canada. Our analysis will attempt to show the way in which the nature of relations between ethnic collectivities (inter-ethnic relations) and within ethnic collectivities (intra-ethnic relations) interact to shape varying expressions of ethnic identity.

Notes

1 It is important to emphasize that all of the criteria used to identify specific components of ethnicity—whether by ethnic insiders or outsiders—are based on *actual* or *assumed* characteristics.

2 This observation notwithstanding, it should be noted that, even in the early period, the Protestant/Catholic division subsumed different ethnicities under each religious rubric.

3 The difficulty in finding a multipurpose term which is both succinct and precise in its reference to the ethnically dominant, White, English-speaking, Christian Canadian of British or Northwest European origin, has led scholars to employ such inaccurate terms as WASP (White Anglo Saxon Protestant), WACP (White Anglo Celtic Protestant) and the like. For the sake of simplicity, in this connection, we will employ the term Anglo-Canadian in those contexts where English/French differences are relevant; the broader term, Euro-Canadian, will be used otherwise.

4 While the focus of this book is on *ethnic* collectivities, it is important to note that sub-ethnic minorities, like persons with disabilities, women, aged, gays and lesbians and others, can make similar claims on the basis of categorical human rights.

5 There were also a number of peace and friendship treaties negotiated between Crown representatives and aboriginal leaders, but only the land cession treaties abrogated aboriginal title to the land.

6 Bill C-31 redefined Indian status and created new categories of Indian. Some of the key changes introduced by Bill C-31 will be discussed in the following section of this chapter. However, we will not attempt to address all of the complexities of reinstatement and of transmitting one's status, which vary for different categories of claimants. For a detailed discussion of these issues, the reader is referred to Frideres, 1993: 34-8.

7 The one exception being that all non-Status Indian women (and non-Indian women, as well) do acquire such Status through marriage to a Status Indian male.

CHAPTER FOUR

Ethnicity and Ethnic Identity

All human beings have a number of different social statuses and identities based upon a variety of human attributes. Some scholars of ethnic relations argue that one's ethnic status and identity is a person's most basic (primordial) group identity (see Isaacs 1977). This line of argument suggests that, in any given social context, one's ethnic attributes will predominate over all one's other human attributes and will, invariably, provide the primary basis for one's group identity. It follows from this position that (for example) a lesbian medical doctor of Jewish origin would identify first and foremost as a member of the Jewish ethnic group, regardless of the social context (synagogue, hospital operating room, or gay and lesbian rights organization).

In contrast to this position, following the theoretical approach of the new ethnicity presented in Chapter Three I propose that which of one's various social identities will come to the fore at any given time or place will vary with the social context and situation. Thus, for example, while one's ethnic identity may be very strong in the context of one's family and ethnic community, in one's public or professional life one's identity may become de-ethnicized.

Factors Affecting Expressions of Ethnic Identity

From a dynamic perspective, taking into account both subjective and objective factors, ethnic identity may be seen as an outcome of the impact upon the individual or ethnic collectivity of the interrelationship between the diachronic and synchronic dimensions of ethnicity, as illustrated in Figure 1, overleaf.

The diachronic dimension of ethnic identity refers to the actor's selective process of perception and evaluation of the various components of the old ethnicity, that is the ancestry, homeland, and culture associated with his or her ethnic origin group. Those components of the old ethnicity selected as core diacritica link the actor with the historical ethnic origin group and provide an expressive focus for his or her sense of ethnic group belongingness and continuity. Those components of the old ethni-

Figure 1 Ethnicity and Ethnic Identity in Canada

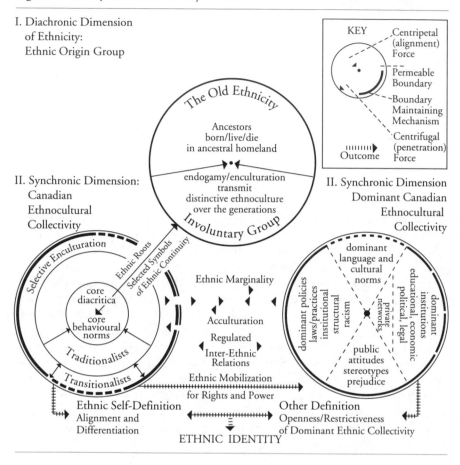

city selected as core 'rules of the game' serve as boundary-maintaining behavioural norms, which simultaneously align the actor with the ethnic origin group—the diachronic dimension—and with the Canadian ethnocultural collectivity—the synchronic dimension, and differentiate the actor as an ethnic insider from outsiders.

The synchronic dimension of ethnic identity refers to the ethnic definitions and priorities governing the selective process of interaction with outsiders and the boundary-maintaining mechanisms employed by the actor to maintain ethnic group alignment and differentiation. Here, a very important factor impacting upon ethnic identity is other-definition, i.e., the way in which the individual or ethnic collectivity is defined, evaluated, and treated by outsiders. Put another way, with reference to the synchronic dimension of ethnic identity the social construction of ethnic identity by ethnic insiders at any given time and place, is highly contingent upon the social construction of ethnic identity by ethnic outsiders.

As illustrated in Figure 1, under social conditions where dominant policies, laws, and practices are predicated on institutionalized forms of racism, and where these racist ideologies and structures are supported by public attitudes of prejudice, the boundaries of the dominant institutions become ossified and virtually closed to penetration by ethnic minorities. Under these conditions, the minority actor becomes highly dependent on his or her ethnocultural collectivity for satisfaction of both expressive and instrumental needs; ethnic identity is likely to gain in strength and salience. Alternatively, where the dominant ethnic group accords legitimacy to ethnic group differentiation, the boundaries of the dominant institutions may become more penetrable by ethnic minorities. Under these conditions, the minority ethnic actor may seek satisfaction of his or her instrumental needs in the dominant institutions. Concomitantly, other social identities—occupational, political, and so forth— may become more salient than ethnic identity in public life, and the actor's ethnic identity may become privatized.

Whether or not the actor aligns her/himself with ethnic networks and/or institutions (structural ethnicity), the established social scientific literature supports the view that ethnic as compared to other collective identities are uniquely able to satisfy members' human need for roots: symbolic ethnicity.

The degree to which members of ethnic collectivities adjudge that their expressive and instrumental needs and goals can best be met by ethnic, in contrast to other, group membership, will influence the degree to which they desire and attempt to shift their primary focus of identification and allegiance from ethnic to other social collectivities.

Dominant ethnic actors in Canadian society are most likely to find their needs and goals furthered by ethnic group membership. Thus, they tend to identify and align positively with their ethnocultural collectivity. Members of ethnic minorities, on the other hand, and especially those whose characteristics are in any way stigmatized by the dominant group, are far more likely to perceive that their instrumental goals are hampered or blocked by ethnic group membership. However, the way in which this perception influences or triggers the actor's ethnic priorities will depend, in part, on the centrality of his or her ethnic, as compared with other, social identities.

Enculturation and Acculturation: Identity-Shaping Processes

Herman (1977: 50-2) delineates three qualitative dimensions of ethnic self-identity: (1) salience or intensity of awareness; (2) centrality or extensity of influence; and (3) valence or positive/negative value. While the salience of the actor's ethnic identity is highly contingent upon the restrictions of the dominant society and culture, the centrality of ethnic as compared with other social identities is largely a function of the relative effectiveness of the processes of enculturation—learning the ways of one's own ethnic collectivity—and acculturation—learning the ways of the larger society.

In the Canadian context, the process of selective enculturation involves a distinctive, yet changing, ethnic socialization through which ethnically valued symbols, 'rules of the game', and life skills are transmitted from one generation to another. To the degree that this process is effective, the younger generation comes to identify first and foremost with the ethnic collectivity, in both its diachronic and synchronic dimensions, and develops a central, personal sense of ethnic alignment and differentiation. The process of enculturation thus generates the crucial centripetal or pull forces, keeping members identified and aligned with the ethnic collectivity.

For members of the dominant ethnic collectivities, the processes of enculturation and acculturation may, to a large degree, tend to be mutually reinforcing phenomena. Hence, the line between the actor's ethnic and national identities may blur, and ethnicity may become salient in only a few contexts. Alternatively, for members of ethnic minorities, the processes of enculturation and acculturation may generate opposing (push and pull) forces. In this context, ethnicity may be rendered highly salient in a great many situations.

For ethnic minorities, acculturation exposes the younger generation to cultural alternatives and to new societal reference and membership groups which may compete with their ethnic counterparts as foci for primary identification and allegiance. Most importantly, it is through the process of acculturation that the younger generation acquires the specialized skills and life ways necessary for effective participation in modern, post-industrial society. By exposing the younger generation to compelling new options, and by equipping them with new, transnational skills, the acculturation process generates the crucial centrifugal or push forces attracting members geographically and/or ideologically away from their ethnocultural collectivity.

Fragmentation: Traditionalists and Transitionalists

The ongoing tension between centrifugal and centripetal forces, characteristic of the synchronic dimension of ethnicity in Canadian society, may fragment the ethnic collectivity in many ways. Most important, for the present discussion, are the lines of fragmentation between traditionalists—those actors closest to the ethnic core, for whom ethnic identity is central and for whom ethnic alignment takes precedence over penetration of dominant institutions, and transitionalists—those actors (usually the numerical majority) for whom ethnic identity is less central and for whom the choice between ethnic alignment and penetration of dominant institutions is situationally determined. While transitionalists may not be as strongly ethnically identified as traditionalists, the valence of their ethnic identity tends to remain positive, despite the fact that their instrumental priorities may favour participation in the public sector of society, as opposed to ethnic participation (see Figure 1).

On the other hand, some ethnic actors may perceive that their desires for societal participation are threatened by their minority ethnic status. Concomitantly, they may become negatively identified with their ethnic collectivity. Negatively identified ethnic actors may seek to adopt the ethnocultural characteristics and life styles of the dominant group in order to improve their social positions and to gain power. However, the impermeable boundary erected by the dominant group may serve to severely limit or entirely prevent penetration by ethnic outsiders. Thus, some ethnic actors who identify primarily with the dominant group and shed their ethnic dia-critica, in the hope of abandoning their ethnic status, are nevertheless prevented from leaving their ethnic collectivity. They are kept within the fold by the dominant boundaries isolating them from without.

Ethnic Marginality

Individuals who have been rebuffed in their attempts to penetrate dominant institutions may experience this rejection as a form of relative status deprivation. They are caught in a status dilemma: rejected by those with whom they aspire to align, and thrown back upon the ethnic collectivity that they themselves have rejected. If they fail, over the long term, to resolve their status dilemma, this can lead to the psychosocial condition of ethnic marginality.

Ethnic marginals are characteristically self-conflicted people. They are persons caught between the equally compelling push and pull forces of two incompatible ethnocultural worlds. Unable to fully satisfy the disparate expectations and requirements of both, yet unable to choose between them or break the ties with either one of them, ethnic marginals may live out their lives in a state of identity confusion. They may become marginal men or women (Stonequist 1937), having a partial status in two ethnocultural worlds, but not fully accepting or being accepted in either.[1]

Levels and Expressions of Ethnic Identity

The foregoing analysis of the relationship between ethnicity and ethnic identity draws attention to the contingent nature of ethnicity and ethnic identity in the current Canadian context.

In order to understand this relationship in any given empirical case, we must also take into account (a) the structural level with which the ethnic collectivity is identified, and (b) the distinction between individual and collective forms of ethnic identification at all social structural levels.

Structural Levels

For analytical purposes, we can distinguish at least four important levels at which ethnicity operates in providing expressive/symbolic foci for ethnic identity, and at which ethnic identity may be mobilized in pursuit of individual or collective instrumental goals: (i) the micro-level, or local level of intra- and inter-ethnic relations,

Figure 2 Lineage Organization on the Principle of Segmental Opposition

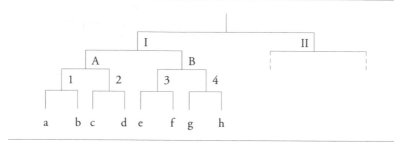

(ii) the regional or provincial level of intra- and inter-ethnic relations, (iii) the state or national level of intra- and inter-ethnic relations, (iv) the macro-level, or international level of intra- and inter-ethnic relations.

Individual and Collective Ethnic Identity

For analytical purposes, we can distinguish two forms of ethnic identity which are manifested at all social structural levels: (i) Individual ethnic identity refers to the relationship of the individual to the ethnic collectivity and its presumed attributes at a given structural level. (ii) Collective ethnic identity differs from the individual form in that it implies a certain degree of consensus among members regarding the criteria selected as paramount symbols for collective identification at a given structural level.

In both its individual and collective forms, changes in ethnic identity tend to reflect shifts in the actor's priorities governing intra-ethnic and inter-ethnic relations at all social structural levels. Ethnic priorities and patterns of group differentiation and alignment, in turn, are particularly responsive to changes in the restrictions of governmental and public ideologies, policies, and practices concerning ethnic diversity.

Shifts in expressions of ethnic identity from one social structural level to another frequently take on a pattern of 'segmentary opposition' or 'fission and fusion' (Despres 1975). In the anthropological literature, the classic formulation of this pattern is found in the principle of Nuer lineage organization described by Evans-Pritchard (1940) and here represented schematically in Figure 2 above.

Put simply, the principle of segmentary opposition is based on the notion of situational in-group 'unity in defence' against a perceived threat from a given out-group. The underlying assumption behind the model is that intra-group conflict, rather than cohesion, is the normal state of affairs at all social structural levels; it is the perception of a threat to a given in-group that spurs members to align themselves in terms of their common interest and affective ties, over and above factional concerns, at the level of the threat from the out-group.

In Figure 2, for example, 1 and 2 may be quarrelling brothers, but as sons of father

Figure 3 Levels of Jewish Ethnic Identification and Alignment Based on the Principle of Segmental Opposition

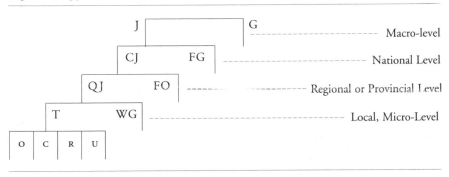

A, when A gets into a fight with his brother B, they align themselves with A against B. Similarly, A and B are sons of father I and when I is threatened by his brother II, or by members of his brother's lineage, A, B, 1, and 2, as members of I's lineage, align on the side of I against II. This pattern of kinship relations has been called 'fission and fusion' because the same principle, i.e., conflict, separates subgroups at one social structural level and unites them at another.

In a somewhat adapted form, this scheme may be used to illustrate shifts in patterns of ethnic identification and alignment at different social structural levels. Figure 3 illustrates this principle, using the example of Canadian Jews.

Beginning our analysis at the local level of the Jewish ethnic collectivity, say, the city of Toronto (T), we find that religious denominational differences between subsectors of the Toronto Jewish community Orthodox (O), Conservative (C), Reform (R), and unaffiliated (U) provide local bases for intra-ethnic antagonisms and conflicts. However, when Torontonian Jews perceive themselves as common victims of an anti-Semitic attack, for example, the defamatory hate propaganda messages broadcast over the telephone by the Western Guard (WG), they will unite, over and above religious and other factional interests, to protect the fundamental human rights of all members of the Toronto Jewish community. Similarly, at the provincial level (for example, Quebec), local Jewish communities will unite above local and factional interests in order to protect all Quebec Jews (QJ) from anti-Semitic policies and attacks: for example, the protest against the vilification of Jews by Neo-Nazi, Fascist organizations (FO) in the 1930s. At the national level, Canadian Jews (CJ) will unite above provincial, local, and factional interests to promote broader corporate ethnic interests and concerns: for example, petitions to the federal government (FG) for the admission of Jewish political refugees to Canada prior to and during World War II. Finally, at the macro- or international level of the Jewish ethnic collectivity, national differences between Canadian, German, Argentinian, and Israeli Jews, for example, will disappear when the continued existence of a Diaspora Jewish community (say, Jews in the former Soviet Union), is threatened and/or when the existence of the State of Israel is threatened (for example, by repeated attacks from Palestinian terrorist groups bent on Jewish genocide). In this event, Jews will unite as Jews, at the macro-level of ethnic identification where the salient in-group/out-group distinction is between Jews (J) (all Jews throughout time and space) and all outsiders conceptualized as Gentiles (G).

This fission and fusion phenomenon highlights the contingent nature of ethnic identities and alignments and emphasizes the crucial role of the out-group in spurring ethnic mobilization in response to a perceived threat.[2]

What this implies at the synchronic level of ethnicity in Canada is that one potential outcome of ethnic relations in a racist society is the mobilization of the ethnic collectivity toward recognition of human rights and toward ethnic group empowerment (see Figure 1 on page 80).

The Development of Ethnic Group Consciousness

Initially, an ethnic category may consist of an unorganized aggregate of persons such as the French in Toronto, or Americans in Canada, or as various dispersed, fragmented ethnic groupings defined, classified, and treated in like manner by outsiders. It is not until members of arbitrary ethnic categories become consciously aware of the fact that they are being evaluated and treated as alike by outsiders, because of assumed common ancestry, that they begin identifying on this arbitrary basis. In many cases, a sense of shared ethnic identity gradually emerges in response to the social disabilities that result from this common labelling. One of the main criteria of minority ethnic group belongingness is this recognition of like, differential, and discriminatory treatment based on like evaluation and labelling by dominant outsiders—what Kurt Lewin (1948) has termed 'inter-dependence of fate'.

Once people categorize themselves as members of a particular ethnic category, they have the potential to transform themselves from a loose ethnic aggregate to an organized ethnic group capable of concerted action. For the definitive characteristic of an ethnic group is in the fact that it is a category of ascription and identification by its members and thus capable of organizing interaction between people. The essential prerequisite for the effective internal organization and integration of any ethnic group is the transformation of the developing sense of consciousness of kind into positive ethnic identity.

Ethnic symbols play an important part in this process, for they become rallying points for positive identification and group mobilization. Newly charged with affective content, race, religion, language, and cultural heritage take on a new collective import and spur the process of in-group coalescence. Efforts directed toward intragroup communication become intensified as the loosely connected ethnic category becomes welded around a common cause. However, mobilization of members of an ethnic category for a specific collective purpose, particularly in response to an external threat, is far easier than gaining their long-term commitment to the ethnic collectivity. An important variable, in the latter connection, is the valence of ethnicity for members. The greater the proportion of members having a negative identity, the more difficult is the effective organization of the ethnic collectivity. The organization of ethnic categories held together only or mainly by outside pressures (such as expressed attitudes of prejudice or acts of discrimination by dominant powers) is characteristically weak. Such collectivities lack unity of purpose and tend, as a result, to become easily fragmented or factionalized within. On the other hand, those ethnic collectivities in which substantial numbers of members are strongly positively identified are more likely to become and remain effectively organized and cohesive. While a strong sense of ethnic group consciousness is a critical factor in the process of transformation from ethnic category to ethnic group, once members of an ethnic collectivity have become collectively mobilized, the degree to which they can continue to unite, over and above factional interests, in pursuit of corporate ethnic goals, as well as the effectiveness of their concerted action, will depend upon a host of other social-psychological, structural, and demographic factors.

The key variables affecting ethnic group viability through time relate to the expressive, organizational, and instrumental strengths of the ethnic collectivity. In the following pages, we will examine the question of objective assessment of ethnic group viability in Canada in the light of these variables.

Factors Influencing Ethnic Group Viability Through Time

Both laypersons and scholars interested in ethnic relations and human rights concerns often question the obvious disparities among ethnocultural communities in their ability to remain cohesive over time; to retain the strong commitment of their membership; to protect the individual and collective human rights of their members; and to improve their group status in Canadian society. In short, the key queries here relate to differences among ethnic collectivities in their degree and patterns of group viability through time.

In this section, we will delineate some of the important cultural and social structural factors influencing ethnic group viability through time, with examples of the principles from Canadian case study materials.

Objective Indices of Ethnicity and Ethnic Group Viability

The viability of a given ethnic collectivity may be assessed in terms of its expressive, organizational, and instrumental strengths. In the conceptual scheme delineated in Table 3 presented on page 88, the first two sets of variables, Degree of Cultural Pluralism and Degree of Ethnic Closure, provide indicators of the potential expressive strength of the ethnic collectivity, that is, the strength of ethnic alignment and ethnic differentiation, through boundary-maintaining mechanisms, in keeping mem-

Table 3 Factors Influencing Ethnic Group Viability Through Time

I Expressive Strengths	**II Expressive Strengths**
(1) Degree of Cultural Pluralism	(2) Degree of Ethnic Closure

I Expressive Strengths

(1) Degree of Cultural Pluralism

    a) Alternate and/or Parallel Cultural Ethos and Institutions*

    Religion: Values and Activities

    Language: Use and Fluency

    SES: Education, Occupation, Income

    Politico-Legal: Idealogy and Activities

    Folk Custom: Food, music, costume etc.

    Country of Origin

    Wave/Period of Immigration

    Generational Continuities/Disparities

    Degree of Acculturation

    Degree of Assimilation

    Ethnic Diacritica (outward display of distinctive group symbols)

    b) Demographic Factors

    Population Numbers

    (Size of Community)

    Age and Sex Ratios

    (Endogamous Potential)

* Ethnic institutions may take the form of alternate and/or parallel structures, i.e., they may diverge from or converge with outside institutions in both form (organization and status structure) and meaning (cultural context and moral values).

II Expressive Strengths

(2) Degree of Ethnic Closure

    a) Boundary Maintaining Mechanisms: Ideological

    Criteria for group membership (ascribed/involuntary or achieved/voluntary)

    Mythological charter for peoplehood

    World view: Degree of ethnocentrism

    Degree of prejudice toward out-group(s)

    Nature and comprehensiveness of ethnic norms/rules of the game and screening devices regulating and restricting inter-ethnic relations

    Gravity and strength of sanctions against deviance from group norms regulating intra-ethnic and inter-ethnic relations

    Value placed on endogamy

    Gravity and strength of sanctions against inter-ethnic marriage

    b) Boundary Maintaining Mechanisms: Behavioural

    Degree of adherence by membership to core 'rules of the game' regulating intra-ethnic and inter-ethnic relations

    Degree of voluntary/preferred residential enclavement (ethnic segregation)

    Nature and proportion of social contacts and institutional activities within versus outside the ethnic context

    Degree of intimate relationships (close friendships) and marital relationships with insiders versus outsiders

    Degree of institutionalization of practices of discrimination against outsiders (ethnic exclusion)

Table 3 (Continued)

III Organizational Strengths	IV Instrumental Strengths
Degree of Structural Pluralism	*Degree of Economic and Political Power*
Alternate versus parallel institutions	Demographic strength/voting power
Degree of institutional completeness	(population numbers; age and sex ratio)
Degree of active participation of members	Nature of ethnic status in Canada
in ethnic versus outside institutions	(charter, immigrant or aboriginal ethnic
Degree of compartmentalization versus	collectivity)
overlap of membership in ethnic	Rank of ethnic collectivity within strati-
institutions	fication system
Range and scope of ethnic institutions	Collective economic resources
(local, provincial, regional, national,	Collective political resources (educational,
cross-national, international)	professional and leadership skills)
Degree of polarization or co-ordination	Collective political skills
of activities of ethnic institutions	a) legitimacy accorded ethnic leaders and
Use and proficiency of ethnic commun-	professional ethnics by insiders and
ication channels (media, newspapers,	outsiders
telephone hotlines, etc.)	b) knowledge of Canadian political and
The number and variety of spheres in	economic bureaucracy; where and
which concerted action is taken at a	whom to lobby
community-wide level	c) nature and degree of personal and
The degree of acknowledged representa-	organizational links with influential
tion and credibility of ethnic leadership	outsiders/outside bodies
The effectiveness of ethnic leadership in	d) degree of ethno-politicization of
mobilizing members in support of	members
issues involving individual and/or	e) degree of consensus among leaders and
collective rights	members on corporate ethnic strategies,
	interests, and goals
	f) degree of formalization and regularity
	of re-assessment of corporate ethnic
	goals

bers positively identified with and strongly committed to the ethnic collectivity.

The third set of variables provides indicators of the corporate, organizational strength of the ethnic collectivity—the degree of self-sufficiency and independence of the collectivity and its ability to provide for and satisfy the needs of its members through internal ethnic institutions and services.

The fourth set of variables in the table provides indicators of the potential instrumental strength of the ethnic collectivity—the nature and extent of internal resources and the ability of ethnic leaders to mobilize resources from within and outside of the ethnic collectivity in the pursuit of corporate ethnic goals.

Caveat

It should be noted that the division between various sets of variables in the foregoing conceptual scheme, while somewhat arbitrary, is designed to facilitate social scientific analysis. In actuality, many of these variables overlap different sets and they can be expected to affect the viability of the ethnic collectivity in more than one area.

A second caveat, here, concerns the limitations of this conceptual scheme, in which the strength of ethnic identity and commitment of members is seen as a function of ethnic group viability. In utilizing this approach, it is important to reiterate our major premise regarding the contingent nature of the new ethnicity: the salience, valence, and centrality of ethnicity and ethnic identity are contingent upon the prevailing social environment, and particularly upon prevailing public attitudes, policies, and government legislation concerning ethnic diversity. Thus, the expressive and/or instrumental strength of the ethnic collectivity necessary to maintain ethnic group viability, ethnic identification, and commitment of members over time will vary with changing social conditions.

Expressive Strengths of an Ethnic Collectivity: Degree of Cultural Pluralism and Ethnic Closure

Distinctive ethnic identity is a function of both intra- and inter-ethnic variables. In the context of inter-ethnic relations, the factors influencing the expressive strength of an ethnic collectivity, delineated in Table 1 (p. 76), will apply simultaneously to all ethnic units in contact. In this light, our first proposition, relating to ethnic distinctiveness, is that the expressive strength of a given ethnic unit will be augmented by (1) the degree of congruence among the internal (cultural and institutional) characteristics within the ethnic unit, and (2) the degree of disparities between the characteristics of the different ethnic units in contact.

Our second proposition, relating to ethnic closure, is that the expressive strength of a given ethnic collectivity will be augmented by (1) the recognized legitimacy and demonstrated proficiency of the boundary-maintaining mechanisms employed by insiders to maintain ethnic closure, and (2) the recognized power and demonstrated proficiency of the boundary-maintaining mechanisms employed by outsiders to maintain ethnic closure.

Boundary Maintenance and Social Distance

Boundary-maintaining mechanisms are ideologies and practices which serve to maintain ethnic group distinctiveness and exclusiveness by minimizing the degree of social distance in relations between insiders—intra-ethnic relations—and by maximizing the degree of social distance in relations between insiders and outsiders—

inter-ethnic relations. Our third proposition, in the light of the above principles, is that the lower the degree of social distance in intra-ethnic relations, and the higher the degree of social distance in inter-ethnic relations, the greater the potential expressive strength of the ethnic collectivity.

In short, the propositions offered in this section suggest that the expressive strength of a given ethnic collectivity is a function of its ability to maintain ethnic distinctiveness, on the one hand, and to maintain ethnic exclusivity, on the other. To illustrate these principles, we will draw upon selected sources dealing with the Hutterites.

The Hutterites: Religious Sectarianism and Ethnic Group Viability Through Time[3]

The Hutterites in Canada are a religiously-defined ethnic collectivity whose distinctive ethnoculture developed within the environmental context of sectarian agricultural communes in Europe, the United States, and Canada over a period of some 400 years. During this time, the Hutterites were persecuted, even burned at the stake, for their religious doctrines. Consequently, they fled from one European country to another, and then from the United States to Canada, where they now live in agricultural communes in the Western Prairies.[4]

The Hutterites represent an unusual case of successful ethnic group persistence achieved by a unique pattern of religious boundary maintenance and voluntary ethnic enclavement. This population provides an outstanding example of the theoretical principles to be delineated; because it is atypical, it can provide a fruitful basis for comparison with other more typical Canadian ethnic groups.

The Hutterian World View

Like the disciples of Christ who had 'all things common' (Acts 2:44), and in contradistinction to the individualistic ethos of society at large, the Hutterites choose to reside in voluntary, egalitarian 'communities of love' based on communal ownership of property and possessions, and dedicated to peace, social harmony, and a life of simplicity and austerity. Because they insist that membership in their communities be voluntary, they have rejected infant baptism in favour of adult baptism, a rite which signifies a voluntary choice by mature persons.

Because the Hutterites are dedicated pacifists whose religious ethos precludes acts of violence, they refuse to actively participate in military service. These key Hutterian doctrines not only provide the core values behind the distinctive Hutterian world view, they also provide the basis for a unique way of life: the Hutterian way.

From their beginning as a distinct Anabaptist sect in 1528, Hutterian doctrines directly challenged the values and authority of established Christian Church States in Europe. Consequently, the Hutterites were persecuted for their religious beliefs, first in Germany and later in the other countries of Europe to which they fled. Historically, the nature of their relations with host nations was one of broken promises, persecution, and flight. Various countries offered them religious freedom and exemption from military service, but inevitably these privileges were withdrawn (Bennett 1969).

In Canada, today, the Hutterites constitute a religious sect in the sociological sense of the term. The sect, in contrast to the church form of religious organization, requires separation from the greater society which it sees as sinful, evil, and contaminating (Yinger 1970: 252-80). The Hutterite religious world view provides the underlying moral rationale and mythical charter for rejection of the outside world in favour of their distinctive ethnocultural way of life. Viewed from the Hutterian perspective, people were created to worship God, and the true believer's prime orientation is toward everlasting life after death rather than enjoyment of the present, temporal life on earth. The outside world of the non-believer, with its competitive individualistic, materialistic norms and its emphasis on self-gratification is considered sinful, and all true believers must withdraw and isolate themselves from its corrupting influences. The Hutterian way is thus in the world, but not of it (Bennett 1969). The ethnocentric premise of Hutterian doctrine is implicit in the contrasting conceptions of virtue embodied in the Hutterian way, and the temptations of sin embodied in the outside way of life. Prejudice toward non-Hutterites is implicit in the categorical application of the notions of sin and corruption to all outsiders by virtue of their association with the vices of society. Ethnocentric and prejudicial Hutterian beliefs and attitudes serve to sustain a high degree of social distance in inter-ethnic relations; they also lend legitimacy and salience to Hutterian ethnic boundaries.

Maintaining Ethnic Distinctiveness

Hutterites' insistence on maintaining an austere, traditional, and frugal way of life is reflected in what neighbours view as their plain, old-fashioned clothing (e.g., women wear kerchiefs and long skirts; men wear long beards, dark suits, and outmoded hats). This distinctive attire serves as symbolic ethnic diacritica, distinguishing Hutterites from outsiders in virtually all social contexts. Thus, dress provides an important cultural boundary marker, rendering highly visible members of an ethnic collectivity whose physical characteristics are essentially similar to those of their Euro-Canadian neighbours.

Another key boundary-maintaining mechanism employed by the Hutterites is their use of a distinctive language, i.e., an archaic form of German. For Hutterites, English is a second language necessary for basic communication with the outside; but within the ethnocultural collectivity at home, at church, and in religious school archaic German is used as a language of ritual, a language of everyday conversation, and a language of instruction for children. Within the self-contained Hutterite communities, the use of a distinctive language, intricately interwoven with a distinctive and exclusive way of life, has been strongly reinforced by long-term endogamy. Thus, cultural and biological forces have worked together to create ethnic homogeneity out of cultural diversity. Consequently, from its sixteenth-century origins as a Christian Anabaptist religious sect, whose members stemmed from various ethnic and national groupings, the Hutterites have become a single, full-fledged Canadian ethnic group.

Because of their *gutergemeinschaft* (community of goods) commitment, there are no categorical internal disparities in socio-economic class among Hutterite colony members. Similarly, in keeping with their common religious stance of rejecting the outside world, Hutterites share a common negative political ideology. They refuse to participate in military service, to hold political office, and to take legal oaths. As a rule, they even refuse to exercise their right to vote, except in the case of local elections where the interests of Hutterite colonies are directly involved (Sanders 1964). Most importantly, because they constitute total *gemeinschaft* communities, they have the requisite age and sex ratios to ensure perpetuation of the ethnic collectivity through recruitment of members from within the sectarian community and through Hutterite ethnoreligious endogamy.

Maintaining Ethnic Closure

Probably the most important mechanism of boundary maintenance employed by Hutterites to preserve the integrity of the Hutterian way, is the strategy of geographical and social isolation of their colonies. Each colony buys a huge tract of land consisting of thousands of acres in an area as isolated as possible from the more highly populated local or regional centres.[5] Moreover, the typical plan of the colony is to place the buildings—church, residences and so forth—in the middle of the tract of land, a design that serves to further isolate Hutterites from their neighbours. Residential concentration also maximizes daily contact between Hutterites (intra-ethnic relations) and facilitates *gemeinschaft* modes of social control (e.g., gossip, scolding, shunning, and so forth) which curb deviance from Hutterian norms. Communal living patterns further reinforce the collective Hutterian ethos, which recognizes status distinctions only in terms of age and sex.

In direct contrast to the intensive and extensive nature of interactions between members within the Hutterite colony, relations between Hutterites and outsiders are sharply limited and carefully controlled by the colony's leaders. In the past, visits to local towns were generally made by only the most clearly committed (hence, least corruptible) leaders of the colony, and were dictated almost entirely by requirements that could not be supplied by the colony, e.g., purchase of farm machinery. Increasing pressure on ministers and elders to allow colony members to go to town or to visit neighbouring non-Hutterite farms has resulted in some relaxation of the stringent prohibitions in this area, but requests are still carefully screened. For example, in one colony requests are typically mediated through community leaders who hold the keys to the colony's only station wagon or to the house containing the colony's only telephone (Flint 1975: 25).

The emphasis on maximization of intra-ethnic relations, together with the severe curtailment of all but the necessary minimal amount of formalized contact with outsiders, dovetails well with the norm of endogamy. For colony members, outsiders remain strangers, removed from everyday reality and stigmatized by their association with the allegedly corrupt ideas and life ways of the outside world. The likelihood that a Hutterite would be able to break through the religiously legitimated barriers of social distance and engage in intimate social relations with non-Hutterites is thereby minimized (Peter 1980a).

The technique of controlled acculturation (Eaton 1952) whereby Hutterites selectively accept, adapt, and integrate outside ideas and practices into their own value system, gives the Hutterian way a limited but important degree of flexibility enabling them to 'bend and not break' under the ever-increasing pressures posed by compelling outside alternatives. Hutterites have successfully managed to screen, limit, and control the process of secular education for their young; they have continually adapted to the use of farm machinery; some colonies have allowed the limited introduction of outside leisure activities, e.g., holding Hallowe'en parties and reading farm magazines (Flint 1975: 121). In all of these new kinds of activities, Hutterite leaders, under pressure for change, have exerted control by defining the areas in which changes can be introduced without sacrificing core religious principles.

To a large extent, the strategy of ethnic enclavement of Hutterite colonies within the Canadian context has been a voluntary mechanism designed to carry out the moral imperatives of the Hutterian world view. This is not to suggest, however, that discrimination against the Hutterites has not occurred; indeed, discriminatory laws and/or practices are a continuing part of their everyday social reality. But, like all outside influences, Hutterites have managed to incorporate the social fact of discrimination within their own religious value system. For many years, there were discriminatory land laws in Alberta that impeded the expansion of Hutterite colonies. Hutterite leaders interpreted those laws as Divine warnings of the evil intent of 'outsiders who hate us' (Eaton 1970: 167). Thus, legal discrimination functioned to increase in-group solidarity and to maintain ethnic closure among Hutterites.

Ethnic closure has also been reinforced by the propagation of membership from within the Hutterian ethnic collectivity. Until the last two or three decades, Hutterites were reported to have the most rapid rate of population growth of any social collectivity in North America (Bennett 1969). According to Peter (1980b) and Boldt and Roberts (1980) advances in agricultural technology have necessitated changes in the division of labour which are antithetic to a high population growth. Concomitantly Hutterites have begun to adopt various strategies, among them family planning and postponement of marriage, to limit population growth. Nevertheless, population growth rates remain more than adequate to ensure that membership in the community of Hutterian Brethren is largely based on ascribed criteria, i.e., birth or early socialization within a Hutterite colony.

Hutterites no longer actively proselytize, as this religious activity is perceived to dangerously increase the exposure of group members to corrupting influences. Consequently, conversion to the Hutterian way, while possible, rarely occurs.

Within their colonies, Hutterites employ a great many mechanisms of social control with strong sanctions against deviance from core religious rules. Particularly important, in terms of maintaining ethnic closure, are the rules and sanctions which severely restrict social interaction with outsiders (inter-ethnic relations) and thereby serve to reinforce the principle of ascribed group membership. Among these, the most important is the norm of endogamy (intra-ethnic marriage); the penalty for its violation is excommunication. For a Hutterite, this is the most severe punishment that can be imposed, for it not only means banishment from the Hutterian fold and the good life in this world, but also, and more importantly, it implies banishment from the fold of the elect and exclusion from their extraterrestrial paradise in the everlasting life to come (Hostetler and Huntingdon 1967).

Despite these stringent sanctions, religious defections have from time to time occurred. Peter (1987) projected a current estimate of 300 defections out of a total population of more than 21,800. From the Hutterian view, such defections help to maintain the traditional cohesiveness and continuity of the colonies by eliminating the religiously alienated members.

Organizational Strengths of an Ethnic Collectivity

The corporate, organizational strength of a given ethnic collectivity is a function of its self-sufficiency and independence of outside institutions, on the one hand, and of the continuing viability of its internal institutions, on the other. The organizational strength of a given ethnic collectivity is indicated by the extent to which it is able to provide for and satisfy the needs of its members through internal institutions and services. Factors influencing ethnic organizational strength are delineated in Table 1 (p. 76). To illustrate these principles, we will again refer to the literature dealing with the Hutterites.

Maintaining Self-Sufficiency and Independence

The ability of Hutterian communities to maintain high degrees of cultural pluralism and ethnic closure is made possible by their continuing high levels of economic, political, and social self-sufficiency and independence. Each colony is virtually institutionally complete. It has its own political, economic, religious, and educational institutions and each employs similar religiously legitimated mechanisms of social control.

Politically, each colony is organized on the basis of managed democracy (Bennett 1969), i.e., a combination of egalitarian decision by group consensus and patriarchal authority. Hutterian interpretation of Christian religious doctrine legitimizes colony arrangements in which the egalitarian, economic *gutergemeinschaft* is governed by an internal hierarchy of elected adult males.

Culturally, Canadian Hutterites are divided into three highly endogamous 'Leuts' or branches which are based on the three major waves of migration from Russia through South Dakota to Canada. Each Leut comprises a number of virtually self-sufficient agricultural colonies, each consisting of several extended families with a total population ranging from 120 to 150 persons. Each colony is organized economically on the Hutterian *gutergemeinschaft* model, i.e., all major forms of property are owned and shared communally.

Today, colonies market their economic surplus in dairy and meat produce and in grain and vegetable produce in order to purchase the latest and best in modern agricultural machinery and equipment, but they attempt insofar as possible to produce all the necessities for life in the colony. Most colonies produce their own foods, make their own shoes and clothing, build and repair houses and tools, and painstakingly inculcate in their children all of the essential religious values and practical skills necessary for the perpetuation of their distinctive, peaceful, frugal, and religiously committed life style.

Each colony has its own informal network of kinship and friendship, and its own patterns of leisure activities—reading, singing, sports, visiting, and so forth. Thus, in both the secondary and primary spheres of social life, Hutterites are only minimally dependent on outside institutions: in the main, they confine their participation to the economic sphere. They also use the health services of the outside as required by members, but even here, only when deemed absolutely necessary. Hutterite norms mitigate against outside interference in their internal affairs. Accordingly, most colonies refuse to accept government assistance such as family allowances, old age pensions, tax exemptions and/or government welfare payments; such outside interference is perceived as undermining their norms of self-help, self-sufficiency, and communal responsibility for the welfare of all Hutterites (Peter 1980a).

Within Hutterite colonies, the various institutions are highly co-ordinated: each is based on the same core Hutterian religious values—co-operation, consensus, love, frugality, simplicity, self-discipline, and—most importantly—the value of deference of the will of the individual to the will of the group. All colony members participate, to the extent that they are able, in a great variety of colony institutions, along lines of age and sex. Thus, there is a high degree of overlap in institutional participation. Because Hutterian institutions are alternate structures, differing in form and meaning from outside institutions, intensive and extensive participation by colony members provides a strong integrating mechanism reinforcing core religious principles and sustaining bonds of social solidarity within the colony. At the same time, common participation in the overlapping life spheres of a distinctive ethnoculture provides a strong segregating mechanism, distinguishing Hutterites from outsiders, and keeping them a people apart.

In this *gemeinschaft* community, intra-ethnic communication takes the form of continuing, face-to-face (primary) interaction within the idiom of kinship. Leaders, like other members, are exposed to the constant flow of information that circulates within the colony. Thus, their decisions, reached through a process of consensus, can take into account and represent the voiced opinion(s) of the community at large.

For the most part, the leadership of Hutterian elders involves decisions concerning the ongoing internal life of the colony. When, however, Hutterian religious principles are threatened by outside sentiments and actions (for example, acts of discrimination on part of neighbouring farmers, anti-German alien sentiment during World Wars I and II, discriminatory land laws, conscription laws, and so forth) leaders act to represent Hutterian interests to the outside.

The most outstanding case in point is provided by Hutterian opposition to Alberta's Communal Property Act. Several times in its long term of office (1935-1971) the Social Credit government of the Province of Alberta responded to public pressure against the Hutterites by enacting discriminatory legislation (Flint 1975). In 1947, in response to widespread public accusations of Hutterite 'land grabbing', the Communal Property Act was put into force. This Act, which prevented anyone from purchasing or owning land communally in the Province of Alberta without government permission, virtually put an end to the expansion of Hutterite colonies in the province.[6] Hutterite attempts to circumvent the Act by individual purchases of land used for communal farming led to a general build-up of hostility, culminating, in 1964, in a formal complaint lodged by a local of the farmers' union, and the laying of charges against Hutterites by the police.

In response, Hutterite leaders broke with their long-term stance against using the courts, a stance which went beyond fundamental religious dictates, and tested the constitutionality of the Act. They argued that common ownership of land was a basis tenet of Hutterite faith and that the Act violated their human right to religious freedom. Further, they argued that since only the federal government could rule on religious matters, the provincial law in question was void. The case was contested as far as the Supreme Court of Canada, in 1969, but the Hutterites lost on the grounds that relations concerning land ownership were a provincial concern. It was not until 1973, under the Conservative government of Premier Lougheed, that the Communal Property Act of Alberta was repealed. At that time, the provincial legislature agreed that the Act violated both the Canadian Bill of Rights (1961) and the Provincial Human Rights Act of Alberta (1966, 1971). Unfortunately for the Hutterites, since the Act has been repealed, their new-found freedom to purchase land communally has not signified an increase in public tolerance. Just the opposite has been the case. The establishment of new colonies has engendered continuing public hostility and tirades against the repeal of the Act on the part of envious non-Hutterite farmers who feel threatened (Flint 1975: 116-17).

Instrumental Strength of an Ethnic Collectivity

The instrumental strength of an ethnic collectivity is a function of its ability to mobilize political and economic resources from within and from without the ethnic collectivity. Ethnic resources may be mobilized in order to defend or promote the individual and/or collective human rights of its membership as well as to improve the group status of the ethnic collectivity in Canadian society. The instrumental strength of an ethnic collectivity is indicated by the strength of its political and economic resources that can be mobilized in order to defend or promote corporate ethnic goals.

Mobilizing Economic and Political Resources

Strict adherence to the religious principles embodied in the Hutterian way requires that Hutterites withdraw from all but the necessary minimum of contact with the outside world. This means that the instrumental strength of the Hutterite ethnic collectively is, for the most part, dependent on the ability of colony members to mobilize collective resources from within. Concomitantly, the instrumental strength of the colonies is a direct function of their political, self-governing independence and their economic self-sufficiency. These, in turn, are dependent on the efficiency of colony management and the maintenance of the co-operative ethos and spirit of social solidarity among members.

Hutterite success in maintaining the instrumental strength of its colonies can be attributed to the viability of a unique, planned, branching-out method of colony expansion. The continuing population growth among Hutterites enables the parent colonies to plan new daughter colonies, in advance. This strategy ensures that each colony does not exceed the maximal optimum population size of approximately one hundred and fifty persons. The decision to branch out is based, in part, on economic viability. The Leut must subsidize new colonies initially; the annual operating cost of a colony in 1974 was estimated at around $300,000 (*Weekend Magazine*, 1974: 7). Other considerations include the availability of land (an increasing problem), population pressure, and the politics of colony management. With regard to the latter, the branching-out process is a customary procedure for resolving internal factionalism among leaders by providing new positions of authority to be filled.

Because Hutterites do not have and refuse to make use of outside resources and connections, they must ensure continuing recruitment of membership from within the group. Their steady population growth ensures a continuing supply of potential members and their strictly enforced norm of endogamy mitigates against loss of committed adult members through intermarriage. Yet Hutterites are aware that the voluntary nature of group membership, predicated on the rite of adult baptism, opens the way for defection of young persons during adolescence when they are not yet fully committed to the Hutterian way and when the attractions of the outside world are most compelling.

In keeping with their 'bend but not break' ethos of controlled acculturation, Hutterian elders accept the fact that the 'foolish years' (Hostetler and Huntington

1967: 79) are a time for 'trying the boundaries'. Thus, parents have come to look at the in-between years—the interval between leaving school and adult baptism—as a temporary, experimental time when young people are allowed to be 'tourists' in the outside world. It is generally accepted that young people will engage in normally unpermitted indulgences such as listening to rock music, taking personal photographs, owning cameras or transistor radios, earning some pocket money, and wearing unorthodox attire.

In recent years, teenagers have been allowed to adopt contemporary North American dating patterns. Peter (1987) suggests that this new practice has resulted in an increase in pre-marital pregnancies. However, there is no evidence to suggest that this has led to social ostracization of the teenage partners. Hutterite adults believe that as the young Hutterite weighs the value of these 'indulgences' against the full life of the Hutterite community, and as participation in the daily round of co-operative activities of the colony grows, the long-term satisfactions of colony life will far outweigh those of immediate self-gratification.

The other side of the coin of Hutterian distinctive enculturation, however, lies in the unpreparedness of Hutterian young people for life on the outside (Peter 1980a). Without more than a rudimentary education, without sophistication in the ways of urban living, and without the economic means to set up a home or business, Hutterites must carefully weigh a decision to leave colony life. For when a Hutterite withdraws or is expelled, the sect is under no legal obligation to offer any kind of recompense for his or her contribution (Flint 1975: 27).

Despite all of their ingenious and time-tested mechanisms for ensuring the continuing commitment of members over the generations and for ensuring the continuing expressive strength and instrumental viability of the colonies, the ethnic status of the few thousand Hutterites within Canadian society is that of a small, isolated, and relatively powerless immigrant minority. Thus, the viability of the ethnic collectivity is highly contingent on public, and especially provincial, tolerance. Because they insist on maintaining an isolated alternate way of life, and because they have grown in numbers and have prospered economically (more so than their neighbours) they tend to be regarded with suspicion. They are perceived as an unknown, mysterious, ethnic collectivity, whose economic success poses a potential threat to neighbouring farmers. Sporadic outbreaks of public hostility toward Hutterites in Canada's western provinces have served as a perpetual reminder to the Hutterites of the evils of the outside world and have indirectly reinforced their alternate religious values and increased their social solidarity. Discrimination against Hutterites has also served as a constant reminder of their immigrant minority status in Canada. Hence, periodic violation of their minority rights has kept alive the option of leaving Canada and of migrating, once again, in search of a climate of national tolerance that would allow them to pursue their plain and peaceful life of religious commitment with a minimum of outside interference.

Are the Hutterites Unique? Some Comparisons

The Hutterite case study raises some interesting questions. Perhaps most important-ly, from a theoretical view, the Hutterite example clearly demonstrates the vital role played by religion in creating and sustaining a distinctive ethnic group identity. This principle, strongly articulated by Millet (1968) with regard to Canadian ethno-reli-gious communities, has for a long time received considerable support among North American social scientists. Indeed, there is a substantial amount of data, based upon case studies of ethnic communities, which provides evidence to support the general principle that religiously-defined ethnic groups, and particularly, religious sectarian communities, tend to remain more viable over time then do ethnic groups without a distinctive religious basis.

While both research studies (see Richard 1991) and media reports indicate that increasing numbers of Canadians have forsaken their former religious affiliations through such influences as secularization, conversion and, especially, intermarriage, in those ethnic communities where religion and other criteria of ethnicity (e.g., lan-guage) remain intimately linked, the pattern of ethnic group persistence appears to remain strong. Millet (1979), for example, argues that in the prevailing Canadian context minority Christian churches operating in non-official languages constitute a strong, religious-linguistic force for ethnic group persistence. Shaffir (1980) empha-sizes the vital role played by the ethno-religious educational institution in resisting outside, assimilative influences. He argues that religiously-based communities, far more than other ethnic groups, are organized to actively, rather than passively, resist outside influences which run counter to core ethno-religious values. Like Hostetler and Huntington's materials on the Hutterites (1968) and the Old Order Amish (1971), Shaffir's (1974, 1980) data on the Lubavitcher Chassidim, an ultra-ortho-dox Jewish sect in Montreal, demonstrate clearly that a key, identity-sustaining ethno-religious institution is the separate school, where comprehensive screening mechanisms ensure that undesired outside influences (e. g., scientific theories chal-lenging religious values, morally and culturally offensive passages in books, and so forth) are effectively censored, and that priority is accorded religious over secular cur-ricular studies.

A common finding in a wide range of materials on religiously-defined ethnic groups in Canada is the feature of internal religious institutional differentiation. Data from several studies on the Mennonites (Epp 1974; Fretz 1974; Anderson and Driedger 1980; Driedger 1988), the Doukhobors (Hawthorne 1955; Woodcock and Avakumovic 1968; Mealing 1980), and the Jews (Glickman 1976; Kallen 1969, 1977; Taieb-Carlen, 1992) indicate that the traditional, unitary religious institution among these populations has become fragmented along lines of greater or lesser retention of traditional beliefs and practices and greater or lesser introduction of out-side values and forms. While these studies tend to suggest that, in general, ethnic group identity is strongest among the most traditional sector of the community and weakest among the most acculturated, these data also demonstrate clearly the way in which religious institutional differentiation has served to hold the ethnic community together, by diversifying the services offered, and thereby meeting the needs of a wider spectrum of its ethnic membership.

Probably one of the most fruitful comparisons for the reader to engage in as a learning exercise here would be to make a comparative study of two Anabaptist sects, for example, a Hutterite community and another community such as Mennonite, Doukhobor, or Old Order Amish. Using the variables delineated in Table 3 on page 88 as a conceptual framework, the reader could make a fairly detailed comparative assessment of the factors influencing ethnic group viability through time in two different religiously defined ethnic communities.

Concluding Comments

In this chapter, we have examined the ways in which ethnic priorities, on the one hand, and dominant ideologies, policies, and practices, on the other, influence expressions of ethnic identity among members of Canadian ethnic collectivities. Our analysis thus far has indicated that a major variable affecting both the nature and the outcome of inter-ethnic relations is the relative rank or social status of different ethnic collectivities within Canadian society.

In the next chapter, we will examine the role played by racist-motivated violations of the human rights of particular ethnic collectivities in creating and sustaining group-level ethnic inequalities in Canada. We also will examine the social processes through which violations of the human rights of particular ethnic collectivities lead to the social construction of ethnic minority status.

Notes

1 In Canada, as elsewhere, this phenomenon is often found among aboriginal youth, especially those who have returned to the relatively traditional ethno-worlds of their isolated communities after spending several years in urbanized Euro-Canadian schools and workplaces (see Kallen 1977: 129-43). Ethnic marginality has not infrequently led conflicted youth to adopt self-destructive coping mechanisms such as alcohol and drug abuse and suicide (see Condon 1987: Ch. 8).

2 While the primary thrust of this scheme is that of in-group unity in defence (or offence) against the out-group, the reader should keep in mind certain caveats.

With specific regard to the Jewish example, at the international level, members were clearly united in support of the creation of the State of Israel, in 1948. At present, however, there are serious lines of division among Jews, within and outside Israel, with regard to the question of Palestinian self-determination. At the time of writing, peace negotiations between Israel and the P.L.O. continue to be thwarted by dissidents on both sides, unable to compromise with the 'enemy'.

3 The case study presented here represents a generalized picture of Hutterian communities,

which does not take into account differences among the various Hutterite colonies. In particular, the degree of adherence to traditional religious norms and the degree of acculturation to contemporary Canadian norms varies, sometimes markedly, from one colony to another.

There is an extensive literature on Anabaptists of various sectarian persuasions, and on the Hutterites, in particular. The main sources drawn from for illustrative purposes include Bennett (1969); Eaton (1970); Flint (1975); Hostetler and Huntington (1967); Peter (1980a, 1980b, 1987); and Sanders (1964).

4 The Hutterite sect originated as part of the Anabaptist Reformation movement in sixteenth-century Europe, which also included the Mennonites, Doukhobors, and Old Order Amish. With the possible exception of the latter sect, the Hutterites have been the most successful of all Anabaptists in maintaining a viable and highly distinctive religious ethnoculture over time.

5 This strategy is becoming more difficult to realize as such tracts of land become less available in Canada's West. Indeed, Peter (1987) suggests that some Hutterites have had to move to agriculturally marginal areas. Nevertheless, recent studies on Hutterite settlement and dispersion patterns (Thompson 1984 and Evans 1985) reveal that the method is still viable.

6 The long-term result of the Act was to encourage Hutterites to set up colonies in the neighbouring province of Saskatchewan as well as in the American states of Montana and Washington. Today, about one-third of the Hutterites live in Montana.

CHAPTER FIVE

Social Stratification, Human Rights Violations and the Social Construction of Ethnic and Other Minorities

In the previous chapters, we examined the ways in which presumed racial and ethnocultural differences between human populations affect the nature of social relations across ethnic boundaries. We have shown how invidious distinctions based on
assumed or perceived racial or ethnocultural differences are used to justify the denial
of human rights of members of particular ethnic collectivities.

In this chapter, we will examine the way in which human rights violations of
members of ethnic and other social categories have produced group-level inequalities
across Canada. Inequalities in political, economic, and social power have led to the
development of Canada's system of social stratification and, at the same time, have
played a major role in the social construction of ethnic and other minorities.

Dimensions of Social Stratification

Systems of social stratification can be based on a wide variety of criteria: race, ethnicity, gender, sexual orientation, age, class, and/or other factors. Any individual,
social, or cultural attribute accorded social significance in a society based on unequal
power relations can provide the basis for differential and unequal treatment of less
powerful populations by more powerful ones.

Regardless of the criteria used as the basis for social ranking, a society predicated
upon unequal power relations can be termed a socially stratified society.

The concept *social stratification* refers to the hierarchical structuring of society
which ensues from the differential ranking of various social collectivities with regard
to their members' degree of political, economic, and social power.

From a human rights perspective, equal access of all individuals to these three
dimensions of power has been conceptualized as political, economic, and social
rights, respectively. Insofar as these rights of all members of society are respected,
and, taking into account the ubiquitous range of variation in motivation, interests,

skills, and abilities among members of every human population, one would expect to find members of all social categories represented, in proportion to their numbers in society, at all ranks (strata) in the hierarchy. Where one finds, instead, differential ranking of various social collectivities, it may be hypothesized that group-based inequality is the long-term consequence of categorical discrimination—the denial or restriction of the political, economic, and/or social rights of members of particular social collectivities.

Political, Economic, and Social Power

The concept of *political power* refers to the ability of some people to control the life chances of others. The prime social indicator of political power, in a modern industrialized society such as Canada, is the attainment of strategic decision-making positions within major societal institutions. Through the attainment of these high-ranking positions, members of some social categories are able to make the crucial decisions which affect the life chances (opportunities and rewards) of others.

The concept of *economic power* or privilege refers to the accumulation and means for accumulation of the valued material and technological goods or resources of society. Social indicators of economic power in Canadian society include wealth, property, income, education, and occupation. Non-Marxian sociologists often refer to this dimension of a stratified system as 'socio-economic class'. Scholars who favour a Marxian or quasi-Marxian approach to social scientific analysis tend to emphasize one aspect of economic class, namely, economic control. The latter dimension of economic power is seen largely as a function of the ownership of the means of production in a society.

The concept of *social power* or prestige refers to the social recognition of honour (dignity) accorded members of society by others on the basis of their particular status, i.e., their culturally-defined position in society.

Parsons (1953) delineated three sets of social attributes which may be used as bases for prestigious evaluation and status ranking in any society: possessions—impersonal items people own (houses, businesses, patents, and the like); inherent (ascribed) personal attributes (age, gender, race, and ethnicity); acquired personal attributes (specific abilities or skills); and performances—demonstrated proficiency in the performance of particular social roles (the behavioural expectations associated with different status positions).

Curtis and Scott (1979) suggest that in Canadian society, prestige is based largely on widely understood evaluations of statuses based on such criteria as political power, economic control, education, wealth, and income, as well as race, ethnicity, gender, and age. In short, Curtis and Scott argue that prestige is premised on social evaluations of persons on the basis of their multiple achieved and ascribed statuses in society.

What appears to be lacking in all of the foregoing definitions is some way to conceptualize the fact that prestige, *at the level of the social collectivity*, is a socially constructed phenomenon, derived from a composite of status attributes, but signifying something more than a mere sum of its components. Viewed in terms of concepts of majority/minority relations, we suggest that social categories accorded prestige (majorities) are thereby *superiorized*; those denied prestige are thereby *inferiorized*. The implications of superiorization and inferiorization are to socially construct *superior* and *inferior* categories of people, with majority and minority status, respectively.

From a human rights view, it may be argued that the denial of prestige (social rights/human dignity) has more enduring disadvantaging effects on minorities than the denial of political and economic rights. For *denial of the human right to dignity* begets inferiorization, and *inferiorized minorities* become branded as *inferior by ascription.*

Social Stratification: Intersecting Dimensions of Ethnicity, Gender and Class

Systems of social stratification can be based on a wide variety of criteria: race, ethnicity, gender, sexual orientation, age, class, and/or other factors. In a society predicated on unequal power relations, any human attribute accorded social significance by dominant powers may be subject to arbitrary inferiorization or superiorization, and thus can provide the basis for differential and unequal treatment of particular populations. Members of social categories assumed to share the inferiorized version of the attribute will be unfairly disadvantaged; those assumed to share the superiorized version of the attribute will be unfairly advantaged. In both cases, the dominance and control of the powers-that-be is maintained.

In recent years, social scientists and other scholars have expressed a growing interest in the inter-linkages among multiple dimensions of social stratification. In particular, there is a growing body of literature which embodies the contemporary search by social analysts to conceptualize the links among relations of inequality based on race, ethnicity, gender, and class.

It is beyond the scope of the purposes of this book to address the many scholarly debates which have informed efforts to theorize connections among the different variables. However, in order to whet the scholarly appetite of the interested reader, I will offer a preliminary look at some of the central issues in the debate. My digest is derived in large part from Stasiulis (1990).[1]

The debates highlight the disagreement among scholars as to which of the variables (if any) assumes priority. Which of these variables—race, ethnicity, gender, or class—logically precedes the others in structuring relations of group-level inequality?

Stasiulis' review of the literature reveals that, on the race versus class question, there are two main opposing positions. The first position holds that social class is logically prior to race. The most extreme version of this view holds that race and ethnic relations are epiphenomena which can be understood solely within the analytic constructs of historical materialism, class, and production relations. More moderate versions of this position vary with respect to the amount of autonomy from class-based social relations they accord the analytic constructs of race and ethnicity.

The opposing view holds that race and ethnicity are logically prior to class. The most extreme version of this view accords full autonomy to the analytic constructs of race and ethnicity and denies any influence of class or economic relations. More moderate versions of this position consider race and ethnic relations to be relatively autonomous forces that are independent of class factors.

A third position, a move away from the determinism and reductionism of both extreme positions on the debate, holds that race and class represent independent but interacting forces which structure relations of inequality. While race and class are held to be separate analytic constructs, this view posits that they interact in a multi-faceted way to generate autonomous but inter-related systems of social stratification.

As compared with the substantial literature on race/ethnicity and class, the litera-ture on gender and race/ethnicity is only in its infancy. Stasiulus contends that the omission of gender in theories dealing with the race versus class question reflects, in part, the immensity of the scholarly challenge posed in the attempt to develop an integrated analytic framework which takes into account two or more social dimen-sions of stratification, both as separate analytic constructs, and in their complex interaction.

Stasiulus observes that, within feminist literature, socialist-feminist theories have incorporated the analytic construct of class as a key explanatory variable, but, until recently, they have been silent on race and ethnicity. The attacks on 'White femi-nism' (feminist writing by white women which ignores or marginalizes race and eth-nicity) by women of colour, has sparked the counter-theorizing of 'Black feminism' (feminist writing by women of colour which incorporates race and ethnicity as key explanatory factors). In the political arena, as well as in theoretical debates, black feminists have criticized the bias within white feminism which prioritizes gender divisions and sexism (or, in socialist feminism, gender and class divisions) over race divisions and racism. Moreover, black feminism challenges the eurocentric premises even of the central concepts within white feminism: analytic constructs such as 'the state', 'reproduction' and 'the family' are all held to embody white racist logics.

Stasiulus criticizes the approach of black feminism on two counts. First, she chal-lenges its implicit black/white dichotomy, frequently assumed to structure the racist and sexist subordination of women of colour. Secondly, she challenges its treatment of women of colour as a homogeneous social category, thus avoiding analysis of the mediating role of class on the disadvantaging effects of race and gender.

The linkages between ethnicity and gender (or femininity) have been theorized in two different ways. Gender has become incorporated into the ethnicity literature and ethnicity has become incorporated into feminist analysis. A special issue of *Canadian Ethnic Studies* (xiii, 1, 1981) which focused on the relationship between ethnicity, femininity, and class, provided an opportunity for scholars with opposing perspec-tives on the debate to present their views. Some argued that ethnicity, race, and fem-ininity were separate but interacting analytic constructs, which combined to doubly or triply disadvantage immigrant women, women of colour, and immigrant women of colour (the double or triple jeopardy thesis). Others argued that race and ethnicity were simply epiphenomena of the fundamental forces of class relations in Canadian society.

Stasiulus (1990) contends that the growth of ethnic feminist historiography in Canada has enabled scholars to challenge the double or triple 'jeopardy' (disadvantage) thesis. These newer analyses of the multiple disadvantages faced by immigrant women have addressed both the similarities and the differences among women differentiated on the basis of immigrant status, race, ethnicity, and class. Stasiulus concludes that the very different circumstances of distinct categories of immigrant women defy analyses based on essentialist conceptions of women, black women, or women of colour.[2]

In her discussion of the race and class debates, Stasiulus points out that at both the political and analytical levels, the arguments have been weighted in terms of the greater or lesser 'evil' (or, in my way of conceptualizing the issues, greater or lesser human rights violations). Which 'evil' (or area of human rights violations) is the more 'primary'?

My own response to this question is simple: Ask the person who has experienced the human rights violations. In my view, it is incompatible with a human rights framework of analysis to socially construct a *hierarchy* of 'evil', which can then be used to socially construct a hierarchy of human suffering based on different, majority-imposed, criteria for inferiorization and unequal treatment

From a human rights view, my own position on the debate would clearly favour a perspective that considered each analytic construct (race, gender, class, and so forth) as autonomous, but that also took into account the complexity of interaction between the separate systems of social stratification predicated on the different analytic constructs.

Regardless of the variables singled out for analysis, systems of social stratification share one common denominator: they are built on unequal power relations between members of superiorized and inferiorized social categories in the society. Social scientists have conceptualized inter-group relations based on inequalities in political, economic and social power as majority/minority relations.

Social Stratification and Majority/Minority Relations

While systems of social stratification may be based on a wide variety of criteria, the concept *majority*, or dominant collectivity, within any system of social stratification refers to the social category with superordinate social status at a given structural level or regional sector in the society, whose members wield the greatest degree of political, economic, and social power. By way of contrast, the concept *minority*, or subordinate collectivity, refers to the *corresponding* social category (with regard to the same ranking criteria) with subordinate social status *relative to the majority*, and whose members wield a lesser degree of political, economic and/or social power.

It is important to emphasize that *majority/minority relations*, as conceptualized by social scientists, are inter-group relations predicated on demonstrable disparities in political, economic and/or social power. They are not necessarily predicated on disparities in population numbers. This point differentiates the social scientific usage of the concepts of majority and minority (to refer to power disparities) from their political application and from their use in common parlance (to refer to numerical disparities).

The Development of the Minority Concept

Social scientific interest in the study of minorities began and for a long time remained closely connected with the field of race and ethnic relations. Culture contact between different ethnic populations and the consequent development of multiethnic societies has frequently, indeed commonly, given rise to some form of ethnic stratification. Concomitantly, scholars interested in the study of ethnic relations, as well as those whose interests focused on the areas of social stratification and social change, almost inevitably become involved in the study of ethnic minorities (Wagley and Harris 1958; Marden and Meyer 1973; Simpson and Yinger 1972; Makielski 1973). An unfortunate consequence of the long-term association between the concepts of 'ethnicity' and 'minority' is the general tendency among scholars and laypersons alike to conceive of all minorities as ethnic collectivities and to conceive of all ethnic collectivities as minority groups. The misleading use of the term *ethnics*, to set apart ethnic minorities from the dominant population in a society—a common tendency among Canadians—is simply erroneous, for it suggests that members of ethnic majorities like Anglo-Canadians are not 'ethnics' (i.e., that they do not stem from or belong to any ethnic collectivity).

The long-term association of the term minority with ethnic differences is similarly misleading, for it suggests that there are no other subordinate and inferiorized populations within the society. Within the current UN framework for human rights, ethnicity is particularly relevant for the question of minority claims based on *collective* cultural rights; but characteristics other than ethnocultural ones (race, sex, age, sexual orientation, disability) are as relevant as ethnicity for the question of minority claims based on *individual* and *categorical* rights.

The Social Construction of Minority Status

Minorities are not 'natural' entities; they are socially constructed categories of people. No human population is innately or 'naturally' superior or inferior to others. However, some populations have more power than others, and those with superior power (majorities) are able to impose *inferiorizing* labels on those with less power on the basis of their own unsubstantiated assumptions about minority group attributes.

Minorities are not 'inferior' by nature, in any of their group attributes, but they become 'inferiorized' by majority definition. The point I want to emphasize here is that it is *not* distinctive minority attributes, in themselves, that are responsible for the social construction of minority status: it is unsubstantiated majority assumptions about group attributes. However, once *inferiorizing* labels are imposed, majority authorities are able to rationalize human rights violations—denial of political, economic, social or cultural rights—to populations *arbitrarily defined as* inferior.

Human rights violations act to discriminate against minorities, to deny their members the opportunities and rewards accorded majority members. The long-term consequence of human rights violations is that minorities become collectively disadvantaged. They come to occupy a subordinate and inferiorized status in society which we conceptualize as *minority status.*

Definition of Minority Concept

The minority concept can be defined from an objective and/or a subjective perspective. In order to include all minorities within a comprehensive, *objective* definition, we will define a minority as any social category within a society (1) that is set apart and defined by the majority as incompetent/inferior or abnormal/dangerous on the basis of assumed physical, cultural, and/or behavioural differences from majority norms; (2) whose members are categorically discriminated against by the majority on the basis of arbitrarily imposed, inferiorizing labels; (3) whose members are subject to some degree of oppression (denial of political rights), neglect (denial of economic rights), diminution (denial of social rights/human dignity) and/or deculturation (denial of cultural rights); and (4) which, as a consequence of the self-fulfilling prophecy of systemic discrimination, comes to occupy a socially subordinate, disadvantaged, and inferiorized position within the society.

The foregoing definition of minority differs from the now classic definition of Louis Wirth[3] in three important ways. First, it utilizes only objective criteria, whereas Wirth employed both subjective and objective criteria; second, it is more inclusive than Wirth's definition with regard to the range of minorities which may be subsumed under it, and third, it includes both minority *categories* and minority *groups.*

The comprehensive definition of minority which I have proposed reveals the three stages or steps in the process through which minority status is socially constructed: labelling as inferior; categorical discrimination/human rights violations and the self-fulfilling prophecy of collective disadvantage which results in minority status.

Majority and Minority: Relative Concepts

Like ethnicity, the minority concept is a relative notion which, even more than ethnicity, is meaningful only in relation to a corresponding out-group. In the case of minorities, the salient out-group with regard to any given human attribute is the corresponding majority or dominant population whose members enjoy a greater degree of political, economic, and social power in the society, and whose particular physical, cultural, and behavioural attributes provide the recognized, legitimate norms for all populations in the society (for example: white/black, male/female, English-speaker/Italian-speaker, Protestant/Moslem, adult/child, heterosexual/homosexual, Euro-Canadian/Inuit). It is important to note, here, that it is the majority who define the normative order in society. Thus, for any socially significant human characteristic, the majority attribute provides the 'normal' (more accurately, normative) referent in relation to which minority differences are defined as 'abnormal' and/or 'deviant' (non-normative).

We will define a majority as a social category (1) whose members have the legitimate power (or authority) to define themselves as normal and superior and to define all social categories (minorities) which are presumed to deviate from their physical, cultural, and behavioural norms as abnormal and/or inferior; (2) whose members are able to justify unequal and inferiorizing treatment of minorities through the use of invalidation ideologies or 'ISMS'—like racism, sexism, and ageism—which provide falsified 'evidence' for the inherent abnormality or inferiority of assumed minority attributes; (3) whose members are able to impose their will, norms, and laws on the society at large and to deny or suppress the expression of alternate, minority ideas and life ways; and (4) whose members exercise the greatest degree of political, economic, and social power in the society and are able to control the life destinies of minorities.

Because minorities are assumed to harbour characteristics that differ from the norms of the dominant population in undesirable or unacceptable ways, minority members tend to be regarded and treated by the dominant population as unworthy or undeserving of equal societal opportunities. It follows from this premise that the more abnormal or inferior the alleged minority attributes are considered, the more pernicious will be the forms of discrimination against minorities. Put another way, insofar as minorities are branded as *less-than-human* by majority powers, then the stage is set for the rationalization that such populations are not entitled to claim the same rights as *fully human beings.*

Inferiorization versus Stigmatization

In general, minorities presumed to be dangerous tend to be treated more inhumanely than those presumed to be inferior but relatively harmless. Dangerous minorities are those perceived by majority authorities as a threat to their entrenched power, i.e., minorities perceived to threaten majority political, economic, and social control in the society. Also seen as dangerous are minorities perceived to threaten established majority racial, ethnic, cultural, and moral norms.

Minorities may be labelled as dangerous on the basis of physical attributes (e.g., race), cultural attributes (e.g., religion) and/or behavioural attributes (e.g., lifestyle). The more dangerous the minority is presumed to be, the more likely that discriminatory treatment against its members by dominant powers will involve the use of punitive legal sanctions backed by armed force (police, military, security guards).

Minorities labelled as dangerous and threatening to society tend to be viewed not just as inferior human beings, but as sub-human or even anti-human beings. They are not just inferiorized; they are *stigmatized.*

According to Goffman (1963) the term, stigma, in its original Greek meaning, referred to forcibly imposed bodily mutilations (e.g., cuts or burns) which publicly announced that the bearer was a morally blemished (or ritually polluted) person—a slave, criminal, or traitor—to be shunned by members of society-at-large (and, we would add, to be summarily denied human rights). Today, in social scientific parlance, the term generally refers to any deeply discrediting human attribute, rather than to any visible bodily evidence of it.

Stigmatization serves to dehumanize the minority in the eyes of the majority audience. This can be explained, in part, with reference to the nature of stigma. A central quality of stigma is that of contagion: stigma deriving from one discrediting characteristic tends to spread to other characteristics. This leads to the imputation of a wide range of discrediting attributes on the basis of the original one: blacks are slow-witted and lazy, they hang around in gangs and push drugs, they are the cause of violence and crime in Canada; Indians have only a primitive mentality, they can't hold down a job, they are just a bunch of drunken welfare bums who get into fights and end up in jail. In this way, a highly distorted and wholly discrediting group stereotype of an anti-human or sub-human minority is generated. Once minorities are categorized as less-than-human, majority authorities are able to rationalize flagrant human rights violations with impunity.

During World War II, those minorities stigmatized by Nazi authorities in Germany as inherently evil, depraved, sub-human, and polluting creatures (for example, Jews, homosexuals, gypsies) were singled out for extermination in death camps. While Canada never adopted such a policy of genocide, during World War II, when Canada was at war with Japan, Japanese-Canadians—most of whom were Canadian-born citizens and many of whom had never seen Japan—were defined as dangerous enemy aliens, traitors to Canada. While no evidence of treason had been found by Government authorities, Japanese-Canadians collectively stigmatized as dangerous enemy aliens were incarcerated under armed guard in internment camps for the duration of the war. This case will be elaborated in the next chapter.

The point of this example is to demonstrate the way in which majority authorities can employ the notion of 'dangerousness' in order to rationalize discriminatory public policies and practices which entail pervasive violations of minority rights. In this connection, it is important to differentiate between 'real' and 'apparent' danger, and to take into account the fact that what is 'real', within the context of majority/minority relations, tends to be what is presumed/alleged to be real by majority authorities.

Master Status and Multiple Minority Status

In the preceding pages, we have argued that the discriminatory implications of minority status vary with the degree of presumed deviance of minority attributes from majority norms; with the nature of majority-imposed labels (inferior versus dangerous); and with the degree of discreditation of minority attributes (inferiorized or stigmatized).

In the pages to follow, we will examine the way in which inferiorization and stigmatization impact upon the personal and social identities of minority members. We also will analyse the discriminatory implications of multiple minority status.

Master Status

Social scientists apply the concept of master status to explain the phenomenon which occurs when the inferiorized or stigmatized minority attribute comes to constitute members' overriding, defining characteristic; when it comes to assume precedence over and above all the other human attributes of minority members. This conception of master status focuses on the way in which majorities create minorities through singling out particular attributes as the basis for inferiorization and categorical discrimination.

Another conception of master status focuses on the way in which minorities react to inferiorization. When inferiorized or stigmatized minority attributes become perceived by minority members as central to their self-definition; when they come to provide the overriding basis for minority members' self-identification and group identification, then the attribute/s can be said to have achieved a master status from the subjective point of view of the minority member. When this happens, minority members have come to *internalize* the inferiorizing labels imposed upon them by the majority. They not only have become acutely conscious of their minority group status and identity, but it has come to supersede all other statuses and identities.

To illustrate this point, I will offer a quote taken from an autobiographical essay by Chief Dan George, a Canadian Indian:

Do you know what it is like to have your race belittled and to come to learn that you are only a burden to the [white man's] country? . . . We were shoved aside because they thought we were dumb and could never learn . . . What is it like to be without pride in your race, pride in your family, pride and confidence in yourself? . . . I shall tell you what it is like. It is like not caring about tomorrow for what does tomorrow matter . . . It is like having a reserve that looks like a junk yard . . . It is like getting drunk . . . an escape from ugly reality . . . It is most of all like awaking next morning to the guilt of betrayal. For the alcohol did not fill the emptiness but only dug it deeper. (Waubageshig, 1970: 186)

Multiple Minority Status

The effect of an overriding master status is to obscure the fact that all human beings have a number of different social statuses and identities based upon a variety of human attributes. Some of these statuses may be based on minority attributes; others, on majority attributes. Therefore, the same individual may, at the same time, have minority status on the basis of some attributes and majority status on the basis of others.

In the following section, we will examine the social significance of multiple minority status. We will analyse the implications of multiple minority status both in terms of its impact on personal and social identities and in terms of its discriminatory manifestations.

Insofar as individuals may belong to several minorities at the same time, the question arises: which of one's minority attributes will assume master status?

Within the context of majority/minority relations, the notion of master status provides a parallel to the notion of primordiality emphasized by some scholars (e.g., Isaacs 1977) in connection with ethnicity and ethnic identity.

In Chapter Four I suggested that if we adopt the approach of scholars who hold that one's ethnic identity is a person's most basic—primordial—group identity, the argument would follow that, in a case of multiple minority status, one's ethnic attributes would override other minority characteristics and would invariably provide the underpinnings for one's master status, at least from the subjective point of view.

In contrast to this position, I propose that the extent to which it holds true in any given empirical instance must be taken as problematic, since both ethnic and other minority group identities are highly contingent upon the nature of the prevailing social environment. I submit that the particular human attribute which will assume master status at any given time will vary with the specific social context and situation.

A number of variables could have bearing here. For example: Which of the minority attributes deviates most markedly from majority norms? Which is most inferiorized or stigmatized? Which minority attribute is at issue in the situation at hand? Which majority group is represented in or relevant to the situation? A black lesbian woman may be discriminated against in the Canadian context on the basis of race, sexual orientation, and sex, but whether one or more of these human attributes provides the basis for her over-arching master status in a given situation is contingent upon the relevant variables in that situation.

In cases where an individual has multiple minority status, the various statuses may or may not overlap in their discriminatory implications, under different social conditions. In the case of one black lesbian woman, blackness may provide the overriding attribute for self-identification and thus may come to assume a master status which remains salient even in situations focusing on either women's or lesbian rights. In another case, this may not hold true. A black lesbian woman may be involved in the women's movement, the movement for gay/lesbian liberation, and a black women's organization, all of which involve the attribute of sex; but it may only be in the context of the women's movement that the attribute of sex, rendered salient by a focus on gender discrimination, assumes master status.

The main point of this example is to show that the way in which multiple minority status impacts upon a person's various social identities varies from one individual to another and from one social context to another. Which, if any, of a given person's minority attributes will assume master status in a given social context is something that must be empirically determined.

In addition to the question of the impact of multiple minority status on one's personal and social identities, a second question arises: that of its discriminatory impact. Does multiple minority status inevitably beget multiple disadvantage?

Multiple Minority Status/Multiple Jeopardy?

The multiple jeopardy thesis has been put forward by social scientific researchers to test the theory that multiple minority status has both objective and subjective disadvantaging effects. The disadvantaging consequences of categorical discrimination on the basis of multiple criteria have thus been measured both in terms of reported fulfilment of life-needs and in terms of reported life-satisfaction.

However, to date, research studies attempting to test the multiple jeopardy thesis with regard to the variables of sex, ethnic status, and/or age have not been able to provide convincing evidence for this thesis with regard to subjective indicators of disadvantage. While research results clearly support the multiple jeopardy thesis with regard to the inadequacy of fulfilment of the life-needs of multiply inferiorized minorities, findings do not provide similarly strong support for the thesis with regard to their subjective feelings of life-satisfaction.[4]

How can we explain this seeming inconsistency in research findings?

A number of factors can be taken into consideration. First, minority categories—whether based on race, gender, age, ethnicity, or other attributes—are not homogeneous groups, as inferiorizing minority stereotypes suggest. Within each category are individual human beings with individual ways of coping with the disadvantages of their minority status. Some members internalize majority-imposed inferiorizing labels, others come to reject these derogatory labels. This observation has been documented in the research studies designed to test the multiple jeopardy thesis.

Differences in the strength of an individual's ability to cope with multiple minority status may vary in relation to lines of differentiation within minority communities. Class (socio-economic status), for example, is important here. Despite the collective disadvantage of minorities as collectivities, some members of ethnic and other minorities occupy a superior or élite economic status within their own minority communities. Clearly, such minority members have greater means than do others with which to cope with inferiorization. Another important variable is the availability of minority support systems. Minority members who can rely on minority support networks can find a great deal of help in coping with the dehumanizing effects of oppression, neglect, and diminution.

There also are inter-ethnic group differences with regard to collective disadvantage, In Canada, European ethnic groups are the least inferiorized and disadvantaged and aboriginal ethnic groups are the most inferiorized and disadvantaged. Among immigrant ethnic minorities, racial visibility is an important differentiating variable: racially visible minorities tend to be more inferiorized and disadvantaged than do other ethnic minorities.

All of these variables must be considered in order to account for the patterns of disadvantage resulting from the combined effects of multiple minority status, particularly when multiple jeopardy rests in part on *ethnicity*.

Multiple Minority Status/Multiple Jeopardy: Immigrant Women in Canada

The diversity in the extent and in the patterns of disadvantage associated with multiple minority status can be well illustrated by the case of immigrant women in Canada.

Some immigrant women have achieved a status in Canada comparable to their middle-class or upper-middle class Canadian counterparts: in particular, immigrant women with professional skills who migrated to Canada as independent immigrants, and immigrant women who came to Canada with considerable wealth (for example, under the business class). Most often, however, immigrant women's status in Canadian society is lower than that of Canadian-born women as a result of their differential treatment under Canada's immigration law and in the labour market.

Boyd (1987) documents the disadvantaging impact upon two categories of immigrant women—domestic workers and permanent residents—of systemic discrimination which has resulted from the intersection of immigration policy with existing settlement/integration policies.

The potential and actual exploitation of immigrant women, many of whom are women of colour, under Canada's Foreign Domestic Worker program provides a glaring example of multiple jeopardy based on gender, race, ethnicity, and class. The program was designed to curb the exploitation of temporary domestic workers which occurred in the past either from the actions of employers or from successive renewals which kept domestics in Canada without any guarantee of permanent residency. Under the current program, permanent residency may be sought by workers admitted to Canada on a temporary basis, and minimum standards for their living and working conditions while employed as temporary workers have been established. Nevertheless, employer exploitation of temporary domestic workers under the program continues to be documented. The potential threat of deportation of temporary domestic workers gives employers—mostly well-to-do white women—the power to exploit and to silence domestic workers—mostly poor women of colour (Hurtado 1989). Boyd (1987) raises several concerns about the FDW program itself, among them low wages, and the need to monitor employer compliance with the terms of the work agreement. She also points to the negative effects on women workers of the dependency relations and privatized work setting—attributes of women's traditional gender roles which confined them to the private sphere where they worked as unpaid domestics.

Immigrant women who have the status of permanent residents are eligible to participate in a number of settlement/integration programs, but in practice, many experience difficulties in accessing these programs. Many immigrant women cannot attend training programs or language classes during the day because they work; at night, they are just too tired to learn anything (Das Gupta 1986). Moreover, Boyd (1987) points out that, under current programs of settlement/integration, female permanent residents who enter Canada in the family and assisted relative classes may not be eligible for certain program entitlements, such as basic training allowances associated with the CEIC language training programs and provincial or municipal social welfare programs. Additionally, as elderly immigrants entering Canada, some immigrant women will receive no Canada Pension Plan benefits or (depending on the country of origin) old age supplements. Immigrant women may also face systemic barriers to accessing job skill or job development programs because economic pressures force them to take any job rather than to be unemployed.

Many working immigrant women find themselves at the bottom of the heap in the labour market. A disproportionate number get stuck in the rut of poorly paid, dead-end, non-unionized, insecure jobs with unsafe working conditions. Immigrant women, immigrant women of colour, and visible minority women tend to be over-represented at the bottom of 'pink ghettos'. Immigrant women are concentrated in textile, garment and electronic factories, food-related services, and domestic and farm work (Das Gupta 1986).

The situation of refugee women is in some respects even more vulnerable than that of immigrant women. Boyd (1993) notes that the observation that approximately 80 per cent of the world's refugees are women and children is an often repeated one. Yet among migrants admitted to Canada on humanitarian grounds, the statistical data indicate clearly that men are greatly over-represented, relative to women. A number of factors related to the process of refugee selection account for this seeming contradiction: taken together they highlight the systemic gender bias in the procedures.

In Canada, the patterns of disadvantage which mark the experience of refugee women are somewhat different from those of their immigrant women counterparts. Like refugees, immigrants have experienced being uprooted from their country of origin. However, as Das Gupta (1986) points out, the relocation of refugees is exacerbated by the abruptness of the experience, the lack of choices on their part, as well as the all too frequent experience of violence and murder. The refugee experience is one which leads to extreme forms of depression, insecurity, and vulnerability.

In response to their diverse experiences of multiple jeopardy, based on gender and/or ethnicity, class, race, or age, immigrant and refugee women have created organizations representing their various voices.

One issue which has raised organized concern among immigrant women is that of unequal access to the federal Language Training programs associated with Employment and Immigration Canada. Immigrant men and women are eligible for the program if they intend to enter the labour force and if (1) their lack of language skills prevents them from securing employment in their usual occupation or (2) they are unskilled and their lack of skill prevents them from obtaining employment (Boyd 1987). Although the program does not explicitly discriminate on the basis of sex, two features of the program curb its accessibility to immigrant women. First, if an applicant is unskilled or has limited skills, she or he will not likely qualify for language training if the ability to speak one of Canada's two official languages is not necessary for the employment. Accordingly, seamstresses, hotel maids and domestics, for example, who can perform their jobs without comprehensive language skills may be denied entry into the program. Secondly, immigrants who enter Canada in the family class and assisted relative class are not eligible for the basic training allowance provided through the program, because their sponsors have agreed to be financially responsible for them. However, women tend more than men to be sponsored immigrants and their ineligibility for the training allowance means that these women will not generate income during the training period. For many immigrant women the economic pressure to work for income precludes their participation in the program.

In addition to their unequal access to language training and their marginalization in employment, many immigrant women experience violence and abuse at home. While violence against women is an increasing concern for all women in Canada, Boyd (1987) points out that immigrant women are particularly vulnerable to entrapment in an abusive situation because of two difficulties in obtaining assistance. First, shelters for battered women in Canada have limited resources and frequently lack the necessary multilingual and multicultural staff who could understand and address the particular needs of immigrant women from diverse cultures. Second, existing sponsorship relationships can restrict assistance. Currently, the sponsorship relation can continue for up to ten years after arrival. As mentioned earlier, this legal relationship precludes government financial assistance to sponsored immigrants. Women in this relationship may also be intimidated by sponsors who threaten them with deportation if they leave an abusive relationship. Sponsored immigrant women, like female domestic workers, are extremely vulnerable to this kind of intimidation, and associated exploitation, by their 'masters'.

Two major concerns of immigrant women have been raised in the form of Charter challenges which claim that two federal government programs for immigrants—the language training program and the fiancée sponsorship program—violate the equality rights (under s.15 of the Charter) of sponsored immigrant women. The first claim argues that the CEIC language training program discriminates against women on the basis of the ineligibility criteria discussed earlier. Immigrant women argue that English as a second language is a necessity for full participation in Canadian society. The exclusion of immigrant women on the ground that language skills are unnecessary to their jobs has the effect of freezing them in their marginalized employment and preventing them from improving their labour market opportunities. They are thereby excluded from participation in the mainstream of Canadian society.

The focus of the second claim is on the potential for abuse of fiancées (and wives, should they marry sponsors) under the fiancée sponsorship program's provisions. The unintended effect of the provisions is to force fiancées to marry abusing sponsors within 90 days of arrival and to remain with the abuser after marriage or face deportation (*Canadian Human Rights Advocate*, March 1988).

These two charter challenges highlight the common goal shared by immigrant women, namely, to achieve recognition and protection for their equality rights. Nevertheless, immigrant women are highly cognizant of their diversity, and they are also concerned that their diversity—based on ethnicity, class, race, age, sexual orientation, and other variables—should be recognized and addressed.

In 1988, organizations representing immigrant women sharply criticized a newly released policy report published by the CACSW on immigrant women in Canada, saying that it ignored the issues of racism and systemic discrimination seriously disadvantaging immigrant women, and also that it lumped all immigrant women together (*Canadian Human Rights Advocate*, April 1988). Immigrant women's organizations criticized the report for ignoring differences between earlier and more recent immigrants, between immigrants from different countries of origin, and between white and non-white immigrants. Accordingly, they argued, the statistical interpretation offered in the report presented a highly distorted picture. Immigrant women demanded that the CACSW halt distribution of the report, but the Council did not do so (*Canadian Human Rights Advocate*, April 1988).

The sharp difference in perspectives on the CACSW report, on the part of its professional drafters, and on the part of representatives of immigrant women, can be seen to parallel the tensions within the women's movement as it attempts to accommodate immigrant women and women of colour within a movement designed to express the particularistic concerns of white, middle-class Euro-Canadian women.

Black feminists, speaking for women of colour, have criticized the women's movement for failing to address the situation of double jeopardy facing non-white women who are discriminated against on the basis of both race and sex (Das Gupta 1986; Stasiulus 1990). Black feminists have been especially articulate in pointing out that mainstream middle-class white feminists frequently display an insensitivity to the enormous power differential between black and white women manifested in the lower income and restricted options of black women. Echoing these sentiments, immigrant women, together with women of colour, have begun to challenge the women's movement's strong middle-class and racist biases. They have drawn attention to the fact that demands of the women's movement such as pay equity have been defined solely in terms of white middle-class women's priorities. How (they ask) can immigrant women make demands for pay equity when the dead-end jobs to which so many of them are confined are largely non-unionized, and when they live in constant fear of being laid off?

Spokespersons for immigrant women and women of colour argue that they have been doubly discriminated against and that only they, themselves, should be responsible for making decisions with regard to ways of addressing the 'double whammy' of racism and sexism. In an article in the *Toronto Star* (28 Nov. 1992) headed 'Feminism's Faultlines', a black female professor is quoted as saying: 'In Canada, white women have claimed the right to define what feminism is about . . . that right to define has never been ours.' Another woman of colour pointed out that white women often say, 'Let's deal with women's issues first, then we'll take on racism.' 'Well (she asked), which line do I stand in? The women's line or the racial minority line? You *can't* separate the two.'

Concluding Comments

The foregoing analysis of multiple minority status and multiple jeopardy draws attention to the fact that inferiorized minority attributes such as race, ethnicity, sex, age, or class often are complexly linked, rather than discrete phenomena, in their empirical manifestations. Nevertheless, for analytic purposes, we can single out *ethnic* minorities from other types of minorities in Canada, whose inferiorized attributes have somewhat different implications for social ranking.

Where ethnicity constitutes an important criterion for social ranking, as in Canada, the society can be said to be ethnically stratified and the system of social stratification may be viewed and studied, for analytic purposes, as a system of ethnic stratification.

In the next chapter, we will analyse the origin and development of the Canadian system of ethnic stratification, and we will delineate the factors influencing different patterns of majority/minority *ethnic* relations in Canada.

Notes

1 For a thorough and intellectually incisive overview and analysis of the debates, see D.K. Stasiulis, 'Theorizing Connections: Gender, Race, Ethnicity and Class', in P.S. Li (ed.), *Race and Ethnic Relations in Canada.* Toronto: Oxford University Press, 1990.

2 In a later section of this chapter, I will address the issues of multiple minority status and the multiple jeopardy thesis, in some detail.

3 Wirth's definition of a minority reads as follows: 'We may define a minority as a group of people who, because of their physical or cultural characteristics, are singled out from the others in the society in which they live for differential and unequal treatment and

who therefore regard themselves as objects of collective discrimination' (quoted in Hacker 1951: 60).

4 See, especially, two special issues of *Canadian Ethnic Studies: Ethnicity and Femininity* (XIII, 1, 1981) and *Ethnicity and Aging* (xv, 3, 1983); Gee and Kimball 1987 and Driedger and Chappel 1987.

CHAPTER SIX

The Vertical Ethnic Mosaic: The Canadian System of Ethnic Statification

In the last chapter, we introduced the concept of social stratification and we showed how it is manifested, in Canada, in unequal relations between majority and minority populations. We examined the way in which majority authorities use invidious distinctions, based on unsubstantiated assumptions about group attributes, to inferiorize particular populations and to justify denial of their human rights. We emphasized the important role played by human rights violations in the social construction of ethnic and other minorities, and we demonstrated how human rights violations based on invidious group distinctions have produced group-level inequalities across Canada.

In this chapter, our discussion of social stratification and majority/minority relations in Canada will focus on ethnic criteria for social ranking. Accordingly, we will limit our examination of the Canadian structure of social inequality to an analysis of Canada's ethnic stratification system.

Racism, Human Rights Violations, and the Social Construction of Ethnic Minorities in Canada

Within the human rights perspective adopted by the International Bill of Human Rights (IBHR), the very existence of ethnic minorities is in violation of their members' fundamental human rights. The Universal Declaration of Human Rights (UDHR) proclaims that all members of every human society should have equal access to political, economic, and social power. Yet, wherever they are found, ethnic minorities are categorically and systemically restricted or excluded from such access on the arbitrary basis of the racist views of the majority, which are used by dominant authorities to rationalize categorical discrimination against minority target groups. Within the context of majority/minority ethnic relations, racist ideologies are transposed into potent political instruments wielded by the dominant ethnic collectivity to oppress (deny political rights), neglect (deny economic rights), diminish (deny social rights), and deculturate (deny cultural rights) members of ethnic minorities.

In addition to the protection of *individual* human rights and freedoms accorded every human being *qua* human being under the IBHR, members of ethnocultural minorities also are accorded protection for their *collective* cultural, linguistic, and religious rights. Article 27 of the International Covenant on Civil and Political Rights (ICCPR) states that ethnic, religious, and linguistic minorities, wherever they exist within states, should not be denied the right to collectively express and enjoy their own distinctive culture, religion, and language.

Current interpretation of this article, as expressed in the *Declaration on the Rights of Persons Belonging to National or Ethnic, Religious and Linguistic Minorities*, adopted by the UN General Assembly on December 18, 1992 (see Appendix D), indicates that it is the *ethnocultural* underpinnings of minority status which provide the justification for *collective* minority rights. What distinguishes *sui generis* ethnocultural minorities from other (non-ethnic) minorities is the attribute of 'living' culture, i.e., culture (or ethnoculture) in the trans-generational, anthropological sense of the term. It is this attribute which provides the currently recognized basis for the *collective rights* of ethnic minorities, under United Nations Human Rights Codes and Covenants.[1]

This distinction is a critical one for our examination of Canada's system of ethnic stratification, for it sets apart *sui generis* ethnocultural minorities from other collectively disadvantaged and inferiorized minorities, as indicated in Tables 1 and 2 (pp. 76 and 77). Only ethnocultural minorities can, justifiably, put forward collective cultural rights claims.

The Development of Ethnic Stratification in Canada

The mere existence of ethnic differences between co-existing human populations within a multi-ethnic society such as Canada's does not mean that ethnic criteria will provide bases for social stratification, and that majority/minority ethnic relations will inevitably follow. It is only when assumed ethnic differences are utilized by dominant ethnic collectivities to create and sustain legitimate bases of social stratification that the ethnic 'minority syndrome' (Glaser and Possony 1979: IX) develops.

When one or more ethnic collectivities, such as the English outside Quebec and the French in Quebec, become powerful enough to define the societal/province-wide situation, to impose their will, their cultural standards, and their laws on all ethnic collectivities within their sphere of jurisdiction in society, and when less powerful ethnic collectivities presumed to differ from majority norms in undesirable ways are thereby denied their political, economic, social, and cultural rights, then the ethnic minority syndrome becomes full blown.

Canada's Vertical Ethnic Mosaic

In *The Vertical Mosaic* (1965), the late John Porter described the nationwide hierarchical structure of the Canadian ethnic stratification system at that time. Based on the findings of a national survey conducted over a period of almost ten years, Porter reported that members of Canada's various ethnic collectivities were differentially and unequally represented (in proportion to their numbers in the population) within the Canadian ethnic hierarchy, which consisted of three broad social categories:

1) Charter or founding populations (English and French), together with immigrants from the British Isles and those from Northern and Western European countries whose biocultural characteristics were similar to those of the charter populations, were disproportionately represented at the top, within the ranks of the majority or dominant social category.
2) Later immigrant populations, largely from Southern and Eastern European countries, whose biocultural characteristics diverged in varying degrees from those of the dominant populations, were found in the middle ranks among Canada's ethnic minorities.
3) Aboriginal populations (Indians, Inuit, and Métis), whose biocultural characteristics diverged most markedly from those of the dominant ethnic categories, were found at the bottom of Canada's ethnic hierarchy. At the time of Porter's study, Canada's aboriginal peoples constituted a racially stigmatized and structurally dependent ethnoclass having the lowest status of all minorities.

Porter noted that there was a tendency for the vertical structure of the ethnic mosaic to persist, in much the same form, over time. Despite considerable upward and downward status mobility and inconsistency in the middle ranks, Porter pointed out that the ethnic composition of the very top ranks and that of the very bottom tended to remain relatively stable and consistent on the three dimensions of stratification (political, economic, and social power).

The survey indicated that a high degree of status consistency was associated with ethnic rank stability. At the very top, the dominant English élite were characterized by superordinate levels of political, economic, and social power; the aboriginal minorities at the bottom were characterized by low status and power on all three dimensions. In the middle ranks, however, there tended to be a higher degree of status inconsistency, a factor which may have introduced an element of instability not found to nearly the same degree at the top and bottom levels. Thus, for example, the Jewish ethnic minority was very high in economic power, but somewhat lower in terms of political power, and decidedly lower in prestige. The French, as an ethnic majority, were high in terms of political and social power, but lower than many immigrant populations in economic power.

Over the more than two decades following the publication of Porter's work, the Franco-Québécois have come to assume economic as well as political control *in Quebec*, but, as 'founding peoples', they have not achieved equality with the English at the national level. With regard to the later immigrant category, since the inception of Canada's 'open' immigration policy, the incoming population has become increasingly diversified, both racially and culturally. While generalization across racial and ethnic groups is problematic, among new immigrants, including refugees, those whose physical and cultural differences from majority norms are greatest tend to experience the most formidable barriers to upward mobility.

Porter's observation regarding the stability of the top and bottom levels of Canada's vertical mosaic has been supported by several later studies (including Kelner 1969; Richmond 1971; Clement 1975; Ponting and Gibbins 1980; and Lautard and Guppy 1990). However, his explanation for the persistence of the vertical mosaic (1979: v) has engendered considerable social scientific debate.

The debate has focused largely on the economic dimension of stratification, specifically the question of the association between ethnicity and socioeconomic class. Porter believed that ethnocultural factors (differences in value priorities) impede economic mobility in a universalistic society. A well-documented critique of this view was provided by Darroch (1979), who argued that it was primarily structural factors (discrimination, job opportunities), rather than ethnocultural ones, that were responsible for the long-term (albeit diminishing) association between ethnicity and economic class in Canada.[2]

This debate notwithstanding, Porter's observation regarding the stability of the top and bottom levels of Canada's ethnic hierarchy has significant import for our analysis of the origin and development of the Canadian system of ethnic stratification.

The Development of the Canadian System of Ethnic Stratification

In the initial stages of development, the two founding populations, English and French, wielded their vast power to usurp the territory which was later to become Canada from the aboriginal peoples then residing in the area. Moreover, these newcomers established political, economic, and cultural hegemony over the aboriginal populations. In order to understand how and why this happened, we will first consider the theoretical prerequisites for ethnic stratification; secondly, we will look at the empirical realities underlying the origin and development of the Canadian ethnic hierarchy.

Prerequisites and Initial Patterns of Ethnic Stratification

Despite ethnic differences between coexisting populations in the same region, majority/minority relations do not develop until one population imposes its will on another. When distinct ethnocultural collectivities come into continued first-hand contact, a system of ethnic stratification will generally follow, given three conditions: (a) a sufficient degree of ethnocentrism; (b) competition for scarce, mutually valued resources; and (c) differential power (Noel 1968).

Noel argues that without a sufficient level of ethnocentrism, social distance between the populations in contact would be minimized, categorical discrimination would not develop, and competition would not be specifically structured along ethnic lines. Without competition for scarce, mutually valued resources there would be no motivation or rationale for establishing the ethnic hierarchy. Without superior power it would be impossible for any one population to become dominant and impose its will and standards (and eventually its laws and institutions) upon the other(s).

Once ethnic collectivities aligned by ethnocultural differences begin to compete against one another, the most important variable in determining which collectivity will emerge as dominant is differential power. Power may derive from the superior size, weapons, property, economic resources, technology, education, skills, customary or scientific knowledge of a group, but whatever its basis or bases, superior power is crucial not only to the establishment of a system of ethnic stratification, but also to its maintenance and development.

Competition between distinct ethnic collectivities for scarce, mutually valued resources may take place in many contexts: for example, war, territorial expansion, or migration. Over time, competition leads to an unequal distribution and control of resources with the more powerful ethnic collectivity emerging as dominant. Once established, these distributive patterns are maintained through continued control of society's major institutions. The majority ethnic collectivity confers the status of society-wide norms upon its own culture, social institutions, and laws and requires conformity to these standards by all other ethnic collectivities. Eventually, prestige becomes associated with control of the society's major resources and social institutions. Thus, the dominant group becomes vested with a relative monopoly of political, economic, and social power.

Origin of Ethnic Stratification in Canada

The development of the contemporary system of ethnic stratification in Canada began around the mid-fifteenth century with continuing contact between the English and French and the aboriginal peoples in a context of European territorial expansion. Initially, the superior power of the Europeans derived from their possession of firearms, as well as their superior economic and technological skills and resources. Competition between Europeans and Indians resulted in the unequal distribution of land and natural resources, with the potentially most productive areas taken by the more powerful Europeans.

Patterson (1972: Part 2, I) provides persuasive historical evidence which shows that the French newcomers inaugurated a reserve system whereby Indians from various aboriginal ethnic collectivities were removed from their aboriginal lands or confined to delimited areas within them, in order to accommodate French settler expansion; the English soon followed suit.[3]

Reserves were typically established in the more isolated, less productive areas of the regions of English and French settler expansion. As English territorial sovereignty expanded, more and more lands traditionally occupied by Indians came under English jurisdictional control, and from 1763 to 1923 land cession treaties with the British Crown formalized the process of Indian land alienation. Through these initial processes, French and English conquerors and settlers acquired not only the most desirably located and the most resource-plentiful Indian lands, but by far the greatest proportion of this new territory (Patterson 1972).

Initially, contact between Europeans and Inuit populations was sporadic and limited to economic interaction between these aboriginal peoples of the Far North and the whalers or fur traders. The remote Arctic lands of the Inuit were not considered desirable for European habitation, nor valuable in terms of natural resources, fur-bearing animals being the one exception. Traditionally, Inuit peoples moved in small bands within a fixed radius and rarely tied themselves down to definite localities. Their nomadic and semi-nomadic patterns were predicated on the migratory movements of their animal resources. Today, as a consequence of the early nature of inter-ethnic contact with Europeans most Canadian Inuit live in permanent settlements selected, designed, and controlled by the dominant Euro-Canadians.

Initially, European trading companies interested in exploiting the valuable resources of Arctic fur-bearing animals selected permanent location sites which were readily accessible by sea, possessed safe anchorages, and were located in areas of sufficient population to be profitable to the fur trader (Nichols 1971). At first, European outposts serving the dispersed Inuit bands of the region were administered by a single European agent (e.g., the Hudson's Bay Company fur-trader). Gradually, however, the areas of European institutional control grew and outposts came to be dominated by the Big Three of the North—the Hudson's Bay Company fur-trader, the Anglican and/or Catholic missionary, and the RCMP officer (Hughes 1965). With the post-World War II introduction into the North of federal government health and welfare services, the institutional spheres of Euro-Canadian control expanded to include nursing stations, schools, and government administrative centres. Later, with the implementation by the federal government of a large-scale rental housing scheme for the Inuit (after 1965), the outposts became (from the Euro-Canadian point of view) the natural choice for the location of permanent Inuit settlements. Frequently, however, the animal resources of the permanent settlement locality were not sufficient to provide enough food to support the Inuit population for more than a short time. Thus, the Inuit have come to rely increasingly on European food and later on scarce jobs and government welfare cheques to purchase food (Vanstone 1971; Paine 1977; Frideres 1993).

Inuit, like Indians, have become more and more dependent on the Euro-

Canadians for their survival. The important point here is that the original decision as to allocation of land for both residence and economic exploitation lay with the most powerful ethnic collectivities, and these initial distributive patterns, once established, were perpetuated through the continuing exercise of institutional control by the Euro-Canadian majority.

Differential Patterns of Majority/Minority Relations: Dominant/Aboriginal versus Dominant/Immigrant Models

Dominant/Aboriginal Relations

Lieberson (1961) contends that in the initial period of contact between two ethnic populations with dissimilar social orders, the critical problem for each population becomes that of maintaining a social order compatible with pre-contact life ways. Whether or not ethnic collectivities will be able to successfully resolve this problem will depend largely on the nature and form of dominant/subordinate ethnic relations that develop. Like Noel, Lieberson posits the existence of a significant power differential—particularly with regard to superiority in technology (weapons) and tightness of social organization—as a major factor in the origin and development of ethnic stratification. Further, Lieberson makes a critical distinction between the nature and form of ethnic stratification which emerges from contact between aboriginal peoples and early migrants (migrant superordination), on the one hand, and between established migrants and later immigrants (indigenous superordination),[4] on the other hand.

In the case of the pattern of migrant superordination, Lieberson argues that maintenance of the subordinated, aboriginal social order becomes threatened by a number of ensuing social conditions: the numerical decline of aboriginal peoples through warfare and introduced diseases; the disruption of aboriginal social institutions by the imposition of a dissimilar (migrant) social order; and the alteration of aboriginal ethnopolitical boundaries by the incorporation of diverse aboriginal populations with a newly created and larger geopolitical society. Because aboriginal peoples have been subordinated at home, i.e., while living in their aboriginal territories or homelands, Lieberson contends, relations between migrants and aboriginal peoples tend to give rise to ethnic conflict as aboriginal peoples tend to resist incorporation into the new economy developed by dominant migrants and attempt to carry on their traditional economic pursuits.

With the advent of settlers from the migrants' homeland the conflict between migrants and aboriginal peoples becomes exacerbated in the competition between settlers and aboriginal peoples for the most resource-plentiful land in a given region. In this struggle the intra-ethnic priorities of superordinate migrants operate to favour settler interests over the claims of aboriginal peoples, with the consequence that the aboriginal populations become geographically displaced, socially and politically disrupted, and economically impoverished. In short, aboriginal peoples become relegated to the lowest rungs of the developing ethnic hierarchy where their potential for participation in the developing society is marginal, at best.

Dominant/Aboriginal Relations: The Pattern of Migrant Superordination

Lieberson's outline of the social conditions which threaten maintenance of aboriginal cultures in the early stages of migrant superordination can be amply documented with reference to Canada. Surtees (1971: III) demonstrates that a marked decline in Indian populations followed directly from Indian involvement in English/French warfare. Entire Indian nations—the Huronia and Nipissings for example—were annihilated through attacks and starvation ensuing from European-generated wars. Disease, however, was the greatest killer, for Indians had never been exposed to European diseases and had no immunity to them. Heagerty (1928, Vol. I: 56) graphically documents the decimating effects of the smallpox epidemic. In his words: 'it played no mean part in the reduction to a mere handful of the once numerous tribes that roamed the plains.' Among the Inuit, epidemics of diphtheria and tuberculosis similarly extracted a heavy toll, sometimes destroying entire camp communities (Jenness 1964).

The Canadian evidence also supports Lieberson's contention that aboriginal peoples inevitably 'lose out' in the competition with technologically superior migrants for control over land and resources, and that they come to represent economically marginal populations, incorporated only peripherally into the public life of the new society. In the Canadian case, the alteration of aboriginal geopolitical boundaries through the establishment of Indian reserves and Inuit settlements, together with their political incorporation into the Canadian state, has had disastrous economic and sociocultural consequences for aboriginal populations. The long-term effect of geosocial isolation and economic depression among aboriginal peoples has been to create structurally dependent welfare populations subsisting on the largess of government hand-outs. Thus, Canada's aboriginal peoples have come to constitute a stigmatized ethnoclass at the very bottom of the vertical ethnic mosaic (Carstens 1971; Paine 1977; Frideres 1993).

Dominant/Aboriginal Relations: The Pattern of Ethnic Segmentation

Breton (1978) points out that the pattern of migrant superordination outlined by Lieberson bears striking resemblance to the pattern of ethnic relations which emerges through amalgamation of contiguous territories following shifts in political boundaries through other means, such as dynastic alliances, wars of conquest, and colonial administration. An essential characteristic of all of these processes, says Breton, is that they bring together populations that already exist as societies, each having a full-fledged, or total, institutional structure. Under these conditions, majority/minority ethnic relations between superordinate migrants and subordinate aboriginal peoples tend to take the form of *ethnic segmentation*. In this pattern, each ethnic collectivity tends to maintain both a high degree of ethnic closure and a high degree of ethnic compartmentalization.

As employed by Breton, the concept *ethnic closure* refers to the enclosure of social networks along ethnic lines, and the concept *ethnic compartmentalization* refers to ethnic institutional or structural pluralism. Under relations of ethnic segmentation, these two sets of boundary-maintaining devices function as mutually reinforcing social processes. Each ethnic segment encapsulates separate inclusive networks of social affiliations, separate total institutional structures, and separate total ethnic identities within its ethnic boundaries. Inter-ethnic relations are mutually regulated to preserve the boundaries and to maintain the dichotomous structure of ethnic interaction between the segments.

Breton's model of ethnic segmentation may be applied to inter-ethnic relations between segments with different and/or unequal ethnic status (e.g., French or English majority and aboriginal minority), as well as to relations between segments with similar and/or equal ethnic status (e.g., French and English as charter groups in Canada). In both sets of cases, Breton argues, members of each segment relate to members of other segments categorically, in ethnic terms.

The pattern of ethnic segmentation, as outlined by Breton, rests on two fundamental assumptions: first, that each ethnic segment is demographically and institutionally capable of maintaining ethnic closure and compartmentalization; second, that all or most members of each ethnic segment want to preserve ethnic boundaries. Here, it is suggested that another feature of the pattern of ethnic segmentation is critical to its maintenance, i.e., territorial integrity, and it is the strong association between ethnicity and territory in the pattern of ethnic segmentation that gives rise to nationalism.

Breton distinguishes between territorial and ethnic forms of nationalism. In the former, ethnic segment and national territory are coterminous phenomena; in the latter, the ethnic segment constitutes a legally autonomous, self-governing unit within a larger geopolitical territorial unit. The argument, here, is that both forms of nationalism are predicated on the territorial integrity of the ethnic segment. In the current Canadian context, all of the major nationalistic movements among minority ethnic segments, like the Franco-Québécois and the Nunavut, are predicated on an assumption of ethnic territorial integrity.

Dominant/Aboriginal Relations in Canada: Colonizers versus Colonized

Lieberson and Breton both adopt an essentially structural approach which downplays the significance of racial and cultural differences in the pattern of migrant superordination. This approach also neglects the very important role played by dominant cultural policies in the early stages of ethnic stratification. Alternatively, Blauner (1972: 11) contends that aboriginal racial visibility and migrant cultural policy are critical variables in the origin of ethnic stratification. Aborigines are 'people of colour' and as such, says Blauner, they have been subjected to a special pattern of migrant superordination, namely, colonization. Unlike other populations, colonized peoples are subject to three conditions. First, they become part of a new larger society through coercion. As the case of the Canadian Indians well demonstrates, colonized peoples are conquered, enslaved, or pressured into movement. Secondly, colonized peoples are subject to various forms of unfree labour that restrict their mobility and power (e.g., Panis [Indian slaves] in early French Canada). Thirdly, the cultural policy of the colonizer disrupts and ultimately destroys the aboriginal way of life (cultural genocide).

The Canadian Indian leader Harold Cardinal (1969) was one of the earliest aboriginal spokespersons to charge that the Indian Act has long served as a powerful legal instrument of colonization locking Status Indians into the position of a colonized people. Earlier, Harper (1945) argued that the primacy of the long-term federal government policy of Indian assimilation (the covert agenda behind the Indian Act) gives credence to Indian claims that cultural genocide has been an implicit goal in Indian administration throughout the years.

The colonizer/colonized pattern of ethnic relations will be elaborated further in Chapter Eight, in discussion of the Paternalistic/Colonial model of ethnic integration in Canada. At this point, we want to address a fourth condition of colonization which Blauner (1972) briefly mentions: the experience of the colonized in being managed and manipulated by outsiders in terms of ethnic status.

The experience of Canada's aboriginal peoples as members of colonized minorities currently provides the subject matter of a growing literature by Canadian Indian, Inuit and Métis authors. While the following excerpts provide only a glimpse at this experience, they serve, nevertheless, to illustrate the profound psychic ramifications of inferiorization on members of colonized minorities:

> As an Indian, it has been very difficult for me to begin thinking about my place in society. It is very difficult because I have been told from early childhood by white teachers and clergymen and community officers that my background is one where people are stupid. (Pelletier 1974: 101)

> The white man saw that it was a more powerful weapon than anything else with which to beat the Halfbreeds, and he used it and still does today. . . . They try to make you hate your people. (Campbell 1973: 47)

> The thing I remember the most was being called dirty Indian kids . . . I also remember going home and trying to wash it off . . . I was one of the darkest ones at school . . . there was definite favoritism shown for the lighter ones . . . Even the Indian people would, and still do, make jokes about those who are darker . . . [Why?] . . . Maybe they've had good training from the nuns and the white people from close by communities or television. (Bear 1987: 55-6)

Dominant/Immigrant Relations: Established Migrant Superordination

Lieberson (1961) maintains that in the initial stages of ethnic stratification, relations between established migrant populations and immigrants are characterized by considerably less conflict than are relations between migrants and aboriginal populations. Unlike aboriginal peoples, immigrants cannot 'opt out' of the dominant economy since none of the aboriginal economic options are open to them. On the other hand, should immigrants become dissatisfied with their subordinate status and/or other life conditions in their new country, they may elect to leave, either to return to their home country or to migrate elsewhere.[5] By way of contrast, aboriginal peoples are not likely to leave their aboriginal territories voluntarily, and their continued presence, together with their refusal to enter the dominant economy, provides a continuing source of conflict.

A second difference between dominant/aboriginal and dominant/immigrant relations, posited by Lieberson, is that immigrants tend to be under much greater pressure to assimilate and tend to do so much more rapidly and extensively than do aboriginal peoples. While Lieberson makes no attempt to account for this difference, it seems obvious that the explanation lies, in large part, in the far greater degree of ethnocultural compatibility between dominant and immigrant populations than is found between dominant and aboriginal populations.

A third difference relates to the control of immigration which ensures the ethnic hegemony of the established dominant population. Immigrants perceived as a biological, cultural, or numerical threat to dominant superiority can be collectively restricted or excluded from entering the country. This strategy cannot be applied to aboriginal populations, however, since these populations were resident in the area long before the arrival of the now dominant migrants.

Dominant/Immigrant Relations in Canada

The development of early English Canadian immigration policy illustrates Lieberson's model of dominant/immigrant relations. Following Confederation, the English became the dominant ethnic group at the national level. Although Confederation gave English and French Canadians equal status as the two 'founding races', English Canadians have increasingly assumed institutional control—culturally, linguistically, and economically—outside the province of Quebec. As the dominant national group, English Canadians have, from the beginning, exercised control of federal immigration policies responsible for determining which ethnic groups would be allowed into Canada, where they would settle, what jobs they could assume, and what ranking and social position would be accorded them within the existing system of ethnic stratification. In order to ensure the dominance of the English majority culture and social institutions, and thus to maintain their dominant position, the English Canadians accorded 'preferred status' to linguistically, culturally, and socially similar immigrants from the British Isles and northern and western

Europe. Less preferred ethnic groups assumed an 'entrance status' which implied lower level occupational roles and social position (Porter 1965: 63-4).

Changes in immigration policies are indicative of the disposition of the dominant group, under changing social conditions, toward admittance of ethnic groups highly dissimilar to themselves in their physical, cultural, and/or behavioural characteristics. Richmond (1970: 86) points out that until 1962, the Canadian Immigration Act was clearly administered to discriminate against non-European and especially non-white immigration. Immigrants from Britain, northern, and western Europe and white immigrants from the Commonwealth countries had preferred status; those from eastern, central, and southern Europe were in a secondary position; and those from Third World countries—potential migrants whose racial and cultural traits diverged more markedly from the characteristics of the established dominant population(s)—were accorded lowest priority.

The long-term consequences of the differential treatment by the dominant English and French of various ethnic categories within the immigrant population sector, together with the differential treatment accorded immigrants as a whole in contrast to aboriginal peoples, produced the vertical mosaic described by Porter (1965).

The Pattern of Ethnic Heterogeneity

Breton (1978) points out that patterns of immigrant adaptation to the new society can be highly varied. He distinguishes between two main categories of migrants: those who are able and willing to establish a full-fledged institutional structure (like the English and French in Canada), and those who cannot or do not wish to do so. (This includes most Canadian immigrants, except for the established dominant populations and some sectarian minorities like the Hutterites.) Most immigrants lack a full-fledged institutional structure, hence they are unable to maintain the high degree of ethnic closure and compartmentalization that characterizes the pattern of ethnic segmentation. Breton refers to their typical pattern as one of *ethnic heterogeneity*. This pattern is characterized by the fragmentation or partialization of immigrant ethnicity and ethnic identity. Some areas of the immigrant's life may involve his or her ethnicity, while other areas may not. Typically, in the pattern of ethnic heterogeneity, ethnic ties are principally maintained in private relations of kinship and friendship. In the public sphere (work, politics, and so forth) the immigrant's relationships become de-ethnicized. Even within the boundaries of the immigrant ethnic collectivity, personal networks and institutional affiliations are selectively chosen, and the various sets of ties and relationships activated by different members tend to become dissociated from one another. At the macro-level of the ethnic collectivity, ethnic organizational structures may serve only limited aspects of social life (e.g. recreational, religious).

Breton argues that the pattern of ethnic heterogeneity, as opposed to ethnic segmentation, is possible only to the extent that society is functionally differentiated so that some roles are performed in one organizational context, and others are performed in another. In other words, Breton argues that the pattern of ethnic heterogeneity is only possible in a large-scale *gesellschaft* society, where people relate to each other in terms of specific segmented roles, rather than as whole persons. For only in a large-scale society can people establish fundamental role relationships independent of their ethnic identities. In contrast, Breton argues, a society based on non-segmented, overlapping relationships between whole persons (i.e., a small-scale or *gemeinschaft* society) could not integrate members of different ethnic collectivities without assimilating them completely or allowing them only peripheral, marginal status as strangers. This is clearly supported in the anthropological literature which indicates that in ethnically homogeneous, small-scale societies, ethnic outsiders, like women and children captured in war or marital partners brought into the society through strategic political alliances, were frequently 'adopted' by a particular kin group as full-fledged members of the ethnic collectivity.

Breton's distinction between the patterns of ethnic segmentation and ethnic heterogeneity seems to be predicated largely on the degree to which the members of ethnic collectivities are able and/or willing to maintain holistic *gemeinschaft*-like ethnic relationships, institutions, and identities within the greater social environmental context of a *gesellschaft*-like society such as Canada's. Clearly the dominant ethnic collectivities—French in Quebec and English in the rest of Canada—are in the most advantageous position to maintain a holistic pattern of ethnic segmentation, for it is their ethnocultural ideas, values, and patterns which are represented in the public institutional structures of Canadian society. For ethnic minorities, cultural discrimination denies the institutional expression of their ethnicities in the public sphere, and the degree to which their ethnicity becomes partialized will depend on their ability to maintain group viability in their private lives.

Variations in the Patterns of Ethnic Segmentation and Heterogeneity in Canada

In the early period, Canada's immigration practices reflected not only the dominant English population's desire to maintain their cultural hegemony over British North America, but also their strong desire to spur the economic development of the new nation. This latter aspect led to marked regional differences in the ethnic composition of Canadian society, as immigration priorities responded to both changing social conditions and continuing marked regional variations in Canada's resources and economic needs. Over time, the differential regional distribution of Canada's ethnic collectivities has created what Driedger (1978: 10-12) has termed a 'regional mosaic', characterized by different patterns of ethnic segmentation and heterogeneity within each region.

Intra-Regional Differences: The Case of Toronto

The regional mosaic elaborated by Driedger (1978) is only one level of the Canadian ethnic mosaic. Another important dimension of ethnic diversity is found at the level of the local community. Within each region of Canada there are significant local variations in the patterns of relations between different ethnic collectivities. Thus, for example, while the region identified by Driedger as Upper Canada may be characterized by a pattern of ethnic heterogeneity which is close to that of ethnic segmentation, at the local level of the city of Toronto, ethnic collectivities differ markedly in the degree to which they represent ethnic 'segments' or ethnic 'fragments' (to paraphrase Breton's terminology). In part, these differences derive from the institutional completeness or incompleteness of the immigrant ethnic collectivity in the early period following arrival in the new country. Over time, however, other factors (for example, population numbers and sex ratio, wave of immigration, duration of residence, degree of acculturation, and experience of discrimination) influence the pattern of dominant-immigrant relations. Thus, at any given time and in any given locality, each observed pattern of dominant-immigrant relations will be a function of multiple variables.

Within the increasingly multi-ethnic and multi-racial context of Metropolitan Toronto, studies published in the 1970s revealed striking variations in patterns of dominant-immigrant relations. Among the older European immigrant populations, the Jewish ethnic collectivity (Richmond 1972; Glickman 1976; Kallen 1977) and the Italian ethnic collectivity (Jansen 1978; Zeigler 1972) were characterized by a pattern closely approximating ethnic segmentation, while the Polish ethnic collectivity (Radecki and Heydenkorn 1976; Matejko 1979) was characterized by a far less enclaved pattern of ethnic heterogeneity. The Toronto Francophone population appeared to be among the least cohesive of the older European immigrants and, accordingly, was characterized as 'invisible' (Maxwell 1979). Among the more recent European immigrants, the tendency toward ethnic enclavement remained strong. Spanish and Portuguese-speaking populations, for example, closely resembled ethnic segments within the city (Anderson 1979).

Striking differences also were found among the various 'visible minorities'— racially-defined immigrant ethnic collectivities whose numbers had increased substantially following the implementation of Canada's open door policy on immigration. In the case of the Chinese ethnic collectivity, the arrival of new immigrants served to strengthen the historical pattern of ethnic segmentation (Lai 1971). The Japanese ethnic collectivity, on the other hand, had changed, over the generations, from a pattern of ethnic segmentation to a pattern of ethnic heterogeneity (Makabe 1976).

More recently, Herberg (1989), utilizing 1971 and 1981 Census data, described the shifting patterns of ethnic cohesion among Canadian ethno-racial collectivities. The findings of his analysis, which applied seven central cohesion variables (two language retention factors, residential proximity, religion, two media indices, and endogamy), revealed significant differences in ethnic-cohesion rates among various ethno-racial collectivities across Canada. Asian (East Indian, Indochinese and Chinese), Jewish, Italian, French, Greek, and Portuguese exhibited high cohesion for most factors. Conspicuously absent from this category were three visible minorities: Japanese, aboriginal peoples, and blacks. With regard to the latter finding, Herberg maintains that racial visibility *per se* clearly does not lead to ethnic cohesiveness (1989: 275-9).

On the basis of the data in his book, as well as external information on institutional development within ethno-racial collectivities, Herberg suggests that continuing evidence of ethnic cohesion and enclavement among many Canadian minorities does not indicate retention of traditional or immigrant values. Rather, he argues, present forms and methods of group cohesion represent values adapted to the dominant urban Canadian societal context. Moreover, Herberg argues, ethnic communities today are developing group enclosure and compartmentalization mechanisms not to maintain their separation from other Canadians, but to enable integration (ibid.: 306).

While it would be difficult to argue against the evidence for value adaptation among virtually all ethno-racial minorities, Herberg's assimilationist stance is inconsistent with the current demands of many immigrant ethnic minorities (not to mention aboriginal peoples) for increased constitutional recognition of their collective religious, linguistic, and (broader) cultural rights (see Chapters Nine and Ten).

Dominant/Aboriginal versus Dominant/Immigrant Relations: Implications for Collective Minority Rights Claims

Mede (quoted in Leavy 1979: 3-4) draws a distinction between two kinds of ethnic minorities:

1) Voluntary minorities, composed of those who, individually or in families, left their country of origin and moved to another country where they live as a community. They preserve certain parts of their own culture and transmit them to their descendants, while integrating to a certain degree with the majority culture of the new country.

2) Involuntary minorities, those groups which for reasons of war, territorial conquest, or frontier adjustments find themselves in a state where their culture is in a minority situation.

Involuntary minorities (e.g., Canada's aboriginal peoples), Mede argues, are justified in making more collective human rights claims than are voluntary minorities (e.g., Canada's immigrant ethnic collectivities). Voluntary minorities would be justified in claiming the right to institutional autonomy, e.g., ethnic schools or social services; but only involuntary minorities would be justified in claiming the right to a measure of jurisdictional cultural autonomy, e.g., the right to establish standards applicable to their ethnically distinctive school system. The rationale for this distinction, Mede argues, is that there can be no cultural autonomy without territorial autonomy.

Mede's argument supports our conceptual distinction—outlined in the Typology of Rights put forward in the Introduction—between collective claims based on cultural group rights (immigrants) and those based on national group rights (aboriginal peoples, charter groups). At the level of rhetoric, this distinction between the range and types of potential human rights claims which may, justifiably, be made by immigrants versus aboriginal peoples is clearly weighted in favour of aboriginal peoples. However, at the level of societal reality, we must take into account the differences in patterns of dominant/immigrant versus dominant/aboriginal relations which may significantly affect the viability of minority ethnic claims. Here, if we accept the thrust of the arguments put forward by Lieberson and Blauner, the pendulum clearly swings in favour of immigrants over aboriginal peoples, at least in the early stages of ethnic stratification. The salient point of distinction is that aboriginal peoples, racially stigmatized as sub-human 'savages' with primitive cultures, would never have been welcomed as immigrants.

In the next section of this chapter, we will look at how early patterns of dominant/immigrant and dominant/aboriginal relations become institutionalized within the structure of ethnic inequality, and we will assess the differential human rights implications of institutionalized racism for Canadian immigrants and aboriginal peoples.

The Persistence of Systems of Ethnic Stratification

The long-term persistence of a system of ethnic stratification depends not only upon the will of its majority group(s) but also upon the tacit compliance of its ethnic minorities. In order to ensure that members of various ethnic minorities 'know their place' and 'stay in their place', dominant populations must be able to justify the existing structure of ethnic inequality; they must be able to imbue the system with recognized social legitimacy so that minorities come to accept the stratified order as a moral order. Unless the system of ethnic stratification is based on a high degree of consensus regarding *place*—the position of various ethnic collectivities within the established hierarchy—the built-in potential for minority ethnic protest can only be contained through coercion.

The case of South Africa under *apartheid* illustrates the latter point; for close to thirty years, the dominant white population was able to rationalize and maintain a relatively stable system of ethnic stratification by institutionalizing *place* for each of the socially defined racial categories in the society, through the racist ideology and policies of *apartheid*. But when consensus began to break down and black minority protest intensified, coercive measures were increasingly adopted, culminating in the declaration of a state of emergency giving police authorities virtually unlimited powers to suppress minority activism.

Isaacs (1977: 4-5) contends that the global picture of escalating ethnic tension and violence is the result of the world-wide collapse of dominant power systems whose survival was only contingent on competition with external rivals and on the compliance of their dominated populations. The established power systems, says Isaacs, managed to hold together their structures of ethnic inequality under the control of a single dominant population or coalition by incorporating the 'rules of the game' into mystiques and mythologies based on assumptions of cultural and racial superiority/inferiority. Racist myths legitimating place were internalized and accepted by all—rulers and ruled, majority and minority, colonizers and colonized. And racist ideologies legitimating the whole structure of inequality were built into the system's institutions to keep it working. Isaacs is arguing that in all of the world-wide systems of ethnic stratification—including such diverse forms as the Hindu caste system in India, *apartheid* in South Africa, black slavery in the Americas, and all of the systems of ethnic inequality predicated on Colonial rule—the persistence of the structure of inequality was predicated upon the institutionalization of racism, by building into the system policies and practices of institutional, systemic, and cultural discrimination.

Institutionalized forms of discrimination against ethnic minorities provide the majority group(s) with legitimate techniques of domination and social control. Historically, the particular techniques of domination discussed in the following pages have provided ethnic majorities in Canada and elsewhere with effective means of guaranteeing their ascendancy.

Institutionalized Racism: Majority Techniques of Domination

Denial of Franchise

Denial of franchise is an institutionalized form of oppression that denies ethnic minorities the fundamental political right of access to political participation and decision-making power. In some provinces, and on a federal scale, Chinese, Japanese, Hutterites, and Doukhobors have at one time or another been denied the right to vote in Canada. Inuit, as full citizens of Canada, have always had a federal vote, but it was not until 1962 that they were given the right to vote in provincial elections as well. Status Indians were denied the franchise until 1960; then pressure from Indian organizations won them federal voting rights, under the (then) new Canadian Bill of Rights.

Control of Land Ownership and Use

Control of land ownership and use is an institutionalized form of neglect that violates the fundamental economic rights of minority members by restricting their access to economic maintenance and opportunities. The usurpation of the lands of aboriginal peoples and their subsequent confinement on reserves and settlements, frequently without a viable economic base, provides the most flagrant example of economic neglect of ethnic minorities in Canada. Less drastic, but nevertheless highly discriminatory, have been the repeated attempts of dominant populations (neighbouring farmers and provincial governments) to control the purchase and use of lands by Hutterite colonies in the Canadian West (see Chapter Four).

In both cases cited, the control of land ownership and use by dominant power groups not only violates the minorities' fundamental economic rights, but also infringes upon their collective minority cultural rights. For in the cases of both aboriginal peoples and Hutterites, their distinctive ethnocultures and economies are rooted in group norms and practices of communal land use and occupancy.

Denial of Educational Opportunities

Denial of educational opportunities is another institutionalized form of neglect of ethnic minorities. Because knowledge and skill acquired through formal education are the keys to upward mobility in our modern, industrialized society, denial of equal educational opportunities sets off a self-perpetuating cycle of economic deprivation—one of the concrete manifestations of the self-fulfilling prophecy of racism.

Separate and unequal educational opportunities have been largely responsible for the consistent records of low academic achievement, high rates of failure, and early school drop-out among aboriginal children (Ponting and Gibbins 1980; Frideres 1993). Until the 1950s, the government delegated the responsibility for educating aboriginal children largely to religious institutions whose missionaries stressed religious indoctrination of the alleged 'savages' and minimized secular curriculum content to fit what they felt was the inferior level of educability of these students (Cardinal 1969).

When local secular schools were set up on Indian reserves, the quality of Indian education did not improve appreciably because of inadequate resources such as buildings, equipment, books, etc., as well as poorly trained and often highly prejudiced teachers. By the mid-1960s, Indian parents, where possible, began enrolling their children in nearby off-reserve integrated schools. But within a decade this trend reversed itself in response to new sets of problems encountered by Indian parents: alienating curricula, prejudices of non-Indian school children, and lack of input into the decision-making processes of school boards (Ponting and Gibbins 1980: 55). In the case of Inuit and other aboriginal peoples living in the Northwest Territories, Canadian government educational policy, until the end of World War II, was largely one of neglect (Jenness 1964). Inuit were expected to live off the land and their education was left to a small number of missionaries and mission schools which served only a minute fraction of the aboriginal children in the Canadian Arctic. As late as 1944, ninety-three per cent of Indian and Inuit children in the Western Arctic and MacKenzie Delta Regions were receiving no formal education. It was not until

1947 that the federal government built the first public school for its Arctic peoples. Although there has been a considerable increase in the number of schools and the proportion of school-age children regularly attending these schools over the years, the problems of inadequate school facilities, curriculum, and a continuing high rate of teacher turnover remain particularly acute in the Arctic.

Until recent decades, no attempt was made by the Canadian government or by Euro-Canadian educators to accord recognition to the collective linguistic and cultural rights of aboriginal minorities, Indian or Inuit. Euro-Canadian educational policies were not only imbued with racist assumptions about the limits of educability of the 'natives'—assumptions which tended, eventually, to become self-fulfilling prophecies—but also they were imbued with similarly negative assumptions about the inferiority of aboriginal cultures. Historically, provision of education to aboriginal children by federal and provincial governments was designed 'to eradicate the "native problem" by destroying native culture' (Canadian Council on Children and Youth 1978: 137). Early boarding schools were 'little more than prisons where their cultures were denigrated and they were punished for speaking their own languages' (ibid.). Since the late 1960s, there has been a shift towards the development of aboriginal-controlled schools in aboriginal communities, which has resulted in higher retention rates for students but, beyond the elementary level, the drop-out rate for aboriginal students is markedly higher than that of the general population. Frideres (1993: 183) reports that nearly 40 per cent of Indians have less than a Grade 9 education, which is double the national rate. Inuit have the highest proportion of adults who are functionally illiterate.

Denial of economic and cultural rights within the sphere of education has also been the characteristic experience of blacks in Canada until recently (Krauter and Davis 1978: 48-51). Throughout Canada from 1850 to 1965, blacks were customarily excluded from the dominant, Euro-Canadian educational structure and relegated to segregated, all-black schools, typically inadequate in space, facilities, and staff. In Ontario the last segregated black school closed in 1965, but in Nova Scotia, despite the abrogation of educational segregation in 1963, several all-black schools, serving black communities, were in operation until the 1970s. Where discrimination against blacks takes the form of long-term structural racism, as for example in Nova Scotia, the ending of *de jure* segregation does not necessarily guarantee the ending of *de facto* segregation. Further, while high-level public education is now, theoretically, open to blacks throughout Canada, awareness among blacks (as among aboriginal peoples) of persistent high levels of discrimination in jobs dampens motivation toward continuing education and encourages early school drop-outs.

Studies of the treatment of blacks within the Canadian educational system provide continuing evidence of racial discrimination and denial of cultural rights. Until recently, cultural discrimination has been manifested in the total omission of historical and current cultures of Canadian blacks in school textbooks (Head 1975: 89). Racial stereotyping and prejudice on the part of teachers continues to be revealed in the common 'expectation' that blacks will be 'slow learners', and racial discrimination is evident in the practice of 'streaming' black students disproportionately more than others into non-academic schools and classes (Hill and Schiff 1988: 20).

Hill and Schiff (1988: 20-1) draw attention to the difficulty, facing the schools today, in overcoming the built-in, long-term effects of cultural and systemic discrimination within the Canadian educational system. Canadian-born blacks, like aboriginal peoples, lag far behind non-black, Euro-Canadians in educational attainment. Moreover, for these victims of the self-fulfilling prophecy of racism, denial of economic and cultural rights remains part of their daily Canadian educational experience.

Denial of Employment Opportunities and Wages

Denial of employment and wage opportunities probably provides the most blatant and direct indicator of neglect of ethnic minorities. Without jobs and earned income, members of ethnic minorities are without access to economic power. In order to subsist, they become economically dependent on 'benevolent' welfare handouts from the dominant controllers of the welfare state. But the syndrome of dependency deriving from denial of economic rights reaches even more deeply into the human psyche. Beyond objective economic measures is the subjective reaction to racial and ethnic inferiorization and stigmatization—the syndrome of psychological dependency.

Internalization of the negative identity associated with inferiorizing and stigmatizing labels breeds alienation, apathy, and acceptance of place. Over the long term, economic dependency breeds political and social dependency. The psycho-social correlates of dependency—alienation, alcohol and drug addiction, violent crimes— are used, in turn, to 'justify' discriminatory treatment of minorities by dominant powers. 'Blaming the victim' is a well-honed technique of domination: it enables majorities to ensure that the self-fulfilling prophecy of racism is fully realized.

The current syndrome of economic dependency among Canada's aboriginal peoples is clearly rooted in the multidimensional cycle of denial of opportunities associated with the self-fulfilling prophecy of racism. Long-term denial of educational opportunities means that most aboriginal people today lack the knowledge, training, and skills which would qualify them to compete for jobs with other Canadians in the southern Canadian context. In northern areas, graduates of special (separate and unequal) training programs for aboriginal peoples often experience difficulty in finding jobs because of the dearth of employment opportunities on Indian reserves and in small, isolated Inuit settlements. Severe competition from Euro-Canadians, plus discrimination against aboriginal peoples in hiring practices, in the more urbanized areas further restricts job opportunities (Brody 1975; Kallen 1977; Frideres 1993).

The long-term consequence of denial of educational and occupational opportunities is that aboriginal peoples are over-represented at the lowest strata of the occupational and income hierarchy in Canada. Those who are fortunate enough to hold jobs tend to be over-represented in the unskilled and semi-skilled occupations (e.g., services, construction, logging, and fishing) and under-represented in the higher level managerial and professional occupations. Virtually none of Canada's aboriginal peoples are represented in the upper echelons of the business ownership ranks (Ponting and Gibbins 1980: 53-4). According to Frideres (1993: 170), the rate of aboriginal participation in Canada's labour force is 20 per cent lower than the national rate. Moreover, Frideres points out, aboriginal persons usually work at seasonal or part-time jobs without job security. The low income of aboriginal peoples as a category reflects both seasonal work and job discrimination: aboriginal persons are less likely to be hired than Euro-Canadians, and when hired they are likely to be paid lower wages than their Euro-Canadian counterparts. As a result, aboriginal peoples remain at the lowest rungs of Canada's income hierarchy, and the disparity in income between aboriginal peoples and other Canadians appears to be growing larger (Frideres 1993: 162).

Among Canada's immigrant ethnic groups, those peoples categorized by the majority as Oriental or Black have, historically, been accorded the highest degree of discrimination in employment and wages. In the nineteenth and early twentieth centuries, Chinese and Japanese lumped together under the misleading label 'Oriental' were subject to severe job discrimination, particularly in the province of British Columbia. Denied the franchise, they were excluded from the voting lists and thus from licensed professions. Moreover, they were directly prohibited from other licensed occupations, such as the fishing industry, by the customary manipulation of special regulations. They were also denied other positions such as public school teaching. Forced to accept any job at any wage, Chinese and Japanese immigrants fell victim to the self-fulfilling prophecy of white racism: they became, in fact, as in stereotype, 'cheap labour'. Because they accepted low wages, they were perceived as a threat to prevailing wage standards by Euro-Canadian workers and by organized labour. As a result, they were excluded from membership in labour unions, and at times were victims of open and devastating racist mob attacks and violence. It was not until the end of World War II that formal union opposition to Chinese and Japanese immigration in large part disappeared (Krauter and Davis 1978: v).

Prior to 1833, black immigrants to Canada were 'employed' as slaves. Since that time, Canadian-born blacks have tended to occupy the very bottom rungs of the urban occupational ladder. Blacks were, for a long time, accorded stereotyped occupations such as railway porters and household domestics. For most Canadian-born blacks, present occupational prospects remain poor due to lack of education and training as well as continuing high levels of job discrimination. Even where educational qualifications are adequate, however, as in the case of many West Indian immigrants, job discrimination persists (Henry and Ginsberg 1988).

A cross-country survey conducted in Halifax, Toronto, Winnipeg, and Vancouver by the Canadian Civil Liberties Association (CCLA), in the fall of 1980, revealed a remarkably high level of racial discrimination among the employment agencies questioned (CCLA News Notes, June 1981: 2). Seventeen of the twenty-five randomly chosen agencies expressed a willingness—in response to a telephone enquiry from a purported new client—to accept 'white only' job orders. More than ten years later, in January of 1991, the results of a CCLA telephone poll revealed that 12 out of 15 employment agencies across Ontario would comply with requests to refer only white candidates (*Toronto Star*, 17 Feb. 1991).

Denial of Adequate Housing

Economic neglect in the control of land ownership and use, denial of educational opportunities, and denial of employment and wage opportunities go hand in hand with denial of the fundamental economic right to adequate housing. Substandard housing breeds sickness and disease; ill health results in high rates of absenteeism, lowered motivation, and poor performance both for adults at work and children at school; poor performance results in loss of jobs and school drop-outs; and the crippling cycle of economic dependency perpetuates itself.

For decades the housing demands voiced by Canada's Indians have been ignored, resulting in wide disparities in housing conditions between Indians and other Canadians. National Indian housing survey data for 1977 indicated that only half of Indian houses had potable water, fewer than half had indoor plumbing, and fewer than half were linked to a sewage disposal system. By way of contrast, over ninety per cent of non-Indian housing had all of these amenities (Ponting and Gibbins 1980: 48-50). In June of 1985, an evaluation of on-reserve housing estimated that about three quarters of the existing housing failed to meet basic standards of safe and decent living (Frideres 1988: 193). A severe overcrowding situation was also documented: one in six homes on Indian reserves as compared with one in forty-three in the general population was found to be overcrowded. Frideres (1993: 196) reports that, while there has been an improvement in household amenities (running water, electricity, sewage disposal), aboriginal peoples have overall the most unfavourable housing conditions of any ethnic group in Canada.

The problem of housing among the Canadian Inuit is a relatively new phenomenon. It has not, therefore, received the attention accorded the parallel Indian situation. The major movement of Inuit from traditional hunting and trapping camps, where they dwelt in temporary snow-houses or tents, depending on the season, to permanent settlements, where they reside in prefabricated housing, followed the implementation of a large-scale housing program initiated by the federal government in 1965. This housing scheme was predicated on the belief that their traditional housing conditions were responsible for the high incidence of disease, especially tuberculosis and influenza, and premature death among the Inuit population (Ottawa 1960).

Although the relocation of the Inuit has coincided with a decrease in disease and premature death rates, this improvement may be due to vastly improved medical services, rather than the change in housing. The problem of adequate housing remains acute. The expansion of medical services in the Arctic has resulted in a steady increase in population numbers and family size among the Inuit.

Consequently, the demand for more and larger houses far exceeds the present supply. Most Inuit families cannot afford to pay more than a part of the rental cost even of a very small house, but most houses are, therefore, at least partially government subsidized. While Inuit families have become increasingly dependent on government assistance to meet their housing needs, the tremendous cost of both transportation and maintenance of houses in the Arctic, coupled with the continually increasing need for housing, has created the current situation in which government supply lags far behind Inuit need and demand. This has produced a growing problem of overcrowding, similar to that found on Indian reserves, particularly in the more remote Arctic settlements (Frideres 1993: 195).

Control of Communications Media

Denial of the fundamental human right to dignity and denial of minority cultural rights are effected through control of the communications media, a powerful technique of domination. In recent times, technological innovations have increased the salience of the communications media as agents of racial and cultural discrimination. In our discussion of cultural discrimination in Chapter Two, we suggested that the ethnic image of Canadian society promulgated by the media in newspapers, magazines, children's books, textbooks, radio and television programs, and so forth typically contained two kinds of errors—errors of omission and errors of commission. Despite Canada's increasingly multi-ethnic character, the primary Canadian image portrayed in the mass media remains white Euro-Canadian. Other minorities, particularly the racially visible, are infrequently represented and when portrayed at all are still largely depicted in terms of segregated, racially stereotyped roles and images.

The increasing tendency of the media to sensationalize controversial and violent events in their news coverage has focused public attention on recent incidents of ethnic conflict and violence in Canada. Ethnic tensions, exacerbated by the continuing increase in the population of visible minorities, have exploded into the kind of confrontation and violence which alerts the attention of the media. The OKA crisis in the summer of 1990, (discussed on page 46) focused media attention on armed Indian 'warriors' in confrontation with police; the expulsion of a Sikh veteran by an Alberta Legion Hall because he was wearing a turban drew media attention to the continuing controversy over the change in rules allowing RCMP and other police officers of the Sikh faith to wear turbans; the protest of black community leaders, enraged by a series of misguided killings of black youths by police in Toronto and Montreal, during 1990 and 1991, inadvertently afforded the media with an opportunity to stereotype blacks as dangerous and threatening (*Toronto Star, passim*). The important point here, with regard to the critical role of the media as an agent of racial and cultural discrimination, is that the white Euro-Canadian audience sees, hears, and reads about visible minorities such as aboriginal peoples, Sikhs, and blacks only or largely in the negative context of racially motivated controversy and violence.

Repeated media portrayal of visible minorities as perpetual victims of racial violence does not induce full sympathy in the viewer. On the contrary, it nourishes the 'new racism' (discussed in Chapter One) in that it leads viewers to 'blame the victim'—to believe that something inherently wrong, bad, or worth hating in the victim provokes the violent attack. And the obvious difference between victim and victimizer is racial visibility.

Racial prejudice against visible minorities in Canada, fed by highly negative media images, takes its most insidious form in slogans like 'Keep Canada White'. Such attitudes surfaced in the nation-wide debate preceding the adoption of Canada's current immigration policy (Richmond 1975: 9-12). While most Canadians did not openly favour a return to an expressedly racist policy, increasing numbers of Canadians were of the opinion that Canada had too many immigrants and favoured a more restrictive policy. What seemed clear from the general thrust of the public debate was that racial visibility linked with ethnic violence provided the single most important perception behind the public attitude of 'too many immigrants'.

By the early 1990s, the white majority 'backlash' against increasing non-white immigration and related policies of multiculturalism and anti-racism had seriously escalated. In February of 1990, an Angus Reid-Southam News poll found that most Canadians believe that intolerance toward ethnic minorities is on the rise and that recent incidents of racial discrimination and violence indicate a darkening mood in race relations. A majority of respondents (roughly 60 per cent) agreed with the view that ethnic minorities should abandon their customs and language and change to be more like 'most Canadians'. As well, some 35 per cent of respondents agreed with the platform of Vancouver-based groups who want Canada to limit immigration of non-whites (*Ottawa Citizen*, 22 Mar. 1990).

Control of Immigration

Control of immigration, viewed from a human rights perspective, is an area where various principles may come into conflict. Under the normative imperatives of the present United Nations human rights codes and covenants, the principle of non-intervention in the domestic affairs of states is honoured. Thus, the territorial integrity and political independence of all states is recognized and protected. Further, as Richmond (1975: 121) points out, the economies and social systems of western societies are based not only upon the assumption of national sovereignty but also upon the desire to maintain existing standards of living (i.e., levels of wealth, health, and welfare). The modern idea of a 'welfare state', Richmond argues, necessarily implies a certain degree of control over population and labour force growth in order to maintain economic and social stability. These societal ideals are directly opposed to an uncontrolled flow of immigration. Yet, when a state adopts a racist immigration policy which excludes or restricts the immigration of certain categories of people on ethnically-defined grounds, it clearly contravenes the anti-discriminatory intent of the International Convention on the Elimination of All Forms of Racial Discrimination. Under the latter convention, any exclusion, restriction, or preference based on ethnic criteria constitutes a violation of fundamental human rights. Taking these different considerations into account, we will argue that a state has the right to screen potential immigrants with regard to their economic contributions, but that it has no right to exclude immigrants on the arbitrary basis of ethnic criteria.

A racist immigration policy is one of the most invidious techniques utilized by those in power to guarantee their ethnic ascendancy in any society. Historically, in Canada, immigration restrictions have most sharply discriminated against non-white immigrants categorized as Orientals and Blacks. Prior to 1953, the inclusion of the notion of 'climatic unsuitability' in the Immigration Act furnished the legal justification for barring non-white people from non-western countries (presumably with hot climates). During the nineteenth and early twentieth centuries, the Canadian Immigration Act contained a number of regulations specifically designed to restrict Chinese and Japanese immigration (Krauter and Davis 1978: 63). In 1886, a federal head tax was imposed on Chinese immigrants entering Canada. From 1898 to 1903, the head tax increased from $50 to $500 per head. In 1907, Canada entered into a 'gentlemen's agreement' with the government of Japan restricting Japanese entry to an initial maximum of 400 families per year, later reduced to 150 families. No such pact was possible with China and because of the continuing high level of anti-Oriental prejudice, especially in British Columbia, Chinese immigration was perceived as a major problem. By 1903, it was clear to the Canadian government that increases in the Chinese head tax were not discouraging the flow of Chinese immigrants. Accordingly, the Canadian Parliament passed a new law requiring every Asian (except those covered by a special treaty or international agreement) to have $200 in his or her possession upon arrival in Canada. When this deterrent proved to be no more successful than the head tax, the government took more drastic measures. One important tactic, designed to limit population growth, was to prohibit immigration of wives or families of Chinese persons. Between 1906 and 1923, only seven Chinese wives were admitted. Finally, in 1923, the Chinese Immigration Act (colloquially referred to as the 'Chinese Exclusion Act') was passed; this Act, which prohibited all Chinese immigration, was not rescinded until after World War II.

Li (1980) argues that institutional racism as manifested in the immigration system produced far-reaching consequences through the subsequent disruption of Chinese family life, long after the obstacles were removed. The patterns of 'separated families' (spouse in China) and 'married bachelor' society persisted until well after World War II, when changes in immigration policy allowed the reuniting of marital partners and families.

Richmond (1975: 115) contends that the year 1967 was a major turning point for Canadian immigration policy. At that time specific ethnic and national criteria for the selection of immigrants were abolished in favour of a points system based largely on educational, professional, and occupational achievements. The only residual basis of discrimination lay in the uneven distribution of Canadian immigration offices abroad, most of which were located in Britain and in European countries. However, even this was modified when new offices were opened in Asia, Africa, and South America.

The present legislation, enacted in 1978, has tightened up the points system through more stringent economic requirements, and institutionalized the anti-discriminatory thrust of the policy. The one loophole in the 1978 legislation is the 'personal quality' clause (up to fifteen points) which gives arbitrary, discretionary powers to immigration officers. Because this clause involves a subjective evaluation on the part of the officer, personal prejudice may influence the selection process.

The *Immigration Act* entrenched the humanitarian goals of Canadian immigration policy by incorporating the UN Convention on Refugees and opening the doors to Indochinese refugees and many others. Three main categories—economic migrants, family class and assisted relatives, and refugees—have characterized the intake of immigrants throughout the 1980s. Additionally, a notable change in this period has been a deliberate policy to encourage 'business immigrants' willing to invest substantial capital in Canada. Overall, the immigration trends in the 1980s have been characterized by the increasing intake of non-white immigrants from non-Western countries (Lam and Richmond 1987).

The white majority backlash to the increasing numbers of non-white immigrants in Canada was noted previously in our discussion of media portrayal of visible minorities. Here, we note also the parallel backlash to the increasing intake of refugees and to the attendant problems of refugee determination and backlog, highlighted by the media (*Toronto Star*, 8 Feb. 1989). Finally, we note the voices of protest raised by MPs and other Canadians against preferential treatment accorded 'business immigrants' under the present Act. Protestors claim that poorer, hardworking immigrants are discriminated against, because rich, business immigrants can 'buy their way in' . . . 'Big money' , they claim, 'is the quickest ticket into the country' (*Toronto Star*, 5 August 1989).

On 28 December 1993, a report in the *Toronto Star*, headed 'Ottawa girds for big battle over future immigration policy', proposed that Canada could be about to embark on an immigration policy debate such as has not been heard in decades. The report noted that annual immigration levels had tripled to about 250,000 in ten years, allegedly because the major political parties all had supported high immigration levels. The report suggested, however, that the October, 1993 election of 52 MPs from the Reform Party, a new party committed to cutting immigration by up to half, could force a debate on the subject in the near future. Moreover, the report noted that the Reform position, which posits that high immigration is putting a strain on the system, especially in terms of funding for social programs, is consistent with the findings of recent public opinion polls which suggest broad displeasure with high levels of immigration.

While deep-seated public concern with potential cuts in funding for social programs may be raising 'genuine fears' regarding immigration levels, more suggestive of the 'new racism' is the recent finding of a national survey which indicated that 41 per cent of respondents thought Canada's immigration policy 'allows too many people of different cultures and races to come to Canada' (*Toronto Star*, 14 Dec. 1993).

Dissemination of Hate Propaganda

The dissemination of hate propaganda—materials characterized by 'a generally irrational and malicious abuse of certain identifiable target groups' (Cohen 1966: 11)—constitutes a violation of the categorical right to dignity of target group members and a violation of the right of the minority collectivity to freedom from racial hatred, harassment and degradation.

Hate propaganda represents probably the most malignant expression of racist invalidation ideology, for it not only inferiorizes target populations, but it also stigmatizes them as *threatening and dangerous to society*. Not surprisingly, it follows from this premise that hate propaganda urges its readers to take steps to eliminate the purported threat. What begins as racial prejudice is thus translated into racial discrimination through hate propagandizing activities which incite action against the target group.

The proliferation of organized racist and fascist hate groups throughout Canada over the last two decades has been well documented (Cohen 1966; Daudlin 1984; Barrett 1987). Whether the invalidation myths and ideologies promoted by these groups are religious (Aryan Nations Church) or political (Edmund Burke Society) in thrust, their common premise is racist and their common message (as detailed in Chapter One, pages 23-8) is to *remove* the target group (and, thereby remove the alleged threat), for the good of society.

A current example is provided by the Heritage Front hotline. The white supremacist Heritage Front, styling themselves as a White-Rights advocacy group, has been charged with violating the federal Canadian Human Rights Act by communicating taped telephone messages which promote 'white rights' and which make racist comments about Jews, blacks, aboriginal peoples, immigrants, and others (*Toronto Star*, 15 June 1993). The hate hotline routinely defames Jews and non-whites and warns of a coming apocalypse brought on by creeping multiculturalism and unfettered immigration from non-white countries. The implied message is clear: prevent the apocalypse/remove the 'alien' ethnic threat.

That hate messages almost identical to those expressed by the Heritage Front were disseminated throughout Germany by the Nazi party and their sympathizers during World War II should come as no surprise to the reader. The Nazi apparatus for Jewish genocide was rationalized by just such hate-propagandizing activities.

Persecution, Extermination, and Expulsion

The ultimate denial of human rights lies in the denial of the right to life. At the level of the ethnic collectivity, denial of this right constitutes the act of *genocide*. Individually or collectively, denial of the right to life is a crime against humanity under present United Nations human rights instruments. The Convention on Punishment of Crime of Genocide describes the crime of *genocide* as measures taken against national, religious, racial, or ethnic collectivities with a view to exterminating the entire population against whom the measures are directed.

This Convention was adopted by the United Nations following World War II in response to the atrocities of the Holocaust and to ensure that state policies of genocide, like those adopted in Germany under Hitler's Nazi régime, would never again be enacted. The death of millions of Jews in concentration camps probably provides the single most insidious act of deliberate genocide in modern history, but it is by no means the only such act in modern times. Policies and practices of 'ethnic cleansing', in the former Yugoslavia, provide a current case in point.

While deliberate acts of persecution, extermination, and expulsion are not characteristic of the treatment of ethnic minorities in this country, Canada, like many other countries, has at times singled out particular minorities for cruel and inhumane treatment. In the case of Canada's aboriginal peoples, the extermination of the Beothuk Indians provides a horrendous example.[6]

Historically, a major reason for immigration to Canada of Hutterites and other ethnic minorities was to escape persecution in the country of emigration. Canada was viewed as a land of safety and opportunity, where people could live without fear of discrimination on religious and/or racially defined grounds. Although Canada has not fully achieved this ideal, the techniques of domination employed by Canadian majority group(s) have tended to be covert, rather than overt, and customary rather than legal.

An outstanding exception to this general principle was the deliberate persecution of Japanese-Canadians, during World War II, which involved wholesale violations of the political, economic, social, and cultural rights of members of this stigmatized minority. In this particular instance, the combined forces of government policy and public opinion, strongly influenced by the traumatic political climate of the times, vented the fear of the nation upon one ethnic minority. As the national focus for persecution, all Japanese Canadians were lumped together, labelled, and discriminated against as undesirable 'enemy aliens' (Krauter and Davis 1978: 66-72). Within one day of the Japanese attack on Pearl Harbor, there was an attack on Hong Kong, in which an Canadian contingent of two thousand was killed or captured. Fear of Japanese invasion spread rapidly throughout the west coast of Canada and quickly found a target in the large and highly visible Japanese-Canadian population. In British Columbia, the Japanese minority, citizen and non-citizen alike, was immediately branded as a subversive 'fifth column of aliens' and was subjected to a concerted program of official human rights violations including wholesale evacuation.

Rigid limits were imposed on the amount of goods evacuées could take with them, and they had little time to dispose of surplus. As a result, their property was frequently sold at a fraction of its market value. Although this program was primarily enacted under British Columbia provincial policy, the federal government did not intervene and eventually supported it. Indeed, as Krauter and Davis point out, the legal justification for the entire episode was provided by the War Measures Act.

All persons of Japanese origin were forcibly evacuated from the west coast defence area and relocated in internment camps in the interior of Canada where they were subjected to neglect, through harsh living and working conditions; to diminution through lack of personal privacy, and to oppression through their constant surveillance by guards to ensure strict obedience to repressive rules.

Persecution of Japanese Canadians during the war was followed by policies aimed at their expulsion later on. Following the surrender of Japan in 1945, the Canadian government ordered the deportation of all persons of Japanese ancestry. Almost four thousand Japanese Canadians were thus repatriated (allegedly voluntarily) prior to the revocation of the deportation order in 1947. The fact that the deportations were ordered after the war and despite any evidence of subversive, pro-Japan activities on the part of ill-treated Japanese-Canadian internees, indicates clearly that the government and the Canadian public were motivated more by anti-Japanese racism than considerations of wartime security. In contrast to the persecution of the Japanese, little was done to Canadians of German origin although almost all of Canada's armed forces were engaged against Germany in the war. It seems clear that the racist colour bias which was directed against the Japanese did not apply to 'White' Germans. During the war period, repressive steps were enacted against some members of other Canadian ethnic groups, for example, Germans and Italians alleged to belong to fascist organizations and some members of pacifist religious groups, such as Hutterites, but discriminatory measures against the Japanese minority were far harsher than those accorded any other group.[7] Only the Japanese were subjected to 'ethnic cleansing' measures against the population *as a whole.*

Conclusion

Techniques of domination provide institutionalized, socially 'legitimate' forms of racism, whereby the human rights of ethnic minorities are systemically violated. Such techniques provide 'built-in' guarantees for the perpetuation of dominant group ascendancy, thus they serve to maintain the existing structure of ethnic inequality.

Our analysis of the origin and persistence of the Canadian system of ethnic stratification has shown that, from the very beginning, discriminatory treatment toward aboriginal peoples, as compared with immigrants, has been rooted in more insidious racist assumptions, and its disadvantaging consequences in terms of access to political, economic, and social power have been far more devastating.

Among immigrants, visible (racially defined) immigrants from non-Western countries, i.e., those ethnic minorities whose racial and cultural attributes have been presumed to deviate most markedly from majority norms, have been most restricted in their access to political, economic, and social power.

Institutionalized forms of ethnic discrimination, elaborated in the last part of this chapter, have served to maintain a vertical ethnic mosaic in which, despite some mobility in the middle ranks, the superordinate status of those at the top (founding partners and immigrants most like them) and the marginalized status of those at the bottom (aboriginal peoples) has remained relatively stable over time.

Institutionalized techniques of domination not only thwart or restrict upward mobility of minority members within the ethnic stratification system but also impede the processes of *ethnic integration* of minorities within Canadian society. Accordingly, the continued application of these institutionalized forms of discrimination serves to prevent the realization of the Canadian democratic dream of ethnic equality and national unity.

In the next chapter, we will examine some of the major assumptions behind this Canadian dream and we will attempt to account for the empirical gap between the egalitarian myth of Canadian democracy and the reality of Canada's institutionalized structure of ethnic inequality.

Notes

1 Elsewhere, I have attempted to demonstrate that the concept of collective minority rights can (and should) be extended to include instances where *non*-ethnic minorities develop and sustain viable and distinctive sub-cultures and communities (e.g., gays and lesbians in large urban centres of Canada). See Kallen 1989: 171-6.

2 For a recent re-assessment of the post-*Vertical Mosaic* literature on the topic, see Lautard and Guppy in Li (ed.) 1990.

3 Early French/English differences in patterns of majority/minority relations with aboriginal peoples notwithstanding. Patterson (1972) and Wade (1970), among others, have argued that the French were far more assimilationist than the English, seeking to absorb rather than to subordinate (or exterminate) the aboriginal population. One outcome of this policy was the creation of the Métis population.

4 Lieberson's use of the term 'indigenous' to refer firstly to aboriginal populations, and secondly to established, dominant migrants (in the common sense of 'native' inhabitants) is confusing. In our analysis we will therefore substitute the term 'established migrant' for 'indigenous' in the second sense of the term, and 'aboriginal' will be used in place of 'indigenous', in the first sense of the term.

5 Lieberson's model does not address the special status of refugees. According to the 1951 UN Convention on Refugees, refugees are defined as persons with a well-founded fear of persecution by reason of race, religion, nationality, membership in a social group, or political opinion, who are outside their country of nationality or habitual residence and who are unable or unwilling to return.

6 While the Beothuk example is regarded as the classic case of genocide in the Canadian

context, historical evidence now indicates that European-introduced diseases played an important part in the demise of this population (see Marshall 1981).

7 For readers who wish to pursue this subject in greater detail, there are a number of key works available. Recommended here, are: Adachi 1976; Broadfoot 1977; La Violette 1948; and Sunahara 1979, 1981 (for a discussion of federal policy).

CHAPTER SEVEN

Ethnic Integration: Models, Policies, and Realities

In the previous two chapters, we have examined social and ethnic stratification in the Canadian context. We have shown how ethnic majorities are able to use racist invalidation ideologies to justify discriminatory policies which serve to disadvantage ethnic minorities, thus maintaining the existing ethnic hierarchy and their superordinate status at its apex.

In this chapter we will examine the various national ideologies—both egalitarian and non-egalitarian—which dominant ethnic authorities have used to justify policies of ethnic integration in Canada.

This book utilizes the concept *ethnic integration* in a holistic sense, namely, to refer to the entire set of social processes whereby continuing interaction between members of different ethnic collectivities within a society leads to changes in the cultural content, structural form, and ethnic identities of the interacting individuals or groups. As an outcome of this process, some participants may become self-identified, accepted, and socially recognized as full-fledged members of an ethnic collectivity or a society other than the one into which they were born or raised.

In an ethnically diverse, post-technological society like Canada's, ethnic integration may be conceptualized and analysed in terms of four interrelated sets of social processes. First, members of different ethnic collectivities come to learn and absorb a common set of cultural values, skills, and life ways—society-wide attributes which constitute the cultural prerequisites for effective participation in the public sphere of society at large. Second, they come to participate in the secondary institutions (economic, political, legal, and educational) of society at large by attaining recognized social positions at various levels or ranks of the society-wide hierarchy. Third, by continuous interaction in public life with ethnic outsiders, they may come to learn and absorb some of the distinctive cultural attributes of an ethnic collectivity other than their own. Fourth, their participation in the private sphere of primary ethnic institutions (religious, friendship and kinship, familial, and marital) of another ethnic collectivity may eventually lead to membership in that ethnic collectivity.

The first two sets of processes of ethnic integration involve the *secondary* integration of members of different ethnic collectivities into the public sphere, i.e., into the secondary institutions of society at large. The third and fourth sets of processes involve *primary* integration into the private sphere, i.e., into the primary institutions of another ethnic collectivity.

Theoretically speaking, all processes of integration are two-way processes whereby members of different ethnic collectivities interact, exchange views, learn new values and lifestyles, acquire new skills, participate in new institutions, and acquire new reference and membership groups. As a consequence of this ongoing two-way exchange, changes occur in the culture and social institutions of society at large and in the ethnocultures and institutions of the interacting ethnic collectivities. These changes, in turn, impact upon ethnicity and generate shifts in both ethnocultural and national loyalties and identities among society's members.

In reality, in an established ethnically stratified society like Canada's, processes of secondary ethnic integration tend to be largely unidirectional; access to positions of political, economic, and social power is limited and controlled by established majority ethnic élites. Moreover, the culture and form of public institutions largely represent the historical outgrowths of the ethnocultures and institutions of the dominant ethnic collectivities.

Some scholars maintain that all Western and Westernized societies in today's post-technological era share a common, universalistic, society-wide, technological or mass culture (Isajiw 1978). However, such a contention requires qualification, at least in the Canadian context. In Canada, the distinctive imprints of the historical ethnocultures and institutions of the dominant English and French ethnic collectivities remain strongly entrenched in public life, outside and inside Quebec, respectively.

In somewhat similar fashion, yet in highly varying degrees, processes of primary integration in an ethnically stratified society tend to be limited and controlled by the different interacting ethnic collectivities, majority and minority alike. Here, rank and status disparities as well as ethnocultural and organizational differences between ethnic collectivities often impede primary ethnic integration. Most importantly, the relative strength of ethnic boundary-maintaining mechanisms (elaborated on pp. 161-2) as well as the spheres of ethnic interaction they control, will affect the permeability of ethnic group boundaries and the nature and extent of inter ethnic relations.

In short, in an ethnically stratified society, the particular patterns of ethnic integration that emerge are fashioned by the degree of accessibility of various ethnic collectivities to societal opportunities and institutions controlled by dominant ethnic élites, as well as by the permeability of the group boundaries of interacting ethnic collectivities, whether majority or minority.

The Rhetoric of Ethnic Integration: Key Variables

In both public and private spheres of life, ethnic integration involves two kinds of social processes—cultural exchange and institutional participation. These will be referred to as *cultural integration* or *acculturation,* and as *structural integration* or *assimilation,* respectively.

Cultural Integration/Acculturation

The concept *acculturation* or cultural integration, in its broadest sense, refers to the process whereby selected objects, ideas, customs, skills, behaviour patterns, and values are exchanged among different ethnic collectivities. In this process, each population acquires from the other new cultural attributes that may eventually be absorbed into its own system.

Viewed as part of a general learning process, acculturation refers to the process of learning those cultural ways of an ethnic collectivity to which one does not belong, in much the same way as the concept *enculturation* or *socialization* refers to the broad process of learning the cultural patterns of the ethnic collectivity to which one does belong.

Within an established system of ethnic stratification, the prime direction of change in the process of acculturation in the public sphere is toward the norms, values, and patterns of the majority society. Most members of ethnic collectivities seek to learn the dominant language and cultural patterns in order to participate in public institutions and to improve their socio-economic position and life chances. Thus, for example, immigrants to Quebec prior to the passage of Bill 101, which made French the official public language in the province, tended to learn English in order to gain entrance to public life. Since the passage of Bill 101—and with its later reinforcement by Bill 178, Quebec's French-only sign law—new immigrants became more inclined to learn French.

Acculturation, in the direction of majority societal values, refers not only to the acquisition of the dominant cultural attributes, but also to the attainment of a level of proficiency in utilizing these attributes for effective participation in the public institutions of the society at large. Hence, the degree of acculturation of a particular individual or ethnic collectivity can be measured in terms of the degree of acquisition of cultural attributes, and the degree of proficiency in utilizing these acquired cultural attributes, commensurate with that of people socialized from birth or early childhood into that ethnoculture or society. To return to the French language example, full linguistic acculturation would necessitate that one lose any trace of a foreign accent and become as fluent in speaking French as one's Francophone counterparts, in public life.

Structural Integration/Assimilation

In its broadest sense, the concept *assimilation* or structural integration refers to the social processes whereby relations among members of different ethnic collectivities result in the participation of these individuals in ethnocultural institutions other than those of the ethnic community in which they were raised. For analytical purposes structural integration can be broken down into three broad subprocesses: secondary structural integration, primary structural integration, and identificational integration.

1) Secondary Structural Integration in Relation to Social Mobility
The degree of structural integration of individuals and/or ethnic collectivities can be measured in terms of their degree of participation in the major secondary institutions (i.e., economic, political, legal, and educational) of the society. Secondary structural integration is commonly confused with the concept of social mobility because, in practice, the two social processes to which they refer are frequently linked. However, the two concepts relate to different social phenomena and should be distinguished for analytic purposes.

Secondary structural integration refers to the overall extent of social participation regardless of the rank of the social position attained in public life. It can therefore be measured horizontally in terms of *proportionate representation*, i.e., statistical measures of positional attainment by various social categories and/or members thereof, in relative proportion to their actual population size in the society, in the available range of social positions within the different sectors of public life.

Social mobility, on the other hand, refers to the extent of vertical movement between the ranks in a socially-stratified society. It can therefore be measured vertically in terms of proportionate representation of various social categories, and/or members thereof, in the rank order of social positions at various status levels in society.

What this distinction implies is that an ethnic collectivity, or an individual member thereof, can be highly structurally integrated within a stratified society at low levels of the social hierarchy, i.e., without achieving marked degrees of upward social mobility. Many members of majority ethnic collectivities in Canada participate in public life at low positional levels, while, at the same time, the ethnic category as a whole is over-represented at the topmost ranks.

Alternatively, an individual or ethnic collectivity cannot achieve high degrees of upward social mobility (i.e., attain top ranking positions) in a stratified society like Canada's without a high degree of cultural and structural integration. For the attainment of élite status, both demonstrated skills in the use of valued society-wide cultural attributes, and social acceptance in high-ranking membership groups, are necessary prerequisites (Porter 1965; Clement 1976).

Phrased in terms of human rights concepts, we may say that, to the degree that the fundamental right of equality of opportunity is honoured in Canadian society, it opens the door for Canada's citizens to participate in public life at various positional levels. However, it does not guarantee upward mobility through the ranks. To obtain high-level societal positions and the advantages associated with them requires the acquisition of prestige, which is based on possession of valued cultural attributes over and above those basic skills required for entrance into the system.

Moreover, it is here that the empirical reality of the Canadian ethnic hierarchy diverges sharply from the national egalitarian ethos of equality of opportunity. For as Porter, Clement, and others have shown, it is in the area of prestige evaluation that ascribed characteristics, like race, ethnicity, religion, family, and social class background become crucial criteria for social acceptance and high positional ranking.

To the degree that ethnic minorities have been denied their fundamental right to dignity and have come to represent stigmatized populations in society, then—regardless of their economic and/or political attainments—this kind of prestige recognition will be lacking in all but the most exceptional, individual cases. The continuing inability of ethnic minorities, especially racially defined minorities, to penetrate the ranks of Canada's uppermost corporate élites despite their increasing upward mobility in the political and economic spheres, speaks to this important point.

2) Primary Structural Integration

The degree of *primary structural integration* of individuals and/or ethnic collectivities can be measured in terms of their degree of participation in the private ethnic institutions (i.e., religious, social, and recreational institutions; friendship and kinship networks; family and marital alliances) of an ethnic collectivity other than their own. The ultimate step in the process of primary structural integration—*reproductive integration*—awaits the offspring of inter-ethnic marriage. Reproductive integration occurs when the progeny of the partners of an inter-ethnic marriage become integrated either into one of the parental ethnic communities or into a community of ethnic hybrids like themselves (e.g., Métis, in Canada; Eurasian, in Asia; Cape Coloured, in Africa). The reader should note, here, that while *ethnic hybridization* is the natural, biocultural result of inter-ethnic mating, it does not necessarily lead to primary structural integration. Only when the progeny of ethnic hybrids marry and become integrated into a particular ethnic community, may primary structural integration ensue.

3) Identificational Integration

Identificational integration is a function of both cultural and structural integration. The concept of identificational integration refers to the process whereby an ethnic collectivity other than one's own comes to provide one's primary source of expressive/symbolic ties and roots, and also becomes one's primary reference group.

The social scientific concept of *reference group* refers to that social category whose cultural standards provide the normative guidelines for one's behaviour and whose core values provide the ethical and status criteria used to evaluate and rank oneself and others. The reference group need not be the actual group to which one belongs. For example, an aspiring member of the English élite may use this social category as a behavioural referent, even though he or she belongs to a working-class Italian family.

Identificational integration is a subjective, experiential phenomenon which can best be assessed by attitudinal indicators. For the individual, it can be measured in terms of the extent to which one thinks, feels, and acts in relation to an outside ethnic referent, and the degree to which one's sense of group identity is transferred from one's own ethnic collectivity to another.

In the public sphere of society at large, *secondary* identificational integration can be measured in terms of the degree to which one's national/citizenship ties and loyalties come to supersede one's ethnic or national/ancestral alignments. In the private sphere of interacting ethnic collectivities, *primary* identificational integration can be measured in terms of the degree to which one's primary social alignments and commitments have been transferred from one's original ethnic collectivity to another ethnic collectivity.

At the level of the ethnic collectivity, the degree of identificational integration can only be indirectly measured, i.e., it can be inferred from objective measures of ethnic group viability (see Chapter Four).

Integration, Ethnicity, and Ethnic Identity

Profiles and Discussion

The following excerpts from *The Immigrants* by G. Montero (reprinted by permission of James Lorimer and Company) are drawn from the reported experiences of Canadian immigrants and are presented to inform conceptual discussion.

Carmen, an immigrant from Spain:

> I didn't speak any English . . . I realized that I had to learn English and applied for government-sponsored classes . . . in the classes you are taught to love the country . . . But the moment . . . you get involved in Canadian life [outside of school] things change . . . The people you bump into at your work place or your neighbours . . . very often discriminate against you because of the colour of your skin or because they don't like your accent . . . You realize this isn't the multicultural Canada you were taught about. (Montero 1977: 38-41)

Ida, an Italian married to a Euro-Canadian:

> I was born in Italy . . . I later went to England where I met my husband, a Canadian, and

I came to Canada with him . . . I love Italy. I like the spirit of the people. But I love Canada, too. It took me a while to get used to it. (Ibid.: 85)

Glenna, a Chinese high school student:

My mom brought me up to date Chinese boys . . . if I were to marry another colour, she'd disown me . . . this Chinese girl went by [our house] with a black guy. My grandmother said 'Look at that, she's out with a black boy. If I ever see you doing anything like that I'll kill you.' If some Hong Kong guy sees a Chinese girl going out with a white guy . . . [they] call us bananas. They say we're yellow on the outside and white on the inside. (Ibid.: 186-7)

Emmy, an Austrian married to an Ukrainian/Dutch farmer:

Only 46 years ago I was born and 16 of them now I have been in Canada . . . I had learnt some English [before coming to Canada] but still it did not exactly prepare me for the strangeness of the accents I heard when I reached Calgary . . . [it] was very difficult for me . . . [I married a farmer of mixed Ukrainian and Dutch parentage and we have two adopted sons] . . . We are a family. A Canadian family. This is my country now. There is no doubt of it at all. (Ibid.: 21-3)

Processes of cultural integration and secondary structural integration in the public sphere of society at large do not require a significant shift in ethnic identity or ethnic membership for members of ethnic collectivities. Although acquisition of new reference groups and entrance into new membership groups are inevitable concomitants of ethnic integration, these new referents and social institutions may be political, legal, economic, occupational, or educational rather than ethnic in self-identificational focus and/or membership criteria. As the profile of Ida illustrates, one may acquire a variety of new reference and membership groups without necessarily abandoning old ones and without any significant dislocation in one's ethnic reference or membership group.

Alternatively, primary structural integration is predicated on the occurrence of some degree of shift in one's ethnic reference group. Primary structural integration requires that social distance between the interacting ethnic collectivities be minimized and that inter-ethnic relationships become more intimate and personalized. When this happens, ethnic group boundaries weaken; subjective indicators of ethnicity lose salience; identification of ethnic outsiders as potential insiders is facilitated; and a major shift in ethnic reference group orientation may occur. The testimonies of Ida and Emmy demonstrate different degrees of identificational integration: partial, in the case of Ida, and virtually total, with regard to self-definition, for Emmy.

A radical shift in ethnic reference group orientation may result in one being an insider in terms of continued membership in one's original ethnic collectivity, but an outsider in primary reference group orientation. This shift in ethnic reference group requires a shift in ethnic self-definition. However, for a change in ethnic membership group to occur, an alteration in both self- and other-definitions of ethnicity is required; one must identify one's self and be identified by others as a member of the aspired-to ethnic collectivity. Glenna's profile provides an excellent illustration. 'Bananas' may identify themselves as white but they are identified by others as yellow. And it is this other-definition that provides the barrier to ethnic integration.

For *full integration* in the primary sphere to occur, aspiring members must be accorded the status of insiders by members of the aspired-to collectivity. This means that ethnic outsiders aspiring to gain membership in another ethnic collectivity must ultimately be deemed suitable as potential marital partners and as *bona fide* members of the group.

As stated earlier, an inter-ethnic marriage does not necessarily lead to the full primary integration of either partner. Where the marriage takes place within a broader familial or community context of cultural and/or religious conflicts, the outcome, for one or both partners, may be one of socio-cultural *marginality*. In this situation, one or both partners may harbour a deep-seated feeling of ambivalence toward, or alienation from, both ethnic communities. On the other hand, the partners may seek a new synthesis, without total disavowal for either ethnic tradition. The histories of Ida and Emmy illustrate this latter pattern. Both women came to Canada as immigrants and both married men of different ethnic backgrounds from their own. While Emmy's self-identity is clearly more fully Canadian than is Ida's, neither woman (from the full account of their stories) has totally disavowed her own ethnic tradition.

Is Full Integration Possible?

Even the ultimate step in primary integration, i.e., reproductive integration, does not categorically ensure loss of their original ethnic identities by the offspring of inter-ethnic marriages. The classic anthropological view that a culture must be transmitted over at least three generations before it becomes a 'genuine' ethnoculture may provide an appropriate analogy here: hypothetically, the progeny of inter-ethnic marriages only cease to identify significantly with the separate ancestral heritages of their forebears after a transitional period of at least three generations.

But what happens when future generations of mixed ancestry are singled out by powerful outsiders as racially blemished because of one strain in their ethnic heritage? The example of fully assimilated Jews in Nazi Germany is instructive. Among the persons identified by Hitler's ss agents as 'Jewish' were many individuals of Jewish and part-Jewish ancestry, but of Protestant persuasion, whose families for at least three generations had identified themselves and been identified by society at large as German Protestants. Nevertheless, these 'Jewish' individuals were subjected to the same programs of internment, torture, and extermination as were self-professed Jews. And many of these fully assimilated Jews who survived the horrors of Nazi concentration camps have re-affirmed their Jewish identity in the strongest terms.

Assumptions Behind the Concept of Total Integration

In reality the rhetoric of total integration is rarely achieved. Insofar as societies are socially stratified along *ethnic* lines, barriers to full integration are posed by boundary-maintaining mechanisms employed by both majority and minority ethnic collectivities.

Total integration in the process of acculturation requires changes in the cultures, reference groups, and ethnic identities of the members of the interacting ethnic collectivities. At both the individual and collective levels, full acculturation assumes that members of ethnic collectivities are both willing and able to acquire outsiders' cultural attributes, and that there are no barriers of individual, institutional, structural, or cultural discrimination which prevent them from so doing.

Regarding the process of secondary structural integration (secondary assimilation), total integration requires changes in the secondary institutions, membership groups, and group identities of members of interacting ethnic collectivities.

The degree of acculturation of members of ethnic collectivities has an important bearing on the question of their potential for secondary assimilation. For it is through acculturation that members of ethnic collectivities acquire the language(s), skills, and qualifications required for proportionate representation in the major secondary institutions of the wider society. But total acculturation is not coterminous with, nor does it ensure, total secondary assimilation. At both the individual and collective levels, total secondary assimilation assumes that members of ethnic collectivities are both willing and able to participate effectively in the secondary institutions of society at large, and that there are no barriers of individual, institutional, structural, or cultural discrimination which prevent them from so doing.

Total integration in the process of primary structural integration (primary assimilation) requires changes in the primary institutions and informal networks, ethnic identities, and ethnic membership groups of the members of interacting ethnic collectivities. At both the individual and collective levels, total primary assimilation assumes that members of ethnic collectivities are both willing and able to shift their ethnic alignments and allegiances from their ethnic origin group to another ethnic collectivity, and that there are no barriers of individual, institutional, structural, or cultural discrimination which prevent them from so doing.

Implicit in the notion of total integration are two assumptions: the willingness and ability of members of ethnic collectivities to interact with outsiders and to engage in a mutual process of cultural exchange and institutional participation; and the absence of barriers posed by individual, institutional, and systemic forms of discrimination which impede integration. The empirical observation that these two assumptions are not, characteristically, built into the reality of inter-ethnic relations renders the application of the theoretical concept of total integration problematic.

With regard to majority/minority ethnic relations, in the context of an ethnically stratified society like Canada's, minority ethnic boundary-maintaining mechanisms, together with continuing majority violations of the political, economic, social, and cultural rights of ethnic minorities present formidable barriers to total integration.

One-Way and Two-Way Processes of Ethnic Integration: Differential Outcomes

The Level of Rhetoric

Theoretically, the social processes involved in ethnic integration are two-way processes of cultural exchange and institutional participation. This observation notwithstanding, the direction of ethnic integration in any given empirical instance is a variable influenced by the relative strength of push and pull forces impacting upon each of the interacting ethnic collectivities. Should the ethnic collectivities be relatively equal in expressive and/or instrumental strength, then ethnic integration will tend to be a two-way process. However, should the ethnic collectivities be unequal, then the process of ethnic integration will tend to be unidirectional, favouring the stronger ethnic collectivity.

Hypothetically, the outcome of a two-way process of ethnic integration could take two forms: (1) the *fusion* of the original ethnic collectivities and the creation of a new, ethnically homogeneous society (*melting pot* or amalgamation); (2) the retention and *federation* of the original ethnic collectivities and the creation of an ethnically heterogeneous, multi-ethnic society (*cultural pluralism* or mosaic).

Hypothetically, the outcome of a one-way process of ethnic integration could take two forms: (1) the *absorption* of the weaker ethnic collectivity by the stronger one, and the creation of an ethnically homogeneous society modelled upon the characteristics of the (original) stronger ethnic collectivity (*dominant conformity* or absorption); (2) the institutionalized and/or coerced *suppression* of the weaker ethnic collectivity by the stronger one, and the creation of a caste-like society dominated and controlled by the stronger ethnic collectivity (*paternalism* or colonialism).

The Reality of Minority Ethnic Integration in Canada: Barriers and their Human Rights Implications

In reality, society-wide processes of integration within Canada's ethnic hierarchy are limited and controlled by the dominant ethnic élite(s) through a broad range of techniques of domination. These institutionalized forms of racism, detailed in Chapter Six, enable dominant powers to restrict and/or exclude minorities, thereby ensuring their own continuing political, economic, legal, social, and cultural hegemony in the society.

Barriers to secondary structural integration violate the fundamental human rights of ethnic minorities by restricting or denying their access to political, economic, and social power in the society. Alternatively, barriers to primary structural integration do not, directly, violate human rights, as all ethnic collectivities have the internationally recognized right to maintain their group distinctiveness. Yet, in Canadian society, the primary ethnic networks of the dominant élite overlap public and private institutional spheres (Kelner 1970). Thus, exclusion of ethnic minorities from these primary relationships indirectly restricts their social mobility by denying them access to powerful contacts and connections at high positional levels (Porter 1965; Clement 1976).

Barriers to primary integration are also self-imposed by minority ethnic collectivities, but minority ethnic closure devices lack both the power and the scope to impact upon opportunities in the society at large. Membership in élite social clubs within the minority ethnic community, for example, does not generally provide the kinds of social contacts and connections necessary for entry into the élite positions of public life.

To summarize: processes of ethnic integration within an ethnically stratified society are limited and controlled by various boundary-maintaining mechanisms—restrictive ideologies, policies, and practices—imposed by both majority and minority ethnic collectivities. However, it is the barriers arbitrarily imposed by majority powers that restrict minority opportunities in public life. Accordingly, these are the barriers that violate the fundamental human right of all citizens to equality of opportunity for participation in public life. And it is these majority barriers that present formidable obstacles to upward social mobility for ethnic minorities, thus impeding their attainment of the prestige and advantages associated with the top-ranking social positions.

Models of Ethnic Integration: The Accommodation of Ethnic Diversity within Society

To account for this gap between the rhetoric and the reality of ethnic integration, we must give serious attention to the dominant ideologies and models of ethnic integration that underscore and legitimate public policy, legislation, and practice.

In North America, scholarly attention has focused on four models of integration.[1] These models, referred to earlier as resulting from ethnic integration processes, are: Melting Pot (Amalgamation), Cultural Pluralism (Mosaic), Dominant Conformity (Absorption), and Paternalism (Colonialism). Each of these models contains somewhat different assumptions about the nature of ethnic integration processes, and about the kind of society predicated upon them or resulting from them. It is important to remember that these conceptual constructs do not exactly correspond with the empirical picture of ethnic integration within any society, at any given time; nor do they exhaust the range of conceptual possibilities. Moreover, the model emphasized in public policies and government legislation in a given society may be discarded, under changing social conditions, for another. The model implicit in majority policy and practice as well as the response of minorities to it may also vary from one ethnic collectivity to another, from one region to another, and/or from one time period to another.

'Models of' and 'Models for' Reality

The term 'model' has two senses—an 'of' sense and a 'for' sense. In the first (inductive) sense a model is a schematic representation of reality, based upon empirical observation. It purports to explain how the reality it represents really works. In this sense, a model of ethnic integration is a conceptual scheme derived from repeated observations of many societal realities and elaborating upon the basic principles behind these realities. In the second (deductive) sense, a model is a prescriptive plan or blueprint for reality, based upon valued ideals. It purports to represent the ideal version of reality and to show how it can be attained. In this sense, a model of ethnic integration is a social doctrine that provides guidelines for the attainment of an ideal mode of accommodation of ethnic diversity within society.

The four models of ethnic integration to be presented in this chapter and summarized in Table 4 (p. 164-5) have been considered both 'models of' and 'models for' social reality in the Canadian context.

Melting Pot and Mosaic: Twentieth-Century North American Myths

The Level of Reality

In contemporary parlance, the melting-pot and mosaic models of ethnic integration have come to assume the status of national myths in the United States and Canada. But on neither side of the Canadian/American border have these essentially egalitarian ideals ever closely represented societal reality. That is to say, neither in Canada nor in the United States have all citizens been accorded full equality of opportunity with full human dignity regardless of ethnic classification.

In the United States for example, blacks, originally racially defined as Negroes, were never expected to 'melt'. Under the racist laws governing slavery, they were defined and treated as subhuman 'chattels'—things to be bought and sold in the marketplace. It follows that a society need not accord full human rights to populations defined as less than human. Similarly, in both Canada and the United States, aboriginal peoples were not included under the ethnic (a term erroneously reserved for immigrants) rubric because they were not deemed fully 'educable' and 'assimilable'.

In reality, the concept of ethnic integration was, from the beginning, a racially and culturally exclusive notion: it was restricted in application to those immigrants whose physical, linguistic, cultural, and behavioural characteristics were considered

Table 4 Assumptions Behind Models of Ethnic Integration in North American Meritocracies

Variables	Melting Pot (Amalgamation)	Mosaic (Cultural Pluralism)	Dominant Conformity (Absorption)	Paternalism (Colonialism)
1. Societal Goal: (Ethnicity and Nationality)	one nation/one people/ one culture	one nation/many peoples/ many cultures	one nation/one people/ one culture (dominant)	one dominant nation/ people/culture subordinated minorities
2. Symmetry/Asymmetry of political, economic, and social power	symmetric (all populations relatively equal)	symmetric	asymmetric (dominant population is superordinate)	asymmetric (dominant population monopolizes power)
3. Ethnocentrism (and) willingness/ability to maintain/shed ethnocultural distinctiveness	low ethnocentrism, willing and able to shed distinctiveness (*all* populations)	high ethnocentrism, willing and able to maintain distinctiveness (*all* populations)	*dominant* – high ethnocentrism, willing and able to maintain distinctiveness / *minorities* – low ethnocentrism, willing and able to shed distinctiveness	*dominant* – high ethnocentrism, willing and able to maintain distinctiveness / *minorities* – low ethnocentrism, but unable to shed distinctiveness (racial/ascribed)
4. Levels of prejudice and discrimination	non-discriminatory; low or absent prejudice	prejudice and discrimination not institutionalized; moderate or low (tolerance possible)	institutional and cultural discrimination; level of prejudice and discrimination: *dominant* – high (intolerant); *minority* – low (willing to conform to majority norms)	institutional, cultural, and structural discrimination; level of prejudice and discrimination: *dominant* – high (intolerant); *minority* – stigmatized permanently

Table 4 (continued)

Variables	Melting Pot (Amalgamation)	Mosaic (Cultural Pluralism)	Dominant Conformity (Absorption)	Paternalism (Colonialism)
5. Criteria for social mobility	achieved	achieved	achieved and ascribed	*dominant* – achieved *within* dominant stratum *minorities* – ascribed status is permanent: no mobility possible
6. Spheres of ethnocultural distinctiveness	none	– *variable* – *public* (political, economic ard / or linguistic pluralism) *private* (multiculturalism) *territorial* (nationalism)	*dominant* – public & private; *minority* – acculturation required	*dominant* – public & private *minority* – deculturation promoted/partial acculturation required
7. Collective identity	national identity (de-ethnicized)	hyphenated-identity ethnic-national	national identity = dominant ethnic identity	*dominant* – national entity = dominant ethnic identity *minority* – negative valence of marginal identity
8. Human Rights	individual human rights	individual and collective rights (collective, cultural and collective, national)	individual rights of minorities predicated on dominant conformity; collective rights of dominant group entrenched at societal-wide level	*dominant* – individual and collective rights *minority* – no human rights, systemic violation of rights

congruent, or similar enough, to deem them meltable or compatible. When immigration laws were relaxed so as to admit racially visible minorities, both countries were faced with severe problems with regard to the reality of ethnic integration.[2]

Democracy and Human Rights: Canadian and American 'Models for' Reality

Both the melting pot and the mosaic ideologies are rooted in some common, liberal, North American assumptions about democracy. Canada and the United States share the same democratic ideal of an open class society in which all citizens are accorded equal individual human rights and equal opportunities for the acquisition of cultural skills, for societal participation, and for social mobility within the public sector. The North American ideal of democracy is predicated on the competitive economic notion of free enterprise, which emphasizes the value of individual achievement. This means that, in public life, each person should be evaluated and rewarded *as an individual* for his or her *demonstrated qualifications*, without reference to ethnic or other group membership.

Another assumption built into the democratic ideal is that of a *meritocracy*, i.e., a stratified social order in which the various social positions are unequally ranked and rewarded on the basis of their socially recognized value to society at a given time.

At the level of societal reality, should the meritocracy truly be based only on individual achievement, given the ubiquitous range in skills, abilities, motivations, and interests among members of every human population, it would follow that members of the country's various ethnic collectivities should be proportionately represented, according to their numbers in the society, at *all* status levels throughout the ranks of the social hierarchy. Put another way, should the fundamental political, economic, and social rights of all citizens be fully and equally respected, some members of every ethnic collectivity will merit greater social rewards and gain greater advantages than others, in recognition of their superior achievements. Accordingly, individuals, rather than social collectivities, will acquire greater or lesser access to political, economic, and social power as the rewards of achieved higher social position.

In short, the North American democratic ideal is egalitarian with regard to the distribution of *opportunity* but it is élitist in terms of the distribution of social rewards. This distinction is an important one, because such a meritocracy can only be democratic in practice if all citizens are given equal opportunity to acquire the values, skills, and qualifications that would enable them to compete for valued social positions in all spheres of public life and to achieve upward social mobility within the ranks of the meritocracy.

While Canada and the United States share this common democratic ideal, prevailing ideologies of ethnic integration north and south of the border have diverged markedly at times. Canadians, in the middle decades of this century, tended to picture Canada as a mosaic in contrast to the alleged American melting pot. Ideally, as 'models for' reality, both the melting pot and the mosaic are egalitarian blueprints designed to create national unity and ethnic equality in a multi-ethnic, democratic society. Where they differ is in their *cultural* goals: the melting pot is designed to create 'unity in homogeneity', while the mosaic is designed to create 'unity in heterogeneity'.

The Melting Pot: Assumptions Behind the Amalgamation Model

The melting pot concept achieved public approbation in the United States with the instantaneous success of Israel Zangwill's Broadway play *The Melting Pot*, first performed in 1914. The play focused on the total integration of a Jewish immigrant, who happily abandoned the yoke of persecution historically associated with his minority ethnic status in Europe in the hopes of becoming a one-hundred-per-cent (de-ethnicized) American citizen.

In conceptual terms, the goal of this American melting-pot dream was a society comprised of one people/one nation/one culture, i.e., a society in which national unity was predicated on a goal of ethnic homogeneity.

As a *model for reality* the melting-pot ideology assumes first and foremost that members of all ethnocultural collectivities are both able and willing to abandon their ethnically distinctive characteristics. Hence, the distinctive characteristics must be similar enough or at least congruent enough to be 'meltable'. Moreover, the degree of ethnocentrism must be fairly low as all cultural contributions to the 'pot' must be equally valued. Secondly, the melting-pot model assumes at least a rough equivalence in degrees of power between ethnic collectivities, so that no one group can easily become dominant. Thirdly, it assumes a virtual absence of prejudice and discrimination; members of all ethnic collectivities are expected to interact freely and equally, without social barriers of any kind, in both the public and private sectors of their lives. Given these assumptions, the ongoing processes of social participation, the formation of friendships across ethnic lines, and the eventual mating and marriage between members of the various ethnic collectivities should lead to a total merging and blending of peoples and cultures. Over time, a new, ethnic entity should be created: a new, biologically and culturally homogeneous society in which all traces of former ethnic cultures, institutions, and identities have disappeared. In this new society, members' national and ethnic identities would be coterminous. Both citizenship and opportunities for social mobility in the new society would be based solely on individual qualities and achievements.

This ideal is predicated on equal recognition of the fundamental political, economic, and social rights of all individual citizens in the society. It leaves no place, however, for the recognition of the collective cultural or national rights of the various ethnic collectivities contributing to the societal melting pot.

The Level of Reality

In the United States, the melting-pot ideology has been a popular myth that has never corresponded to or even approximated social reality. However, scholars generally agree that at the level of interaction between specific ethnocultural collectivities, it has been more typical of inter-ethnic relations between European groups in the United States than in Canada.

In Canada, an unique example of a melting-pot aftermath is provided by historical communities of Métis on what is now Canada's Western prairies (Sealey and Lussier 1975; Sawchuck 1978). In the nineteenth century, in the Red River area of what is now Manitoba, the Métis constituted a distinct ethnocultural and political community—a 'new nation' which, for a short-lived period, could successfully assert political and legal rights against the national government (Daniels, March 1979: 7). The political autonomy of the Red River Métis was shattered with their defeat in the Riel-led rebellion of 1869. From 1870 to 1930, government authorities tried to eradicate Métis claims to aboriginal rights and, in 1940, erroneously convinced that they had succeeded, federal officials abolished the special legal Status of the Métis people. Today, a number of Métis organizations are attempting to reclaim a distinct status for descendants of the Métis people as 'First Nations', under Canada's Constitution (*Toronto Star*, 13 Aug. 1991).

The Mosaic: Assumptions Behind the Cultural Pluralism Model

Despite popular belief, the concept of cultural pluralism is not a uniquely Canadian phenomenon, nor does it clearly differentiate Canadian from American thinking about models of ethnic integration. Indeed, the first spokesperson for cultural pluralism was the American philosopher, Horace Kallen. Writing in 1915, Kallen pictured the ideal American civilization as a 'multiplicity in a unity . . . an orchestration of mankind based on the co-operative harmonies of European civilization, with the elements of poverty and persecution eliminated'.[3] However, this approach, which favoured retention of ethnic distinctiveness, was met with widespread criticism. Early in the twentieth century, the melting-pot ideology, while never enshrined as policy, was clearly favoured as the most appropriate image for an America bent on shedding its multi-ethnicity.

In contrast, the concept of cultural pluralism in Canada represents a fairly recent outgrowth of the historical ideal of 'cultural dualism'—the original myth legitimating the constitutional separation and guarantees underlying English/Protestant hegemony outside Quebec and French/Catholic hegemony within the Province of Quebec.

Early in the twentieth century, with the arrival of large numbers of non-English and non-French immigrants, the myth of cultural dualism began to lose popularity, and, by the third and fourth decades the mosaic myth was increasingly lauded in the speeches of politicians and other dignitaries (Burnet 1981: 29).

However, while the mosaic and melting-pot myths flourished in the rhetoric of public life in Canada and the United States, respectively, public policy continued to be governed by the concept of dominant (Anglo) conformity. In Canada, the assumption was that immigrants would assimilate to the British institutional and cultural model, which included the English language and the Protestant religion. Not until the early decades following World War II did the mosaic rhetoric take on serious multicultural policy implications.

The mosaic myth was strengthened by the negative reaction of immigrant ethnic minorities to the reports of the Royal Commission on Bilingualism and Biculturalism, in the late 1960s. However, the abridged version of the mosaic myth, legitimated by the federal government policy of multiculturalism in 1971, deviated markedly from the original ideal. The multicultural policy and the 1988 Act which put the policy into a statutory framework will be discussed later in this chapter. At this juncture, we will examine the theoretical assumptions behind the mosaic/cultural pluralism ideal.

As a model for reality, the mosaic ideology is predicated on a national goal of one nation/many peoples/many cultures, assuming that members of all ethnocultural collectivities are both able and willing to maintain their ethnocultural distinctiveness. The implications of this assumption are manifold. First, it implies that all ethnic collectivities are willing to adopt a *laissez-faire* stance toward ethnocultural collectivities whose values and life ways differ markedly from their own. The second implication is that levels of prejudice and discrimination between ethnic collectivities are low enough to allow mutual tolerance. Thirdly, it assumes a rough equivalence in the distribution of power, so that no one ethnic collectivity can assume dominance and control. Finally, it implies mutual agreement among members of various ethnic collectivities to limit and control the extent, spheres, and nature of their interaction. Thus, processes of acculturation and assimilation will be mutually restricted by the interacting ethnic units.

Given these assumptions, inter-ethnic relations within the mosaic society would take the form of ethnic segmentation (Breton 1978). Each ethnic collectivity would be institutionally complete, and ethnocultural distinctiveness would be maintained through separate ethnic institutions. As an outcome of this cultural and structural pluralism, every citizen's identity would become hyphenated, i.e., ethnic-national, with equal weights on both sides of the hyphen. With regard to human rights, the society would recognize both the individual human rights of all its citizens and the collective cultural rights of all its ethnic collectivities. Given the basic assumption of equality of opportunity built into the notion of a meritocracy, the social position attained by individuals within a mosaic—as within a melting-pot-society—would be based on individual talents, capabilities, and skills on the one hand, and their assigned cultural value on the other. Ethnicity would not be a criterion for personal evaluation or for positional attainment in public life. It would, however, provide the recognized basis for collective rights, in that all ethnic collectivities would be guaranteed the freedom to express their religious, linguistic, and cultural distinctiveness.

The most important variable in the operation of this model is the relative weights assigned to unity and diversity. The importance of ethnic diversity is reflected in the spheres in which collective rights may be guaranteed. Should the mosaic take the form of pluralism in the public sector, then ethnocultural rights could be guaranteed through political representation, economic control in specified areas, recognition of linguistic rights, and, in its most extreme form, territorial autonomy. This latter form of pluralism supports nationhood based on geographical separation of ethnic collectivities sharing language, culture, and territory. If viable for all ethnic groups, it could lead to multi-nationhood—a multinational society within a common political administrative framework—in which the national group rights of all ethnic collectivities would be recognized.

In Canada, the myth of the mosaic was not initially conceptualized by majority powers in *nationhood* terms for populations other than the English and French charter groups. Rather, the mosaic model relegated cultural and structural pluralism for ethnic minorities to the private sphere of life; within the public sector, all *individuals* would be accorded equal opportunities without reference to ethnic classification. But, with regard to collective rights, the public sector was envisaged as an Anglo or Franco Canadian cultural monolith; thus attainment of social positions within secondary institutions would be predicated on acculturation to prevailing Anglo or Franco norms and practices. It is this abridged version of the mosaic model which has informed Canada's multicultural policy over the years, and which is still reflected in Canada's Multiculturalism Act (1988).

To help understand how Canada's particular version of the mosaic ideology came into being, the following pages offer a brief historical overview of the development of multiculturalism in Canada.

From Cultural Dualism to Multiculturalism: The Historical Background of the Canadian Mosaic Ideology[4]

As a national ideology of ethnic integration, multiculturalism represents a fairly recent outgrowth of the constitutionally entrenched ideal of cultural dualism. The ideal of Canada as a bilingual and bicultural society has its roots in the Confederation pact between Canada's two 'founding partners', English Protestants and French Catholics. It was not until the late 1960s that the ideal of multiculturalism took on serious policy implications.

Until this time, government policy was predicated on the ideal of assimilation or dominant conformity. It was assumed that all ethnic minorities would willingly abandon their 'inferior' cultural baggage—their traditional language, religion and customs—in favour of the 'superior', dominant-Canadian model. For most immigrants to Canada, the dominant model to which they were expected to assimilate was English-Protestant for, historically, immigration was a primary concern only of

English Canada. French Canada's population growth was ensured by a continuing high rate of natural increase. Few immigrants chose to reside in Quebec, and those who did tended to assimilate to the English-Protestant rather than to the French-Catholic cultural milieu within the province.

Over the decades, from the period of massive early-twentieth-century immigration to the post-World War II period, public support for multiculturalism among immigrant ethnic groups grew perceptibly. In response, a new 'Canadian mosaic' ideal was increasingly lauded in speeches by politicians and other dignitaries. But, as conceptualized by these dominant authorities, the mosaic version of multiculturalism digressed radically from the egalitarian cultural pluralism ideal, for it totally *privatized* the cultural claims of minority ethnic groups. The right of non-English and non-French ethnic groups to freely express their cultural distinctiveness was relegated to the private sphere only. Public institutions, it was assumed, would continue to be predicated on the established model of cultural dualism. For ethnic minorities, then, opportunities for advancement in public life would continue to be predicated on dominant conformity—required linguistic and cultural assimilation to entrenched Anglo or Franco majority norms.

My argument, here, is that *even as an ideal* multiculturalism in Canada did not replace dominant conformity as a blueprint for ethnic integration. It was just an addendum to the principal national agenda which continued to endorse the entrenchment throughout public life of the linguistic and broader cultural rights of Canada's founding partners.

During the 1960s, the period of the 'Quiet Revolution' in Quebec, French-Quebeckers began to collectively vocalize their discontent with their subordinate status, as 'founding peoples', relative to the English within Canada *and* within Quebec. They began to voice strong demands for equality of political and economic power with the English, under threat of separation from the Canadian federal state. The federal government response to French-Quebec's demands was the creation of a Royal Commission with a mandate to inquire into and report on the state of bilingualism and biculturalism in Canada.

The impetus for Canada's multicultural policy lay in the negative response of non-English and non-French immigrant ethnic minorities to the mandate and the recommendations of the Royal Commission on Bilingualism and Biculturalism (The Bi and Bi Commission). The reports of the Commission supported policy changes designed to entrench a Canada-wide policy based on an ideal of cultural dualism, i.e., institutionalized English/French bilingualism and biculturalism across Canada. Spokespersons for a Third Force of immigrant ethnic minorities (a growing population sector already representing more than a quarter of Canada's total population, at the time) adamantly rejected the bi and bi model. They argued that it was an élitist model that reinforced the established dominant ethnic status of English- and French-speaking Canadians and relegated non-English and non-French Canadians to the status of second-class citizens in Canada. Immigrant demands for cultural equality and for an equitable distribution of power across all ethnic groups escalated. In response, the government extended the mandate of the Bi and Bi Commission and, in 1970, the Commission produced Book Four of the Bi and Bi Reports, entitled: the Cultural Contribution of the Other Ethnic Groups.[5] This report contained 16 recommendations which, had they been implemented, would have necessitated a federal government policy of multilingualism and multiculturalism.

Prime Minister Trudeau's October 1971 announcement of a multicultural policy for Canada[6] was the official response of the federal government to the recommendations contained in Book Four. Mr Trudeau made it clear that although the government endorsed the 'spirit' of Book Four, it did not support the position implicit in its recommendations that language and culture are indivisible. The federal government rejected the notion that multiculturalism necessitates multilingualism and proposed that the multicultural policy be implemented within a bilingual framework.

Multiculturalism as Public Policy in Canada

The Prime Minister emphasized the fact that, under the terms of the new multicultural policy, the preservation of cultural distinctiveness and of ethnic ties and identities, by individuals or by groups, was to be a *voluntary* and *private* matter. In public life, all individuals were to be free to participate as Canadians without regard to ethnic or other group classification.

The government's policy statement on multiculturalism set forth four objectives: 1) to provide resources for the cultural development of those groups which demonstrate a desire to maintain a distinctive culture and a need for assistance in doing so; 2) to assist all Canadians to overcome cultural barriers to full participation in Canadian society; 3) to promote creative intercultural exchange between groups in order to foster national unity; 4) to assist immigrants to acquire at least one official language (English or French) in order to become full participants in Canadian society.

The cultural priorities of the federal government are clearly revealed in this fourfold package of multicultural policy objectives. Only the first of the stated objectives affords any basis of support for minority cultural diversity. Objectives two and three are clearly designed to foster national unity. The final objective supports the central cultural aim of the policy, namely, the preservation of majority (English and French) linguistic/cultural dualism in public life.

Trudeau's announcement of the multicultural policy sparked vociferous debate among scholars and concerned citizens alike. The disagreement between the policy's supporters and its opponents sustained heated public controversy about multiculturalism for more than a decade. In the following analysis, we will offer only the gist of the bases of contention in the multiculturalism debate.

With regard to the first policy objective, support for cultural diversity, there was a clear line of division in both academic and public opinion. Those who expressed support for this objective tended to support Trudeau's argument that ethnicity serves to meet an individual's expressive needs for emotional security and support.

Maintenance of ties to distinctive ethnic communities and cultures, it was argued, provides an important sense of group belongingness and identity necessary in order to counteract the impersonal and alienating environmental influences of a post-technological workaday world. Notwithstanding this symbolic dimension of ethnicity, opponents contended that maintenance of distinctive cultural values impedes upward mobility in a society predicated on dominant conformity in public life. Moreover, they argued, preservation of cultural differences impedes the development of national unity.[7]

The first policy objective also was attacked by opponents who rejected the government's shallow interpretation of the concept of 'culture', as reflected in the nature of early programs of implementation. Critics argued that multicultural programs fostered the conception of Canada as a kind of ethnic zoo[8] where the function of the zookeeper was to accumulate ethnic exotica and to exhibit them publicly once a year. For example, critics pointed to government-funded ethnic festivals, where the audience could go from one display to another, sampling such ethnic tidbits as wonton soup, pizza, Madras curry, kosher pastrami, and the like.

In similar vein, critics pointed to government-funded programs focusing on traditional, artistic expressions of ethnicity—what one sociologist called the 'just keep dancing' version of multiculturalism.[9] The focus of criticism, here, was on the backward view of ethnoculture as museum culture. Critics argued that this view of multiculturalism nourished stereotypes of minority ethnic groups as strange upholders of quaint customs. At the same time, it denied them support for language, religion, and other institutions essential to their living ethnocultures.

In Michael Hudson's view, the multicultural policy's failure to address the linkage between culture and language and its favouring of bilingualism 'created a major lacuna in the government's response to the "Third Force"' (Hudson, CHRF 1987: 64). By neglecting non-official languages, he argued, early multicultural programs 'denied an essential element of self-identification for many ethnic groups'.

In response to expressed minority ethnic dissatisfaction with the linguistic focus of early multicultural programs on French/English bilingualism, and the cultural focus on folk art and museum culture, multicultural programs were expanded to offer limited support for private non-official language schools as key institutions of 'living' ethnocultures. Since 1973, the policy has supported heritage language teaching in private schools through the Cultural Enrichment Programme, but the funding for this endeavour has been minuscule in comparison to that afforded French and English language education (Hudson 1987: 68). Moreover, ethnic minority representatives have continued to argue that failure to provide support for maintenance of language and culture in public institutions—in primary and secondary schools, community colleges and universities, and in public broadcasting and other media—perpetuates the minority status of non-English/non-French immigrant ethnic groups (Burnet 1981: 31). For the most part, provincially-supported 'heritage language' programs are offered outside the public school system. For example, in Ontario, these classes are offered after regular school hours and on weekends or, where numbers warrant, by an extension of the school day (Hudson 1987: 81). Only in a few larger communities in Alberta, Manitoba, and Quebec is funding proffered for public bilingual schools.

The most biting criticism of the first multicultural policy objective was raised by opponents who argued that the emphasis on culture deflected attention from inequalities in political and economic power across ethnic groups, and did nothing to improve opportunities for empowerment of immigrant ethnic minorities. Taking this line of argument a step further, a number of social scientists suggested that the multiculturalism/bilingualism policy represented the government's attempt to 'appease and contain' the conflicting empowerment demands of immigrant minorities, on the one hand, and of French-Quebeckers, on the other. In order to contain the political and economic demands of both, the government made some concessions to their cultural demands. To appease the immigrants, the government offered some support for the maintenance of minority ethnocultures, in the private sphere. To appease the French-Quebeckers, it offered nation-wide bilingualism. Through this strategy of appeasement and containment, the policy was designed to ensure the continuation of English dominance and control in Canada at the national level.[10]

It should be noted, here, that this entire argument did not address aboriginal peoples' concerns, for aboriginal peoples' demands focused on their special status and rights which were not addressed in the multicultural policy. Indeed, aboriginal peoples did not want to be 'lumped together' with immigrants as ethnic minorities under the multicultural policy, because they feared that this would jeopardize their claims for special status and their aboriginal and treaty rights.

To return to the debate over the multicultural policy: the second and third policy objectives, designed to reduce cultural discrimination and to foster national unity, were accorded virtually unanimous scholarly and public support. However, critics were soon to point out that these objectives were not adequately implemented, for it was in this area that multicultural programs were most neglected. Another source of criticism relating to these objectives emerged from representatives of Canada's growing population of visible minorities. Spokespersons for groups such as Chinese, West Indians, and South Asians argued that early multicultural programs did not place enough emphasis on eliminating racial discrimination. In this connection, it is important to note that it was not until 1981—ten years after the policy of multiculturalism was established—that the government finally responded to the escalating demands of visible minorities for anti-racism (rather than cultural retention) programs. In this year, a race relations unit was instituted within the Multiculturalism Directorate, and a national program to combat racism was inaugurated.

Over the ensuing decade, critics have asserted that the anti-racism initiatives increasingly emphasized under the policy have failed to halt the escalation of prejudice and discrimination against visible minorities across Canada. Moreover, some critics have argued that the state, through its funding of multicultural and anti-racism activities, is able to officially define program priorities, and thus to exercise fiscal control over ethnic organizations (Li 1990: 14-15).

The fourth and last multiculturalism objective, bilingualism, proved to be the most contentious aspect of the entire policy. Multiculturalism within a bilingual framework simply did not seem to make sense to anyone. In the view of critics, even today, the only viable options are Bi and Bi or Multi and Multi. Supporters of the egalitarian multiculturalism ideal argue for multilingualism and multiculturalism.[11] Supporters of the élitist ideal of English/French cultural dualism argue for bilingualism and biculturalism.[12] It is important to note, however, that supporters of multilingualism and multiculturalism are not making demands for minority language guarantees equal to those afforded the English and French majorities. Spokespersons for immigrant ethnic groups are asking for *non-official language* rights. Thus, the privileged position of Canada's two official languages is not challenged by minority demands.

Summary: The Canadian Mosaic and Multiculturalism Policy

Clearly, the federal government policy of multiculturalism has not gained the unqualified approval of Canadian scholars or Canadian ethnic communities. Assessed in terms of the prerequisites of the egalitarian multicultural ideal, the policy is an abject failure. While it affords symbolic endorsement for immigrant ethnocultures, it provides no concrete guarantees of support for ethnic institutions, such as language and religion, vital to the maintenance of distinctive, living ethnocultures. With regard to immigrant group demands for political, economic, and social equality within Canada, the policy is silent. By both commission and omission, Canada's multicultural policy perpetuates the 'vertical Canadian mosaic'. It reconfirms the superordinate ethnic status of Canada's two 'founding' partners and it relegates later immigrant groups to the inferior status of ethnic minorities. This observation has been substantiated by the marked priority in government funding accorded 'official languages' over multicultural programs.

On the positive side, critics have pointed out that, despite its serious shortcomings, the multicultural policy has given immigrant ethnic minorities a legitimate basis for making claims on public policy and public funds. Indeed, it was in response to the vigorous, organized lobbying efforts of immigrant ethnic minorities that the Government established the Cultural Enrichment Program, giving support for heritage language teaching (Hudson 1987: 68). More recently, in response to continued ethnic lobbying, in 1988, Canada became the first country in the world to adopt a national Multiculturalism Act.

Legislated Multiculturalism: The Canadian Multiculturalism Act (1988)[13]

By the mid-1980s, it was obvious to all concerned that the 1971 multicultural policy had become insufficient and out of date. In response, the Canadian government authorized a number of politically appointed commissions to assess the policy in light of submissions from ethnic minorities and to provide recommendations for improvement.[14] The recommendations submitted to the Government addressed the major criticisms of the multicultural policy over the years and provided a substantive blueprint for a new, egalitarian Canadian mosaic.

Unfortunately, but certainly not surprisingly, the response of the federal government essentially has been to protect established ethnic priorities. The government legislated a Multiculturalism Act (passed by the House of Commons on July 12, 1988) which recognizes multiculturalism as a fundamental characteristic of the Canadian heritage, but which does so within the 'official' framework of English/French linguistic and cultural dualism. Critics of the Act argue that it incorporates 'motherhood' statements made since 1971, but that privatization of multiculturalism continues. Once again, critics argue, the multicultural rhetoric of intention is not followed through by concrete guarantees for implementation. In short, critics argue that the Act perpetuates the old government strategy of giving in to unthreatening cultural demands in order to appease and contain threatening demands of immigrant groups for equal economic, political and social opportunities within Canada.[15]

Notwithstanding these critical comments, there are some positive features of Canada's new Multiculturalism Act. Unlike the original multiculturalism policy, the Act includes reference to *racial* as well as cultural equality and includes reference to non-official as well as official languages. It also includes mention of aboriginal peoples. In a word, the rhetoric of the Act, unlike that of the original policy, suggests that it applies to all of Canada's ethnic groups. Again, unlike the original policy, the Act supports measures designed to achieve the *equality* of all Canadians in the economic, social, cultural, and political life of Canada. Thus, the Act can be seen to reflect Charter-endorsed equality rights (under s.15) as well as multicultural rights (under s.27). Most importantly, the Multiculturalism Act provides a *legal* basis for minority ethnic claims at the federal level and, like other federal legislation, it may serve as a model for parallel legislation by particular provinces. At the time of writing, only the province of Saskatchewan has passed a Multiculturalism Act, although five provinces (Alberta, Saskatchewan, Manitoba, Quebec, and Ontario) have adopted multicultural policies.

The federal Multiculturalism Act recognizes multiculturalism as a *fundamental characteristic* of the Canadian heritage. This acknowledgement builds on the constitutional commitment to multiculturalism afforded by s.27 of the Charter. The question now arises: how strong are the protections for multicultural rights afforded by the Charter? Does the Charter endorsement of both equality rights and multicultural rights signify Charter protection for the multicultural ideal of *ethnocultural group equality* across Canada? These questions will be addressed in our analysis of the Charter's provisions for minority rights in the final chapter of this book.

Dominant Conformity: Assumptions Behind the Absorption Model

When we contrast the dominant conformity model with that of multiculturalism, we find that the two models reflect alternate cultural visions of Canada: an élitist vision of one nation/two cultures (Anglo/Franco conformity) as opposed to an egalitarian vision of one nation/many cultures—multiculturalism. While multiculturalism is predicated on the achievement of national unity through the fostering of respect for cultural diversity, dominant conformity is predicated on the achievement of national unity through the cultural assimilation of all ethnic groups to one of the two dominant groups (Anglo- or Franco-conformity).

The dominant conformity model of ethnic integration provides the underlying rhetoric which, historically, has legitimated a large part of public policy and practice directed toward the integration of immigrants in Canada. The concept, dominant conformity, assumes an existing system of ethnic stratification predicated on a highly ethnocentric stance of the established dominant ethnic élite. Majority/minority relations are structured on the assumption of the inherent superiority of established dominant peoples, ethnocultures, and institutions over all others. Given this premise, dominant conformity as a mode of ethnic integration posits a total one-way process of acculturation and assimilation whereby all newcomers abandon their alleged inferior original ethnocultures, institutions, and identities in favour of the alleged superior societal and ethnic model posited by the established dominant group.[16]

Like the melting-pot model, the dominant-conformity model is built on a societal goal of unity in homogeneity, i.e., one nation/one people/one culture. But, unlike the egalitarian melting pot which envisages a 'new nation' created from the equal contributions of all its original ethnic components (a two-way process of acculturation and assimilation), the dominant conformity model is asymmetric and unidirectional: it envisages the absorption of all newcomers through one-way processes of integration to the dominant blueprint.

Early in this century, the dominant-conformity model was rationalized, at least in part, through direct reference to the alleged failure of the American melting pot. R. B. Bennett, for example, used this tactic to support his argument that Canadians must endeavour 'to maintain our civilization at that high standard which has made the British civilization the test by which all other civilized nations in modern times are measured . . . We desire to assimilate those whom we bring to this country to that civilization . . . rather than assimilate our civilization to theirs' (House of Commons Debates 7 June 1928: 3925-7).

In similar vein, but in even stronger words, J.W. Sparling (Woodsworth 1909: Introduction) warned that the massive waves of immigrants to Canada from the alleged backward non-Protestant countries of southern and eastern Europe posed a national danger. Thus, he cautioned: 'Either we must educate and elevate the incoming multitudes or they will drag us and our children down to a lower level. We must see to it that the civilization and ideals of Southeastern Europe are not transplanted to and perpetuated in our virgin soil' (Woodsworth 1909: Introduction).

As a model for reality, the dominant-conformity ideology assumes, first, that the established dominant ethnoculture and institutional framework is inherently superior to that of newcomers; second, that all newcomers will realize and appreciate the superiority of established dominant ways and will be both willing and able to shed their inferior ethnocultures, institutions, and identities in favour of the dominant model. These assumptions in turn are predicated on the existence of a significant political, economic, and social power differential that enables the dominant group to require conformity to its language, religion, laws, ethical standards, rules of etiquette, and customs. In conceptual terms, the model of dominant conformity is predicated on highly institutionalized forms of cultural discrimination: social participation and mobility are conditional on required acculturation to dominant norms. The dominant-conformity model also assumes a high degree of ethnocentrism among the dominant ethnic collectivities and a low degree among immigrant ethnic minorities. Most importantly, it assumes that immigrants are not only willing but also able to become absorbed into the dominant ethnic collectivity and society, that all immigrants are both educable and assimilable.

Given this assimilationist premise, potential immigrants whose ascribed characteristics (race, physical or mental disability) assume them incapable of adapting to dominant norms are denied entry. Dominant conformity also sanctions highly exclusive institutional forms of discrimination (such as expulsion, extermination, or incarceration) against non-conformist minorities whose unwillingness to embrace dominant norms marks them as culturally and/or behaviourally deviant. In short, the degree to which ethnic and other minorities are accorded fundamental human rights and societal opportunities is predicated on the degree to which they are both able and willing to shed their distinctive/deviant attributes and to conform to the dominant ethnic/societal model.

On the question of collective rights, the dominant-conformity model is clear: ethnic minority rights are not recognized; the collective cultural and national group rights of the dominant powers are permanently entrenched. Given these assumptions, ethnic integration would result in a society in which all citizens would be absorbed through one-way processes of acculturation and assimilation to the dominant ethnic collectivity. The society would be characterized by national unity in dominant homogeneity and each citizen's ethnic identity would be coterminous with that of the original dominant population.

The Dominant-Conformity Model at the Levels of Public Policy and Societal Reality

As suggested earlier, Anglo Canadians wished to dissociate themselves from the alleged failure of the American melting pot and to legitimate the separate existence of Canada as a British preserve. The Anglo Canadians' sense of nationalism linked pride in their new country with continuing pride in their alleged Anglo-Saxon ethnic heritage, both of which were strongly associated with ties and loyalties to the British Crown. Thus, from the beginning, many Anglo Canadians were supportive of the view that Canada should develop as a British preserve and an Anglo-Saxon nation. Racial extremists of the day argued that *non-Nordics*[17] were racially inferior, thus they could not be assimilated to the Anglo-Saxon model. They should therefore be barred from immigration to Canada. Their admission might lead to 'miscegenation' and its alleged inevitable consequences—the corruption of the 'pure' Anglo-Saxon stock, the destruction of the 'higher' Anglo-Saxon civilization, and the decay and ruination of the new Canadian nation. Most Anglo Canadians, however, were more optimistic about immigration. They assumed that the superior initiative and strength of the Anglo-Saxon 'race' would acculturate the lower characteristics of the European 'races' to its higher ideals and standards. This position was less overtly racist than that of the extremists, implying cultural rather than biological Anglo-Saxon superiority, and thus allowing for possible acculturation of educable and assimilable newcomers.

The immigration policy predicated on this view welcomed only those immigrants willing to conform to the distinctive and superior, White, Anglo-Saxon, Protestant values, cultural standards, and life ways. Non-Anglo-Saxon Protestant immigration was not considered a real danger as long as it was believed that new immigrants could be acculturated to the ways of the majority through the concerted efforts of dominant group agents, especially educators and Protestant missionaries. However, not all were believed capable of acculturating. Distinctions were clearly drawn between the supposedly lower ethnic groups (peoples from southern and eastern Europe) believed capable of acculturation, and the alleged inferior races (peoples from less civilized regions, marked and isolated by a skin colour barrier) considered incapable of so doing. This racist ideology—one version of the White supremacy theory—was used to justify exclusion of many peoples racially defined as Negroes and Orientals.

While changes in immigration policy over the last decades have markedly reduced the racist bias in the present Act, the treatment of visible immigrants after their arrival in Canada indicates that racial barriers continue to impede ethnic integration. Moreover, as argued earlier, the federal government multicultural policy and the more recent Act, as implemented to date, do not appear to have significantly reduced racial/ethnic antagonisms or shifted the balance of power between majorities and minorities within the racial/ethnic hierarchy. Thus, the goal of immigrant *absorption* continues to be impeded by individual, institutional, and systemic forms of racial discrimination.

Paternalism: Assumptions Behind the Colonialism Model

In our discussion of the origins of ethnic stratification (Chapter Six), we suggested that Blauner's (1972) model of colonizer/colonized relations could be applied to the origins and early development of dominant/aboriginal relations in the Canadian context. Further, in keeping with the stance increasingly documented by spokespersons representing various organizations of Canada's Status Indians, we argued that the cultural policy of the colonizers—that of cultural genocide—was most starkly epitomized in Canada by the paternalistic conditions for the treatment of Status Indians set forth under the Indian Act.

Following from this, the paternalistic model of ethnic relations to be outlined in the following pages will be based on the rhetoric underlying dominant/aboriginal relations in Canada, and, especially, underlying the legal conditions of the Indian Act.

The paternalistic model is highly asymmetric, assuming vast disparities in political, economic, and social power between interacting ethnic collectivities. In a paternalistic relationship the more powerful dominant population is highly ethnocentric: it perceives itself as a superior category of human beings and the less powerful minority population as subhuman or less than human beings. Van den Berghe (1966: 27-9) suggests that the paternalistic model of ethnic relations is based upon the master-servant relationship. From the master's point of view, the minority population is stereotyped as 'childish, immature, irresponsible, exuberant, improvident, fun-loving, good-humored, and happy-go-lucky; in short as inferior but lovable as long as they stay in their place'.

The concept, paternalism, stems from Latin: of or belonging to a father. In practice, a paternalistic system of ethnic relations is one in which the dominant population takes on the role of an authoritarian father toward his children—the childish minorities. The dominant population creates policies, rules, and laws based on a paternalistic ideology of *benevolent despotism* (Van den Berghe: 27): the ruling powers of the father are absolute; the children are denied the fundamental right of self-determination and are required to give unquestioned obedience to the dominant authority. As long as they comply with the dominant 'rules of the game', they will be cared for and protected by the dominant power.

In the colonial era paternalism was rationalized through racist ideologies of White Supremacy based on the equation: White = Might = Right. Paternalistic relations were predicated on two further assumptions held by dominant European powers, i.e., *the white man's burden* and *noblesse oblige*. The white man's burden was to civilize the savages; noblesse oblige meant that privilege, the white man's prerogative, entailed responsibility for the care and protection of the childlike savages. In short, based on the primary assumption that aboriginal peoples were not quite human, the dominant Europeans assumed the obligation of humanizing them. This pattern of paternalistic relations is analogous to the way an authoritative father, operating on the assumption that children are born bad and wild, attempts to morally indoctrinate and control his children.

The Canadian historian, John Maclean, reacting against the overtly paternalistic treatment of aboriginal peoples by early Euro-Canadians, attempted to focus public attention on their way of life. In the preface to his book *Canadian Savage Folk* (1896) he argued:

Close contact with our native tribes shows the mistake we have been making in deciding that ignorance, superstition and cruelty belong to these people . . . A faithful study of the languages and customs compels us to acknowledge that . . . *under the blanket and coat of skin there beats a human heart* . . .[18]

As late as the 1950s, overtly racist views such as those expressed by the French-Canadian writer, Yves Thériault were typical. In *Agaguk* (1971) he says of the Inuit:

Now, Eskimos are unpredictable beings, capable of uncontrolled rage, particularly when they are together in a group. Just like animals who are normally easily frightened or inoffensive but become dangerous when surprised. (p. 186)[19]

Given these racist assumptions, it is not difficult to understand the zeal with which Christian missionaries undertook the civilizing mission behind their white man's burden. Katherine Hughes, in her book *Father Lacombe, The Black-Robe Voyageur* (1920) recounts:

With all the ardors of his warm nature, Father Lacombe burned to reach every tribe on the plains—group after group, to gather these poor nomads in fresh colonies . . . while he pushed again into the wilds with his Red Cross flag and his plough to bring into Christian submission still other bands of savages. (p. 106)

Clearly, the civilizing goal of Christian missionaries extended far beyond their efforts at religious conversion. Bringing the 'savages' into submission entailed a high degree of institutional control over the relocated aboriginal peoples; a concerted effort to eradicate aboriginal customs; and an attempt to induce dominant conformity in all life spheres.

The paternalistic model of ethnic integration resembles the dominant conformity model in terms of asymmetric power relations, a high degree of ethnocentrism among dominant populations, devaluation of minority ethnoculture(s), and required acculturation to dominant norms. In other respects it is based upon significantly different assumptions.

The paternalistic model assumes first and foremost that 'subhuman' aboriginal minorities have permanently limited human capacities. They are not expected to reach maturity; they are regarded as *permanent children*, inherently unable to fully acculturate and assimilate to dominant ways. Operating on these racist assumptions, dominant agents and agencies promote total deculturation, but only partial acculturation. The civilizing mission is thus characterized by a high degree of cultural, institutional, and systemic discrimination against aboriginal minorities. Strictures on the educational process ensure that minorities do not acquire sufficient knowledge and skills to enable them more than minimal participation in dominant institutions. Thus, access to political, social, and economic power is virtually denied and the self-fulfilling prophecy of White Racism is guaranteed. Aboriginal minorities are relegated to the lowest rungs of the ethnic hierarchy, where they are tolerated as long as they 'stay in their place' and are 'seen but not heard'.

Under the paternalistic model of ethnic integration aboriginal minorities come to occupy a permanently inferiorized and stigmatized status, marginal to the dominant society. Their collective stigma is rooted in racial and cultural characteristics assumed by dominant powers to be associated with their 'savage' origin, and which serve to define them as *less than human*. Because this dehumanizing stigma is a permanent one, dominant powers are able to rationalize and eventually to legitimate wholesale violations of the individual and collective human rights of aboriginal minorities. In consequence, aboriginal minorities become *marginalized*—suppressed populations, *in* but not *of* society at large. The paternalistic model thus ensures that the control wielded by dominant powers is not threatened by minority subordinates and that only the individual and collective rights of the dominant population are recognized and respected in society at large.

The outcome of the paternalistic model for ethnic and national identities is very different, in the case of majority as opposed to aboriginal minority populations. For the dominant ethnic collectivity—recognized as human beings—it parallels that of the dominant conformity model, i.e., unity in dominant homogeneity—one dominant nation/culture/people.

For minorities whose aboriginal identities have been stigmatized and dehumanized, whose cultures and institutions have been denigrated and destroyed, and whose identification with the oppressor (Fanon 1967) has been repudiated, the outcome is one of ethnic and national marginality.

Paternalism/Colonialism: Canadian Public Policy and Societal Reality

In Canada, the paternalism model has historically provided the rhetoric behind virtually all varieties of aboriginal policy. In the various Indian Acts (1896-1950), federal policies specifically designed for so-called 'Native Peoples' have given racist, paternalistic assumptions their clearest institutional expression. Waubageshig (1970: 97) argues persuasively that the Indian Act is the 'principal variable of colonialism in Canada'. Further, he contends that the cultural and geographical fragmentation of Canadian aboriginal peoples that has ensued from Colonial 'divide and rule' policies has eased the way for the long-term continuance of Colonial relations between administrative authorities and aboriginal peoples in Canada. Ponting and Gibbins (1980) have provided a socio-political profile of Indian affairs in Canada which affords clear documentation for Waubageshig's view from a non-Indian perspective. And Weaver (1981) has published an excellent analysis of the 'hidden agenda' behind the making of Canadian Indian policy.

Weaver's book was based on several years of intensive research into the politics of the formulation of the 1969 White Paper in Indian Policy. This draft policy statement, designed to terminate special Indian Status in Canada and to assimilate all aboriginal persons, as individuals, to the dominant cultural and institutional blue-print, was proposed by the federal government in 1970. But negative, indeed hos-tile, reaction from nascent Indian organizations and (later) other aboriginal groups, together with widespread public sympathy in favour of aboriginal peoples' expressed desire to preserve their distinctive communities and cultures, led to its withdrawal.

Although the policy outlined in the 1969 White Paper was never formally imple-mented, Ponting and Gibbins agree with Weaver's contention that it has had a last-ing, assimilative influence on federal Indian policy. And, as an indirect consequence, it engendered increasingly stronger, organized aboriginal protest. The relationship between the federal government/majority and aboriginal minorities in the context of the aboriginal protest movement is discussed at length in Chapter Eight.

At this juncture, it may be appropriate to note, in advance, that attempts by abo-riginal political leaders, as well as by a growing cadre of aboriginal cultural élites, to articulate the distinctive cultural value premises behind aboriginal demands for self determination have had little success in persuading federal authorities that aborigi-nal peoples *as nations* should be constitutionally recognized as 'distinct societies' within Canada.

The Status Indian Reserve: A Total Institution[20]

The Indian Act has been the legal instrument responsible for the encapsulation, oppression, neglect, and diminution of Status Indians within the total institution of the reserve. Under this Act, the federal minister of Indian affairs, until recently, has had the ultimate authority over all decisions affecting the lives and destinies of Indians residing on reserves. Throughout the years, the minister and his agents have dominated and controlled all of the bands' resources—land, housing, capital and income, livestock and equipment—and have wielded decision-making authority over medical services, employment, education, wills, and virtually all aspects of Indian life. Even the decision of a Status Indian to give up legal Indian Status has had to be approved. While their special legal Status gives reserve Indians some eco-nomic benefits, such as certain tax exemptions, it systemically violates their funda-mental human rights by heavily restricting their freedom and by keeping them in a perpetual state of dependency (Wilson 1974: 20-2). Under increasing pressure from Indian leaders, Indian affairs ministers have turned over more and more of the responsibility for the everyday administration of reserves to their elected band coun-cils. Yet, ultimate decision-making authority remains in the hands of federal author-ities. In response to increasingly vociferous demands for Indian self-government, the federal government has agreed to turn Indian reserves into self-governing units. But their model (based on delegated authority) still leaves ultimate control in the hands of the state, thus it has been rejected by those Indian leaders who seek independent 'First Nation' status and self-government on the basis of national group rights.

The long-term, unintended, yet disastrous consequence of policies, laws, and practices toward Indians—epitomized by the reserve—is the ugly reality of the self-fulfilling prophecy of White Racism, under the model of paternalism. Treated as irresponsible children, Indians living on reserves have suffered oppression: they have been denied their human right to make the critical decisions affecting their own lives. Assumed to be naturally racially inferior in intelligence to Euro-Canadians, they have been denied equal educational and economic opportunities, and reserves have become riddled with neglect. Substandard housing, breeding disease and death; closed schools due to lack of teachers, heat, and/or running water are but a few examples of continuing dehumanizing life conditions on many reserves.

Status Indians' human right to dignity and respect as persons has been violated at every turn: it has been violated every time an adult Indian has had to ask permission to go about the ordinary business of life. It is not surprising, given these long-term paternalistic conditions, that many reserves have become centres of Indian cultural alienation, characterized by all of the symptoms of the self-fulfilling prophecy of paternalism—poverty, crime, alcohol and drug addiction, apathy and anomie.

Paternalism destroys incentive, stifles initiative, and breeds dependency and despair. Over the years, the more the Canadian government pursued its paternalistic policies, the more the Indians' self-confidence and self-respect were undermined and the cost of paternalistic hand-outs increased. Nevertheless, as Wilson contends, the administration probably found it less expensive to keep them on welfare than to make the huge capital expenditure required to make Indian reserves self-sufficient, independent communities.

While this paternalistic picture of dominant-Indian relations is slowly changing, the long-term outcome of paternalism was to create a stigmatized, dependent, welfare population, whose very existence at the margins of Canadian society demonstrated unequivocally the dehumanizing consequences of denial of human rights and the utter failure of policies predicated on the paternalistic ideology of the white man's burden.

Models of Ethnic Integration: Comparative Implications for Human Rights

The four models of ethnic integration outlined in the foregoing pages have different implications for the kinds of human rights recognized in societies as well as for relationships between ethnic units predicated upon them. All of these models have, in varying degrees, underscored relations between ethnic collectivities in Canadian society. At the level of societal reality, the melting-pot and mosaic models have remained largely mythical, while the dominant-conformity model has underscored dominant/immigrant relations, and the paternalism model has underscored dominant/aboriginal relations.

At the level of rhetoric, the melting-pot and mosaic models are essentially egalitarian with regard to individual human rights and individual opportunities for social mobility, both of which are accorded all citizens regardless of ethnic classification.

Ethnicity does not provide a recognized criterion in either model for social stratification. In their North American, democratic versions, both models are rooted in assumed meritocracies in which differential rewards are accorded on the basis of positional attainment of individuals on criteria of specified qualifications and demonstrated performance. Social stratification in both models thus derives from unequally rewarded social positions based on achieved criteria.

The essential difference between the melting-pot and mosaic ideals lies in their evaluation of ethnocultural distinctiveness and in their assumptions about processes of acculturation and assimilation of ethnic collectivities. The melting pot devalues ethnic distinctiveness and posits total two-way acculturation and assimilation; the mosaic values ethnic distinctiveness and posits partial (mutually controlled and restricted) acculturation and assimilation. Accordingly, in the former model, there is no place for collective rights of distinctive ethnic collectivities; in the latter, the collective rights of all ethnic collectivities are recognized and protected.

In contrast, the dominant-conformity and paternalism models of ethnic integration are essentially inegalitarian or asymmetric in their ethnic orientation. Both models are predicated on racist assumptions which serve to underscore and legitimate a system of ethnic stratification based on ascribed and achieved criteria.

The essential difference between these two models lies in their evaluation and accommodation of ethnic distinctiveness. In the dominant-conformity model, non-violation of the political, economic, and social rights of members of various ethnic minorities is conditional upon their willingness and ability to acculturate to dominant norms and life ways. This implies that various ethnocultural minorities are unequally evaluated in terms of their members' presumed educability and assimilability; presumed non-educable and non-assimilable ethnic collectivities are excluded from the society. In this model, the collective rights of the dominant ethnic collectivity are permanently guaranteed and protected. Alternatively, the collective rights of ethnic minorities are not recognized and institutionalized forms of cultural discrimination ensure denial of minority cultural rights within the society. While the dominant-conformity model makes human rights conditional on acculturation to dominant norms, the paternalistic model goes much further in violating the human rights of minorities. Under paternalism, aboriginal minorities are defined as subhuman and are, accordingly, denied the human rights accorded human beings. Racism provides the ideological underpinnings for a comprehensive system of institutional, systemic, and cultural discrimination against subhuman minorities; institutionalized racism, in turn, ensures that aboriginal minorities become permanently locked into a stigmatized marginal status in society. By way of contrast, the individual and collective rights of the dominant ethnic collectivity are permanently entrenched and strongly enforced throughout the society.

The paternalism model has special implications with regard to the collective aboriginal and national group rights of aboriginal peoples. Because it denies the validity of aboriginal cultures it fails to recognize the vital link between aboriginal peoples, their distinctive ethnocultures and institutions of self-government, and their aboriginal territories. Paternalistic relationships, predicated on cultural genocide, thus give rise to aboriginal claims to nationhood.

While the melting-pot and mosaic models are clearly far less discriminatory in their ideological intent than are the dominant-conformity and paternalism models, they nevertheless can be seen to violate the individual and/or collective human rights of members of some social categories. The melting-pot model clearly denies the collective rights of its constituent ethnocultural collectivities; thus it discriminates against minority members who are unwilling to abandon their distinctive ethnocultures and life ways. In both melting pot and mosaic models, equality of opportunity is conceptualized in terms of standard (same) rather than equivalent (special) treatment. Thus, they both discriminate against those individuals whose authentic disabilities disadvantage them by impeding their access to the opportunities accorded others. At the level of rhetoric, these models do not address the *categorical rights* claims of disabled minorities for whom actual (as opposed to rhetorical) equality of opportunity necessitates equivalent (as opposed to standard) treatment, including the provision of specialized, affirmative measures designed to compensate for and overcome the handicapping effect of their disabilities.

Concluding Comments

In this chapter, we have examined the four major models of ethnic integration which have provided the ideological rhetoric for social policy in North America. In the following chapter, our focus will shift from the level of rhetoric (societal ideals) to the level of reality (societal action). We will analyse the social conditions which give rise to minority protest movements and we will examine the factors responsible for their ultimate success or failure. Minority rights movements, as a particular form of ethnic protest, will be analysed with specific reference to aboriginal peoples, immigrant ethnic minorities, and the Franco-Québécois in Canada.

Notes

1   In the North American context, the classic statement concerning these models is provided by Gordon (1964). Palmer (1976) provides a critical review of the scheme with particular relevance for Canada.

2   The same phenomenon has occurred elsewhere. Britain, for example, has experienced severe problems culminating in sporadic race riots. Richmond (1975-76) gives an excellent comparison of the circumstance in Britain and in Canada.

3   In Canada, Sir Wilfrid Laurier made a strikingly similar analogy, albeit in British cultural terms. He pictured the Canadian mosaic in terms of the Gothic architecture of England, as a cathedral of marble, oak, and granite with each element distinct, yet moulded into a harmonious whole (Yusyk 1967: 7).

4   The arguments in the section to follow represent a distillation of the author's published

commentary on multiculturalism over the last decade. For further elaboration, see Kallen 1982, 1987, and 1990.

5 Report of The Royal Commission on Bilingualism and Biculturalism, *Book IV: The Cultural Contribution of the Other Ethnic Groups*, Ottawa, Information Canada, 1970.

6 *House of Commons Debates (1971)*, Statement of Prime Minister P.E. Trudeau, October 8, 1971.

7 This view was strongly voiced in a number of writings by the late sociologist, John Porter. See, for example, 'Melting Pot or Mosaic: Revolution or Reversion?' in *The Measure of Canadian Society*, Toronto: Gage, 1979.

8 The 'ethnic zoo' analogy was put forward by the political scientist Howard Brotz, in his article on multiculturalism in *Canadian Public Policy* VI, 1 (Winter, 1980).

9 'Just keep dancing' is attributed to Alan Anderson (personal communication).

10 See, especially: K. Peter, 'The Myth of Multiculturalism and Other Political Fables' in Dahlie and Fernando (eds) 1981.

11 This position was forcefully presented by Manoly Lupul in 'Political Implementation of Multiculturalism' in *Journal of Canadian Studies* 17, 1 (Spring, 1982).

12 See, especially: G. Rocher, ' Multiculturalism. Doubts of a Francophone'. Ottawa: Canadian Consultative Council on Multiculturalism, 1976.

13 *House of Commons*, Bill C-93: An Act for the preservation and enhancement of multiculturalism in Canada, The Secretary of State of Canada, 22427-27-11-87.

14 *Equality Now!*, Report of the Special Committee on Visible Minorities in Canadian Society, B. Daudlin, MP (Chair), March 1984; *Multiculturalism: Building the Canadian Mosaic*, Report of the Standing Committee on Multiculturalism, G. Mitges, MP (Chair), June 1987.

15 The *Toronto Star*, 6 February 1988. Reported response of various scholars and spokespersons for Canada's ethnic communities to Bill C-93.

16 Because the model was originally conceived within the North American societal context in which the dominant population was ethnically categorized as Anglo-Saxon, the particularized concept Anglo-conformity was employed to refer to the broader notion of dominant conformity.

17 The racially-intensive label Nordics referred exclusively to Anglo-Saxon Protestants from the British Isles and countries of northern and western Europe. Racial extremists of the day argued that these northern races and northern civilizations were superior to all others (Woodsworth 1972: 164).

18 Emphasis is that of the author. While Maclean's view indicates that he considered the aboriginal peoples to be *human beings*, as such, the tone of the book suggests they were still somewhat childlike and inferior in nature.

19 English translation.

20 The concept *total institution* refers to a physical and social environmental context in which the lives and destinies of insiders are completely controlled and regulated by more powerful outsiders. The concept had its origins in the literature on physically confined populations, in jails, mental institutions, and the like, which documents the paternalistic model of treatment and its self-fulfilling outcome—a syndrome of social and psychological dependency. (See Gove 1976.)

CHAPTER EIGHT

Minority Protest Movements:
The Politicization of Ethnicity

The preceding chapters have illustrated the ways in which institutionalized forms of racism within Canadian society have impeded the processes of ethnic integration and social mobility for members of various ethnic minorities. Institutionalized racism has provided majority authorities with powerful techniques of domination and control over ethnic minorities, and these instruments of human rights violation have enabled ethnic majorities to maintain the established ethnic hierarchy and their superordinate status at its apex.

As long as ethnic minorities accept the existing ethnic hierarchy as legitimate, or as long as they are prevented from acquiring competitive advantages which bring them into direct power struggles with the dominant populations, the established structure of ethnic inequality remains unchallenged.

Within a highly institutionalized system of ethnic stratification, ethnicity may serve the expressive needs of members of ethnic minorities by providing them with a source of roots and a sense of primary group belongingness. For most members, however, it is unlikely fully to meet their instrumental needs, for the corporate ethnic interests of the minority are denied expression in the society.

Earlier, it was suggested that the new ethnicity is highly contingent upon the prevailing social environment. Hence, not until social conditions change markedly, throwing the very legitimacy of the structure of ethnic inequality into question, can the politicization of ethnicity take root among inferiorized and suppressed ethnic minorities.

Sources of Minority Ethnic Protest

Minority ethnic protest develops when social conditions change so suddenly or radically that new alternatives, hopes, and competitive advantages become available for minorities. Such major changes may be a result of forces emanating from outside a community or society. Natural disasters, like floods, famine, or disease, may wipe out entire communities or populations. Similarly, human atrocities such as war and conquest may upset the demographic balance as well as the relative balance of power among the ethnic groups in contact. The influx of new ethnic groups and the exodus of others, urban migration, and shifts due to transient or migrant labour can result in important demographic changes, which in turn can result in positional changes of different ethnic collectivities within the overall hierarchy.

Today, with the increasing modernization, urbanization, and industrialization of societies throughout the world, scientific, economic, and technological developments have emerged as major forces of inter-ethnic conflict and change. In a modern nation such as Canada, there is an ever-increasing demand for new kinds of skills and abilities and a decreasing demand for the traditional artisan. Education assumes a heightened role to satsify the increased demand for highly skilled specialists. When members of ethnic minorities acquire new skills crucial to the economy, they become vitally important to the labour force. Similarly, when ethnic minorities gain purchasing or bargaining power they acquire new competitive advantages. All of these changes can increase the instrumental strength of ethnic minorities and can further the process of politicization of ethnicity.

One of the major modern developments affecting inter-ethnic relations on a global scale is the tremendous advance in the fields of transportation and communication. Whether through travel or telecommunication members of ethnic minorities are today exposed to a plethora of new values, ideas, and standards that challenge established ways and entrenched authorities. Since the 1972 launching of the Canadian satellite, Anik, even the most remote Inuit community in the high Arctic now has access to radio and telephone communication, and most settlements also receive television programs from southern Canada. Exposure to new ideas and values, and comparisons with other ethnic minorities who have improved their status, raise expectations. As a result, many aboriginal and immigrant ethnic minorities have become critical of the existing hierarchy and discontented with their lowly position in it.

In today's global village, ethnic tensions in other countries as well as voiced minority discontent within Canada have an immediate impact on Canadians. The media focus on violence and sensationalism makes events depicting ethnic conflict prime targets for daily news coverage, editorials, television documentaries, and so forth. In turn, this constant exposure renders the instrumental aspect of ethnicity highly salient. Most important for this discussion are the political strategy models provided minority ethnic leaders for the pursuit of instrumental corporate ethnic goals. Guerrilla tactics, hijackings, and myriad other acts of sabotage are globally communicated in vivid media imagery on an almost continuous basis.

Provision of successful role models for emulation by minorities throughout the world is a crucial aspect of modern communication. The post-World War II achievement of independence and nationhood by formerly colonized peoples throughout Africa had a marked influence on the global development of Black Nationalism. Black Power movements in the West Indies, the United States, and Canada have in turn influenced protest movements among other ethnic minorities, such as nationalist movements in Quebec, and among Canada's aboriginal peoples. In Quebec, members of the ill-fated FLQ (Front de Libération du Québec) initially identified themselves as the alleged 'White Niggers of America' (Vallières 1971), and early nationalist movements among Canada's Indians emphasized 'Red Power' (Stewart 1970).

The spread of the minority coalition idea—as exemplified in the concepts of Third World (developing countries, previously subject to overseas colonialism) and Fourth World (aboriginal nations, subject to internal colonialism)—can be largely attributed to developments in transportation and communication. Identification with the plight of similarly disadvantaged and inferiorized minorities throughout the world has sparked efforts of leaders of ethnic minorities to expand their power bases by forming coalitions to pursue common ethnopolitical goals.

The Quest for Roots, Rights, and Empowerment

Minority ethnic protest movements represent a particular kind of social movement, one which arises in response to long-term collective disadvantage and inferiorization of minorities, resulting from *racist-motivated* forms of discrimination.

Clark *et al.* (1975: Introduction) define a social movement as a social process through which substantial numbers of participants attempt to bring about or to resist social change. It is a conscious effort to create new social and cultural frameworks or designs for living, or to restore old ones. Following the approach of the 'Chicago School' these scholars argue that minority discontent is rooted in profound dissatisfaction with prevailing life conditions arising out of perceived value inconsistencies. Discontent may arise from a perceived conflict between values, from a perceived discrepancy between values and their implementation, from a perceived gap between expectations and achievements, from status inconsistency, and from a host of similar variables. Whatever its perceived source, discontent is expressed in a rejection of societal values, norms, and/or leaders and an attempt to find meaningful alternatives.

The process of organization of the minority in order to achieve better life conditions involves the formulation of guidelines for new lifestyles (group ideologies) and the gaining of the discontenteds' commitment to the new designs for living. Minority discontent is initially unfocused. Before demands for change can be made, it must be mobilized and directed toward clearly defined goals. Central to this initial phase of minority organization is the rejection by minorities of majority-imposed *inferiorizing* labels and their replacement with positive minority self-definitions. This change in nomenclature—from Nigger to Black, from Indian to First Nation, from Jap/enemy alien to Japanese Canadian—symbolizes a shift from negative to positive minority identities, a shift which is essential in order to mobilize minority discontent around human rights and empowerment goals.

When more and more members of an ethnic minority regard the existing system of ethnic stratification as unjust and corrupt, *contrast conceptions* develop which stereotype the majority as evil perpetrators of human rights violations and the minority as virtuous victims of majority discrimination. Such contrast conceptions heighten *consciousness of kind* among members of the minority ethnic collectivity and strengthen the salience of ethnic group boundaries. They also reinforce positive minority identities and, at the same time, provide moral justification for concerted, aggressive action against the alleged enemy. In this way, contrast conceptions facilitate mobilization, focusing and directing minority discontent toward the alleged majority persecutors.

Examples of contrast conceptions abound in the protest literature. The following illustration is fairly typical. Here the contrast is between the Euro-Canadian majority (paleface) and the aboriginal minority (Red People) depicted in Caibaiosai's 'The Politics of Patience' (Waubageshig 1970): 'YOU RED PEOPLE ARE STRONG . . . much stronger than PALEFACE' (p. 146). 'We have survived over four hundred and seventy years of the worst treatment possible, and we still are STRONG. All the paleface has to show for these years is his loot, but . . , his putty hands grow more and more spastic, his lies more and more obvious' (pp. 151-2).

Minority ethnic protest movements often gain impetus from marginal members, highly assimilationist in orientation, who realistically assess their own chances for status improvement in terms of the collective advancement of their ethnic community. Frustrated ethnic marginals, prevented from attaining majority ethnic status, may seek to assume leadership of their own ethnic group in order to mobilize members around collective empowerment goals. Early leaders tend to stem from the ranks of the well-educated and politically sophisticated ethnic élites capable of manipulating their ethnicity to further their own political and economic interests. In order to win and hold the collective support of members of their communities they must establish personal credibility. This involves convincing ethnic compatriots that their personal goals are coincident with the ultimate goals of the movement and that both are legitimate.

A second and critical task of leaders of minority protest movements is the mobilization of members to participate in activities designed to effect social change. Clark *et al.* (1975) posit four key variables affecting the potential for success of a social movement's mobilization of members: the development of a unifying ideology; the recruitment of willing, able, and representative leadership; the availability of channels for communication and the existence/cultivation of networks of co-operative relationships; the development of an autonomous organizational base.

In the case of minority ethnic protest movements, we would posit three additional variables: formulation of a *legitimating* (as well as unifying) ideology, to justify protest; formalization of corporate ethnic strategies and goals; and organization of the ethnic collectivity as a pressure group.

Another factor in the effective organization of minority protest movements is the nature and extent of social segmentation (cleavages between groups) in the society at large. Minority discontent is more likely to give rise to protest movements in strati-fied societies marked by great disparities in cultural values and in political, econom-ic, and social power between groups. Further, in stratified societies minorities will be more likely to have a heightened sense of collective consciousness, agreed-upon group values and goals, existing channels of communication, and networks of co-operative relationships with which to build an organizational base for protest move-ments.

The conceptual distinction between 'communal' and 'associational' forms of minority organization (the *gemeinschaft/gesellschaft* typology) has important implica-tions for mobilization and retention of members of protest movements (Clark *et al.* 1975). Communal groups are based on traditional cultural and kinship linkages between people (ethnicity). Associational groups are based on special interests (polit-ical, economic, religious, civic). Communal groups are more likely than association-al groups to have value consensus beyond one set of issues, and are more likely to have developed an organizational base for a protest movement.

These observations are closely related to the conceptual distinction between [eth-nic] *group* and *category* (see pages 67-8). Members of minority *groups* with the re-quisite institutional infrastructure for maintenance and transmission of a distinctive subculture or ethnoculture are more likely to have and/or to develop the collective consciousness and the organizational basis for a successful protest movement than are members of minority *categories*. A minority category represents a conceptual or statistical classification of a population based on one or more criteria (race, age, gen-der) which may or may not give rise to a sense of collective consciousness or to minority organization. Minority categories (e.g., aboriginal people) are more likely than minority groups (e.g., Inuit of Nunavut) to be represented empirically by dis-persed, fragmented population aggregates whose members' only common attribute is the inferiorizing label imposed upon them by majority authorities. The propensi-ty for factionalism to impede organization for minority protest is, therefore, much greater within minority categories than within minority groups.

The course and potential success of a minority protest movement is determined by the continual interaction of internal (minority) and external (majority) forces as well as by changes in the broader environment. A crucial task for minority leader-ship is to create and maintain in-group solidarity. Lines of fragmentation based on differences in values, interests, priorities, and sources of discontent among minority members must be contained through the development of a strong collective com-mitment to the ideology and goals of the movement. Rivalries among minority lead-ers must be resolved so that leadership is perceived by both insiders and outsiders as representative of the membership of the movement.

Lobbying efforts by minority representatives must convince majority authorities that minority demands are valid and must be dealt with. When minority ethnic lead-ers begin to lobby influential majority bodies and governmental officials in pursuit of corporate ethnic goals, the relative success of their early efforts will depend on many factors, including the key instrumental variables associated with ethnic group viability, outlined in Chapter Four (see Table 1; pages 164-5). Two of the most important factors influencing minority lobbying efforts will be: (1) the credibility of ethnic leaders and the legitimacy of their cause, as perceived by the majority bodies being lobbied; and (2) the demonstrable strength of minority ethnic political, economic, and social power, and the degree to which majority bodies regards minority protest as a palpable threat to their entrenched societal dominance and control.

Dominant bodies may perceive ethnic minority demands as both legitimate and threatening but they may, nevertheless, be unwilling and/or more realistically unable to accede to these demands, at least in the short term. In response, they may attempt to appease and contain minority ethnic demands through strategies designed to maintain majority hegemony. They may, for example, accede to limited, expressive (cultural) demands of ethnic minorities in order to contain more threatening instrumental (political) demands. As pointed out in Chapter Seven, some scholarly critics have suggested that the federal policy of multiculturalism within a bilingual framework essentially represents a strategy of appeasement and containment, designed to contain the conflicting empowerment demands of the Third Force (see p. 211) and the French nationalists through limited appeasement of the cultural demands of the Third Force, and through major concessions to the linguistic demands of French supporters of bilingualism and biculturalism.

Another common strategy employed by dominant bodies is to decapitate the minority by co-opting their most effective leaders and incorporating them into positions of power within the dominant establishment. This strategy maintains dominant hegemony by simultaneously depriving the minority of leadership skills and power and buttressing the dominant society with additional talent (Shibutani and Kwan 1965: 334-6). In Canada this strategy may have been utilized to diffuse and contain at least three minority ethnic protests over the last several decades. Three powerful and potentially threatening minority ethnic leaders have been given important governmental posts: Pierre Vallières (Franco-Québécois Independence), Harold Cardinal (Red Power), and Stanley Haidasz (Third Force).

A third technique of dominant management of ethnic minority demands is through government funding of minority ethnic organizations, legitimated under a special policy rubric. Funding bodies are controlling agencies. The dominant fund-giving agency sets the terms under which funds are allotted, selects the recipients, and regulates distribution and expenditure. Hence, government funding allows subtle dominant intervention in minority affairs: the ethnic minority is kept in a dependent position, and minority ethnic protest is diffused.

Earlier, we drew attention to this phenomenon in connection with a critique of multicultural policy (see page 175). Ponting and Gibbins (1980: 124-5) provide incontrovertible evidence of the foregoing principles in their description of the nature of 'socio-fiscal control' exercised by the federal government over Indians. Socio-fiscal control may be exercised in a blatant fashion to curb political deviance, as when the Department of Indian Affairs and Northern Development (DIAND) withheld funds from the Dene and Métis organizations in the Mackenzie Valley until they ended their political squabbling and agreed on a joint position in land claim negotiations with DIAND.

Currently in Canada, minority organizations within the three major ethnic status categories—charter, immigrant, and aboriginal populations—are funded by the Department of the Secretary of State under special policy rubrics. Many minority ethnic organizations (e.g., aboriginal organizations) were virtually created by government funding and remain almost totally dependent on government handouts for their survival. Few Canadian ethnic minorities have sufficient economic power to refuse government funding and the intrusion in their affairs that it entails.[1]

Clark *et al.* (1975) suggest that the response of majority authorities (in most instances, governments) to minority protest may take the form of indifference, accommodation, and/or obstruction. If management techniques—like modes of federal socio-fiscal control—fail to diffuse and contain minority discontent and protest, dominant bodies may resort to more coercive measures, i.e., they may employ various techniques of domination, as outlined in Chapter Six.

A response of indifference is most likely when the movement is not perceived as a threat of any kind by governments (e.g., Jesus Freaks). Accommodation implies a willingness of governments to negotiate, based upon the recognition of some minority demands as valid and based also upon the perception of the minority movement as non-threatening, provided that its demands are addressed (e.g., multicultural movement). A response of obstruction is most likely if the success of the movement is perceived by governments to threaten the social order (e.g., the Front de Libération du Québec). While these conceptual distinctions are important for analytic purposes, in reality a combination of responses may occur. A government may accommodate a minority protest movement (or be indifferent) but it may obstruct particular tactics. For example, the Government of Canada has accepted the demands of the aboriginal movement for settlement of aboriginal land claims and has accepted the *principle* of aboriginal self-government, but the armed protest of Mohawk Indians against encroachment on their alleged lands, during the Oka confrontation, was forcibly curtailed by police and armed forces.

Routinization of Charisma: Prerequisite for Institutionalization of the Minority Movement

When their demands for reform are continually and effectively blocked, the ethnic minority may adopt various strategies of adaptation (Wallace 1956). Original leaders, drawn from the ranks of marginal or assimilationist minority élites, may be replaced by new, charismatic leaders, bent on cultural transformation. The authority of the charismatic leader does not rest primarily on the individual's social status. Initially, the leader's authority derives from a special quality of personality, a personal power of extraordinary magnetism that attracts followers.

A major problem deriving from the nature of charismatic leadership is what Max

Weber termed 'routinization of charisma'. Initially, followers are drawn to the movement more through emotional commitment to the leader than through ideological commitment to the cause. It is, therefore, of the utmost importance that the initial, personal power of the leader be converted into the authority of office within a stable institutional framework. The process by which routinization of charisma is accomplished is a critical issue in movement organization; if it does not occur, leadership authority cannot be delegated and distributed to other personnel, and the movement itself may die with the death or failure of its original leader.

While examples of failure abound, two cases of successful routinization of charisma are provided by the Hutterites (founded by Jacob Hutter) and the Parti Québécois (founded by René Lévesque). The former provides an example of a successful, introverted/expressive, religious revitalization movement, previously discussed in Chapter Four; the latter is an example of a successful, extroverted/instrumental, political movement, to be discussed later in this chapter.

Minority protest movements frequently fail to achieve their original ideals, but some succeed at least in part by compromising ofttimes unrealistic goals and by adapting group ideologies and strategies in order to gain acceptance by insiders and outsiders. When movements succeed, they become 'routinized' (in Weber's classic terms): they become institutionalized in a stable organizational form. They may become absorbed through legislation as part of the majority society; they may develop organizational bases independent of the majority society; they may overthrow the majority order and establish their own organizational base as dominant. Whatever happens, minority protest movements leave their mark on society. They identify an area of perceived human rights violation needing redress; even if they fail to achieve such redress, they provide the inspiration for future movements which may arise to revitalize the quest.

Types of Minority Ethnic Protest Movements: Contention and Revitalization

In broad terms, the goals of minority ethnic protest movements are twofold: (1) to eradicate the cultural and structural bases of minority oppression, diminution, and neglect in the society; and (2) to attain ethnocultural legitimacy, self-determination, and empowerment for the minority ethnic collectivity.

Minority protest in pursuit of corporate ethnic goals may take the form of *contention*, leading to movements for social and political reform, or of *revitalization*, leading to more radical, secessionist, or revolutionary movements.

In *contention*, the ethnic minority protests against its subordinate status and disadvantaged life conditions and demands ethnic group equality within the existing societal order. Contention may be predicated on either a melting-pot or a mosaic model of ethnic integration, depending on the degree of importance attached to ethnocultural distinctiveness by the minority. In the former case, the minority will demand recognition of their fundamental individual human rights; in the latter, demands will be based on recognition of both individual and collective rights.

The evolution of Black Protest in the United States is instructive here. The early Civil Rights Movement, led by the Reverend Martin Luther King, Jr, sought social reforms through legislation aimed at guaranteeing the individual rights of Black Americans—the melting-pot model. Later forms, under the rubric of Black Power, focused on collective economic and political rights—the mosaic model. Full-blown, the Black Power movement became Black Nationalism (Malcolm X 1966; Carmichael and Hamilton 1967) and the minority response of contention gave way to revitalization. Nationalistic revitalization movements among American Blacks have assumed a wide range of forms: separatist, secessionist, religious, and revolutionary (Killiam 1968; Kilson 1975). The Black Muslims (Lincoln 1961) provide an outstanding example of a religious revitalization response, while the now-legendary Black Panthers provide a well-known example of a revolutionary formation among Black Americans.

In *revitalization*, the ethnic minority seeks to establish a viable new ethnocultural form, designed to meet the present and future needs of its members within a new societal order or, failing this, outside the existing social order. Revitalization is predicated on holistic ethnocultural transformation: it presents a design for a new ethnic world order. Revitalization thus necessitates a pluralistic model of ethnic integration or a model of ethnic separation. The ideological orientation is on collective rights, sometimes emphasized at the expense of individual rights. The latter is most likely to be the case in religious revitalization movements, such as the Black Muslims (Lincoln 1961).

A revitalization movement represents a long-term collective response not only to oppression, neglect, and diminution, but also to severe ethnocultural deprivation or alienation. It offers hope to those who had long given up hope for human dignity, cultural legitimacy, and/or status improvement. The theme of revitalization, whether couched in religious or secular terms, is to build a better world. Its premises, strategies, and goals, articulated in a clearly defined ideology, tend to be framed in terms of contrast conceptions; i.e., it conveys a portrait of conflict between the minority ethnic group and its opponent(s) as a historical struggle between the good ethnic insiders and the evil outsiders. The ideology of revitalization not only denies the majority claim to superior status, but affirms the alleged moral and ethical superiority of the minority. The majority is depicted as the evil oppressor and is blamed for the disabilities and sufferings of the allegedly innocent minority victims. Revitalization of the good life of the minority, it is argued, necessitates the expulsion of evil, i.e., the elimination of the majority persecutors and the creation or recreation of the 'just society' by members of the ethnic minority. Revitalization thus involves a deliberate, organized effort by members of ethnic minorities to create a totally new social and cultural world in accordance with their own values, goals, and standards (Wallace 1956).

Revitalization may involve a politically revolutionary response, in which members of ethnic minorities attempt to overthrow the established social order or politically secede to build their own version of the truly just society. These responses are exemplified in the goals of some Black nationalist movements in the USA, as well as some Franco-Québécois nationalists in Canada. It may, on the other hand, lead to a reactionary or counter-revolutionary movement, or to a response of near-total withdrawal from the existing social order through ethnocultural secession. The latter response is typical of religious revitalization movements, particularly in their early stages of development. In the Canadian context, the Hutterites provide a good case in point.

While it is important to distinguish between the models of contention and revitalization for purposes of analysis, the reader should note that, at the level of empirical reality, the boundaries between the two analytic constructs may overlap, particularly with reference to the priority accorded the cultural dimension of protest. Later in this chapter, I conceptualize the multicultural movement in Canada as an example of contention. However, within this overall movement, some ethnic minorities have from time to time revitalized particular aspects of their cultural traditions (religion, language, and nationality, for example) in ways that have markedly altered the lifestyles of ethnic members. Among Jews, for example, religious differentiation, commitment to Israel, and the shift from Yiddish to Hebrew as the 'ethnic' language have led to marked alterations in ethnocultural lifestyles and have increased their diversity (Kallen 1977). Elsewhere (Kallen 1989), I have conceptualized the current Gay and Lesbian Liberation Movement (in contrast to the Gay and Lesbian Rights Movement) as a revitalization movement, on the ground that, in large urban areas of North America, it has led to the creation of new and distinct communities and sub-cultures (without roots in an historical tradition). Moreover, these gay and lesbian communities have developed the necessary institutional infrastructures through which to transmit their distinctive sub-cultural lifestyles through time.

From Contention to Revitalization: The Evolution of Minority Protest

We suggested earlier that movements for social reform generated by ethnic minorities often gain impetus from marginal or assimilationist members, who realistically assess their own chances for status improvement in terms of the collective advancement of their ethnic community. Contention often develops when frustrated ethnic élites, denied access to valued social positions and prevented from attaining majority ethnic status, re-identify strongly with their own ethnic group, assume leadership, and mobilize discontent.

Reformer leaders support the ideals of the established order and thus can often rally support from both dominant and minority ethnic collectivities through mass appeals to public opinion. An outstanding illustration is provided in the case of Martin Luther King, leader of the American Civil Rights Movement. In the Canadian context, William Wuttanee provides an example among Indian leaders (see Wuttanee 1971).

Attempts to overthrow the existing order or secede from it do not usually occur until leaders of ethnic minorities have failed or given up hope of achieving desired reforms. More radical leaders may then attempt to organize subversive revolutionary movements utilizing illegal violent tactics such as terrorism and guerrilla warfare. Militant Black Nationalist movements in the United States, and in Canada, the FLQ (Front de Libération du Québec) and the NARP (National Alliance for Red Power) provide striking examples.

Minority Rights Movements

Minority rights movements represent a particular form and direction of collective minority protest. This type of social movement is most likely to emerge when minority discontent focuses on the inconsistency between declared societal ideals endorsing human rights principles and the non-implementation of these ideals in public institutions and in public practice.

Ironically, as pointed out more than a century ago by Alexis de Tocqueville (quoted in Clark *et al.* 1975: 11): 'generally speaking, the most perilous moment for a bad government is one when it seeks to mend its ways.' When governments begin to replace discriminatory social policies and laws with anti-discriminatory, human rights instruments, the expectations of minorities, the targets of discrimination, begin to rise. When minority expectations rise at a faster rate than actual achievements, the gap between expectations and achievements widens, and minority discontent escalates.

When human rights principles become legally entrenched, it follows that minority expectations will reach new heights. Minority expectations for explicit statutory and constitutional recognition of minority rights and for actual equality of societal opportunities may then come to outstrip the manifest increase in achievements. When this happens, minority discontent rises palpably.

The emergence and proliferation of minority rights movements in Canada over the last two decades provides evidence for this theoretical position. Minority protest on the part of both ethnic and non-ethnic groups initially focused on policy changes. In the 1970s (the 'human rights decade') protest came increasingly to incorporate demands for legal protection for minority rights under the enumerated non-discriminatory grounds of statutory human rights instruments. Since the advent of the Charter in 1982, minority rights issues have become constitutionalized and minority protest has focused on constitutional changes designed to guarantee minority rights. Actual achievements have lagged behind soaring minority expectations. Accordingly, expressed minority discontent, in the form of continued lobbying for change and legal claims for redress against violations of minority rights put forward at both the statutory and constitutional levels, has increased. These general observations will be documented in our analysis of the legal framework of human rights protection in Canada presented in Chapters Nine and Ten.

Minority Rights Movements and Human Rights Claims

The conceptual distinction between contention and revitalization as forms of minority rights movements has important implications for the nature of human rights claims by minority organizations. Drawing upon the typology of human rights claims developed in the Introduction to this book, we will argue that contention focuses on individual, categorical, and/or collective rights claims, while revitalization tends to prioritize collective rights claims, including nationhood claims, over and above individual and categorical rights claims.

Individual rights claims represent demands for recognition and protection of the individual human rights of minority members. Such claims may seek specified changes in constitutional and/or statutory law.

Categorical rights claims represent demands for collective redress against the adverse impact of systemic discrimination upon the minority as a whole. Such claims may seek the implementation of affirmative action measures designed to remedy group inequities. Like individual rights claims, categorical claims do not rest on assumptions about cultural distinctiveness or alternate lifestyles, thus they can justifiably be put forward by representatives of minorities with and without a viable cultural base. Accordingly, members of non-ethnic as well as ethnic minorities may put forward categorical rights claims.

Collective rights claims assume the right of a minority as a collectivity to express and perpetuate a distinctive ethnoculture or sub-culture. Collective rights claims may therefore only be justifiably put forward by representatives of minorities with a viable ethnocultural or sub-cultural base. *National rights* (nationhood) claims, as a distinct form of collective rights claim, are predicated on a demonstrable and integral link between a particular ethnic group, its ancestral territory, and its distinctive ethnoculture. Such claims can only justifiably be put forward by those ethnic groups with an ancestral territorial base (homeland) within the state.

Differential Minority Ethnic Status and Collective Rights Claims: Charter, Immigrant, and Aboriginal Ethnic Collectivities

In the current Canadian context, differential ethnic status, i.e., charter, immigrant, or aboriginal status, has important implications for the kinds of minority protests that arise, and for the kinds of categorical and collective human rights claims proposed by ethnic minority organizations. In the following pages, three minority ethnic protest movements will be examined in light of these considerations. The human rights framework for our analysis is provided in Table 5. Discussion will focus on the collective and categorical human rights claims made by representatives of the three protest movements. Individual claims put forward by particular minority members on the basis of perceived human rights violations are not included in the discussion; cases based on such claims are detailed in Chapter Nine.

Table 5 Minority Ethnic Protest Movements and Human Rights*

Minority Ethnic Status	Categorical	Cultural (Linguistic Religious)	Territorial National	Aboriginal
Charter: Québécois Independence	x	x	x	–
Immigrant: Multiculturalism	x	x	–	–
Aborigines: Aboriginal Rights and New Nationhood	x	x	x	x

x *Kinds of Rights Claimed*

* The discussion of the three minority ethnic protest movements will highlight those aspects most relevant to our focus on human rights. For those readers who wish to pursue the topics in greater depth, selected references are provided throughout the text.

Three Minority Ethnic Protest Movements

Breton (1978: 65) has identified three broad movements of minority ethnic protest operative in Canada: the Québécois Independentist movement, the Multiculturalism movement, and the Red Power movement.[2] These three social movements represent the differential responses of charter, immigrant, and aboriginal minorities to their subordinate status within Canadian society. As Breton points out, each of these movements is heterogeneous, i.e., each rubric covers a variety of different ethnic organizations, platforms, and proposals. Moreover, none of the movements can be taken to represent all of the diverse communities and organizations within the ethnic category as a whole. For the present analysis, which focuses on the human rights implications of the movements, it is the differentiation *between* rather than within these movements which is salient.

Franco-Québécois Independence Movement

The Franco-Québécois Independence movement may be conceptualized as a revitalization movement bent on politico-economic sovereignty and cultural transformation. As such, it represents a politically revolutionary response to long-term ethnic inequality. Franco-Québécois demands for a sovereign Quebec are rooted in claims based on the constitutionally recognized charter group status of the French as one of Canada's two founding nations.

The Franco-Québécois Independence movement germinated in the Quiet Revolution following the election of the Quebec Liberal party in 1962. The electoral slogan of the Liberal party, *Maîtres chez nous* or 'Masters in our own home' symbolized a radical shift in the political, economic, and cultural components of the nationalism of French Quebeckers, away from passive maintenance of the provincial *status quo*—symbolized by the slogan *la survivance*—to active control of the development of the state (Lee 1979). A variety of less radical options to Québécois independence emerged in this period, but widespread disillusionment with their failure led more and more Quebeckers to favour the route of independence (Morris and Lanphier 1977).[3]

Lee (1979) provides an insightful analysis of the evolution of nationalism in Quebec that clearly shows the way in which the Franco-Québécois Independence movement represents a revitalization response to the suppression of long-term yearnings for new nationhood among French Quebeckers.[4]

Traditional Nationalism: La Survivance

Politically, traditional nationalism also emphasized ethnic isolation, as a means of preserving French/English 'unity in duality' within Canada. The mission of Quebec was to guard French-Canadian culture, and to protect and defend provincial rights from federal intervention. Cultural nationalism implied the maintenance of the religious, linguistic, and cultural *status quo* through the continuing battle against assimilation to Anglo influences.

Modern Nationalism: Maîtres chez nous

Lee (1979) argues persuasively that the increasing impact of industrialization, urbanization, and political modernization upon Quebec from without, and later from within, the boundaries of the province, virtually destroyed the bases of traditional nationalism, as its conservative bias proved both inappropriate and ineffective in a modernizing Quebec fraught with radical changes in all spheres of life.[5] Together with *maîtres chez nous*, the liberal slogan of the 1960s was *Il faut que ça change* (Things must change). As the relative isolation of the Quebec French collectivity was penetrated, the goal of self-sufficiency became dissociated from the need to maintain the *status quo* and nationalism was re-defined as the need to control both internal institutions and relations with the outside. Expanding Anglo-American capitalism had created an increasingly economically dependent French urban ethnoclass as the 'habitant' population, without available land to farm and without modern occupational skills, surged to the city. In the face of the subordinate economic status of the French 'in their own country', the modernizing élite took steps to increase the control of the state in economic matters (e.g., nationalization of Hydro Quebec).

Lee contends that new responsibilities in the areas of taxation, health and welfare, and education necessitated a marked expansion of Quebec bureaucracy. Thus, political nationalism included the administration of new spheres of activity associated with expanding industrialization as well as social and welfare services previously managed by the Catholic church. In turn, cultural nationalism meant the assumption of control over cultural matters, and the concomitant breaking of the church's monopolistic front.

With the decline in power and ideological salience of the Catholic church, the focus of French cultural control shifted to issues of language and immigration. In this process, the *maîtres chez nous* nationalism moved from a goal of bilingualism and biculturalism for French Canadians throughout Canada, to one of unilingualism and uniculturalism for the Franco-Québécois in the Quebec state. As the Province of Quebec assumed a more active role in decisions concerning its economic, educational, and health and welfare institutions, it provided a new territorial basis for French ethnic alignment and identification. Ethnic territoriality for the French thus became disassociated from Canada and re-defined in terms of the 'state' of Quebec, since, by definition, a state has jurisdiction over a given territory. In this process, the boundaries of the French-Canadian ethnic collectivity disappeared and new, narrower, group boundaries emerged around a new Franco-Québécois ethnic identity.

According to Lee, the political implications of this shift in ethnic group boundaries are manifold, and all signs point toward the movement for Franco-Québécois independence and nationhood. At the time of writing, Lee asserted that all scenarios concerned the self-sufficiency and self-determination of Quebec, not Canada, and not French Canada. While the modern nationalist options range from the *status quo* to separatism, Lee contended that the options of decentralization, special status, or sovereignty-association were probably among the more viable scenarios in the immediate future.

More than a decade later, the scenarios outlined by Lee were in the forefront of the protracted debate on Canadian unity—an observation to be elaborated later in this analysis.

The Revitalization Option: Conceptualizing Franco-Québécois Independence in Human Rights Terms

The Franco-Québécois Independence movement is predicated on both instrumental and expressive corporate ethnic goals. Demands for political autonomy and control over economic resources rest, in part, on claims for categorical rights as redress for long-term political and economic discrimination. However, an important aspect of alleged past discrimination has been its linguistic basis (Joy 1972); thus, demands for linguistic rights are closely associated with politico-economic demands. Language is also importantly linked with expressive goals: the ethnocultural identity of the Franco-Québécois has a strong linguistic character. Finally, and most importantly, because of their ethnic status as a charter group the Franco-Québécois can make nationhood claims based on collective national group rights. In this connection, the self-definition of the Franco-Québécois as a distinctive ethnocultural collectivity whose ancestral homeland is the Province of Quebec, is critical.

The late René Lévesque, the prime catalyst and charismatic leader of the Franco-Québécois Independence Movement, clearly identified his people's ethnocultural destiny with their right to their ancestral homeland. In his seminal book, *An Option For Quebec* (1968), he asked:

Of all the rights that are recognized—or at least proclaimed—by twentieth century man, is there a more fundamental one than the right to a genuine homeland, the right to live (and hence to work) in one's own language, the right to have a daily environment in harmony with one's culture and mentality, the right to take part in the concert of nations, freely and directly? (Lévesque 1968: 116)

His own answer, succinct and to the point, provided the charter for the Franco-Québécois Independence movement:

If we want to remain French, if we want to conduct our lives in French, like a normal nation, there is no path to take other than that which leads to the political sovereignty of Quebec, along with an economic union with the rest of Canada. This means independence without total separation. This means freedom from our perpetual minority status to associate ourselves in true liberty and equality [with English Canada]. (Ibid.: 118)[6]

With the 1976 electoral victory of the Parti Québécois under Lévesque's leadership, the politicization of the Franco-Québécois Independence movement as a revitalization movement became full blown. While not all Québécois independentists supported the Parti Québécois, as a political party it managed to bring together most of the small, independentist groups under a social democratic program with a strong emphasis on cultural nationalism (Morris and Lanphier 1977: 249). This cultural nationalism was clearly expressed in Bill 101, which made French the single official language in Quebec.

Notwithstanding internal differences regarding the precise blueprint for Quebec's future, Lévesque's sovereignty-association model for Québécois independence was proposed in the historical 1980 referendum question:

The Government of Quebec has made public its proposal to negotiate a new agreement with the rest of Canada, based on the equality of nations; this agreement would enable Quebec to acquire the exclusive power to make its laws, administer its taxes and establish relations abroad—in other words, sovereignty—and at the same time, to maintain with Canada an economic association including a common currency; any change in political status resulting from these negotiations will be submitted to the people through a referendum; on these terms, do you agree to give the Government of Quebec the mandate to negotiate the proposed agreement between Quebec and Canada?

Despite the 59.5 per cent rejection of this option in favour of federalism by the people of Quebec, Lévesque refused to abandon his dream for a revitalized Franco-Québécois nation.[7] To his campaign supporters he offered these words of hope: 'Let us accept, but not let go, never lose view of such legitimate, universal objectives as equality. It will come' (*Globe and Mail*, 21 May 1980).

Into the 1990s: The Québécois Quest for Nationhood, Equality, and Cultural Survival

In the wake of the Quebec referendum in May 1980, the federal government made a commitment to renew Canadian federalism through greater recognition of the needs and aspirations of Quebec. But, in November of 1981, Premier Lévesque refused to endorse the constitutional agreement (enacted on April 17, 1982 as the Canada Act) because it was deemed to abrogate the Government of Canada's commitment of 1980 and to counter the particular interests and historic rights of Quebec society, the only society in Canada with a French-speaking majority (Remillard, in Behiels 1989: 29). Premier Lévesque's refusal to sign the constitutional accord of 5 November 1981 clearly demonstrated his fervent commitment to the principles of Québécois nationhood. At that time, he proclaimed that Quebec, as an equal partner in Confederation, had the right to veto a constitutional package that did not recognize and protect the special status and character of the Quebec nation (*Globe and Mail*, 25 Nov. 1981).

The death of René Lévesque, and the election of a Liberal government under Robert Bourassa in 1985, put Lévesque's dream of sovereignty association for Quebec on hold. Nevertheless, since this time, the Franco-Québécois quest for equality with English Canada and survival as a distinct society within (or in some form of association with) the Canadian state has continued to gain salience in the context of three national debates: the controversy surrounding Bill 101, Quebec's French Language Charter; the constitutional debates over the provisions of the proposed 1987 Meech Lake Accord and the 1992 Charlottetown Accord; and the question of Quebec sovereignty.

Bill 101: Overriding the Constitutional Charter

In the 1980s, negative reaction against the provisions of Bill 101 on the part of Quebec's linguistic minorities, particularly its long-established anglophone population, led to a series of court cases challenging the constitutionality, under the Charter, of section 58 of the Bill that dictates that public signs must be in French. In 1988, the Supreme Court of Canada ruled that section 58 was unconstitutional, in that it violated section 2(b) of the Charter guaranteeing freedom of expression.

The Court held that freedom of expression, under the Charter, includes expression through commercial signs and thus the choice of language of expression (Foucher 1990: 126). The Court argued also that while a province has the authority to require the use of a given language on commercial signs, it does not thereby have the authority to prohibit other languages. The Court asserted that, in order to protect and promote the French language in Quebec—the remaining Francophone bastion in North America—it could have required the *predominant use* of French. By placing a complete ban on other languages, in violation of the linguistic rights of minorities in the province, Quebec went too far.

In rejection of the Supreme Court ruling, Premier Bourassa used the constitutional 'override' provision (Charter s.33) to enable the province to enact a new law, Bill 178, which mandates that public signs (on the outside of buildings) be in the *French language only.*

The enactment of Bill 178 served to heighten the indignation of Quebec's linguistic minorities and sparked organized minority opposition, first, in the form of an English rights lobby group (Alliance Quebec) and then in the form of a new, English rights political party (Equality Party). Additionally, it reinforced the already rising tide of out-migration from Quebec of disenchanted minorities (*Toronto Star*, 11 May 1991). We will return to the latter point at the end of this chapter.

In 1991 a Quebec resident won the right to appeal Bill 178 before the UN Human Rights Committee. The UN gave Ottawa until 11 December 1991 to reply to the charge that the law violates international human rights standards (*Toronto Star*, 21 June 1991).[8]

The Demise of the Meech Lake Accord[9]

In order to break the constitutional impasse between Quebec and the rest of Canada ensuing from the 1982 Canada Act, which Quebec had refused to sign, in May of 1986 the Government of Quebec, under Premier Bourassa, took the initiative to make known to its Canadian partners the five conditions to be met in order for Quebec to support the Act (Remillard, in Behiels 1990: 29). These conditions were: 1) the explicit recognition of Quebec as a distinct society; 2) a guarantee of increased powers in immigration matters; 3) the limitation of federal spending power; 4) recognition of a right of veto; 5) Quebec's participation in the appointment of judges to the Supreme Court of Canada.

On 30 April 1987, at Meech Lake, the First Ministers signed an agreement ratifying the acceptability, in principle, of the five conditions put forward by Quebec. On 3 June 1987 they signed a final agreement, incorporating the spirit and letter of the Meech Lake agreement and reflected in the provisions of the *Constitution Amendment 1987* (Remillard: 30).

The announcement of the terms of the Meech Lake Accord of April 1987 provoked immediate concern among aboriginal and multicultural minorities, and their representatives urged the First Ministers to ensure that a 'distinct society' amendment would not erode or diminish their constitutionally recognized collective rights. In response, then Prime Minister Mulroney and the Premiers added a clause (s.16) to this effect. Women's groups and other minority organizations followed suit, seeking similar protections in an amended Accord.

On 3 June 1987 the Prime Minister and all ten Premiers agreed to place the Accord, the *Constitutional Amendment 1987*, before Parliament and the provincial legislatures for adoption (Government of Canada, August 1987: 1). In the months to follow, Canada's various minorities, notwithstanding their disparate, particular constitutional concerns, were virtually unanimous in their expressed opposition to the provisions the Accord, especially with regard to s.2(1)a and s.2(1)b, recognizing the existence of French-speaking Canadians and English-speaking Canadians as a 'fundamental characteristic' of Canada and recognizing that Quebec constitutes a 'distinct society' within Canada. Minorities feared that if the Accord were enacted, it would elevate the 'distinct society' to an interpretive clause, recasting the entire Constitution and the Charter in the light of special status, and exemptions, for Quebec.

French-speaking Ontarians and English-speaking Quebeckers expressed concern that the Accord's provisions would override or weaken Charter-endorsed constitutional guarantees for their collective and individual rights. Spokespersons for Franco-Ontarians expressed the fear that the 'distinct society' provision would relegate the role of Ontario (and, similarly, the other provinces) to French language preservation without the necessary distinctive cultural context currently provided in French language schools where history and other subjects are taught from a Franco-Ontarian perspective. Accordingly, representatives pressed for positive guarantees for their collective rights.

Anglo-Quebeckers voiced similar concerns regarding the erosion of their constitutionally recognized rights under the Charter by the provisions of the Accord. Alliance Quebec called on Ottawa to amend the Accord so as to make it clear that nothing in the 'distinct society' clause could override constitutional guarantees for English language rights under the Charter.

Representatives of multicultural minorities were even more vehement than spokespersons for 'official language' minorities in declaring their opposition to the provisions of s.2(1) of the Accord. Some argued that this section of the Accord sanctioned the ensconced, superordinate, ethnic status of the French and English majorities, thereby relegating non-English and non-French minorities to the status of second-class citizens within Canada. The Canadian Ethnocultural Council, a coalition of more than thirty national ethnic organizations, contended that Section 2(1) of the Accord clearly gave priority to English/French bilingualism over multiculturalism. Multicultural spokespersons asserted with one voice that the Constitution should be amended so as to include a reference to multiculturalism in its opening clause.

Equally adamant in their rejection of the provisions of s.2(1) of the Accord, representatives of aboriginal organizations contended that the recognition of Quebec as a 'distinct society' without parallel recognition of aboriginal nations as 'distinct societies' seriously undermined constitutional protections for aboriginal peoples' rights. In this connection, a representative of the Inuit Committee on National Issues asked the Joint Committee for some commitment in the Accord which would obligate Ottawa to address the still outstanding issue of aboriginal self-government. Aboriginal leaders also expressed concern that the provisions of s.41 of the Accord requiring amendment by unanimous consent of the provinces would make it more difficult for the Northwest Territories and the Yukon Territory—jurisdictions representing substantial numbers of aboriginal Canadians—to gain provincial status.

Besides the objections voiced by ethnic and other minorities to the provisions of the Accord favouring Canada's 'founding' English and French partners and perceived to undermine their hard-won constitutional rights, there was virtually unanimous condemnation of the undemocratic nature of the amending process which did not allow for the effective input of citizens or minority organizations. This position has become expressed in increasing minority demands for direct participation in constitutional forums and negotiations, as will be shown in our analysis of the aboriginal and multicultural movements to follow.

As the 23 June 1990 deadline for ratification of the Accord approached, the provinces of Manitoba and Newfoundland had not yet signed the agreement. Given the adamant rejection of the Accord by aboriginal representatives, when the final blow was struck by the stalling tactics of Manitoba MLA Elijah Harper, an aboriginal leader who singlehandedly quashed the accord with a wave of his sacred eagle feather, his stature among Canada's aboriginal peoples rose to that of national hero (*Toronto Star*, 23 June 1990). Reaction among the Franco-Québécois, however, was anything but jubilant. The failure of the Accord left little hope for the inclusion of Quebec as a founding nation within Canada and the stage was set for the re-assertion of the sovereignty-association model.

Franco-Québécois Nationhood through Sovereignty Association

Over the decade from the time of the sovereignty association referendum in May 1980 to November 1990, public opinion polls indicated that support for sovereignty-association among Quebeckers had risen from 40 per cent to 66 per cent (*Toronto Star*, 26 Nov. 1990). In light of this political climate, and, in response to public demands for citizen input into further constitutional deliberations, the Quebec government established the Belanger-Campeau Commission on Quebec's political future. After several months of public hearings, culminating in marathon secret deliberations, the Commission overwhelmingly recommended that the National Assembly pass a bill providing for a sovereignty referendum by 26 October 1992 at the latest. The Bill, tabled in the National Assembly on 27 March 1991, also envisioned the creation of a sovereign state within one year of voters' approval of a sovereignty referendum. In practical terms, the Bill gave the rest of Canada 18 months to come up with a proposal for renewed federalism. In the words of Intergovernmental Affairs Minister Gil Remillard, 'I think it's about time Quebec received offers from the rest of Canada . . . ' (*Globe and Mail,* 27 Mar. 1991).

On 9 March 1991, ruling Liberal Party delegates in Quebec accepted virtually all the important recommendations of the Allaire report, a Party committee report outlining future policy directions in relations between Quebec and the rest of Canada (*Toronto Star,* 11 Mar. 1991). The Allaire report called for radical changes, including a dramatic takeover of federal powers by Quebec. The report proposed that Quebec should become an autonomous state and assume exclusive authority over 22 jurisdictions controlled entirely or partly by Ottawa. It also proposed a referendum on sovereignty if negotiations with the rest of Canada failed. On 20 June 1991 the Quebec legislature passed Bill 150, a law that paved the way for a referendum on sovereignty in 1992 (*Toronto Star,* 21 June 1991).

The official federal government response to Quebec's post-Meech Lake proposals were outlined in the document *Shaping Canada's Future Together,* tabled in the House of Commons on 24 September 1991. This document was put forward as a blueprint for 'Canadian unity' and contained 28 proposed Constitutional reforms, including the recognition of Quebec as a 'distinct society', defined *in the Charter of Rights* as including: its French-speaking majority, unique culture, and civil law tradition (*Toronto Star,* 25 Sept. 1991). The immediate reaction of all but a few (Liberal Party) spokespersons from Quebec was negative. The federal government was accused of using the old ploy of making cultural concessions to avoid power-sharing. Indeed, early critics asserted that the document increased the federal government's economic control (*Canada A.M.* CTV Special Program: 25 Sept. 1991).

The terms of the initial federal proposal for Constitutional reform repudiated many of the recommendations of the Belanger-Campeau and Allaire proposals. However, the document was open to amendment in response to views expressed in public hearings. By 31 May 1992—the Government's self-imposed deadline for talks on proposed changes to the unity package—a number of concessions had been made in order to bring Quebec to the table, but several key issues, including Senate reform, a limited veto for Quebec, and increased powers for Quebec over such areas as telecommunications, energy, and family law policy remained unresolved. Additionally, Quebec had served notice that the province was not committed to anything until the Quebec government decided to formally return to the table (*Toronto Star,* 31 May 1992).

Confronted with Quebec's proposed referendum on sovereignty, by May of 1992 the Government had moved to pass legislation enabling a national referendum on Canadian unity to be held before the Quebec vote would take place. On 7 July 1992, while the referendum question was still in abeyance, the premiers representing the nine provinces of English Canada reached an accord to reform the constitution in a way that they hoped would be acceptable to Quebec (*Toronto Star,* 8 July 1992). The agreed-upon Canadian unity package included a veto for Quebec and every other province over future changes to federal institutions. The agreement recognized

Quebec as a distinct society, and affirmed the right of the Quebec government to preserve and protect Quebec's distinct language, culture, and civil code. The distinct society clause was moved from the Charter to the Canada clause, where it could be used by the courts in interpreting the entire constitution. The accord also included a new division of powers between the federal and provincial governments and an elected and equal Senate with substantially increased powers.

In immediate response to the terms of the constitutional proposal, Quebec's Premier Bourassa asserted that clarifications and changes were needed. The Bourassa government set out a list of conditions to be met, including the restoration of Quebec's guarantee of a veto over the creation of new provinces, if Quebec was to consider returning to the bargaining table (*Toronto Star*, 16 July 1992). Prime Minister Mulroney was quick to assure Quebec that the unity package was not definitive and that the constitutional package would be open to further negotiation at a forthcoming First Ministers' meeting, to which Quebec's premier was invited. Premier Bourassa agreed to attend.

A First Ministers meeting, which included representatives of the two territories and four aboriginal groups, met in Charlottetown, PEI during the last week of August. On 28 August 1992 an unanimously endorsed agreement-in-principle was reached, the legalities and exact wording of which were yet to be worked out.

The agreement (the Charlottetown Accord) was designed to incorporate the two fundamental, yet contradictory, principles behind the long-standing unity debate: regional equality across Canada, and the special status of Quebec as one of Canada's two 'founding nations'/partners in Confederation. The equality principle was expressed in the proposed creation of an elected senate, composed of six senators from each province and one from each territory, plus additional aboriginal senators from each jurisdiction (*Toronto Star*, 1 Sept. 1992). The special status principle was expressed in the proposed guarantee that the whole Constitution, including the Charter, would be interpreted in light of the recognition of Quebec as a distinct society. Further, Quebec would be guaranteed 25 per cent of the seats in the House of Commons, regardless of its future population numbers, and the terms of the proposal ensured that a few francophone senators from Quebec would hold effective veto power over any changes to Canada's language legislation and, thereby, to a range of language-related cultural institutions (*Toronto Star*, 3 Sept. 1992).

Not surprisingly, opposition to the unity package was quickly expressed by spokespersons for various women's groups, racial and ethnic minorities, and others who felt that their particular interests and constituencies had been left out of the constitutional deal. In Quebec, the unity package was rejected outright, not only by supporters of the Franco-Québécois movement but also by Jean Allaire and nine members of the Belanger-Campeau Commission, whose 1991 report on Quebec's constitutional future had recommended either a profound reform of federalism or independence (*Toronto Star*, 28 Aug. 1992).

The Government of Canada proposed to hold a national referendum on the 28 August 1992 unity package—the Charlottetown Accord—on the date initially set by Quebec for a provincial referendum on sovereignty: 26 October 1992. The Quebec government proposed to hold a parallel referendum on the unity package, instead of on sovereignty, on the same date.

The result of the national referendum on the Charlottetown Accord was a resounding vote of NO, not only by Quebec voters, but also by the majority of voters across Canada.

For leaders of the movement for Franco-Québécois independence, rejection of the Charlottetown Accord was taken as a clear expression of the extreme dissatisfaction of their Quebec compatriots with the constitutional *status quo*, and an irrepressible desire for change in the direction of sovereignty. This gave the movement renewed vigour for their pursuit of independence, and before long, a new, sovereignist, federal party—the Bloc Québécois, an offshoot of the Parti Québécois—burst onto the political scene. In the federal election held on 25 October 1993, the Bloc Québécois, under the leadership of Lucien Bouchard, captured 54 of the province's 75 seats (most of the province's predominantly French-speaking ridings) and emerged as the federal party with the second largest number of seats. This put the Bloc in position for the role of official opposition party to the new Liberal government, under Prime Minister Jean Chretien (*Toronto Star*, 26 Oct. 1993).

A few days before the federal election, Parti Québécois leader Jacques Parizeau predicted that Quebec would be sovereign by 1995 (*Toronto Star*, 22 Dec. 1993). Parizeau said that the PQ's support of the Bloc is part of a three-stage plan to achieve this goal: 1) strong representation of the Bloc in the federal parliament, 2) victory of the PQ in the next provincial election in Quebec, and 3) a provincial referendum 'to achieve sovereignty'.

At the time of writing, many commentators appear to believe that this is the most likely political scenario in Quebec's future. It certainly bodes well for the prospects of the Franco-Québécois Independence Movement.

The Multicultural Movement: The Search for Eqalitarianism by Non-English and Non-French Immigrant Groups

As a movement of minority ethnic protest, the Multicultural movement represents a response of contention designed to achieve the goal of an egalitarian Canadian mosaic. Immigrant ethnic collectivities' demands for cultural and structural reform within Canadian society involve claims based on both categorical and collective cultural rights. Unlike the Franco-Québécois Independence movement which addresses its design for the future to a single ethnic audience, the Multicultural movement encompasses the diverse and sometimes conflicting claims of a wide range of immigrant ethnic collectivities.

As indicated in Chapter Six, the Multicultural movement emerged in response to the expressed discontent of immigrant ethnic minorities with their relegation to second-class status under the terms of the Royal Commission on Bilingualism and

Biculturalism. The Bi and Bi Commission was instructed to recommend steps for the development of Canadian Confederation on the basis of an equal partnership between the 'two founding races'—a term that confuses race and culture—in reference to the English and French charter groups in Canada (Privy Council 1963: 1106). This bicultural goal, it was argued, relegated all other peoples and cultures to minority status within Canada. Similarly, objections were raised against the goal of bilingualism which supported only the English and French languages, later enshrined in the Official Languages Act (1969).

The earliest and most powerful spokesperson for the Multicultural movement was Senator Paul Yuzyk, who, in his maiden speech in the Canadian Senate (3 May 1964), introduced the idea of a Third Force—a coalition of all non-English and non-French ethnic collectivities in Canada. Yuzyk clearly articulated the instrumental goal of the movement when he pointed out that the Third Force then represented almost one-third of the Canadian population, and as a united organizational force could hold the balance of power between the English and French. The expressive goal of the Multicultural movement soon became evident in demands for the implementation of the Canadian mosaic ideal through a federal policy of multiculturalism and multilingualism. Spearheaded largely by Ukrainian representatives such as Yuzyk, the movement was supported even in its early stages by those of other long-resident immigrant ethnic collectivities, such as Jews, and later by a variety of newer immigrant populations including Italians, Armenians, Portuguese, Greeks, and others.

The majority response to the conflicting demands of the Third Force on the one hand, and of the French nationalists who supported a model of English/French bilingualism and biculturalism, on the other hand, was represented in the compromise policy of multiculturalism within a bilingual framework. Minority ethnic protest against the terms of the policy, since its inception, has indicated clearly that it has not satisfied the demands of either of the constituencies whose claims it sought to address. Just as proponents of bilingualism and biculturalism continue to argue that the latter necessitates the former, proponents of the Multicultural movement continue to argue that language and culture are indivisible; therefore multiculturalism is meaningless without multilingualism. While the early proponents of the Multicultural movement focused on fundamental human rights, especially the right of equal access of all ethnic groups to political, economic, and social power, spokespersons for a variety of ethnic organizations over the years have increasingly made demands for collective minority cultural, religious, and linguistic rights.

Concessions to ethnic minority linguistic demands, in the form of provincial heritage language programs (discussed in Chapter Seven), have not adequately addressed minority concerns. From the viewpoint of the Multicultural movement, unless multicultural policy at both federal and provincial levels affords tangible support for minority cultural maintenance in public institutions, it continues to violate the collective rights of non-English and non-French immigrant ethnic collectivities.

This position was strongly endorsed in minority ethnic representations before the Special Joint Committee of the Senate and the House of Commons on the

Constitution. Witnesses were virtually unanimous in their insistence that multiculturalism be formally acknowledged in the Constitution, and the many witnesses who spoke in favour of non-official language rights indicated clearly that the Third Force was seeking positive, constitutional protection of non-official languages, particularly in education (Hudson 1987: 78). However, the outcome of their efforts was not an amendment to the Charter's provisions for official languages and 'minority' language education rights, which would provide parallel protection for non-official languages and language education, but a separate, vaguely-worded provision on multiculturalism (s.27) which makes no mention of language.

Hudson (1987) and Magnet (1989) agree that there are no clear clues as to how the phrase 'multicultural heritage' in s.27 of the Charter is to be interpreted. Hudson (1987: 78) has argued that the constitutional background sheds no light on the meaning of the phrase, and Magnet (1989: 745) has suggested that the broad range of opinion as to the meaning of s.27 revealed by ethnic lobbying prior to the constitutional entrenchment of the provision allows the courts to interpret the phrase 'multicultural heritage' in a wide variety of ways. In any event, in the view of the Third Force, s.27 of the Charter should be interpreted so as to afford positive protection for collective, linguistic, religious, and broader cultural minority rights. This position will be elaborated in Chapter Ten in our analysis of the constitutional debates and the provisions of the 1982 Charter.

With regard to Government support for minority religious education, the tiny amount of funding for instruction in private minority religious schools afforded under multicultural programs indicates beyond doubt that this is not a priority item on the Government's multicultural agenda. Moreover, any hopes that religious minorities may have had of using the provisions of the Charter to advance their claim to religious educational equality were certainly stifled by the Supreme Court decision which upheld as constitutional Ontario's Bill 30, providing full public funding only for Roman Catholic denominational schools (Ref. re: An Act To Amend The Education Act 1987).

At issue in the case was s.93 of the 1867 Constitution Act which provides the constitutional underpinnings of public support for 'minority' Catholic denominational schools outside Quebec and 'minority' Protestant denominational schools in Quebec. Spokespersons for a variety of religious minorities argued that Bill 30, premised on the provisions of s.93, conferred benefits on Catholics which were not available to other taxpayers and other religious minorities (Shapiro 1986). In a multicultural society, some opponents of the Bill contended, all religious groups should receive equivalent benefits. Accordingly, in order for s.93 to be constitutionally valid, it must apply equally to all religious minorities. The argument presented before the courts was that Bill 30 violated the equality rights and freedom of religion provisions of the Charter. However, the Supreme Court decision held that the Charter was never intended to be used to invalidate other constitutional provisions, particularly those such as s.93, which represented a fundamental part of the confederation compromise (Ref. op. cit. 1987). The ethnic priorities behind this decision are obvious: another victory for Canada's entrenched majority groups; another defeat for her multicultural minorities.

For members of visible minorities, the Multicultural movement represents a forum for protest against racism and an instrument through which to combat racial discrimination. Spokespersons for visible minorities such as Chinese, Blacks, and South Asians argued that early programs of implementation under the multicultural policy did not place nearly enough emphasis on eradicating racism in Canada.

In response to this position, in 1975 the then Minister of Multiculturalism, John Munro, declared a shift in program emphasis from language and culture to group understanding. As pointed out earlier, funding support was given to academic research studies which provided important documentation on the nature and extent of ethnic prejudice and discrimination in various parts of Canada. However, these kinds of studies were not designed to alleviate the collectively disadvantaging consequences of racism for visible minorities. It was not until 1981—ten years after the policy of multiculturalism was established—that the government finally responded to the escalating demands of visible minorities for anti-racism (rather than cultural retention) programs. In this year, a race relations unit was instituted within the Multiculturalism Directorate, and a national program to combat racism was inaugurated.

Over the ensuing decade, critics have asserted that the general anti-racism initiatives—anti-racist educational programs, employment equity measures for visible minorities, sensitivity training for police forces—increasingly emphasized under the policy, have failed to halt the escalation of prejudice and discrimination against visible minorities across Canada. Moreover, some critics have argued that the state maintains fiscal control over minority organizations through its funding of multicultural and anti-racism activities. Because the state can officially define program priorities, it succeeds in managing race and ethnic relations within a state apparatus (Li 1990: 14-15). Thus, while visible minorities have been able to use multiculturalism as a resource in their efforts to combat racism, they have done so at a price: the threat of losing ethnic organizational autonomy.

For visible minorities, the fight against racial discrimination takes precedence over the fight against cultural discrimination. Indeed, more than a few spokespersons for visible minorities have openly declared that the expressive issue of ethnocultural retention should be tabled until the instrumental empowerment goals of visible minorities have been adequately addressed. In the words of one critic: 'By introducing multiculturalism before anti-racism, Canada has put the cart before the horse' (*Toronto Star*, 15 July 1992). The empowerment goals articulated by representatives of visible minorities are based on three institutional imperatives: *access* (openness to visible minorities), *representation* (proportionate to numbers in the population), and *equity* (equality of opportunity and removal of systemic barriers) (Elliot and Fleras in Li 1990: 69).

The competing *collective rights* claims of ethnocultural minorities, on the one hand, and *individual* and *categorical rights* claims of visible minorities, on the other hand, have resulted in a deepening rift between racial and cultural minorities within the Multicultural movement. The difference in priorities between the two factions within the movement is compounded by the fact that they must compete with each other for the very limited government funding available under the multicultural rubric. The implications of this split for the future of the movement are manifold: it has seriously weakened the potential of the Multicultural movement as a Third Force coalition comprised of all immigrant ethnic groups.

Not only internal but also external forces have placed the future of the multicultural movement into serious question. The critical national issue of Canadian unity, confronting Quebec's threat of sovereignty, has made Canadians increasingly wary of the divisive potential of cultural demands. Accordingly, as minority cultural claims have escalated the ideological premises of multiculturalism have come under intensified criticism by dominant Canadians. Rising numbers of non-white immigrants has created a parallel backlash: increasingly, established white EuroCanadians feel racially and culturally threatened. This decrease in tolerance for racial and ethnic diversity, and the concomitant lack of public support for both multicultural and anti-racism initiatives, will be elaborated later in this chapter.

In an article in the *Toronto Star*, 'One final appeal for multiculturalism' (31 Aug. 1991), Andrew Cardozo, retiring executive director of the Canadian Ethnocultural Council, addressed the anti-multiculturalism forces at hand. He reflected bitterly: 'The rest of the world is saying: How do you do this? And we're turning away from the policy.'

In support of his assertion, Cardozo noted the following: 'The Progressive Conservatives voted at their biennial convention this month to "abandon the policy of multiculturalism and try to foster a common national identity".' The Spicer Commission (Citizens' Forum on Canada's Future) concluded, after listening to more than 400,000 Canadians, that 'federal government funding for multicultural activities other than those serving immigrant orientation, reduction of racial discrimination and promotion of equality, should be eliminated.' And the Reform Party (whose openly assimilationist policy would allow immigration only re: economic criteria) 'voted at its annual convention in April to end funding of the multicultural program and support the abolition of the department of multiculturalism'.

As to the future of multiculturalism, Cardozo expressed the view that the government probably 'will move away from the policy gradually and unobtrusively' by cutting or freezing its already inadequate budget and by saddling the department with a succession of low-profile junior ministers (*Toronto Star*, 31 Aug. 1991).

It was not long before the Reform Party's policy stance and Cordozo's prediction, strongly supported by public opinion, would come to pass, at least in part. In 1993, during Kim Campbell's brief reign as Prime Minister of Canada, the two-year-old Department of Multiculturalism and Citizenship was abolished, and multiculturalism was demoted. A new Canadian Heritage Ministry was established, which includes multiculturalism along with parks, culture, sports, official languages, and the status of women. The Ministry was headed by Sheila Finestone, then a low-profile junior minister (Tepper 1993). The new Liberal government, under Prime Minister Jean Chretien, has kept this arrangement. Sheila Finestone has been promoted to the position of Secretary of State, but the Canadian Heritage Ministry has again been placed under a junior minister, Michael Dupuy (*Toronto Star*, 12 Dec. 1993). These recent political manoeuvres do not augur well for the future of the multicultural movement. Also taking into account news reports of increasing public disenchantment with and rejection of multiculturalism, the survival of the multiculturalism movement is highly problematic.

The Aboriginal Nationhood Movement: Focus on Aboriginal Rights and Nationhood Rights

Like the Québécois Independence movement, and in contrast to the Multicultural movement, the Aboriginal movement can be conceptualized as a revitalization movement bent on politico-economic sovereignty and cultural transformation. In one of its early radical expressions, articulated by the Native Alliance for Red Power, it represented a politically revolutionary response to long-term colonial suppression. The goal was separation from Canada, to be achieved through violence, if necessary (Jack 1970). For the most part, however, demands for economic equality and for political and cultural sovereignty voiced by various organizations under the general rubric of the Aboriginal movement represent claims for special status.

As Canada's original occupants, who were self-governing nations before European encroachment into their territories, aboriginal peoples are making national rights claims. The intimate association between aboriginal peoples, their land-based cultures, self-governing institutions, and their aboriginal territories provides the basis of collective national group rights for aboriginal claims to nationhood. Aboriginal peoples also are making aboriginal land rights claims, based on their continuing occupancy and use of their aboriginal lands 'from time immemorial'.[10]

Lastly, given massive, incontrovertible evidence of their collective disadvantage and marginalized social status, consequent upon long-term institutional and systemic forms of racial discrimination against all categories of aboriginal peoples, leaders of the Aboriginal movement advance strongly documented claims based on categorical rights.

The Aboriginal movement arose as a highly negative response to proposals for change in Indian Affairs outlined in the federal government's White Paper of 1969 (Weaver 1981). This document, purportedly intended to accord Status Indians and other aboriginal peoples full ethnic equality within Canadian society, proposed the abolition of the special constitutional and legislative status of aboriginal peoples; the repeal of the Indian Act; the phasing out of the reserve system; and the transfer of responsibility for services from the federal to provincial governments (Jackson 1979: 284).

Ponting and Gibbins (1980: 25-9) argued that the White Paper clearly reflected the liberal ideology of the Liberal government of the time, led by then Prime Minister Trudeau. This ideology strongly endorsed the protection of individual rights but was antagonistic to the notion of collective rights. Thus, the White Paper emphasized the equality of aboriginal and non-aboriginal Canadians as individuals, at the expense of the collective survival of aboriginal ethnic groups as culturally distinctive peoples. With specific reference to Status Indians, the policy paper gave some recognition to treaty rights, but it interpreted the wording of treaties historically negotiated between Indian bands and the Crown as revealing only 'limited and minimal promises' (Government of Canada 1969: 11). Further, it virtually ignored the gigantic liabilities which Indians had accumulated as a long-term result of the self-fulfilling prophecy of racism. It did not attempt to compensate for the economic, political, and social disadvantages which would continue to impede the integration of Indians as 'ordinary citizens' within Canadian society. In a word, it failed to recognize the validity of potential Indian claims based on categorical rights.

In explanation of the negative response of Status Indians to the abolition of the Indian Act, Weaver (1981: 19) argues that while they clearly resent its paternalistic constraints, they embrace the special rights it provides, particularly with regard to the protection of their lands. Their overriding concern—shared by Canada's other aboriginal peoples—is to protect their historical relationship with aboriginal lands, which they view as critical for the survival of their distinct cultures. The White Paper was perceived to pose a direct threat to this valued relationship.

Aboriginal protest to the White Paper surfaced in a number of documents written by angry Indian leaders. In his pathbreaking book, *The Unjust Society* (1969: 1), Harold Cardinal charged that the program suggested by the White Paper represented 'nothing better than cultural genocide'. For the Indian to survive, Cardinal contended, he must become 'a good little brown white man'. In effect, the policy implied 'The only good Indian is a non-Indian'. In another document, *Citizens Plus* (1970), the Indian chiefs of Alberta reinforced Cardinal's position by arguing that Indians should be recognized as 'Citizens Plus', i.e., citizens who possess additional rights as 'charter' members of Canadian society.

The White Paper proposals had their most immediate impact on Registered Treaty Indians, for the recommendations to abolish the special legal status of Indians under the Indian Act threatened their treaty rights. But other aboriginal peoples— Registered non-Treaty Indians, non-Status Indians, and (later) Métis and Inuit— were soon swept up in the aboriginal tide of protest, for the White Paper proposals also threatened any potential claims that might be based on aboriginal rights. These aboriginal fears were intensified by a speech given by then Prime Minister Trudeau, in which he said that his government would not recognize aboriginal rights. However, under mounting and concerted pressure from aboriginal organizations, and after many months of public debate, in 1971 the government finally retracted the White Paper proposals.

Since then, the various associations within the Aboriginal movement have, with one voice, demanded recognition of their special status as First Nations within

Canada. They have argued that they have the fundamental right to political and cultural sovereignty, and that they have the right to retain ownership of sufficient aboriginal lands to ensure their independence and their economic and cultural survival. While there is considerable diversity among the kinds of claims put forward by representatives of particular aboriginal organizations, the concepts of collective aboriginal and nationhood rights underscore them all.[11]

As pointed out in Chapter Three (page 68), spokespersons for aboriginal organizations maintain that sovereignty is a gift of the Creator which has never been and can never be surrendered. Prior to the arrival of European agents, aboriginal peoples were independent, self-governing nations whose members lived and sought their livelihoods within clearly delineated territories. With colonization, they claim, their right to sovereignty was unjustly abrogated and their institutions of self-government systematically dismantled. But, as nations, they assert their sovereignty and their right to create and administer their own forms of self-government. From this aboriginal view, treaties made between aboriginal peoples and Governments should be regarded as treaties between sovereign nations, in the sense of public international law.

This ideological thrust of the Aboriginal movement was most clearly articulated in the initial proposals for settlement of land claims and for self-government put forward by representatives of the Dene Nation (1976) and the Inuit of Nunavut (1979). Both of these proposals have undergone considerable alteration, over the years, in the attempt of the aboriginal nations to achieve negotiated settlements with the federal government. And, in both cases, original nationhood claims have been compromised in the process.

For purposes of illustration, we will focus on the Nunavut proposal. In the author's view, the Nunavut claim represents the strongest single case for nationhood based on the demonstrably continuing links between the Inuit ethnic group, its distinctive ethnoculture, and its aboriginal territory/homeland.

New Nationhood: The Nunavut Proposals (1979-92)

In order for the Inuit to regain aboriginal nationhood status, the national Inuit organization (Inuit Tapirisat of Canada—ITC) deemed it essential that the Inuit people validate their claim to national self-determination and regain political, economic, and cultural sovereignty within their aboriginal territory. This involved, at the outset, documenting that Inuit aboriginal right to their territory had never been surrendered by war or by treaty, and that they had continued to occupy and use their lands in their traditional ways 'from time immemorial'. Inuit representatives had to provide evidence for the continuing integral links between the Inuit people, their aboriginal territory, and their land-based, aboriginal ethnoculture. In other words, the Inuit nationhood claims rested on the premise that the collective cultural, aboriginal, and national group rights of the Inuit people had never been abrogated in any way.

As put forward by the Inuit Committee on National Issues, the Inuit claim was based on an holistic conception of aboriginal and national rights:

> Our position is that . . . aboriginal title to land, water and sea ice flows from aboriginal rights . . . to practice our customs and traditions, to retain and develop our languages and cultures, and the right to self-government . . . In our view, aboriginal rights . . . [are] . . . human rights, because these are the things that we need to continue to survive as a distinct people in Canada. (quoted in Asch 1984: 30)

This position was clearly articulated in the original ITC land-claims proposal which was supported by extensive research studies documenting (among other things) actual Inuit land use and occupancy over the centuries. One study, directed by Dr Milton Freeman, an anthropologist at McMaster University, showed that, from prehistoric times, the Inuit have used and occupied virtually all of an estimated 750,000 square miles of land claimed as their aboriginal territory, as well as an estimated 800,000 square miles of northern ocean. This documentation was essential in order for the Inuit to validate their collective land claim, based on aboriginal rights.

With regard to Inuit nationhood claims, a number of proposals were circulated among the many dispersed Inuit communities before a widely agreed-upon position paper was drafted. The first agreed-upon proposal was put forward by the ITC in 1979, as a position paper entitled 'Political Development in Nunavut'.[12] In this paper, the ITC outlined Inuit demands for a newly defined territory which would assume provincial status over a period of about 15 years. The proposal made several important claims, among them the right to self-determination of the Inuit people, the right of the Inuit to conduct their affairs in their own language (Inuktitut), the right of the Inuit to their traditional lands, waters and resources therein, their right to preserve and use their traditional hunting, trapping and fishing resources, their right to define who is an Inuk (Inuk = singular of Inuit), and their right to economic compensation for past, present and future use by non-Inuit of Inuit lands, waters and resources.

From the beginning, the federal government rejected the conception of Nunavut as an 'ethnic' province, to be administered by the Inuit in ways which differed from that of other provinces. Throughout the 20 years of negotiations, the federal government invariably divided the political and economic package proposed by the Inuit, and focused on providing economic compensation for non-Inuit use of Inuit lands and resources. The Inuit proposals, on the other hand, focused on the sharing of Inuit lands and resources with the federal government and the people of Canada, on the understanding that the Inuit would have a prominent voice on all matters within their territorial jurisdiction (Ittinuar 1985).

The first step toward Inuit self-government was the proposed creation of a new territory, Nunavut, on Inuit aboriginal lands in the Northwest Territories. This proposal envisaged the division of the NWT into two separate jurisdictions, with

Nunavut comprising the Eastern Arctic jurisdiction, north of the treeline. The Inuit proposed an elected system of government, for Nunavut, similar to that of the existing NWT government. Since the vast majority of people within the jurisdiction would be Inuit, the Inuit would assume a substantial degree of control over their economic and cultural destinies.

In 1982, what seemed at the time to be a major breakthrough for the Inuit was the result of a NWT plebiscite which approved division of the NWT into two territories.

The split received federal government approval in principle, subject to agreement on a boundary between the two new jurisdictions, and settlement of outstanding aboriginal land claims in the NWT. Soon after, the Nunavut Constitutional Forum was established to work out the details of a Nunavut Constitution. In 1987, a proposal for a Nunavut Constitution was completed and a proposal for a Boundary and Constitutional Agreement between Western and Nunavut Constitutional Forums was put forward. However, the boundary dispute continued until October of 1990, when Inuit and territorial government leaders finally reached agreement on how to divide the Northwest Territories and create the territory of Nunavut (*Toronto Star*, 21 Oct. 1990).

In December of 1989, agreement in principle was reached between the Tungavik Federation of Nunavut, representing the Inuit in the central and Eastern Arctic regions, and the federal government on the long-standing land claim of the Inuit (*Ottawa Citizen*, 9 Dec. 1989). The terms of the agreement would give the Inuit possession of over 260,000 square kilometres of land, with surface rights to about 225,000 square kilometres of the land, and with sub-surface rights to about 36,000 square kilometres of the land. Additionally, the Inuit would receive $580 million in financial compensation, over 14 years. With indexation for interest rates, the total would be about $1.15 billion (*Toronto Star*, 17 Dec. 1991). In exchange, the Inuit would surrender aboriginal rights and title to the land. The agreement did not address the question of Inuit self-government.

At this point, the entire package still had to clear three outstanding hurdles: 1) a plebiscite on the proposed new borders by voters in the existing NWT; 2) ratification of the agreement by a majority of Inuit voters age 16 and over, not just by a majority of those who do vote; and 3) ratification of the details of the agreement by a vote in Parliament and the passage of legislation to create the territory of Nunavut.

On 4 May 1992, voters in the NWT narrowly supported a controversial boundary to split the NWT into two territories, Nunavut in the east and the Western Arctic (or Denendch, as the Dene prefer) in the west.

The plebiscite saw the eastern NWT, where 80 per cent of the population is Inuit, vote overwhelmingly in support of the boundary, while Western Arctic residents voted strongly against it. Only a low voter turnout in the west, where just 47 per cent of voters cast ballots, allowed for a victory for boundary supporters (*Toronto Star*, 6 May 1992). Rejection of the boundary highlighted several long-term concerns of opponents: 1) complaints by the Dene in Saskatchewan, Manitoba and the NWT that the boundary placed traditional lands used by Dene Indians under Inuit jurisdiction; 2) complaints by aboriginal (Indian) leaders such as Ovide Mercredi, national chief of the Assembly of First Nations, that the Inuit should have reserved their inherent right to self-government as part of the package instead of setting a precedent, abandonment of self-government, which could be harmful to other aboriginal nations seeking self-government as part of their land claim negotiations; and 3) fears of Western Arctic residents of the demise of a central government and the fragmentation of the territory into diverse, regional governments, together with the dire economic consequences of such a an occurrence.

In November of 1992, Inuit residents in the Eastern Arctic voted 69 per cent in favour of the final Nunavut land claim package. The package will give the Inuit clear title to 350,000 square kilometres (140,000 square miles) of land, as well as $1.15 billion dollars in compensation for land ceded, over a period of 14 years (*Toronto Star*, 13 Nov. 1992). The Inuit also will have the right to hunt, fish, and trap in all of Nunavut, a region of 2.2 million square kilometres (880,000 square miles). The agreement includes a phase-in period that will give the Inuit time to set up a new government which likely will be similar to the territorial administration in Yellowknife, NWT. Because the Inuit make up about 80 per cent of the Nunavut population (17,500 out of 22,000), they will be able to dominate the legislature and thus have a form of self-government. An accord signed prior to the vote between federal government and Inuit negotiators calls for the legal establishment of Nunavut by 1999. In the summer of 1993, legislation was introduced to ratify the agreement and to establish the Nunavut territory.

The present Nunavut agreement undoubtedly represents a hard-wrought compromise on the part of the Inuit. The government of Nunavut will be run on the majority (Euro-Canadian) model, not on the model of traditional Inuit self-government. In other words, this model of government is not based on the right of the Inuit to self-determination as a distinctive people, culture, and nation. It represents a compromise position. Nevertheless, given the fact that the Inuit make up some 80 per cent of the population in the proposed territory of Nunavut, their voting power can be used to ensure that the individual and collective cultural rights of the Inuit people are recognized and protected in the future. Inuit nationhood, however, remains a dream deferred.

Government Response to the Aboriginal Movement

To date, government response to proposals put forward by representatives of the Aboriginal movement have favored assimilationist settlements like the precedent-setting James Bay Agreement (1975) and have opposed proposals like the original versions of the Dene and Nunavut claims that seek political self-determination as nations. While the goal of aboriginal nationhood remains elusive, the Aboriginal movement has come a long way toward persuading federal government authorities of the legitimacy of its position. 'Special status' for aboriginal peoples, rejected out of hand in the 1969 White Paper, now has become accepted in principle by Government.

The federal government also has endorsed the principle of limited forms of aboriginal self-government through public policy (Government of Canada 1984), and a number of Indian reserve communities already have established limited forms of self-government. Nonetheless, the federal government's restrictive interpretation of the concept of aboriginal self-government, based on the delegated/municipal model which keeps ultimate decision-making power over aboriginal affairs firmly in Government hands, differs radically from the nationhood model endorsed by the aboriginal movement.

Most recently, during the 1992 round of constitutional negotiations, the principle of an inherent aboriginal right to self-government was accepted by Canada's federal and provincial premiers (*Toronto Star*, 12 May 1992). The final constitutional proposal (Charlottetown Accord) agreed upon by all of Canada's premiers on 28 August 1992 proposed that the Constitution would recognize the inherent right to self-government of all aboriginal peoples, and aboriginal governments would also be recognized as one of three orders of government, the others being federal and provincial. Additionally, under the newly proposed Canada clause, the right of aboriginal peoples to promote their languages, cultures, and traditions and to ensure the integrity of their societies would be guaranteed. The Accord also guaranteed that there would be a political accord which recognized the right of aboriginal peoples to a significant say over future constitutional amendments which affect them.

However, in the national referendum held on 26 October 1992, a significant majority of Canadians voted to reject the Charlottetown Accord. A mixed response from Canada's aboriginal communities revealed that there were sharp lines of division over the aboriginal package. The Inuit of the Eastern Arctic, with the vote on their Nunavut proposal only weeks away after some 20 years of negotiation, voted to support the Accord. On the other hand, most Indians on reserves voted 'no' (*Toronto Star*, 28 Oct. 1992). Ovide Mercredi, national chief of the Assembly of First Nations (representing Status Indians) suggested that Status Indians rejected the Accord for two reasons: first, distrust of the Government and disbelief in good-faith negotiations with governments, and second, dissatisfaction with alleged inadequacies of the proposed aboriginal package, and additional unmet demands.

Prior to the vote, it had been made abundantly clear that aboriginal women were divided in support for the aboriginal package. Indeed, the Native Women's Association of Canada had sought an injunction to block the referendum on the grounds that women's equality rights, under the Charter, would be secondary under the agreement because, under the Canada clause, it would give priority to the upholding of traditional aboriginal values. These could encompass systems of aboriginal government presided over by hereditary male chiefs, in which women historically have been excluded from voting or holding office (*Toronto Star*, 9 Oct. 1992). While not all aboriginal women supported this interpretation of the proposed package, a substantial number were suspicious enough of the possibility of such an interpretation that they put themselves clearly on the 'no' side.

Notwithstanding the failure of the Charlottetown Accord, aboriginal peoples have not abandoned their fight for national self-determination. Indeed, a number of Indian (band) communities across Canada have already stated that they intend to proceed to establish their own nation-like governments unilaterally (*Toronto Star*, 31 Oct. 1992). Aboriginal leaders have pointed out that the federal government has the power to reach self-government agreements with aboriginal groups, outside of the constitutional process. The question is: does the Government have the will to do so? If not, leaders say, aboriginal peoples may use civil disobedience to attain their goals.

Despite internal differences in the positions of representatives of various of aboriginal organizations, there is general agreement that self-government means the right of aboriginal peoples to determine their own destinies. Aboriginal representatives are united in their commitment to the position that aboriginal peoples have an inherent right to self-government, meaning *that it has always existed and was never surrendered.* Whether or not this definition will be accepted by governments is a question for the future. At present, like the constitutionally recognized aboriginal and treaty rights of Canada's aboriginal peoples, their newly accepted inherent right to self-government has not, as yet, been defined.

The hiatus between aboriginal and government positions on definitions of aboriginal rights and aboriginal self-government created a formidable obstacle to progress in the earlier constitutional negotiations of 1980-82, and in the four Constitutional conferences (1983, 1984, 1985, and 1987) convened in order to define aboriginal peoples' rights. However, while the First Ministers' conferences failed to culminate in an agreement on the definition of aboriginal rights, they did reveal a new pattern of interaction between government and aboriginal representatives, one in which the voice of aboriginal peoples is taken into serious account. This new pattern also is evident in the involvement of aboriginal peoples in the formulation and implementation of federal government policy and, most recently, in their involvement in the latest (1992) round of constitutional negotiations. The paternalistic pattern of unilateral policy-making without the participation of aboriginal representatives has given way, under continuing pressure from aboriginal organizations, to a new pattern in which aboriginal input (however circumscribed) is deemed essential.

Having failed to gain recognition as First Nations through the political process of land claim negotiations, aboriginal leaders shifted the focus of their activities to constitutional negotiations. While this strategy, in and of itself, has not yet proved to be successful, it has bolstered the political process and brought to public attention the strength of aboriginal support for some form of self-government. Most importantly, it has given new impetus to the aboriginal movement for new nationhood.

The Future of the Franco-Québécois, Multicultural, and Aboriginal Movements

The three minority ethnic protest movements examined represent the differential collective responses of members of Canada's charter, immigrant, and aboriginal minorities to their subordinate ethnic status in society at large. Ethnic status differences among the three movements are reflected not only in the kinds of collective rights that each can claim, but also in the differing potential for success of the movements.

Both the Franco-Québécois Independence movement and the Aboriginal movement can make collective claims based on national group rights on the evidence of the inextricable link between the ethnic group, its language and culture, and its ancestral territory within Canada. But the enormous difference in power between the two movements indicates that the chances for eventual success are far greater for the Franco-Québécois than for the aboriginal nations, who have modelled their demands for special status as 'distinct societies' on those of the Franco-Québécois.

The Multicultural movement, unlike the others, cannot make territorial claims based on any link with an ancestral homeland in Canada. Thus, proponents of multilingualism and multiculturalism can make collective claims based on minority religious, linguistic, and cultural rights, but not on national group rights. Visible racial minorities, proponents of anti-racism initiatives, cannot make cultural claims on the basis of race: their claims are based on categorical rights. Further, the competing and, increasingly, conflicting interests and claims of visible minorities and ethnocultural minorities within the multicultural movement weaken its political clout and impede its chances of success.

Prospects for the Future of the Three Movements

To some degree, the futures of all three movements are interdependent. A most important factor lies in the question of Franco-Québécois independence. Should the Franco-Québécois achieve their goal of a sovereign Quebec, then the futures of aboriginal and multicultural minorities within and outside Quebec could be quite different. In the case of the multicultural movement outside Quebec, with increased public support it could benefit, indirectly, from the achievement of Franco-Québécois independence, for the bilingual framework of multiculturalism would then lose salience. Within Quebec, the multicultural movement could give rise to an increasing alliance of ethnic minorities with the English Rights bloc. For the aboriginal movement, Quebec sovereignty could give new impetus to nationhood claims of aboriginal peoples within the state of Quebec. However, most aboriginal peoples in the State of Canada would likely continue to pursue less radical forms of self-government.

Finally, in speculating on the future of the three minority protest movements, it is important to take into account the prevailing climate of public opinion with regard to each of the movements.

The preliminary report of the Spicer Commission (Citizens' Forum on Canada's Future)—triggered by the failure of the Meech Lake Accord—underscored the marked disparities in opinion concerning the future of Quebec voiced by Canadians living within and outside Quebec (*Toronto Star*, 21 Mar. 1991). The report stated that while the majority of participants wanted Quebec to stay in Canada, for most participants outside Quebec, Quebec's continued presence in Confederation could not be bought at the price of sacrificing individual or provincial equality. Most participants expressed the view that they would rather see Quebec separate than give it preferential treatment. Additionally, the report revealed that few participants across Canada voiced support for official bilingualism. The majority favoured either delegating jurisdiction over languages to the provinces or having French as the official language in Quebec and English as the official language everywhere else.

Reflecting strikingly similar views, the results of a Gallup poll conducted in June of 1991 indicate that nearly three out of five Canadians disapproved of the inclusion of Quebec in the Constitution as a 'distinct society'. The 59 per cent who disapproved of the distinct society clause represented the highest level of such opposition in nine polls by Gallup over the previous four years (*Toronto Star*, 11 July 1991). Analysed according to mother tongue of respondents, the figures showed that 56 per cent of francophones, as opposed to only 22 per cent of anglophones, supported a distinct society clause for Quebec.

With regard to the climate of public opinion on multiculturalism, support for government programs aimed at cultural retention has all but disappeared. In June of 1991, a two-part feature article in the *Toronto Star* reported that 'multiculturalism is under attack—from an increasingly wide variety of people' (23 June 1991). Michael Adams, president of Environics Research Group, is reported to have said that 'Traditional WASPs are feeling threatened by the loss of dominance of Anglo-Saxon and traditional Protestant values . . . But they're now being joined in their opposition to multiculturalism by baby boomers [and others].' The report also indicated that, while multicultural programs supporting cultural retention continue to be defended by representatives of various ethnocultural minorities, the public backlash against government funding for these activities is widespread.

The final report of the Citizens' Forum on Canada's Future, released at the end of June 1991, raised questions about the effectiveness of both bilingualism and multiculturalism. The report recommended that the federal government should discontinue funding multicultural programs other than those promoting anti-racism, equality, and immigrant integration 'because they are divisive and because new Canadians don't want them' (*Toronto Star*, 29 July 1991). The covert agenda behind the recommendations of the report—to replace multiculturalism with assimilation as a model for public policy—became evident in its recommendation that the key goal of multiculturalism should be to welcome all Canadians to an *evolving mainstream*. Accordingly, the report recommended that maintenance of distinctive ethnocultures should be a voluntary matter for ethnic communities and should not receive government funding.

As reported in Chapter One, a recent national survey on public opinion in the area of inter-ethnic relations, carried out under the auspices of the Canadian Council of Christians and Jews (*Toronto Star*, 14 Dec. 1993) indicated an escalating intolerance among respondents for racial and cultural differences, and a concomitant rejection of both multiculturalism and anti-racism initiatives. Forty-one per cent of respondents believed that Canada's immigration policy 'allows too many people of different cultures and races to come to Canada'. Nearly three quarters of Canadians interviewed rejected the notion of this country as a multicultural nation. Sixty-two per cent of respondents expressed the opinion that people should 'adapt to the value system and the way of life of the majority in Canadian society'. In short, the majority of respondents believed that all Canadians should assimilate to the established racial and cultural norms of the dominant Euro-Christian populations in this country.

With regard to the future of the aboriginal movement, the 1991 Spicer report revealed that while there was strong support among participants in the Forum for the resolution of aboriginal land claims and for the principle of aboriginal self-government, the lack of understanding of these complex issues among participants precluded discussion of detailed recommendations (*Toronto Star*, 28 June 1991). Moreover, there was a sharp difference in views of aboriginal self-government voiced by aboriginal and non-aboriginal participants. Aboriginal participants tended to view self-government (in *legislated* terms) as akin to sovereignty; non-aboriginal participants tended to view self-government (in *delegated* terms) as akin to municipalities.

Prospects for the Future: A Cautionary Prognosis

All things considered, at the present time we are led to conclude that the Franco-Québécois movement is the most likely of the three minority protest movements to achieve its goals (sovereignty, in some form) in the near future. The aboriginal movement is unlikely to achieve sovereignty or full nationhood recognition, but, if particular groups within the movement are willing to compromise, they are likely to attain a limited form of self-government. The multicultural movement is by far the weakest of the three: public sentiment is increasingly assimilationist in orientation, Anglo-conformist outside Quebec and Franco-conformist within Quebec. If this trend continues, instead of a national policy of multiculturalism and bilingualism across Canada, we may well see separate state policies of uniculturalism and unilingualism: English in Canada and French in Quebec.

Concluding Comments

Throughout the foregoing analysis of the protest movements which have emerged among Franco-Québécois, multicultural, and aboriginal minorities in Canada, we have alluded, from time to time, to the attempts by minority representatives to use *legal* (statutory and constitutional) protection for human rights as levers for their particular claims.

In the next two chapters of this book, we will examine and evaluate the legal framework of human rights protection across Canada, in light of the standard provided by the provisions of international human rights instruments. We will pay particular attention to protection for ethnic minority rights and to the ways in which minorities have responded to legal endorsement of human rights by putting forward individual, categorical, and collective rights claims under the provisions of statutory human rights legislation and the constitutional Charter.

Notes

1 A few exceptions are a small number of religious sectarian communities like the Hutterites, to be discussed in connection with minority religious rights, in Chapter Ten. Also notable are the few resource-wealthy Indian bands, such as those from Alberta who reportedly bankrolled Indian lobbying efforts in England at a cost of some $300,000 during the 1980-81 constitutional debate (*Globe and Mail*, 17 July 1981).

2 For purposes of our analysis, we will refer to these three movements as (1) Franco-Québécois Independence, (2) Multiculturalism, and (3) Aboriginal Nationhood.

3 Morris and Lanphier (1977) provide a comprehensive account of the various options to Québécois independence. Their conceptual analysis is framed in terms of a threefold classification of rights (individual, collective, and cultural) which in several ways parallels the author's distinction between individual, categorical, and collective (cultural) rights. However the territorial basis of aboriginal and national rights of aboriginal peoples and charter groups is not differentiated or included in their conceptual design.

4 A brief recapitulation of her argument is given here; however the entire selection is recommended reading.

The literature on the evolution of Québécois nationalism in Canada abounds. The following selections are particularly recommended in conjunction with our present discussion: Rioux 1971; Milner and Milner 1973; McRoberts and Posgate 1976; and Dion 1976. For readers who wish to pursue this topic further, excellent coverage of 'The National Question' can be found in a special issue on Quebec of *The Canadian Review of Sociology and Anthropology* 15, 2 (1978). This issue also contains a well-selected bibliography (Zinman: 246-51).

5 Bernier (1981) takes a somewhat different view, but arrives at the same conclusion with regard to contemporary Québécois nationalism. He argues that capitalistic developments since the Duplessis era eroded the power base of the reactionary petty bourgeoisie class which Duplessis purportedly represented. Contemporary Québécois nationalism, consequent upon modern, capitalistic developments, focuses on the necessity to create a new nation-state within Québécois national territory, the state of Québec. Unlike its reactionary predecessor, contemporary nationalism is a forward-looking activist movement whose ideology is promoted by a new politically-oriented national bourgeoisie and whose main instrument is the Quebec state bureaucracy.

6 Reprinted by permission of The Canadian Publishers, McClelland and Stewart Limited, Toronto.

7 Lévesque took comfort in the fact that, despite considerable support for federalism in some ridings, overall it was clearly the non-French Quebeckers who won the day for the federalists.

8 On 22 December 1993, a new law (Bill 86) came into effect in Quebec which allows languages other than French on outdoor commercial signs, as long as French is predominant (*Toronto Star*, 22 Dec. 1993). However, few store owners are expected to invest thousands of dollars in new signs, as many, reportedly, fear that the new law could be rescinded if the Parti Québécois wins the next provincial election.

9 This discussion of the Accord represents an abridged version of the author's article 'Entrenching a Pecking Order of Minority Rights' in *Canadian Public Policy* (Supplement to xiv, 1988). For a comprehensive analysis of the entire spectrum of issues raised by the Accord, see *The Meech Lake Primer*, M.D. Behiels, ed., University of Ottawa Press: 1989.

10 A comprehensive overview of the rights of Canada's aboriginal peoples, from a legal perspective, is found in B.W. Morse, ed., 1985. Recommendations for 'An Agenda for Action' with respect to aboriginal rights are found in The Canadian Bar Association Committee Report *Aboriginal Rights in Canada* (August 1988).

11 For a comprehensive overview of the historical foundation for aboriginal peoples' collective rights claims based on aboriginal, treaty and national group rights, see J.S. Frideres, 1993 (Chapters 3, 4 , 11, and 12).

12 Nunavut (Our Land) refers to the proposed Inuit province in the NWT. While the NWT is reportedly eighty per cent aboriginal in ethnic composition, it was not until 1979 that an aboriginal majority was elected to the legislative assembly (*Toronto Star*, 24 Jan. 1982. Since that time, with leaders from the four major aboriginal organizations in control of the assembly, the idea of aboriginal political sovereignty has been actively promoted.

CHAPTER NINE

The Legal Framework for Protection of Minority Rights in Canada: Human Rights Statutes

Human Rights Legislation and the Control of Ethnic Discrimination in Canada

The nature and extent of racism at the levels of public policy and practice, before the enactment of anti-discrimination legislation in Canada, has been documented throughout this book. In this chapter, we will examine the historical forces underlying attempts to control ethnic discrimination through the development and implementation of human rights legislation in Canada.

Critics of human rights legislation have long argued that 'You can't legislate morality' (Hill 1977: 23). In fact, as Hill suggests, human rights legislation is not intended to turn self-professed racists into loving ethnic neighbours. Rather, it is intended to reduce discrimination: to ensure fair and equitable treatment of different ethnic collectivities despite the existence of prejudices. Nevertheless, while legislation may not change attitudes, it can introduce a climate in which the possibility of attitudinal change is maximized (Case 1977: 52).

The relationship between prejudice and discrimination, discussed in Chapter One, is instructive here in terms of the differential implications of these two phenomena for programs of social action. In any attempt to combat racism, it is important to recognize that an individual or group may harbour strong ethnic prejudices and yet be *prevented* from acting out these prejudices through overt discriminatory policies and practices (Hill 1977: 2). It is precisely this function of *prevention of discriminatory acts* that is the prime objective behind human rights legislation in Canada.

The British North America Act (Constitution Act 1867) makes no explicit reference to human rights. Further, aside from the provisions protecting English and French languages in s.133 and others protecting the rights of Protestants and Catholics to their denominational schools in s.93, the BNA Act does not address the kinds of collective human rights associated with ethnic group membership.

For almost a century after the British Emancipation Act of 1833, which marked the official demise of slavery in Canada, the trend at the federal, provincial, and municipal levels of Canadian government was to enact discriminatory legislation. Among the most pernicious pieces of legislation was the Indian Act, whereby Canadian Indians were virtually denied all of their fundamental human rights, but many other discriminatory laws impeded the rightful participation of Asians, Blacks, and other ethnic minorities from anything like full participation in Canadian society.

Although there were isolated legislative attempts to overcome ethnic discrimination in Canada as far back as the 1930s, Tarnopolsky (1979: xv) contends that it was not until the end of World War II that an interest in anti-discrimination legislation developed. Knowledge of racist atrocities committed under Nazi policies of genocide began to penetrate the Canadian consciousness, forcing at least some Canadians to reflect on racism within their own borders. Hill (1977: 18) argues that it was during the World War II period that Canadians bore witness to some of the most flagrant examples of racism in this country's history. In 1939, humanitarian petitions for Canadian acceptance of a fair quota of Jewish refugees fleeing the threat of extermination were ignored. In 1942, a policy of forceful evacuation of Japanese-Canadians from west coastal areas led to the confiscation of their property and their internment as 'enemy aliens' in Canadian-style concentration camps.

Following the war, Canadian public opinion became more sensitive to incidents of ethnic discrimination. As various pressure groups began to lobby for anti-discrimination legislation and for more adequate means of implementation and enforcement of the laws, governments ventured slowly and carefully into the area of human rights legislation.

In the 1940s, the provinces of Ontario (Racial Discrimination Act, 1944) and Saskatchewan (Bill of Rights, 1947) enacted quasi-criminal statutes that declared certain practices illegal and imposed sanctions on them. The Ontario Act was very limited in scope: it prohibited only the public display of signs, symbols, or other racially or religiously discriminatory representations. The Saskatchewan Bill was much broader: the anti-discrimination provisions applied to accommodation, employment, occupation, land transactions, and business enterprises, and included the government.

Tarnopolsky (1979: 296) argues that a major weakness with both pieces of legislation lay in their quasi-criminal nature which made many people reluctant to use them. To overcome this impasse, Fair Accommodations and Fair Employment Practices Acts were enacted, first in Ontario in 1954 and, within one decade, in most of the other provinces. Although these acts clearly represented a step forward, they still contained a major weakness in that the victims of discrimination were responsible for lodging the complaint. Racism was their problem and their responsibility.

The major step was taken in 1962, when the Province of Ontario consolidated its legislation into the Ontario Human Rights Code to be established by the then one-year-old Ontario Human Rights Commission. By 1975, all Canadian provinces had established Human Rights Commissions to administer anti-discriminatory legislation. Two years later, the Canadian Human Rights Act established a federal commission.

The Ombudsman

The role of the ombudsman as protector of citizens' rights against abuse by government bodies is a relatively recent development in Canada. As a consequence of the increasingly enormous powers of the modern administrative state over the lives of ordinary citizens, the potential for friction between the individual citizen and the administrative bureaucracy has grown and intensified. A variety of solutions to this problem have been suggested and tried in many of the world's countries and, of these, two have been proposed as potentially most effective: (1) a system of administrative courts and (2) the Ombudsman (Friedmann 1979: 340-3).

The first system, developed by the Roman-law countries of continental Europe, has a decided advantage for the individual in that the onus of proof is on the government administration. However, this system also has some serious shortcomings, such as its enormous costs to all concerned and the complexity of its judicial procedure.

The second system, that of the Ombudsman, has been preferred in common-law countries such as Canada. One of the primary advantages of this system is that its costs to society as compared with those of a system of administrative courts are extremely low, and there are no costs to the complainant. Further, as Friedmann (1979) argues, a one-person institution promises much easier access and inspires far more confidence in the individual citizen than does a vast, impersonal bureaucracy. The major disadvantages of the ombudsman system are twofold: (1) the onus of proof is on the individual complainant, and (2) the ombudsman has the power only to recommend corrective action and to report publicly the findings and recommendations of the investigation; the office does not have the authority to change administrative decisions (Hill 1974: 1077).

The role of the ombudsman is to facilitate the lodging of complaints against public administration (Friedmann 1979: 345). The office of the ombudsman is legally established, functionally autonomous, and external to the government administration. The ombudsman, in short, is an independent and non-partisan intermediary between citizens and their governments, who acts as an impartial investigator of citizen complaints against government administration.

The institution of the ombudsman may be introduced at any or all levels of government. A number of the world's countries currently have ombudsmen at the central government level. Canada, like many other federal states, has instituted the office at the sub-national level. All provinces, with the single exception of Prince Edward Island, adopted ombudsmen between 1967 and 1977. Additionally, at the federal level, Canada has established ombudsmen for two specific and highly sensitive areas of public administration, i.e., a linguistic ombudsman, the Commissioner of Official Languages, and a prison ombudsman, the Correctional Investigator.

The Commissioner of Official Languages

For purposes of this book, with its focus on collective rights, the most relevant Canadian ombudsman is the Commissioner of Official Languages. This office was developed in response to the 1967 recommendation of Book 1 of the Reports of the Royal Commission on Bilingualism and Biculturalism. Specifically, the Commission recommended that Parliament adopt an Official Languages Act and appoint a Commissioner of Official Languages to ensure respect for the equal status of English and French in all federal institutions (Yalden 1979).

The Act, passed in 1969, affirms the principle that French and English enjoy equal status, rights, and privileges in their use as federal languages of work and as languages of service to the public. The commissioner is the legal watchdog of the Official Languages Act for Parliament and has the authority to intervene in linguistic matters in all areas under federal jurisdiction, including Crown corporations. The commissioner is entitled to investigate any complaint involving either lack of recognition of the status of an official language or non-compliance with the spirit and intent of the Act by governmental bodies.

Yalden (1979: 379) points out that the Official Languages Act (and, we would add, the role of the commissioner) continues to be widely misunderstood by the Canadian public, who all too often assert that the federal government is trying to 'force French . . . down the throats' of unwilling Canadians. Yalden, a strong supporter of the Trudeau government position on bilingualism and biculturalism, contends that investing in the future of Canada necessitates more than an Official Languages Act and Commissioner. It means firmer commitments from federal and provincial governments and from educational systems at all levels to producing truly bilingual citizens.

While this position clearly aims to protect the linguistic rights of English and French Canadian citizens, it is vehemently opposed by many non-English and non-French Canadians. Proponents of multilingualism and multiculturalism support the alternative position based on the recommendation of Book 4 of the Reports of the Royal Commission on Bilingualism and Biculturalism, namely that, where numbers warrant, the linguistic rights of all of Canada's ethnic groups must be recognized and respected. It follows from this latter position that the Office of Commissioner of Official Languages should be changed to that of Official and non-Official Languages, and that the mandate of the linguistic commissioner/ombudsman should be expanded accordingly, so as to protect the linguistic rights of members of all of Canada's ethnic communities.

The larger debate concerning non-official minority language rights, to which the foregoing discussion alludes, will be addressed in Chapter Ten, within the broader context of the Canadian Constitutional debate.

Scope of Canadian Legislation Prohibiting Ethnic Discrimination

There are significant differences in detail among current human rights statutes in their enumerated non-discriminatory grounds, areas of application, and so forth. However, with the single exception of British Columbia, statutes at the provincial and federal levels share fundamental similarities in content and administration (Hill and Schiff 1988: 31).

All of the human rights statutes in Canada prohibit discrimination on the basis of race, religion, colour, nationality or national origin, and sex. Discrimination on ethnic grounds is thereby prohibited in the broad sense of the term 'racial' as outlined in the International Convention on the Elimination of All Forms of Racial Discrimination. All the statutes refer to both 'race' and 'colour' as well as to other terms relating to ancestral origin such as 'national extraction (or) origin', 'place of birth (or) origin', 'ancestry', 'ethnic origin', and 'nationality'.

The statutes are designed to ensure equality of access to places, activities, and opportunities. Accordingly, they all prohibit discrimination in hiring, terms and conditions of employment, job advertisements, job referrals by employment agencies, and membership in unions. Most also prohibit discrimination in professional, business, and trade associations.

Both federal and provincial statutes prohibit discrimination in the provision of accommodation, services and facilities to which the public has access. The provinces and territories prohibit discrimination in residential property rentals and sales; many also cover commercial properties (Hill and Schiff 1988).

Administration and Enforcement of Human Rights Codes

Tarnopolsky (1979: 297) argues that the importance of consolidating human rights legislation into codes to be enforced by administrative commissions lies in the fact that this structure ensures community vindication of the victim of discrimination. Human rights legislation recognizes that it is not only bigots but also 'nice guys' who discriminate; most Canadians discriminate not so much because of racist convictions as from fear of loss of comfort, convenience, or monetary revenues.

The philosophy underlying the contemporary human rights approach blends educational and legal techniques in the pursuit of social justice. All jurisdictions except British Columbia and the Territories have full-time staff and citizen commissioners responsible to ministers of government, whose task is to administer the legislation and to act in an advisory and policy-making capacity. In accordance with the legislation, the staff and commissions are required to enforce the acts, carry out research on human rights, and conduct public education programs (Hill and Schiff 1988).

The enforcement process in all jurisdictions typically begins with the submission of a complaint of discrimination to the commission by the alleged victim of discrimination or by interested private groups, third parties, or (in some cases) officers of the administering agency. Following the receipt of a complaint, the commission is required to conduct an investigation and, should sufficient grounds be established to justify the complaint, conciliate the matter or effect a settlement. Terms of settlement vary depending on the nature of the complaint, but may require provision for accommodation, employment, and/or services previously denied. Other forms of redress commonly include recompense for the victim's financial loss and/or injury to dignity. In some cases, respondents also are required to undertake special—affirmative action or pay equity—programs to improve minority opportunity in their establishments (Hill and Schiff 1988: 32).

Initially, those who are found to discriminate are given the opportunity to redress their ways by being confronted with the severity of the injury to the human dignity and economic well-being of the victim as compared with their own real or anticipated loss of comfort or convenience. However, if persuasion, conciliation, and efforts to effect a settlement fail, a board of public inquiry or tribunal may be ordered. The public aspect of the inquiry, especially where the events capture media attention, is considered to be an important component of the public education mandate of commissions.

Ultimately, a discrimination complaint, if not settled to the satisfaction of both parties and/or the commission, may reach the courts. Some statutes empower commissions to bypass public inquiry and take cases directly to court. In any case, upon summary conviction the discriminator may be subject to fines that, depending on the jurisdiction, may range as high as $25,000 (Hill and Schiff 1988).

The Effectiveness of the Current Human Rights System in Canada

Anti-discrimination legislation has clearly served to raise the level of public consciousness of racism in Canada. But how successful has it been in achieving its ultimate goal, that of reducing the societal level of ethnic discrimination? The evidence presented throughout this book demonstrates that while discrimination has lost its public respectability, it has definitely not disappeared in Canada. What has happened is that blatant racism has gone 'into the closet', where it has become transformed into its more subtle counterpart—the 'new racism'.

Human rights advocates have long argued that in order for anti-racist legislation to be effective in practice, it must have teeth in it. The vigorous and intelligent enforcement of human rights legislation, with forceful sanctions against those who discriminate on the grounds of race, ethnicity, or any other prohibited grounds, advocates argue, is the most convincing form of public education.

Limitations of the Current Human Rights System

Since the coming into effect of the equality rights provisions of the Charter, in 1985, the statutory human rights model has come under increasing criticism. Section 15(2) of the Charter allows for the provision of affirmative measures to remedy group-based disadvantage resulting from systemic discrimination. In conformity with this Charter standard, most human rights statutes now allow for the provision of affirmative measures to redress group-based inequalities.

Critics of the current human rights model claim that the individual complaint-based procedure at the centre of the system has failed to adequately address and remedy systemic group-based inequalities. For example, Day (1990: 22) argues that systemic discrimination cannot be addressed effectively by a procedure which is designed for *individuals*, and which is *passive*, coming into play only when a victim of discrimination puts forward a complaint. Nevertheless, she points out, commissions do have the capacity to accept and investigate systemic complaints; they can even initiate such complaints. The failure of commissions to fully and effectively tackle widespread systemic discrimination and group-based inequality stems from the inappropriateness of the procedures, designed for processing individual complaints, as well as the current overload of unresolved individual complaints. Because of inadequate funding resources, Day asserts, there are long delays in the resolution of individual complaints and few resources for anything else (1990: 23). Additionally, she contends, there is a lack of will on the part of commissioners, and more importantly, on the part of governments, to *shift direction* in order to see systemic discrimination effectively addressed. In short, she argues, it is difficult to make the human rights processes match the Charter-endorsed promise of group—as well as individual—equality in the law when procedures are designed for a narrow, individual complaint system, when resources are scarce, and when governments do not provide support for tackling larger, systemic problems (1990: 25).

Day's critique of the human rights system was vividly demonstrated in a recent and scathing report on the practices of the Ontario Human Rights Commission, based on an investigation headed by the Ontario Ombudsman, Roberta Jamieson (*Toronto Star*, 20 July 1991). Jamieson stated that the backlog, at that time, of over 2,800 complaints was so overwhelming that the agency could no longer enforce the law. The investigation of the Commission found that complaints had not been adequately handled. Because the Commission is under-funded, there are virtually no resources for staff training, and because the Commission is understaffed, the workload precludes the adoption of speed-up procedures to deal with the backlog of cases. Clearly, under these onerous conditions, it is all but impossible to tackle larger problems of systemic discrimination and group-based inequality.

Conceptualized in terms of the human rights framework adopted in this book, it can be argued that the current human rights system (given adequate resources) is designed to deal with *individual rights* claims, but not with *categorical* or *collective rights* claims. We will address the question of collective rights claims in our analysis of the provisions of the Charter in Chapter Ten. At this juncture we will turn to the question of categorical rights claims, and examine the types of affirmative measures which have been adopted in Canada to redress systemic discrimination and group-based inequalities.

The Need for Affirmative Action: Collective Adverse Impact of Systemic Discrimination

In the last two decades there has been a marked increase in public awareness and understanding of the damaging effects of systemic or structural discrimination on Canadian minorities *as collectivities*. This mounting recognition of the pervasive discriminatory effects of long-term inequality of opportunity on whole categories of people, as opposed to single individuals, has had an important impact on human rights legislation. At the most fundamental level, it has led to an expansion of the legal definition of discrimination.

Until the nineteen-seventies, in legal terms discrimination tended to be equated with isolated acts, motivated by prejudice (individual discrimination). Yet the cumulative experience of Canada's various human rights commissions in administering anti-discriminatory legislation over the years was demonstrating beyond doubt that the most pervasive discrimination often results from unconscious, seemingly neutral practices and unexamined traditions which have become embedded, even unintentionally, in the everyday operations of employment, education, and other social institutions (systemic or structural discrimination). Human rights commissioners, practitioners, and lawmakers alike, increasingly have come to realize that systemic forms of discrimination impact adversely upon minorities as entire groups, and thereby guarantee the preservation through time of their collective, disadvantaged minority status (self-fulfilling prophecy). Accordingly, human rights legislation no longer defines discrimination simply as individual acts, nor does it identify discrimination simply by intent or motive (prejudice). Increasingly, anti-discriminatory legislation defines discrimination as systemic, and identifies it by results (collective adverse impact).

The fact that a great many historical traditions and public practices embedded in the everyday operations of Canadian public institutions have had and continue to have an adverse impact on whole categories of people clearly demonstrates the need for *intervention*, if these minorities are to enjoy *in fact* the equality promised by human rights legislation and guaranteed under s.15 of the Charter. Even if all minorities were to be afforded explicit protection under the enumerated grounds of non-discriminatory legislation, this would assure non-discrimination only in the future; it would not provide remedies for past human rights violations. The strategy of intervention which has been developed both to counteract and to provide immediate redress for the disadvantaging effects of systemic discrimination is that of *affirmative action*.

Glaser and Possony (1979: 24) have interpreted the concept of affirmative action as a system of positive discrimination in favour of collectivities hitherto discriminated against: compensatory discrimination in favour of disadvantaged collectivities in the society (ibid.: 57). More recently, Hill and Schiff (1988: 35) have defined affirmative action more specifically as 'a program of temporary measures designed to eliminate systemic factors that prevent members of minority or other groups from competing equally with members of the majority for opportunities, usually in employment or education'.

Section 15 of the Charter of Rights and Freedoms in the Canadian Constitution (1982) not only prohibits individual discrimination but also recognizes the validity of laws, programs, or activities designed to ameliorate the disadvantaged conditions of individuals or groups. Section 15(2) thus guarantees that affirmative action programs, designed by government agencies to provide forms of collective redress against the adverse impact of systemic discrimination upon disadvantaged (minority) groups, will be allowed. The guarantee provided by s.15(2) of the Charter was deemed to be imperative in order to ensure that special measures of affirmative action would not constitute 'reverse discrimination' under the non-discriminatory provisions of s.15(1).

The inclusion of s.15(2), in part, represented an attempt to prevent a repetition, in Canada, of the negative backlash to affirmative action which occurred in the United States. Let us, then, consider what happened south of the border, before going on to discuss the process of implementation of affirmative action in Canada.

Affirmative Action in the United States

The concept of affirmative action began to gain public approbation in the United States (at least in liberal sectors) by the 1960s. This development represented public response to a concerted effort on the part of the Government to reduce and eventually to eliminate racial, ethnic, and gender discrimination. In 1964, Congress enacted Title VII of the Civil Rights Act which made it unlawful for employers to discriminate on the basis of race, colour, religion, sex, or national origin. Initially, the Act applied only to the private sector, but in 1972, public sector employers and agencies were included.

There are two major programs enforced under the Civil Rights Act. The Equal Employment Opportunity Commission is responsible for enforcement of the 1964 legislation and also for information gathering. Under this program, every company with more than 100 employees must annually file a form listing the numbers of women and of four major racial and ethnic minorities (Blacks, Spanish-surnamed, Orientals, and American Indians) in their employ (Pie, *Viewpoint*/undated). The other major federal program is administered by the Office of Federal Contract Compliance (OFCC). This program requires that government contractors commit themselves to non-discrimination in business practice and to programs of affirmative action in their companies. Since 1970, each contractor and subcontractor must file an affirmative action plan with OFCC.

During the 1970s, public support for affirmative action fell off sharply, and programs began to be legally contested by non-minorities. Three key court cases challenging the constitutionality of affirmative action programs resulted in decisions specific to the particular case at hand, providing no clear guidance on how far employers could go in giving preferential treatment to minorities.

The Bakke decision (*Bakke v. University of California Regents*) was the first land-mark decision. In this case, a white male student challenged the affirmative action program of the University of California medical school which set aside a certain number of seats for minorities. Bakke was denied admission to the medical school, even though his examination scores were higher than those of the minority members admitted under the affirmative action program. The Supreme Court held that the special program of the medical school was unconstitutional. The Court decided that race could be taken into account in admission programs, but that race could not constitute the only criterion for admission. Two other court decisions, one upholding a special training program for minorities, and the other maintaining that an affirmative action program could not take precedence over a legitimate seniority system, left the question of the limits of affirmative action unresolved.

This lack of clarity as to the limits of affirmative action was one factor feeding the backlash against such programs, but, in the United States, at least two other factors were important. First, unlike the earlier Johnson administration, the Reagan and Bush administrations were not supportive of affirmative action, and, second, the economic climate, during recessionary years when promotional opportunities were limited and layoffs frequent, did not favour preferential treatment for protected classes of minorities.

Affirmative Action in Canada

Unlike the case of the United States, in Canada affirmative action programs for the most part are voluntary, and a set of voluntary affirmative action guidelines have been developed at the federal level. Weinfeld (1981) locates the origin of affirmative action in Canada in the efforts of the Royal Commission on Bilingualism and Biculturalism, in the 1960s, to increase francophone participation in the federal government service. At that time, not only were there disproportionately few francophones employed overall, but those who were employed were concentrated at the lower salary levels. Among senior decision makers, francophone representation was minuscule.

The Bi and Bi Commission, Weinfeld points out, developed the first clear outline of affirmative action principles as a basis for policy making. These principles, which largely followed the American model, involved a major shift in policy emphasis regarding human rights. This shift was threefold: (1) a shift from an emphasis on individual discrimination to an emphasis on institutional and systemic forms of discrimination; (2) a shift from an emphasis on individual rights to an emphasis on collective entitlement. This involved a shift from the individual merit principle to a modified merit principle which took into account the differential nature and impact of collective linguistic and broader cultural considerations; and (3) a shift toward the employment of statistical indicators of under-representation of target populations as a measure of group inequality.

Under-representation of francophones in the federal public service was acknowledged to be a manifestation of systemic discrimination in federal employment systems necessitating affirmative action programs designed to recruit, place and promote francophones (Hill and Schiff 1988: 39). Such programs were put in place, and, by 1977, as a mark of their effectiveness, overall francophone representation in Government employment had almost reached the proportion of francophones in the general population.

At the federal government level, the legal foundation for affirmative action policies was provided in 1977 with the passage of the Canadian Human Rights Act. With regard to employment, s.15 of the CHRA states that it is not a discriminatory practice to carry out a special program, plan, or arrangement designed to prevent, eliminate, or reduce disadvantages suffered by individuals or groups because of race, national or ethnic origin, colour, religion, age, sex, marital status, or physical handicap, by improving their opportunities respecting goods, services, facilities, accommodations, or employment. In short, s.15 of the CHRA insures that programs of affirmative action toward historically disadvantaged populations will not constitute reverse discrimination. Further, under the terms of reference of the Canadian Human Rights Commission that administers the Act, an affirmative action program may be required as part of the settlement of a discrimination complaint, as a measure designed to prevent the future recurrence of discriminatory practices. At the federal level, then, mandatory affirmative action plans may be deemed appropriate as preventive measures when a case of discrimination against an individual is found to be indicative of categorical discrimination against the minority she or he represents. Beyond this, the CHRA allows for, but does not require, affirmative action remedies.

In Canada, following the mandate of s.15(2) of the Charter, human rights codes in the 1980s have increasingly incorporated provisions allowing for programs of affirmative action. In the broader, North American context, affirmative action programs and legislation operate throughout both Canada and the United States. The major difference between the Canadian and the American experience lies in the directive of the regulatory agencies. In the United States, affirmative action is compulsory; in Canada, for the most part, it is voluntary.

The sanction for programs of affirmative action under s.15(2) of the Charter affords a constitutional basis for categorical rights claims, i.e., claims for redress against the collective adverse impact of systemic discrimination on disadvantaged groups. Such redress, in the form of affirmative action programs, may take a number of different forms, depending on the kinds of claims brought forward.

Types of Categorical Rights Claims and Affirmative Action Programs

Programs of affirmative action may be instituted in response to three kinds of claims based on categorical rights: (1) claims for equal (standard) treatment; (2) claims for temporary compensatory treatment; and (3) claims for permanent compensatory treatment.

The first kind of claim applies in cases of institutional discrimination, where, for example, equally or better qualified persons are denied jobs because they are identified as members of a particular racial or ethnic group. These are the kinds of cases typically brought before Human Rights Commissions. While individual cases can be dealt with appropriately by such commissions, larger, collective problems such as those posed by dire poverty on Indian reserves, and by systemic practices of racial discrimination in the work sphere, are not addressed. The latter problem is one which is most amenable to remedy through employment equity programs designed to ensure proportionate representation of minorities at all positional ranks in the society. While the strategy, here, is based on positive discrimination, the long-range goal of such programs is equal (standard) treatment.

The second type of claim applies in cases predicated on the collective, adverse impact of systemic discrimination, for example, where aboriginal or visible minorities, as a consequence of long-term denial of adequate education and training, lack the requisite qualifications and skills with which to compete in the Canadian job market. What is required here is a program of affirmative action through special education and job training designed to provide those minorities who are victims of systemic discrimination with a level of qualifications and skills equal to that of other Canadians. Such programs rest on claims for temporary (compensatory) treatment, but the long-range goal is one of equal (standard) treatment.

The third kind of claim applies in cases of institutional and systemic discrimination where equal (standard) treatment is inappropriate even as a long-range goal because of the permanent handicapping effects of a real mental and/or physical disability. Here, affirmative action programs must permanently provide 'reasonable accommodation', compensatory mechanisms that reduce the handicapping effects of disabilities and enable members of disabled populations to maximize their societal opportunities. Thus the long-range goal is equivalence, rather than equality of treatment.

Implementing Affirmative Action Programs

Affirmative action is a method for identifying and eliminating systemic practices which act as barriers to equality of opportunity across different population categories. It also is a method for assisting minority victims of systemic discrimination to overcome its long-term disadvantaging effects through the provision of special measures. Both of these components (elimination of discriminatory practices and provision of special measures) are deemed necessary in order for affirmative action programs to be effective (SHRC *Newsletter*, 9, 2, 4 March 1980).

Identification of Practices of Systemic Discrimination

In the area of employment, a number of systemic practices have been identified as barriers to equality of opportunity for aboriginal peoples, women, and visible minorities. For example, 'old-boys' networks' among white males have been found to provide convenient channels for word-of-mouth job recruitment in some employment sectors, ensuring that knowledge of job vacancies is confined to the in-group. Women and non-whites are thereby excluded.

Additionally, inflated or non-job related requirements have been found to pose systemic barriers for some minorities. Inflated educational requirements serve to bar competent (but poorly educated) aboriginal peoples and certain non-essential height and weight standards have been found to discriminate against women, some ethnic minorities, and aboriginal peoples. (SHRC, 1980).

Public Education: Practices of Omission and Commission

In the area of education, systemic barriers can discriminate against particular minorities by practices of omission or commission. For example, a number of research studies (Barrie 1982) have identified sex-stereotyping of occupational roles (commission), while others (McDiarmid and Pratt 1971) have revealed the absence of materials dealing with aboriginal peoples' languages, cultures, and histories in standard course curricula (omission).

It has been argued previously that *legislation* is needed to combat and eradicate acts of discrimination. In this section, we will argue that *education* is needed to counteract and eradicate the ideas and attitudes of prejudice which lie behind them.

To meet any kind of reasonable goals, public education must be based on accurate, up-to-date information; hence adequate resources must be allocated to fund research projects designed to provide such information. Further, unless minority members are informed about human rights principles, legislation, and investigative and conciliation procedures, they may well be unaware of the help available to them in an instance of discrimination. Hence, there is a need for much wider publicizing of human rights materials, including codes, cases, decisions, etc. as well as the findings of research studies on human rights issues. Probably the most glaring case of *omission* in this area lies in the neglect of formal instruction about human rights in the curricula of public education institutions in this country.

Within the public education system, it also is essential that textbooks, at all educational levels, be reviewed regularly for errors of omission and commission so as to ensure that they accurately reflect the historical and contemporary character and conditions of Canada's minority groups. Similarly, school facilities, programs, and guidance counselling need to be brought into line with human rights principles. They must be based on equity of access and equity of opportunity for all. The latter point draws attention to the importance of teacher training in the area of human rights. At present, however, this represents another large lacuna in human rights education throughout Canada.

Special Measures: Active Recruitment and Training Programs

The objective of special affirmative action programs is to create a more equitable distribution of opportunities and benefits across diverse social and cultural groups in Canada. Towards this end such measures as active recruitment and hiring strategies have already been undertaken by various governments and private bodies to move qualified aboriginal peoples and visible minorities into labour force positions they have previously been prevented from attaining.

Another special measure already undertaken at various levels of government is the establishment of training programs designed to equip members of long-disadvantaged minorities with skills and qualifications previously unavailable to them.

Planning for Affirmative Action

In both employment and education—the two key areas in which affirmative action programs have been developed—the planning of special programs involves, at the outset, establishing a measuring structure and specifying goals and timetables to meet those goals. The measuring structure is designed to ascertain, on a statistical basis, the distribution of opportunities and associated benefits across the various population groups in the relevant locale (society, region, organization, etc.). Once identification of group disadvantage has been established, corrective action is undertaken through programs designed to redress the identified disadvantaged condition of the target population(s).

The following examples may serve to illustrate the way in which this process operates.

In 1981, approval was granted to the Saskatchewan Piping Industry Joint Training Board to implement a special training program in the North which would increase the number of men and women of Indian ancestry, in the plumbing and pipe-fitting trade. Evidence was provided to show that persons of Indian ancestry composed 11.5 per cent to 14.7 per cent of the working-age population. Statistics revealed that of the 512 journeymen in the pipe trades in Saskatchewan, nine (1.74 per cent) were persons of Indian ancestry. These data demonstrated an under-representation of approximately 13 per cent, which supported the need for a special program in the plumbing and pipe-fitting industry. The program was designed to recruit 30 men and women of Indian ancestry each year into the pipe trades apprenticeship program. It was estimated that by 1989, 14 per cent of the apprentices would be persons of Indian ancestry (BC Human Rights Commission, *Newsletter* 4, 4, Spring 1983).

While women have been the main beneficiaries of affirmative action in Canada thus far, a number of programs have already been put in place for aboriginal peoples and visible (immigrant) minorities (Hill and Schiff 1988: 42). The Vancouver police force is one of several which have launched recruitment drives designed to penetrate visible minority communities and to increase the representation of visible minorities on the force. In 1977, there were only two minority group members on the 1000-member force. In order to facilitate recruitment of minorities, the Vancouver police waived traditional but non-essential job criteria such as height and weight requirements, which systemically discriminated against some visible minorities. By 1982, the force had increased the number of minority members to only 14, but it was stepping up its efforts.

In the early 1980s, the Saskatchewan Human Rights Commission approved several multi-faceted affirmative action projects whose chief beneficiaries were aboriginal peoples (Hill and Schiff 1988). One project was implemented by the Key Lake Mining Corporation in connection with the construction of a uranium mine in a sector of the province where aboriginal persons comprised 70 per cent of the population and where unemployment among them was over 80 per cent. Recruitment officers were sent out to aboriginal communities to contact potential workers, and the work schedules of aboriginal employees were adapted to accommodate the commuting distance between the work-site and the aboriginal community. Additionally, traditional academic requirements that were not essential to the job were waived and advisors were employed to help aboriginal workers adjust to conditions on the site and to protect their rights under the collective agreement.

In 1986, the federal government, through the Treasury Board, initiated a number of affirmative action measures for visible minorities in the Public Service of Canada (Jain 1987: 174). These included a special employment program, a visible minority employment office at the Public Service Commission in Ottawa, regional visible minority co-ordinators, special training for public service managers, a monitoring program for the recruitment, referral and appointment of visible minorities in the public service, and the granting of Canadian educational equivalences for certain foreign university degrees. Further, in August 1987, the Treasury Board established numerical targets for visible minorities. These targets were to be set by occupational category and instituted by departments for a three-year period beginning 1 April 1988.

Contract Compliance: An Alternative to Voluntary Programs

One of the alternatives to voluntary affirmative action, already in use by the federal and some provincial governments, is 'contract compliance'. While there is no comprehensive contract compliance legislation in Canada, the principle of contract compliance has become embedded in some Canadian statutes and embodied in regulations governing dealings of some governments with the private sector. Under contract compliance, any firm to which a government pays public funds for the purchase of goods or services must, as a condition of its contract, comply with the government's human rights requirements (Hill and Schiff 1988: 48-9). In some cases, the requirement may simply be one of non-discrimination in employment and services.

In other cases, however, the firm may be required to undertake a program of affirmative action. Companies with which governments do business may, for example, be required to take positive steps to redress any existing imbalance in what could be reasonably expected to be an equitable distribution of minority members throughout the ranks of their employees. Specific affirmative action programs constitute part of the contract with the government; thus, programs are carefully monitored by officers of human rights commissions. Failure to comply with the affirmative action provisions can result in penalties, which include, at least minimally, cancellation of the contract and exclusion of the firm from future government business.

The principle of contract compliance has become embodied in the federal Canada Oil and Gas Lands Act as well as in provincial regulations in Saskatchewan which require that resource companies who enter into surface lease agreements with these governments hire a certain proportion of their workers from local, disadvantaged groups, usually aboriginal peoples (Hill and Schiff 1988: 49). Similarly, highway construction contracts issued by the Manitoba government in the early 1980s required the hiring of local labour, primarily benefiting aboriginal persons.

Contract compliance, under the regulations of human rights legislation, clearly provides more forceful leverage for affirmative action than does 'permissive' legislation simply *allowing* voluntary programs. One example of human rights compliance regulations is provided by s.19 of the Canadian Human Rights Act. Section 19 of the Act gives the Government of Canada the power to make regulations providing for the placing of terms and conditions relating to anti-discrimination in contracts, grants, or licenses from the federal government. Under such regulations, organizations would be *required* to comply with the affirmative action provisions of the Canadian Human Rights Act (s.9-15).

Hill and Schiff (1988: 49) hold that the principle of contract compliance has broad support throughout Canada. These authors point out that both the Commons Committee on Visible Minorities (1984) and the Abella Royal Commission (1984) recommended the adoption of such policies. Further, policies of contract compliance are advocated by the Public Service Alliance of Canada, the Canadian Civil Liberties Association, and virtually all visible minority organizations. Moreover, Hill and Schiff assert, most advocates of the principle believe that a legislative base for contract compliance is necessary in order to ensure continuance of effective policies over successive governments, and strongly recommend the enactment of comprehensive contract compliance legislation, replete with remedies and enforcement procedures (1988: 50).

Mandatory Affirmative Action: Pros and Cons

Before we undertake a consideration of the policy option of mandatory affirmative action in Canada, it is important to address the basic issues which have plagued the controversy surrounding the policies and programs of mandatory affirmative action south of the border, since their inception in the USA over a quarter of a century ago.

The issues in the debate involve discussion at two levels: the level of ideology, and the level of public practice.

The ideological debate focuses on the meritocracy principle and on the contradictions to this principle posed by programs of affirmative action. The first issue to be addressed in relation to the meritocracy principle is that of the legitimacy of collective redress against the adverse impact of systemic discrimination (categorical rights claims). Opponents argue that when compensation is offered to groups (rather than to individual complainants) it is because of some collective characteristic (disadvantage) members (assumedly) share, not because of demonstrable evidence that, as *individuals*, they were victims of discrimination. Affirmative action programs accordingly are open to criticism on the ground that evidence has not been provided to show that all minority members have been equally subject to systemic discrimination. The possibility exists, therefore, that some minority members without need of affirmative action programs may be unjustly advantaged by them.

Opponents of affirmative action, like the late sociologist John Porter, have argued that American-style affirmative action, with its imposition of quotas for minorities, represents a retreat from the dogmas of universalism, the protection of individual rights and the merit principle which represent the fundamental democratic principles behind North American society. Porter (1980) suggested that affirmative action may have an effect that is opposite to its intention, namely, to force individual minority members to identify, perhaps unwillingly, with their minority collectivity, thus crystallizing the subordinate status of the group and *reducing* its members' prospects for upward mobility.

At the level of public practice, critics argue that problems in determining the extent of group disadvantage caused by systemic discrimination are manifold (see especially Block and Walker 1981.) For example, critics point out that it cannot be safely assumed that in every situation where disproportionate group representation (or under-representation) exists that it is due to systemic discrimination. For, even without systemic discrimination, it is unlikely that a random distribution of different groups would be evident in various sectors of society. Clearly, other variables, such as education, religion, place of residence, and so forth can affect differential outcomes for both individuals and groups. Therefore, before affirmative action programs can be deemed appropriate measures of redress, research must be conducted to identify all the causes of disproportionate representation of minorities within Canadian societal sectors and institutions.

Another set of issues, arising from the American experience with mandatory affirmative action programs, relates to their unintended, harmful, psycho-social consequences. Such programs have been perceived to have negative effects on the self-image of the minority participants and on the quality of inter-group relations. With regard to the first point, opponents of affirmative action have argued that minority participants in these programs are deprived of the feeling of self-worth and accomplishment which comes from achieving one's social position through one's own merit. As there will almost inevitably be some members of any minority target group who have achieved parallel social positions on their own merit, those members given 'special treatment' may come to see themselves as less worthy, less meritorious, than those who have made it on their own.

The other side of the coin of 'special treatment' lies in its potentially negative repercussions on individuals and groups who do not receive such benefits. Both minority and majority members excluded from or by affirmative action programs may harbour resentment towards minority participants and may feel that they have been discriminated against. The American experience reveals that co-workers and fellow students in the institutional settings where affirmative action programs have been put in place have tended to look down upon minority participants and to see them as less meritorious than themselves. These attitudes, in turn, have reinforced the negative self-image(s) of the minority participants.

Finally, when unqualified or less qualified minority participants are selected for an affirmative action program (in the American experience, in order to fill arbitrary quotas) the outcome, in many cases, has been the failure of the participant to fulfil the objectives of the program. The negative consequences of failure have in many instances been psychologically devastating for the participant. In these particular cases, which represent an abuse of the goals of affirmative action, hostile majority backlash has been all but inevitable. The failure of minority members has rendered these programs counterproductive: they have served to reinforce and 'justify' stereotypes of minority inferiority.

In light of the American experience, Glaser and Possony (1979: 325) have argued that the mounting injustice not only to victims of 'reverse discrimination' but even to the beneficiaries of positive programs under policies of mandatory affirmative action renders them inappropriate as a means of achieving equality of opportunity for minorities.

Canadian critics (see Block and Walker 1981) have tended to adopt a more positive, yet cautionary, approach toward mandatory affirmative action programs in this country. Some support the view that small pilot projects should be initiated and should be tested for costs and benefits before large-scale affirmative action programs are put in place. A major reason behind this cautious approach is that costs of mandatory affirmative action programs would be born largely by the taxpayer, through public funding. Before public resources are formally allocated, it is argued, taxpayers should be able to have a reasonable expectation of demonstrable social benefits from mandatory affirmative action programs.

Mandatory Affirmative Action: A Summary of the Issues

Opponents of mandatory affirmative action have argued against this policy option on both ideological and practical grounds. Ideologically speaking, critics have argued that special measures of *collective redress* against the adverse impact of systemic discrimination upon minorities as wholes offends one of the most fundamental principles of North American democratic society, the individualistic principle of meritocracy.

From a practical view, two routine arguments have been raised against legislating mandatory affirmative action in Canada: first, the financial cost and difficulties of implementation of programs and second, the alleged, negative results of such legislation in the USA.

The financial cost of affirmative action, we will argue, must be weighed against the tremendous social costs of maintaining the *status quo*: the cost of systemic discrimination is demonstrably greater than the expense of redressing historic wrongs. In financial terms alone, Canadians pay very high welfare costs when employers categorically exclude various minorities from employment, not to mention the concomitant costs of poor human resources planning and utilization. Accordingly, the Canadian economy suffers when aboriginal peoples, women, visible and other minorities are categorically excluded from various sectors of the work force.

As regards the second point, in the United States, the implementation of mandatory affirmative action has not produced uniformly negative results as its critics are prone to suggest. It has met mixed reactions and has generated vigorous debate. A particular target of attack has been the negative consequences of the imposition of compulsory 'quotas' designed to increase the representation of particular minorities in the employment and education sectors. As alluded to earlier, in order to fill arbitrary quotas, in many instances unqualified or underqualified minority members were accepted (see Kallen 1982: 234-40).

In the Canadian case, what must be considered at the outset is that Canada's legal, social, and economic situation is very different from that of the United States. Moreover, Canadians are presently in a position to learn from the *cumulative* American experience. The negative results of early affirmative-action programs with imposed quotas led to marked policy changes in the USA, favouring the setting of 'reasonable goals'. Canada's voluntary affirmative-action programs have followed this later course rather than the earlier quota system, and also have adopted monitored recruitment, hiring, and promotion strategies in order to reach projected goals. Most importantly, Canada's emphasis has been on education and training programs designed to assist target minority populations in the attainment of trade skills and professional certification which will provide them with legitimate qualifications for jobs. In this way, some of the major problems encountered south of the border, specifically, the filling of educational and occupational 'quotas' with *unqualified* or *underqualified* minority members, have been circumvented.

Affirmative Action and Human Rights in Canada Today

Despite some variation in the scope of human rights legislation and in the powers of different commissions, human rights legislation in Canada is largely permissive rather than prescriptive. Section 15.2 of the Charter and parallel statutory legislation throughout the country *permit* affirmative action by stating that it is not a discriminatory practice to implement special programs for (minority) groups disadvantaged through the effects of systemic discrimination.

While legislation is essentially permissive, federal and provincial governments increasingly have gone on record in favour of affirmative action. The constitutional sanction for affirmative action, given by its incorporation under s.15 of the Charter, makes Canada one of the few countries in the world where programs of affirmative action, including special measures, have gained status recognition under the provisions of the supreme law of the land.

These positive accomplishments notwithstanding, when it comes to assessing the concrete results of voluntary affirmative action programs, their inherent weakness comes to the fore. For more than two decades, the federal government has been actively promoting voluntary affirmative action programs through the Affirmative Action Division of the Canada Employment and Immigration Commission (CEIC). However, only a minuscule number of employers have actually instituted such programs. For example, from 1979 to late 1983, of the 1130 private firms contacted by the CEIC, only 49 agreed to develop an affirmative action plan (Hill and Schiff 1988: 47). The general picture, in all regions of Canada, reveals that while employers may have expressed an interest in actively complying with affirmative action provisions, few have voluntarily initiated programs of affirmative action. At best, it appears that the voluntary approach is working with exceeding slowness and the results remain obscure.

Mandatory Affirmative Action/Employment Equity: The Abella Report

In 1984, the Royal Commission on Equality in Employment, chaired by Judge Rosalie Abella, reported the findings of their national investigation of systemic discrimination in employment. On the basis of their study the Commission recommended that the federal government institute mandatory programs of employment equity in all Crown and government corporations where evidence of systemic discrimination in the form of under-representation of identified target groups was found.

The Terms of Reference of the Abella Commission were to enquire into 'the most efficient, effective, and equitable means of promoting employment opportunities for and eliminating systemic discrimination against four designated [minorities] groups: women, [aboriginal] native peoples, disabled persons and visible minorities'. The Commission examined the labour force profiles of three of the four categories (there being no comprehensive national data on disabled persons). It observed that four factors are statistical indicators of possible systemic discrimination: participation rates, unemployment rates, income levels, and occupational segregation. Census data and other survey data on female, aboriginal, and visible (non-aboriginal/racial) minorities revealed possible systemic discrimination as a determinant of the following general findings (the particular patterns varied from one category to another): under-participation, high unemployment, low wages, and under-representation in high income occupations. Consultations were carried out by the Commission with members of each of the designated minority categories in order to document their experiences relating to discriminatory employment barriers. All three categories articulated the following forms of categorical discrimination: insufficient or inappropriate education and training facilities; inadequate information systems about training and employment opportunities; no voice in the decision-making process in programs affecting them; employers' restrictive recruitment, hiring, and promotion practices; and discriminatory assumptions. On the basis of their findings, the Royal Commission recommended that the federal government put into place mandatory 'employment equity' programs in all Crown and government corporations where under-representation of designated minorities was identified.

Federal Response to Abella: Mandatory Programs of Employment Equity

Since 1986, two mandatory programs of employment equity have been initiated by the federal government.

In 1986, the federal government passed the Employment Equity Act (Bill C-62). This Act applies to Crown corporations and federally-regulated employers with 100 or more employees. The legislation requires that, from June 1988, these employers file an annual report with CEIC providing information on the representation of all employees and members of four designated target groups (aboriginal peoples, women, disabled persons, and visible minorities) by occupational group and salary range. Further information must be provided on those hired, promoted or terminated, month by month, for a full year. Failure to comply with this requirement can result in a maximum fine of $50,000. Annual reports must be publicly available and provided to the Canadian Human Rights Commission which is authorized to conduct an investigation should the data indicate evidence of systemic discrimination. Employers also are required to prepare an annual employment equity plan with goals and timetables. However, employers are not required to submit this plan to the Government and no penalty is imposed for failure to prepare and implement this plan.

The second mandatory federal program is the Federal Contractors' Program (FCP). This program is restricted to contractors with 100 or more employees who bid on contracts for goods and services worth $200,000 or more. Under this program, contractors are required to sign an agreement to design and carry out an employment equity program which will identify and remove discriminatory barriers to the selection, hiring, promotion, and training of women, aboriginal peoples, persons with disabilities, and visible minorities. Failure to implement equity can result in the exclusion of the contractor from future Government business (Jain 1989: 173-4). Unlike the Employment Equity Act, the FCP does not require employers to file an employment equity plan, only to make a commitment to develop a plan.

Critics of the federal government's two employment equity programs argue that these programs, though garbed in mandatory trappings, will remain *de facto* voluntary because they lack mandatory implementation of plans with specific goals and timetables, systematic monitoring mechanisms and effective sanctions for non-compliance (Jain 1989: 175, Stasiulis 1987: 237).

Critics also have pointed out that federal programs do not apply to all agencies under federal jurisdiction. The employment equity legislation applies only to employers under federal jurisdiction, while the federal government's affirmative action program applies only to the federal public service. Neither of these affirmative policies apply to the RCMP or the Armed Forces. Jain (1989: 177) comments that it is ironic that government requires private sector employers to collect and report data on representation of designated minorities in their work force, while an important government agency like the RCMP is not required to do so. The federal government should, he contends, extend its affirmative action mandate to include the RCMP and the Armed Forces.

Furthermore, Jain points out that there are few employment equity programs or contract compliance programs at the provincial level, where affirmative action plans remain voluntary. To remedy this situation, he recommends that provincial and territorial governments introduce mandatory employment equity and contract compliance programs.

Summary: The Advocates' Voice

In recent years, a succession of key reports documenting racism in Canada, including the reports of the Commons Committee on Visible Minorities (Canada. Daudlin, B., Chair 1984) and the Abella Commission (1984) have pressed the case for mandatory affirmative action. Hill and Schiff (1988: 47) state that, in the opinion of most advocates of affirmative action programs, such initiatives will not be assumed by business and industry as a serious obligation unless they are mandatory. Unfortunately, these authors suggest, the model of mandatory affirmative action set by the federal government is most inadequate. In the view of human rights activists, the federal employment equity bill is 'unworthy of the name'. For advocates of affirmative action, the admonition of the Abella Commission still constitutes the last word on the subject:

> A government genuinely committed to equality in the workplace will use law to accomplish it and thereby give the concept credibility and integrity . . . Equality in employment will not happen unless we make it happen. (Hill and Schiff 1988: 47)

Concluding Comments

In this chapter, we have focused our analysis on legal mechanisms designed to prevent and/or eradicate ethnic discrimination in Canada. We have analysed the legal structure of human rights protection at the statutory level, and we have attempted to point out its limitations, particularly with regard to its inadequacy in resolving group-level complaints based on systemic discrimination. In the latter regard, we have examined the continuing debate as to the appropriateness of the remedy of voluntary and/or mandatory affirmative action as a measure of collective redress against systemic discrimination.

In the next, and final, chapter of this book, we will focus on the legal structure of human rights protection at the constitutional level, in Canada. We will examine the differences between statutory and constitutional protection for human rights, and we will critically analyse the provisions of the Charter as an instrument designed to ensure equal protection for the human rights of all Canadians.

CHAPTER TEN

The Legal Framework for Protection for Minority Rights in Canada: The Canadian Constitution and its Charter of Rights and Freedoms

Constitutionalizing Minority Rights: Ethnic Group Equality or Entrenched Minority Status?[1]

Insofar as constitutional provisions are in accordance with fundamental human rights principles, they should afford equal/equivalent protection not only for the individual rights of all persons but also for the collective rights of all ethnic groups within the state. Yet Canada, from Confederation, has been constitutionally predicated on the inegalitarian notion of special group status. Under the Confederation pact and the subsequent Constitution Act of 1867, Canada's 'founding peoples'— English/Protestant and French/Catholic ethnic groups—acquired a special and superordinate status as the majority or dominant ethnic collectivities, each with a claim for nationhood within clearly delineated territorial boundaries (Upper Canada/ Ontario; Lower Canada/Quebec). Moreover, under the terms of s.93 and s.133 of the 1867 Constitution, the collective, religious/educational, and language rights of the two 'charter groups' were protected even outside their respective territorial jurisdictions, in localities where their members constituted *numerical* minorities.

By way of contrast, under the terms of s.94(24) of the 1867 Constitution, aboriginal nations, lumped together under the racist rubric of 'Indians', became Canada's first ethnic minorities. The provisions of s.94(24) gave the Parliament of Canada constitutional jurisdiction to enact laws concerning Indians and lands reserved for Indians. Under ensuing legislation, notably the various Indian Acts, once proud and independent aboriginal nations, living and governing themselves within the territorial bounds of their indigenous homelands, acquired a special and inferior status as virtual wards of the state.

Later immigrant ethnic groups, without constitutional provisions for special status—superior or inferior—have come to constitute a third (multicultural) category of ethnic groups whose collective claims rest on a goal of *equal* ethnic status and *equal* ethnocultural rights (Kallen 1982b).

For purposes of this book, the significance of constitutionally rooted status differences among founding, aboriginal, and multicultural ethnic groups is that they afford differential bases for collective claims: claims based on special (founding or aboriginal) status and claims based on equal (multicultural) status. Moreover, a consequence of this tripartite division is that minority rights claims put forward by representatives of each of the three categories are in competition, if not in direct conflict, with each other.

To what extent were each of the three sets of claims recognized during the 1980-82 constitutional debates, and to what degree have the collective rights of minority claimants been specified and protected through ensuing (1982) amendments? The analysis to follow explores not only the ethnic priorities underscoring the amending process but also the concomitant version of Canadian 'unity in diversity'—on both ethnic and non-ethnic grounds—entrenched through constitutional amendments.

Constitutionalizing a Canadian Charter of Rights and Freedoms (1980-82)

Throughout the 1980-82 constitutional debate legal scholars who voiced support for constitutional entrenchment of a Charter of Rights and Freedoms argued that an entrenched Charter would override existing legislation and render all discriminatory laws throughout the country inoperative. Moreover, it was argued, an entrenched Charter would serve to eliminate existing disparities in the provisions of federal and provincial human rights legislation as it would provide the standard to which all legislation should conform (Kallen 1982: Ch.9).

It follows from this line of argument that a constitutionally entrenched Charter should provide all Canadian minorities with an equal/equivalent basis for making claims for redress against perceived human rights violations. But is this in fact the case? Is the Charter truly an egalitarian human rights instrument, or is it informed by established ethnic and non-ethnic group priorities which serve to render some categories of Canadians *more equal* than others?

In order to answer this question at least three variables relating to the nature of the provisions of the Charter must first be taken into account:

1) Negative vs Positive Protections
Negative protections guarantee only non-interference by the state in the exercise of human rights by individuals or groups. Positive protections, on the other hand, obligate the state to take appropriate measures, including the provision of resources out of public funds, in order to guarantee the full exercise of rights.

2) Specified vs Unspecified Protections
Unspecified protections apply generally; they do not specify particular target populations. Specified protections, on the other hand, apply specifically to particular, enumerated target populations.

3) Undefined vs Defined Rights

Undefined rights are not spelled out with regard to meaning and content. Accordingly, the nature of the state obligations and of the protections to be afforded are neither clarified nor elaborated. Defined rights, on the other hand, are spelled out with regard to meaning and content, and the protections to be afforded by the state are delineated.

When the foregoing variables are taken into account in assessing the provisions of the Charter, it becomes evident that the Charter is not a truly egalitarian human rights instrument. Rather, the Charter, together with related (1982) constitutional provisions, can be seen to perpetuate and to further legitimate long-institutionalized status inequalities between and among different ethnic and non-ethnic populations in Canada.

Ethnic Inequalities

The special and superordinate status of Canada's two founding peoples is reconfirmed and bolstered through Charter provisions protecting their collective rights. Under Charter ss.16-21 and s.23, *positive, specified* protections are afforded for *clearly-defined* English and French language and educational rights. Under Charter s.29, the constitutionally entrenched, positive, specified protections for the clearly defined religious denominational education rights of Protestant and Catholic religious collectivities throughout Canada are reconfirmed.

Conversely, there are no parallel protections for the collective linguistic and religious rights of multicultural or aboriginal minorities. Charter s.27 mentions the 'multicultural heritage' of Canadians, but the vagueness of this provision leaves its interpretation entirely in the hands of the courts. Certainly, s.27 affords no *positive* protections for minority rights as this provision neither specifies nor defines the nature of the rights alluded to. Similarly, Charter s.22 provides only a vague, *negative* protection for non-official language minorities by allowing but neither specifying nor defining their linguistic rights.

Constitutional amendments (s.35 and Charter s.25) represent a positive move to improve the constitutionally entrenched, special, and inferior status of Canada's aboriginal peoples by recognizing their collective aboriginal rights. Yet these provisions afford only *negative* protections for the aboriginal and treaty rights of Indian, Inuit, and Métis minorities. The nature and content of collective aboriginal rights is not elaborated, and, after four constitutional conferences convened for the singular purpose of defining aboriginal rights, they remain undefined.

The unwavering priority given the collective rights of Canada's founding peoples over the parallel rights of multicultural and aboriginal minorities was evident throughout the amending process. In the original (1980) version of the Charter, there was no mention of the notion of 'multicultural heritage'. In response to unflagging lobbying by representatives of ethnic minorities, s.27 eventually was added (in the view of many scholars, as a tokenism—a 'motherhood' statement) (Kallen 1987).

Amendments pertaining to aboriginal peoples' rights proved to be highly vulnerable to the moves of the inter-governmental political chess game, and sections were inserted, deleted, and altered before the undefined rights of aboriginal peoples were finally recognized in s.25 of the Charter and s.35 of the Constitution Act (Kallen 1982).

The end result of the Constitutional amendment process was the enactment of a Charter which both reflects and entrenches the ethnic and non-ethnic priorities informing the entire debate.

My earlier analysis of the Charter revealed an apparent hierarchy of ethnic groups constitutionalized through its protections for collective rights. In the following section, my analysis will reveal a parallel hierarchy in the Charter's protections for the equality rights of members of ethnic vs non-ethnic minorities.

Equality Rights: Constitutionalizing Ethnic and Non-ethnic Inequalities

Section 15(1) and (2) of the Charter, under 'Equality Rights', provides the key constitutional basis for individual and categorical rights claims for equal status and equal/equivalent treatment. While there is general agreement among scholars that the non-discriminatory grounds of s.15 are 'open', i.e., that claims can be put forward by minorities not enumerated in its provisions, enumerated minorities are afforded specified protection for their human rights, while non-enumerated minorities have only unspecified protection. Enumerated minorities, specified on the grounds of race, national or ethnic origin, colour, religion, sex, age, or mental or physical disability, thereby have a firmer basis for claims than have non-specified minorities. Even among the different enumerated minorities, a covert status hierarchy can be found. Ethnic (aboriginal and multicultural) minorities and women have specified human rights protections under other Charter provisions (s.25, s.27 and s.28, respectively), whereas other enumerated minorities do not. In light of the fact that the provisions of s.15 of the Charter are subject to the possibility of provincial government override under s.33, while s.25, s.27 and s.28 are not vulnerable in this respect, it becomes apparent that aboriginal and multicultural minorities and women enjoy greater Charter protections than do other minorities enumerated under s.15.

The foregoing analysis suggests that the provisions of s.15 of the Charter can be seen to underscore a status hierarchy in which enumerated minorities with other constitutional protections (namely, aboriginal and multicultural minorities and women) rank highest; other enumerated minorities (namely, those specified on the basis of race, age, or physical or mental disability) rank second, and non-enumerated minorities (namely, unspecified populations whose minority status is based upon sexual orientation, political belief, criminal record, or other grounds) rank lowest. Given this interpretation, I would tend to agree with Judge Walter Tarnopolsky

(1982: Ch.1) that it would not be surprising if some version of the American approach to equality rights were to be adopted by the courts in assessing equality rights claims. The American model involves three levels of judicial scrutiny: strict, intermediate, and minimal. This model could be applied to claims put forward by non-enumerated minorities, enumerated minorities without other constitutional protections, and enumerated minorities with other protections, respectively. Should this happen, the discriminatory implications for minorities of the inegalitarian nature of the Charter's provisions could be profound. For it would follow that the lower the status of the minority the greater would be the burden of proof upon the victim of discrimination.

Tarnopolsky's suggestion is supported to some extent by judicial interpretation made in connection with the ruling of the Supreme Court of Canada in the Andrews and Kinersly case. In releasing its first judgment under s.15 of the Charter, the court ruled that a British Columbia statute (the Barristers and Solicitors Act) which stipulated that only Canadian citizens could practise law in that province violated s.15 on the basis of citizenship (*Toronto Star*, 3 Feb. 1989). Citizenship is not enumerated in the non-discriminatory grounds of s.15, but the court ruled that it is akin to the kinds of characteristics listed. This case will be elaborated later in this chapter.

Legal observers had been looking to the court for guidance on whether the prohibited grounds of discrimination extended beyond those enumerated in s.15. Judge McIntyre said that, for now, non-enumerated grounds will be judged on a *case-by-case* basis. What this suggests is that claims brought forward on non-enumerated grounds will be more strictly scrutinized than claims brought forward on enumerated grounds (*Toronto Star*, 3 Feb. 1989). Accordingly, s.15 of the Charter will continue to afford clearer protection for the rights of enumerated vs non-enumerated minorities.

Proposed Constitutional Amendments: A Threat to Charter-endorsed Minority Rights?

1) The (failed) 1987 Meech Lake Accord

In discussion of the Accord in connection with the Franco-Québécois movement (Chapter Eight), we pointed out that when the provisions of the proposed Accord were announced, representatives of multicultural and aboriginal ethnic minorities were unanimous in their position that s.2(1)a of the Accord, recognizing the existence of French-speaking Canadians and English-speaking Canadians as a 'fundamental characteristic' of Canada, and s.2(1)b, recognizing that Quebec constitutes a 'distinct society' within Canada, diminished their Constitutionally endorsed rights. Despite the fragility of s.27 of the Charter as a constitutional safeguard for the protection of multicultural values, this Charter provision is strongly embraced by multicultural minorities both as a symbol and as a guarantee for their multicultural rights.

Accordingly, the reaction of ethnic minorities to the *omission* of multiculturalism from the original provisions of the proposed Meech Lake Accord was decidedly negative, if not hostile. A parallel response was voiced by aboriginal representatives with regard to their special rights protected under s.35 and under s.25 of the Charter.

The First Ministers' response to the strongly voiced concerns of multicultural and aboriginal representatives was to add to the Accord section 16, which declares that nothing in s.2(1) of the Accord affects the (specified) provisions of the Charter and the Constitution protecting multicultural rights and aboriginal peoples' rights. But, despite this addendum to the Accord, minority spokespersons continued to be vehement in declaring their opposition to these provisions. The Canadian Ethnocultural Council (CEC) expressed dissatisfaction with s.16 of the Accord because, they argued, while this provision immunizes s.27 of the Charter from s.2 of the Accord, the provisions of s.27 apply only to the Charter, and not to the entire Constitution. Alternatively, if the Accord was ratified, the entire Constitution would have to be interpreted in light of s.2 of the Accord, i.e., in a manner which recognizes English/French bilingualism as a fundamental characteristic of Canada and which recognizes Quebec as a distinct society. Aboriginal representatives echoed these criticisms, pointing out that aboriginal peoples also constituted 'distinct societies' within Canada and should be recognized as such.

What ethnic minority opposition to the provisions of the Accord implied was that this amendment favoured the élitist model of cultural dualism over the egalitarian model of multiculturalism and that, had it been enacted, it would have undermined Constitutionally endorsed multicultural and aboriginal rights. From the view of Canada's ethnic minorities the Accord was seen as a retrogressive amendment harking back to the constitutional priorities behind Canada, vintage 1867.

2) The (failed) 1992 Charlottetown Accord

In the wake of the failure of the Meech Lake Accord, the federal government made a concerted effort to ascertain the views of Canadians on the vision of Canada which should be enshrined through future constitutional amendments, and, as detailed in Chapter Eight, on 24 September 1991 Government tabled the document *Shaping Canada's Future Together*, in the House of Commons (*Toronto Star*, 25 Sept. 1991). The immediate reaction of Canada's three minority ethnic constituencies—Franco-Québécois, aboriginal peoples, and multicultural communities—was decidedly negative.

Let me summarize the proposed constitutional changes and outstanding issues with specific reference to the rights of aboriginal peoples, Quebec, Charter-language minorities, and multicultural minorities:

Aboriginal Peoples
The Constitution would recognize the inherent right to self-government of all aboriginal peoples. Aboriginal governments would also be recognized as one of three

orders of government, the others being federal and provincial. A major issue has been how quickly aboriginal groups would be able to go to court to enforce their right to self-government. The talks agreed in principle that the right to go to court be delayed for three years in order that the process of negotiating the details of self-government could proceed. The exact powers of aboriginal governments would not be defined in advance; instead, aboriginal governments would be described in general terms, and Ottawa and the provinces would commit themselves to negotiating the details of self-government in the future. Outstanding issues here include control over natural resources, justice systems, health care, children, economic development, and recreation. Aboriginal governments would be subject to the Charter, but once they create 'legislative bodies', these would have the same power as other legislatures to override most sections of the Charter. Aboriginal peoples also would have a constitutional guarantee that their cultures, languages, and traditions would not be thwarted by the Charter, including the proposed recognition of Quebec as a distinct society.

Quebec/Meech

Under the new proposals, Quebec would be recognized as a distinct society. Quebec legislation, otherwise deemed unconstitutional, might be permitted in order to promote Quebec's distinctiveness, defined as including a French-language majority, unique culture, and civil law tradition. A separate provision would require the courts to interpret the *entire Constitution*, and not just the Charter, in light of Quebec's 'special responsibility' to preserve and promote its distinct identity. There had been concerns by some that this might give Quebec more power than the other provinces; however, a new addition to the provision, the Canada clause, states that all provinces are equal.

A key issue, still unresolved at this time, was Quebec's demand for the power to veto any future changes to federal institutions such as the Senate or Supreme Court, if it believed that such changes would go against its interests. Also outstanding were Quebec's demands for more control over areas including energy, telecommunications, and family law policy.

Charter-language and multicultural minorities

While Quebec would be recognized as a distinct society, the proposals guarantee that, in interpreting this provision, the courts would also be obliged to take into account the vitality and development of anglophones inside Quebec and francophones outside Quebec. Further, the provisions of the proposed Canada clause would reaffirm Canada's constitutional commitment to racial and gender equality, multicultural diversity, and three orders of government: federal, provincial, and aboriginal.

As the (Government-declared) *last* round of talks began, in June of 1992, representatives of the Canadian Ethnocultural Council demanded 'official observer status', arguing that the then current process, which included aboriginal groups as well as federal, provincial, and territorial governments, 'marginalizes ethnic and racial minorities' (*Toronto Star*, 9 June 1992). CEC also outlined a number of constitutional changes designed to promote racial and ethnic equality. Among these were changes to the preamble and Canada clause of the new constitution to recognize the 'pluralistic and multicultural reality' of Canada, rather than merely recognizing the nation's heritage or cultural diversity.

On 7 July 1992, the premiers representing the nine provinces of English Canada reached an accord to reform the constitution in a way that they hoped would be acceptable to Quebec (*Toronto Star*, 8 July 1992). The Canadian unity package agreed upon included a veto for Quebec and every other province over future changes to federal institutions. The agreement recognized Quebec as a distinct society, and affirmed the right of the Quebec government to preserve and protect Quebec's distinct language, culture, and civil code. The distinct society clause was moved from the Charter to the Canada clause, where it could be used by the courts in interpreting the entire constitution. The Accord also included a new division of powers between the federal and provincial governments and an elected and equal Senate with substantially increased powers.

With regard to aboriginal issues, under the agreement, the constitution would entrench an inherent right to aboriginal self-government. Also, there would be a political accord which recognized the right of aboriginal peoples to a significant say over future constitutional amendments which affect them. The Canada clause would be amended to include wording to guarantee the right of aboriginal peoples to protect and promote their cultures and languages and to act in the best interests of their societies (*Toronto Star*, 8 July 1992).

While aboriginal representatives at the meeting generally applauded these changes, they reportedly expressed some concern about the deletion, in the new agreement, of a 'contextual clause' that in the previous proposals would have detailed some of the preliminary aspects of aboriginal self-government. This exclusion, they said, could make negotiation of self-government agreements more difficult. Additionally, while aboriginal self-government continued to be recognized under the agreement as a third order of government in Canada, the waiting period before courts can be asked to intervene and interpret self-government was extended from three to five years.

In order to finalize the terms of the Accord, then Prime Minister Mulroney invited all of Canada's First Ministers, together with representatives of the two territories and four aboriginal groups, to a meeting in Charlottetown, PEI, and on 28 August 1992 an unanimously endorsed agreement-in-principle was reached.

Reaction of human rights activists and spokespersons for Canada's ethnic and other minorities to the final version of the Accord was decidedly negative. While the Charter-endorsed rights of aboriginal, official language, racial and ethnic and gender-based minorities across Canada were mentioned in the Canada clause, legal scholars and other critics were quick to point out that, once again, the priorities informing the constitutional process had produced a 'pecking order' of human rights. Lawyer Anne Bayefsky, for example, in an article for the *Toronto Star*, argued persuasively that the Canada clause provision contained a list of priorities (*Toronto Star*, 21 Sept. 1992). Of primary importance was Quebec's 'distinct society', and the government of Quebec was given the power to 'preserve and promote' that society. Next in the pecking order were aboriginal peoples, whose governments would constitute one of the three orders of government in Canada, and who would have the power to 'promote' their languages, cultures, and traditions. Next came official language minorities, who have governments' vague commitment to their 'vitality and development', without any specified power to 'promote' or 'preserve' their communities. Much lower down in the pecking order was 'racial and ethnic equality' and 'equality of male and female persons', without any government obligation to 'promote' or any government commitment to these human rights principles. Finally, omitted from the Canada clause was any mention of multiculturalism as a fundamental characteristic of Canada, or any mention of the many other minorities in Canada (based on age, disability, sexual orientation, or whatever), who were thereby excluded from the new pecking order of human rights protection.

Not surprisingly, opposition to the unity package was quickly expressed by spokespersons for various women's groups, for racial and ethnic minorities, for persons with disabilities, and for others who felt that their particular interests and constituencies had been left out of the constitutional deal.

When a national referendum on the 28 August 1992 Charlottetown Accord was held on 26 October 1992, the Accord was defeated, not only in Quebec, but across Canada. Both the YES and NO sides in the campaign which preceded the vote represented an uneasy alliance of interest groups whose reasons for siding with one camp or the other were as diverse as their particular priorities. But what the final vote made clear was that Canadians were suffering from 'constitutional fatigue' and were determined to move on to more immediately pressing concerns, particularly the depressed state of the country's economy. At the time of writing, the constitutional question remains on the back burner. Moreover, Prime Minister Jean Chretien has publicly declared that under the mandate of the present Liberal government, constitutional issues will not be resurrected in the foreseeable future (*Canada AM*: CTV Interview, 7 Jan. 1994).

Until such time as future constitutional amendments are enacted, Canada's Charter of Rights and Freedoms, in its present form, will provide the standard for the legal protection of minority rights in Canada. It may therefore be appropriate, at this juncture, to undertake a brief consideration of its strengths and weaknesses.

The Charter's Protection for Minority Rights: Strengths and Weaknesses

Strengths

1) The Charter primarily applies to actions of governments. As part of Canada's (1982) constitution, the supreme law of the land, its provisions override those of

statutory law. Accordingly, federal and provincial governments must ensure that their laws conform to Charter standards. The Charter has an enforcement provision which authorizes courts to strike down laws which do not conform to its standards (s.52) and to order appropriate and just remedies to complainants (s.24).

2) The Charter also provides private, non-governmental bodies and individuals with a constitutional basis for challenging their federal and provincial governments when their laws or policies do not conform to Charter standards. Prior to the enactment of the Charter, private individuals and organizations could bring forward complaints alleging human rights violations against other private individuals or organizations only under the provisions of statutory human rights legislation at the federal and provincial levels. However, claimants could not challenge any alleged discrimination in the laws themselves, or in government policies and practices under these laws.

3) Because the Charter provides a nation-wide standard for all legislation, once all laws have been brought into conformity with Charter provisions, Canadians should be afforded the same protection for their human rights throughout the country, rather than differential protection from one jurisdiction to another.

Weaknesses

1) Section 1 of the Charter (the 'reasonable limits' clause) limits Charter rights in a number of ways. We know that, even as universal moral principles, human rights are never absolute rights: the justification for imposing limits on rights at the most fundamental level is non-violation of the rights of others. Under s.1 of the Charter, limits must be 'reasonable, prescribed by law, demonstrably justified, and in keeping with the standards of a free and democratic society'. The problem with this articulation of limits on human rights is that it is subject to questionable, *subjective* interpretation by the courts. Three of the four criteria are open to judicial bias in interpretation because of their subjective nature: only the criterion 'prescribed by law' is objective.

2) Section 33 of the Charter (the 'opting out' clause) allows governments to exclude their laws from the requirements of the Charter with regard to s.2 (fundamental freedoms) and ss.7-15 (legal and equality rights) for a period of 5 years at a time.

Minority Rights Cases: Claims under Human Rights Statutes and Charter Challenges

Notwithstanding the previously noted limitations of human rights statutes and of the Constitutional Charter, the following pages present a sample of cases, from across Canada, which serve to reveal the positive benefits for minorities of legal protection for minority rights. But, before we look at particular cases, it is important to distinguish clearly between the nature and scope of human rights protection afforded under constitutional/Charter and statutory legislation with regard to minority rights claims.

Statutory versus Charter Protection for Minority Rights

1) Statutory human rights laws deal with claims of discrimination by and against private individuals or groups; the Charter deals with discrimination by governments (e.g., discriminatory government laws and/or policies).

2) Statutory human rights legislation applies primarily to discrimination in employment, accommodation and public services; the Charter applies to all areas under government jurisdiction.

3) Federal and provincial human rights commissions provide investigative services at no cost to the complainant, but individuals or organizations bringing complaints under the Charter must pay for the costs involved (e.g., hiring a lawyer to defend the case in court). Because this is beyond the means of many persons, particularly members of disadvantaged minorities, the federal government initially provided some funding for selected 'Charter Challenge' court cases at the federal level. However, this program was discontinued in 1992. The substantial court costs of Charter challenges prohibit most minority members and organizations from pursuing this option on their own.

Resolution of Minority Claims

In the following section of this chapter, we will apply the typology of human rights and human rights claims delineated in the Introduction (page 10) in examining legal cases brought forward by minority claimants under the provisions of human rights legislation in Canada.

1) Individual Rights Claims

Our first example deals with a claim of racial discrimination made against a Victoria restaurant and the Victoria police by a black citizen of Canada. The complainant, born in St Vincent, holds a master's degree from two Canadian universities and works as a health co-ordinator in British Columbia (*Canadian Human Rights Advocate*, Feb. 1988). While visiting Victoria, the complainant, a registered guest at a motor inn, went into the restaurant at the inn and sat down at the only available table. All other tables were occupied by non-black patrons. He placed his order with a waiter, but within five minutes was informed by a waitress that he would have to move so that she could seat two other persons at his table. He refused to move because he could see no other table available and because he had not, as yet, received his order. The police were called. Victoria police questioned him about his citizenship, threatened him with deportation, searched and handcuffed him, and then hauled him off and locked him in jail for eight hours. The complainant brought his case to the BC Human Rights Council, which found that the only reasonable inference which could be drawn was that the complainant was the subject of racial discrimination. The complainant was awarded $2000 for humiliation, embarrassment, and damage to self-respect against both the restaurant and the police.

This case, and others like it, reveal that under human rights legislation, the employer is held responsible for the discriminatory acts of employees. Thus, what may appear to be an act of individual discrimination is treated as an act of institutional discrimination, thereby putting the onus on those who control organizations to ensure that they respect the human rights of all persons associated with them.

In our second case, four white men, who had held senior positions with an electronics firm, resigned from their jobs and filed a complaint with the Ontario Human Rights Commission alleging that an untenable work atmosphere had been created after they refused to carry out racist and sexist policies instituted by the president of the company (*Canadian Human Rights Advocate*, Jan. 1989). The complainants alleged that the president customarily made racist remarks and told them not to hire women or visible minorities. When the president discovered that women or members of visible minorities had been hired, he ordered the complainants to fire them. The complainants each alleged a breach of their rights to equal treatment in employment and freedom from reprisal for refusing to infringe the right of another person.

The company was ordered (and agreed) to pay the former employees a total of $293,796 in lost compensation, and the president of the company agreed to send each of the complainants a letter of apology and to personally pay each former employee $8000 in general damages. The settlement also required the company to put in place a comprehensive affirmative action program (in areas of education, hiring, advertising, and recruiting) in order to reach a goal of employment equity for women and visible minorities. As a whole, the settlement acknowledged three forms of discrimination: *individual* (president's directives), *institutional* (company policy), and *systemic* (long-term company practices), and sought to provide remedies for all three.

A third example illustrates the way in which human rights cases are resolved when there is an apparent conflict of rights involved. The Supreme Court of Canada ruled (in the Bindher case) that on a construction site a member of the Sikh faith may not insist that he be allowed to wear his turban (a required religious observance) in preference to a safety helmet ('hard hat') (*Affirmation*, Sept. 1986). The original case was brought forward under federal jurisdiction by a Canadian National Railways employee. The position of the Supreme Court was that considerations of public safety take precedence over religious freedom. This position is consistent with the general human rights principle (derived from the American Bill of Rights) which holds that where there is evidence for 'a clear and present danger', in the interests of the 'greater good', individual rights may be abrogated.

On the other hand, when such overriding considerations are not at issue, under human rights legislation, religious freedom must not be denied. Accordingly, the Metro Toronto Police have amended some of their regulations so as to permit a police officer of the Sikh faith to wear a turban on duty, instead of the customary officer's cap. The turban has been specially designed to accord in colour with the customary police cap and also features the officer's badge. In addition, the clean-shaven rule of the police has been amended to permit a Sikh to wear his religiously required beard.

What these contrasting examples illustrate is the difference, under human rights legislation, between a *bona fide* job requirement, which cannot be held to be discriminatory (the hard hat, in the first case) and a non-essential or non-job-related requirement, which can be held to be discriminatory (the customary police cap and the clean-shaven requirements, in the second case).

2) Categorical Rights Claims

Categorical rights claims may seek redress against the collectively disadvantaging effects of past discrimination through programs of affirmative action (allowed under section 15(2) of the Charter and parallel statutory provisions). This kind of claim has been suggested in the recommendations for mandatory programs of affirmative action for visible minorities put forward in two 1984 federal government reports: the Daudlin (*Equality Now*) report and the Abella (Equality in Employment) report. Both reports identified a variety of systemic discriminatory practices in the work place, including word-of-mouth recruiting, 'Canadian experience' criteria, cultural-ly biased interviews and tests, limited exposure to new job openings, and many other practices which create barriers to hiring and promotion opportunities for visible minorities. Both reports strongly recommended that programs of affirmative action for visible minorities be made mandatory, because the voluntary approach to affir-mative action has not led to widespread adoption of programs for visible minorities. The *Equality Now* report pointed out that a number of Canadian organizations have voluntarily adopted affirmative action programs to increase employment opportu-nities for aboriginal peoples (1984: 34). Even in the case of aboriginal minorities, however, where affirmative action incentives have been in place for almost two decades, the voluntary approach has produced meagre results in terms of redressing long-term, categorical disadvantage.

Another kind of categorical rights claim seeks compensation for the systemic impact on the minority of blatant, past forms of institutional discrimination involv-ing perceived group degradation. The Japanese-Canadian claim for redress against the flagrant violations of the political, economic, social, and cultural rights of the Japanese minority in Canada during World War II provides a stark case in point.

Fulfilling a long overdue promise to representatives of the Japanese-Canadian minority, in September of 1988 the Parliament of Canada rendered a formal apology for the 'savage injustices perpetrated in Canada's name' during World War II (*Toronto Star* editorial, 23 Sept. 1988). Prime Minister Mulroney announced that the Government would 'put things right' by paying $21,000 each to compensate the thousands of Canadians who have survived 'this shameful chapter in our history'.

Representatives of the Chinese Canadian National Council have been (so far, unsuccessfully) seeking a parallel settlement (apology and individual monetary compensation) from the Government for the head tax imposed on all Chinese immigrants to Canada from 1866 to 1923, and in symbolic reparation for the virtual ban on Chinese immigration to Canada from 1923-1947. Like the Japanese-Canadian case, the focus of the Chinese-Canadian claim is on the affront to group dignity experienced by the minority and on the symbolic (rather than monetary) importance of Government recompense (*Toronto Star*, 18 Mar. 1991).

3) Collective Rights Claims

While collective cultural claims have been far less common than individual and categorical rights claims, two important cases have rested at least in part on collective claims. The first case was the Sandra Lovelace case brought forward by an Indian woman who had lost her legal Indian status and her right to reside on her New Brunswick reserve because she married a non-Indian (Kallen 1982: 226-7). After she divorced her husband, she wished to return to her reserve, with her children, to be with her family and ethnic community. She was not allowed to do so because, under the prevailing provisions of the Indian Act, when an Indian woman married out, she and her descendants automatically lost their legal Indian status. Lovelace argued that the relevant provisions of the Indian Act discriminated against women, because, when an Indian man married out, his wife and descendants automatically gained legal Indian status. Thus, the Act endorsed and enforced a sexist double standard. Lovelace took her claim to the New Brunswick Human Rights Commission, and eventually to the Supreme Court of Canada, but was unsuccessful. Having exhausted all legal avenues in Canada, she took her claim to the United Nations Human Rights Committee and she won her case. The interesting aspect of the UNHRC decision was that it did not rest on sexism, but on cultural discrimination. The committee argued that by denying Lovelace (and, by implication, all Indian women who married out) access to her reserve, she and her children were being denied their right to practise their distinctive ethnoculture. This, they argued, was in conflict with article 27 of the International Covenant on Civil and Political Rights, which protects minority cultural rights (see Introduction: page 2).

This was a landmark case for it succeeded, where all previous cases had failed, in persuading the federal government to amend the contested provisions of the Indian Act. As detailed in Chapter Three, in 1985, the Government enacted Bill C-31, which deleted the Act's sexist double standard regarding out-marriage and which enabled the re-instatement of thousands of Status Indian women who has lost legal Indian status through marriage to a partner without legal Indian status.

The second case is again a landmark case with regard to minority cultural rights claims. On 24 April 1985 the Supreme Court of Canada unanimously struck down the federal Lord's Day Act on the grounds that it conflicts with the guarantee of freedom of religion under s.2a of the Charter. This was the first Supreme Court decision interpreting the right to freedom of religion in the Charter, and the Court interpretation represented a sharp break with pre-Charter decisions which had interpreted that freedom very narrowly (*Canadian Human Rights Advocate*, May 1985). What is most interesting about the interpretation is that it took into account equality rights, even though s.15 of the Charter was not yet in effect, and it also took into account s.27 of the Charter, the multicultural provision. By so doing, the interpretation of freedom of religion was broadened from its customary interpretation as an individual right (freedom of choice) to an interpretation reflecting the principle of ethnocultural equality which includes collective religious rights, i.e., the right of minorities to express their difference from the dominant religious culture. This case will be elaborated in our analysis of Charter challenges, later in this chapter.

In connection with this particular case, it is important to point out that it may not necessarily be precedent-setting for parallel provincial legislation, insofar as the Supreme Court has indicated that statutes requiring businesses to remain closed on Sunday may be valid if it can be demonstrated that they are designed to ensure workers a day off (a common pause day) rather than to enforce religious beliefs. In September of 1984, the Ontario Court of Appeal, in considering the Ontario Retail Business Holiday Act which requires many businesses to remain closed on Sunday, found that the purpose of this law was not to protect the Christian Sabbath, but to ensure a day off. For that reason, the Court held that the law was not invalidated by the Charter, for most purposes. However, the Court recognized that the unintended effect of the law was to discriminate against religious minorities whose Sabbath day of rest fell on another day of the week. Therefore, the Court held that those who closed on another day due to religious beliefs were exempted from the law and could remain open on Sunday (*Canadian Human Rights Advocate*, May 1985). The Act is still in effect, but the Ontario government has amended it so as to shift the onus of decision-making on the question of Sunday closing to the municipalities (*Toronto Star*, 8 Feb. 1989).

4) Nationhood Claims

As detailed in Chapter Eight, such claims have been brought forward, for example, by the Dene Nation, by the Inuit of Nunavut, and by the Franco-Québécois. To date, in no case has the desired goal of nationhood (including self-government) been achieved.

In the last section of this presentation of case materials, we will shift the focus of our discussion from the resolution of minority claims *per se*, to an examination of the *conflict of rights* at issue in minority vs majority claims in a number of recent cases (*Zundel, Keegstra, Andrews, Taylor, et al.*) involving hate propagandizing activities.

5) Rights in Conflict: The Hate Propaganda Debate

In the various cases involving hate propagandizing activities, the *individual right* of majority hatemongers—the right to freedom of expression—is in direct conflict with the *categorical right* of identifiable minority target groups—the right to freedom from racial hatred and group defamation. The cases in point all have involved Charter challenges, under s.2b (freedom of expression), by majority respondents, to particular anti-hate propaganda laws, and all have ultimately sought resolution before the Supreme Court of Canada.

In virtually all of the public trials of known hatemongers, the opposing arguments put forward by counsel for the complainant and counsel for the respondent have reflected conflicting ideological positions with reference to the central question: Does the harm to target groups and to the Canadian social fabric engendered by hate propagandizing activities constitute reasonable cause to justify the imposition of limits on freedom of speech?

From the *libertarian* view, the answer is no. Libertarians argue that freedom of speech takes precedence over all other rights and freedoms because all rights and freedoms depend on the existence of an effective right of dissent (Rosenthal 1990: 139). From this view, only a 'clear and present danger' to society at large would justify imposing constraints on freedom of expression.

From the *egalitarian* view, the answer is yes. Egalitarians argue that, in a multicultural society such as Canada, the state has a valid interest in suppressing the dissemination of racist ideas in order to protect minority groups from pain and suffering and in order to promote racial harmony. From this view, Canada's constitutional commitment to the recognition of the right of all Canadians, majority and minority groups alike, to *equal dignity* and to the equal protection and benefit of the law, without discrimination, constrains our federal government to place reasonable limits on racist speech which undermines the country's core human rights values (Rosenthal 1990: 120).

The Public Trials of Zundel and Keegstra: Impact of Hate[2]

During 1985, Canadians were exposed to exhaustive media coverage of the public trials of two known hate propagandists, Ernst Zundel and James Keegstra. The trials of these two men provided a public forum for the hate propaganda debate. Counsel for those bringing the charges against the accused took the egalitarian position in favour of anti-hate propaganda legislation, while counsel for the accused took the libertarian position against anti-hate legislation, arguing that the legislation violates freedom of speech.

Zundel was charged under (then) s.177 of the Criminal Code of Canada with two counts of knowingly publishing false news that caused and/or was likely to cause damage to social or racial tolerance. Two anti-Semitic pamphlets, published by Zundel, were at issue. The first promoted the 'Holocaust hoax' myth; the second promoted the myth of a Jewish-dominated, international conspiracy to control the world. Zundel was convicted on the first charge and was sentenced to fifteen months in jail and three years probation, during which period he was ordered to cease publishing hate propaganda.

Keegstra was charged and convicted under s.281(2)—now s.319(2)—of the Criminal Code of Canada with wilfully promoting hatred against an identifiable target group, Jews, through his classroom teachings at Eckville, Alberta Secondary School. Keegstra's teachings promoted both myths found in Zundel's publications and also perpetuated highly derogatory stereotypes of Jews as 'evil incarnate'. Keegstra was convicted and fined $5,000 to be paid within four months, or six months in jail.

Both Zundel and Keegstra appealed the decisions against them by challenging the constitutionality, under s.2(b) of the Charter—protecting freedom of expression, of the laws under which they were charged. In Zundel's case, the original decision was upheld by the Supreme Court of Ontario. In Keegstra's case the Supreme Court of Alberta overturned the original decision.

The Keegstra case was brought before the Supreme Court of Canada and on 13 December 1991 a judgment upholding the legislation in question and supporting the original decision against Keegstra was rendered. The Zundel case was brought before the Supreme Court of Canada on 27 August 1992, and a judgment striking down the legislation in question and overturning the original decision against Zundel was rendered.

The reasons for the majority and minority judgments in these two Supreme Court decisions reveal that, in the Keegstra case, the majority adopted the egalitarian view, while the minority (dissenting reasons) took the libertarian view. In contrast, in the Zundel case, the majority adopted the libertarian view and the minority (dissenting reasons) took the egalitarian view. In light of the human rights framework which informs this book, these two Supreme Court decisions have differential implications for minority rights. The Supreme Court decision in the Keegstra case will be analysed in some detail in the following section of this chapter.

Charter Challenges: Has the Charter served to protect minority rights?

Hate Propaganda

R v. Keegstra (13 Dec. 1990) S.C.C. file no. 21118
On 5 and 6 December 1989, the Charter challenges in the appeals of Keegstra, Andrews and Smith, and Taylor were brought before the Supreme Court of Canada.

A Supreme Court judgment delivered on 13 December 1990 upheld the anti-hate propaganda laws challenged in these cases. The reasons for judgment written by the majority and the dissenting Justices, in the *Keegstra* case, clearly reflect the egalitarian versus libertarian views on anti-hate legislation.

The reasons for judgment written by the Rt. Hon. Brian Dickson, P.C. and concurred in by the Hon. Mme Justice Wilson, the Hon. Mme Justice L'Heureux-Dubé, and the Hon. Mr Justice Gonthier for the majority, favour the 'egalitarian' view. In contrast, the dissenting reasons, written by the Hon. Mme Justice McLachlin and concurred in by the Hon. Mr Justice Sopinka and the Hon. Mr Justice La Forest, favour the 'libertarian' position. In the following pages, I will attempt to summarize the relevant points of argument for each of the opposing points of view, as articulated in the majority and the dissenting decisions.

The Issues in the Keegstra Appeal

Dickson asserts, at the outset of his analysis, that *Keegstra* (along with *Andrews*) raises the highly controversial issue as to the constitutional validity of s.319(2) of the *Criminal Code*, R.S.C., 1985, c. C-46, a legislative provision which prohibits the wilful promotion of hatred, except in private discourse, towards any group distinguished by colour, race, religion, or ethnic origin. The central issue is whether this provision infringes the guarantee of freedom of expression found in s.2(b) of the Charter in a manner that cannot be justified under s.1.

My discussion of the arguments in this appeal highlights the opposing views on the hate propaganda/free speech debate reflected in the majority and dissenting reasons, and examines only the central issue in the judgment.

McLachlin J.: Dissenting Reasons

McLachlin adopts the libertarian view which ascribes to freedom of expression a central role and enhanced status as the pivotal freedom on which all others depend. Without the freedom to comment and criticize, this view posits, all other rights and freedoms may be subverted by the state.

McLachlin declares that free expression is a fundamental value in Canadian society, but, like other rights and freedoms, it is not an *absolute* value. The question is always one of balance. The law may legitimately restrict free expression where the value of this freedom is outweighed by the risks engendered by allowing it. Accordingly, s.2b of the Charter is subject to s.1, which permits such reasonable limitations on the right as may be justified in a free and democratic society.

In her historical overview of hate propaganda and freedom of speech (pp. 20-38) McLachlin draws heavily upon United States precedent in support of her arguments. Her rationale for subscribing to US rather than international tradition regarding free speech and hate propaganda, is that the United States experience is the most relevant to Canada, since its Constitution, like Canada's, places a high value on freedom of expression.

McLachlin's analysis of the scope of the Charter concludes that s.319(2) of the *Criminal Code* violates s.2(b) (freedom of expression) of the Charter. She then addresses the question of whether or not the legislation in question can be upheld under s.1 of the Charter as a reasonable limit prescribed by law and demonstrably justified in a free and democratic society.

The real question in this case, she contends, is whether the means—the criminal prohibition of wilfully promoting hatred—are proportionate and appropriate to the ends of suppressing hate propaganda in order to maintain social harmony and individual dignity. Arguing from the libertarian view, McLachlin posits two 'unique' characteristics of freedom of expression. First, McLachlin states that free expression is fundamental to a free and democratic society and hence must protect expression which challenges even the very basic values of Canadian society. Second, McLachlin posits that limitations on expression tend to have a 'chilling effect', deterring legitimate expression of law-abiding citizens by uncertainty as to whether they might be convicted. Creativity and the beneficial exchange of ideas, she argues, could be adversely affected.

McLachlin asserts that there is not a strong and evident connection between the criminalization of hate propaganda and its suppression. Indeed, she suggests, s.319(2) may detract from its worthy objectives not only by deterring legitimate expression, but also by conferring on the accused publicity for his dubious causes, through extensive media coverage. Insofar as the criminal process is cast as a conflict between the accused and the state, media exposure may even bring him sympathy. Moreover, McLachlin argues, any questionable benefit conferred by the legislation is outweighed by the significant infringement on the guarantee of freedom of expression. The claims of gains to be achieved at the cost of the infringement of free speech by s.319(2) are tenuous and it is unclear how the legislation fosters the goals of social harmony and individual dignity. Moreover, McLachlin posits, it is arguable whether criminalization of expression designed to promote hatred is necessary. Other remedies, such as human rights legislation—without draconian criminal consequences— may be more appropriate and effective. McLachlin concludes that s.319(2) is not saved by s.1 of the Charter.

Dickson C.J.: Reasons for Judgment

In contradistinction to McLachlin's libertarian position, Dickson's analysis reflects the egalitarian view. At the outset, Dickson emphasizes that the Court must be guided by the values and principles central to a free and democratic society. Such ideals, he asserts, include respect for the inherent dignity of the individual, commitment to social justice and equality, accommodation of a wide variety of beliefs, respect for cultural and group identity and trust in democratic, social and political institutions.

With specific regard to the case at hand, Dickson alleges that those who attack the constitutionality of s.319(2) draw heavily on the tradition of American jurisprudence. In response, Dickson questions this emphasis. He argues that Canada and the United States are not alike in every way and that the documents entrenching human rights in the two countries have not arisen in the same context. Furthermore, Dickson contends, applying the Charter to s.319(2) reveals important differences between Canadian and American constitutional perspectives. First of all, there is no equivalent to s.1 in the United States; s.1 operates to accentuate a uniquely Canadian vision of a free and democratic society. Second, he argues, the international commitment to eradicate hate propaganda and, most importantly, the special role given to equality and multiculturalism in the Canadian Constitution necessitate a departure from the prevailing American view that the suppression of hate propaganda is incompatible with the guarantee of free expression.

Dickson then asks whether there is sufficient harm caused by hate propaganda in Canada to justify legislative intervention. There is substantial evidence, he asserts, that hate propaganda causes harm both to target group members, in terms of degradation and suffering, and to society at large, in terms of its contribution to racial and religious tension and divisiveness. This conclusion, he points out, is strongly supported by international human rights instruments prohibiting hate propaganda. In particular, the relevant provisions of the International Convention on the Elimination of All Forms of Racial Discrimination (CERD) and the International Covenant on Civil and Political Rights (ICCPR) demonstrate that the prohibition of the promotion of hatred is considered to be not only compatible with a signatory nation's guarantee of human rights, but is, as well, an obligatory aspect of this guarantee. In Dickson's view, the fact that the international community has collectively acted to prohibit such expression, underscores the importance of the objective of s.319(2) and the principles of equality and dignity protected by it. In more general terms, the prohibition against the promotion of hatred places a central value on the principles of equality and dignity of all persons that inform both international human rights instruments and the Charter.

In addition to the strong support for the objective of s.319(2) offered by international instruments, Dickson points out that significant support is evident in various provisions of the *Charter* itself. Most importantly, he contends, for the purposes of this case, is the strong commitment to the values of equality and multiculturalism represented by s.15 and s.27. These provisions, he asserts, underline the gravity of Parliament's objective in prohibiting hate propaganda.

Dickson argues that the message of the expression covered by s.319(2) is that target group members are not deserving of equal standing and equal respect with others in Canadian society. The harms caused by this message counter the values of mutual respect and social harmony protected under s.15 and s.27 of the *Charter* and necessary in a multicultural nation that venerates the principles of equality and dignity of all persons.

Dickson then turns to consider whether the means chosen to further the objective are proportional to the ends. He declares, at the outset, (in contradistinction to the libertarian view espoused in the dissenting reasons of McLachlin) that the s.1 analysis of a limit upon s.2(b) cannot ignore the nature of the expressive activity which the state seeks to inhibit. The brand of expressive activity represented by hate propaganda, Dickson argues, is wholly inimical to the democratic aspirations of the free expression guarantee. Such expression subverts, rather than promotes, the central values of a free and democratic society.

In disagreement with the dissenting reasons offered by McLachlin, Dickson argues that the extensive media attention afforded hate propagators by coverage of public criminal trials is not likely to increase public sympathy for their ideas; rather, by highlighting the value of the legislation prohibiting their communications, the severe reprobation with which society holds messages of hate towards identifiable target groups is demonstrated. Moreover, Dickson argues, members of target groups can take comfort from the knowledge that the hatemonger is criminally prosecuted and his ideas rejected. Equally, the community as a whole is reminded of the importance of the societal values of multiculturalism, equality and dignity of person being particularly emphasized.

Dickson also takes issue with McLachlin's dissenting view that anti-hate propaganda legislation is unnecessary because there are more appropriate, alternative modes of furthering Parliament's objective, such as public education and human rights statutes. He agrees that the fostering of tolerant attitudes and the prevention of discrimination among Canadians may best be achieved through a combination of diverse measures, but he argues that the harm done through hate propaganda in some cases may require that especially stringent measures be taken to prohibit and suppress the expressive activity. In order to punish a recalcitrant hatemonger, for example, the more confrontational response of criminal prosecution (as opposed to the conciliatory response of human rights statutes) is best suited. In Dickson's view, in order to send out a strong message of condemnation, both reinforcing the values behind s.319(2) and deterring the few intentional promoters of hatred from causing harm to target groups and society at large, the criminal law will occasionally need to be invoked. Dickson concludes that s.319(2) of the *Criminal Code* does not unduly impair freedom of expression. He then goes on to examine whether the effects of the legislation represent so grave a limitation upon s.2(b) of the *Charter* as to outweigh the benefits to be gained by the prohibition.

Few concerns, states Dickson, can be as central to the concept of a free and democratic society as the dissipation of racism. When the magnitude of the objective of s.319(2) in the context of Canada's multicultural society is taken into account, its effects, in Dickson's view, are not of such a deleterious nature as to outweigh any advantage gleaned from the limitation of s.2(b).

In conclusion, Dickson upholds the constitutionality of the anti-hate propaganda legislation in question—s.319(2) of the *Criminal Code* of Canada.

Implications of the Keegstra *Decision for Ethnic Minority Rights*

An important contention in the argument supporting anti-hate legislation is that it represents Charter values protected under s.15 (equality rights) and s.27 (multicultural rights). Hate propaganda, on the other hand, represents the antithesis of these

Charter values; it infringes on the constitutional rights of the disadvantaged minorities these sections of the Charter were expressly designed to protect. In support of this view, it is argued that any expression which is destructive of Constitutional values is undeserving of Constitutional protection. In other words, the argument goes, 'You cannot use rights to destroy other rights.'

The egalitarian perspective articulated above has been consistently endorsed by spokespersons for racial and ethnic minorities in Canada. As targets for hate propaganda, many minority spokespersons made representations before the Special Joint Committee of the Senate and the House of Commons of Canada on the Constitution in support of a Charter (Cotler, in Abella and Rothman 1985: 119). They saw in the Charter a guarantee against the violation of their equality rights and multicultural rights. Many who sought a specific prohibition against hate propaganda written into the Charter itself were assured by its drafters that the Charter was meant to be a declaration of minority rights.

Similarly, minority representations made to the Special Parliamentary Committee on Visible Minorities in Canadian Society (Daudlin 1984) clearly favoured the egalitarian view in support of anti-hate propaganda legislation. Persuaded by the finding of a 'critical mass' of hate propaganda being disseminated in Canada, the Committee recommended that amendments be enacted to strengthen present Criminal Code provisions against hate propagandizing activities. Further, the Committee strongly endorsed the provisions of article 4 of the International Convention on the Elimination of All Forms of Racial Discrimination (ICEAFRD) which prohibits, as a matter of law, the dissemination of hate propaganda. It recommended that the Government of Canada, after proper consultation with the provinces should make a declaration under article 14 of the ICEAFRD and specify that complaints under article 4 should be considered as subject to the protections of the Charter and the International Covenant on Civil and Political Rights (ICCPR) (Daudlin: Recommendation # 46).

In 1985-1990, the author carried out a research study designed to ascertain the psycho-social impact of hate propagandizing activities, as revealed in the public trials of Keegstra and Zundel, on members of the Jewish-Canadian target group. The study findings provided unequivocal support for the egalitarian perspective on the part of Jewish-Canadian respondents. Despite respondents' reported pain and suffering, engendered by the anti-Semitic revelations (Holocaust hoax; International Jewish conspiracy, etc.) of the trials, study findings revealed their overwhelming endorsement for strengthened anti-hate propaganda legislation. In the view of the minority target for hate, insofar as the state has a duty to protect the inherent group dignity of racial and ethnic minorities, then freedom of expression cannot include words that vilify, maim, and cause demonstrable harm and suffering (Kallen 1992; Kallen and Lam 1993).

In the following section of this chapter we will consider the human rights implications of the recently developed model for Charter interpretation which has been set out by the Supreme Court of Canada. To further our analysis, we will examine the way in which this model has been applied in Charter challenge cases.

Interpreting the Charter: The Purposive Approach

Because the Charter represents a recent amendment to Canada's Constitution, there is little precedent to guide judicial interpretation of its provisions. Interpretive principles are only in their infancy and are by no means unanimously endorsed. To facilitate Charter interpretation, the Supreme Court has sanctioned a *purposive* approach which involves a two-stage process of analysis for the application of the Charter in a specific case (Pentney 1989: 23). At the first stage, the right or freedom involved in the case must be defined and a determination must be made as to whether it has been infringed or abrogated. At the second stage, it must be determined whether the 'limit' on the right or freedom meets the 'reasonable limit' standard set out in s.1 of the Charter.

The model for the purposive approach derives from the view expressed by Dickson, J. in *R. v. Big M Drug Mart* (quoted in Pentney 1989: 24):

> In my view, this analysis is to be undertaken, and the purpose of the right or freedom in question is to be sought by reference to the character and the larger objects of the Charter itself, to the language chosen to articulate the specific right or freedom, to the historical origins of the concepts enshrined, and where applicable, to the meaning and purpose of the other specific rights and freedoms with which it is associated within the text of the Charter.

With reference to the 'character and larger objects of the Charter', Dickson, J. (quoted in Pentney 1989: 22-3) has pointed out that one of the critical features of the Charter as a constitutional rather than a statutory legal instrument is that, once enacted, its provisions cannot be easily repealed or amended. Accordingly, it is drafted with an eye to the future, for it must be capable of application to new social, political, and historical realities unimagined by its framers. In interpreting its provisions, then, the judiciary must adopt a broad approach which will facilitate its application under new and unforseen social conditions.

Pentney argues, with reference to the 'language chosen to articulate the specific right or freedom', that, as a general rule, the exact words of the provision should be adhered to, for these have not been arbitrarily chosen by the drafters. Only if a literal reading of the provision defeats the purpose of the section and detracts from its underlying values, should a departure from a literal interpretation be undertaken.

The purposive approach also requires an examination of the 'historical origins of the concepts enshrined' in order to glean the values underlying the right or freedom and thus to provide an understanding of the concept embodied in it. In some cases, the content of a particular right or freedom may be determined with reference to the 'meaning and purpose of the other specific rights and freedoms with which it is associated within the text of the Charter'. The purposive approach thus requires that the Charter be viewed as a whole so that the meaning and scope of a particular right or freedom is consistent with and in part gleaned from, similar guarantees, usually found under the same heading in the Charter (Pentney 1989: 24-6).

In summary, the purposive approach requires the derivation of the underlying values that a specific right or freedom is intended to protect and an analysis of principles drawn from legal and broader, historical traditions which reflect these values in order to ensure that the interpretation of a particular right or freedom furthers its purpose. Moreover, the purposive approach requires that the interpretation adopted incorporate the forward-looking view appropriate for constitutional judgments and is sensitive to the future political, economic and social implications of the decision (Pentney: 27-8).

The way in which the Charter can be used as a standard in statutory human rights cases is highlighted in the following Supreme Court cases.

Religion

Regina v Big M Drug Mart Ltd. (1985), 18 C.C.C. (3d) 385, 18 D.L.R.(4th) 321, [1985] 1 S.C.R. 295
In their decision on this case, the Supreme Court of Canada struck down the Lord's Day Act, a federal Sunday closing statute, as unconstitutional by reason of its violation of the guarantee of freedom of conscience and religion under s.2a. of the Charter. In reaching their decision, the Court reasoned that the Act discriminated against non-Christians by taking Christian religious values and, using the force of the state, translating them into a positive law binding on believers and non-believers alike. The court also pointed out that to accept that Parliament retains the right to compel universal observance of the day of rest preferred by one religion is not consistent with the values underlying s.27 of the Charter which sanction the preservation and enhancement of the multicultural heritage of Canadians. The protection of the dominant religious culture and the concomitant non-protection of minority religions was held to be inimical to the spirit of s.2a of the Charter and to the dignity of non-Christians. In the words of Justice Dickson : 'A free society is one which aims at equality with respect to the enjoyment of the fundamental freedoms . . . '. For persons of a non-Christian religion, the practice of that religion, it was argued, at least implies the right to work on Sunday if the person wishes to do so. Any law, purely religious in purpose, which denies the person that right infringes on that person's religious freedom.

Moreover, the Court ruled that the Act could not be justified as a reasonable limit under s.1 of the Charter. While the Government sought to support the Act on the basis that it had a secular purpose, namely to provide a uniform day of rest, the Supreme Court held that the Act had never been held by the courts to have this objective. Accordingly, the Court declared the Lord's Day Act to be of no force and effect.

Zydelberg v. Sudbury Board of Education (Director) (1988) 65 O.R. (2d) 641 (C.A.)
In their judgment in this case, the Ontario Court of Appeal held that regulations under the Education Act of Ontario calling for the reading of Bible scriptures and the recitation of the Lord's Prayer or other prayers in public school classrooms contravened the guarantee of freedom of conscience and religion under s.2a of the Charter. The fact that the regulations permitted a pupil or his or her parents to claim exemption from these Christian religious exercises was held not to save it because the existence of the exemption option did not eliminate the pressure on non-Christian and non-religious pupils to participate. The Court reasoned that the peer pressure and the classroom norms to which children are acutely sensitive are real and pervasive and operate to compel members of religious minorities to conform with majority religious practices. Further, they argued, the exemption provision penalizes the non-Christian and non-religious students who utilize it by stigmatizing them as non-conformists and setting them apart from their fellow students. While the principle Charter right invoked by the Court was freedom of conscience and religion under s.2a, it was held that the regulation also discriminated against members of religious minorities by violating their equality rights under s.15.

The Court held that because the purpose of the regulations was religious and the exercises mandated by them were intended to be religious, the regulations could not be justified under s.1 of the Charter. Even if s.1 were available, the Court held that the regulations still could not be justified because opening exercises in public school classrooms can more appropriately be founded on the multicultural traditions of Canadian society, recognized under s.27 of the Charter, than upon the values of one religion.

Hothi et al. v. The Queen et al., [1985] 3 W.W.R. 256, 33 Man. R. (2d) 180 (Q.B.).
In this case the trial judge ruled that the prohibition against an accused person shouldering a weapon during a trial, even if the weapon represents a religious symbol and carrying it is a religious requirement, is a reasonable limit on the Charter right of freedom of religion guaranteed under s.2a. Thus, the prohibition is justified under s.1 of the Charter. Specifically, the judge forbade the accused, a baptized Sikh, to have on his person in the court-room, a kirpan, a dagger with a four-inch blade carried by baptized Sikhs as a religious symbol. The judge held that the kirpan was an instrument capable of use as a weapon. An application to quash the ruling was dismissed, for it was reasoned that the ruling was made in the exercise of a judicial authority recognized by law to maintain order and control the process within the court-room. The ruling was held to serve a transcending public interest that justice be administered in an environment free from any influence which might thwart the process. While the ruling may interfere with freedom of religion, it was held to represent a reasonable limit prescribed by law as can be demonstrably justified in a free and democratic society.

Re McTavish et al. and Director, Child Welfare Act et al. (1986), 32 D.L.R. (4th) 394 (Alta. Q.B.)

There have been a number of cases testing the Charter's protection against religious discrimination which have been brought forward in the context of legislation authorizing compulsory medical treatment or other care or custody for children found to be in need of protection (Gibson, 1990: 198). The earliest of these cases all involved challenges to such laws, or challenges to steps taken under them, by Jehovah's Witness parents who were religiously opposed to the administering of blood transfusions to their children. Almost all of these challenges have been unsuccessful.

In the above-mentioned case, the Alberta Court of Queen's Bench rejected a Charter challenge which alleged that the province's Child Welfare Act violated the equality rights provisions of s.15 by discriminating against a religious minority, Jehovah's Witnesses. The Court reasoned that the Act was not discriminatory, first, because it treated all children in need of protection alike, regardless of religion, and second, because, in any event, it represented a reasonable limit on equality rights, justified under s.1 of the Charter. The Court recognized that the effect of the Act, conferring jurisdiction on the Court to authorize medical treatment of a child notwithstanding the refusal of consent by the child's guardian, is to impinge on the parents' right to direct the medical treatment of their child in accordance with their religious beliefs. Nevertheless, it held that where the Court is satisfied that the treatment is in the best interests of the child, the need to protect the health of the child justifies this infringement on freedom of religion.

Charter Protection for Religion: Discussion

The reasoning behind the judicial decisions in the first two cases (*Regina v. Big M Drug Mart* and *Zydelberg v. Sudbury Board of Education*) provides a clear demonstration of the application of the purposive approach to Charter interpretation. In both cases, the principal Charter right invoked in the challenge was freedom of conscience and religion under s.2a. However, in both cases the Court took into account the 'character and larger objects of the Charter itself' and made reference to values of equality and multiculturalism, protected under other Charter provisions (s.15 and s.27, respectively). As a result, in both cases the ruling of the Court, reflecting the spirit of the Charter as a whole, afforded protection not only for the individual right of freedom of conscience and religion, but also for the collective rights of non-Christian and non-religious minorities.

In the third and fourth cases (*Hothi et al. v. The Queen et al.* and *Re McTavish et al. and Director, Child Welfare Act et al.*) the reasoning behind the judicial decisions revealed how s.1 of the Charter is used to justify the imposition of reasonable limits on Charter rights in order to serve the best interests of a person or a society. In the Hothi case, a restriction was imposed on the guarantee of freedom of religion under s.2a of the Charter in order to serve the 'transcending public interest' of justice at court. In the McTavish case, a restriction was imposed on the guarantee of religious equality under s.15 of the Charter in order to serve a child's 'best interests' through the protection of his or her health.

Race, Ethnicity, and Nationality

There have been relatively few Charter challenge cases based on grounds of race, ethnicity, or nationality. The two cases selected by the author were considered to be instructive for purposes of Charter interpretation.

R. v. Kent, Sinclair and Gode (1986), 21 C.R.R. 372 (Man. C.A.)
In this case, the Manitoba Court of Appeal rejected a Charter challenge which alleged that accused persons of aboriginal origin had been discriminated against, in violation of the equality rights provisions of s.15, by reason of under-representation on their jury of persons with aboriginal backgrounds. The accused were convicted of murdering two prison guards. Counsel for one of the accused (a Status Indian) unsuccessfully challenged the selection of jurors at the beginning of the trial and again, on appeal, on the ground that the jury panel did not adequately represent the accused's 'peers'. The population of Status Indians in the province, at the time, represented approximately 5 per cent of the total population. The panel from which the jury was chosen was drawn from a provincial Health Services Commission list of 150 eligible, adult, health care recipients, only two of whom were Status Indians. One of the latter served on the accused's jury.

The Manitoba Court of Appeal rejected the allegation that the accused had been discriminated against because he had not been accorded a jury of his 'peers'. The Court found no evidence of deliberate exclusion from the jury of persons of a particular race or origin, a finding which clearly would have violated the Charter. The Court held, further, that the equality rights provisions of s.15 of the Charter do not require a jury to be composed entirely or proportionately of persons belonging to the same race as the accused. It was held that to interpret the Charter in this way would run counter to Canada's multicultural and multiracial heritage and to the right of every person to serve as a juror (unless otherwise disqualified). The Court held that the jurors' list in the case was racially neutral and that it must be assumed to provide a fair cross-section of the country and to be reasonably representative.

In his discussion of the Court's ruling in this case, Gibson (1990: 180-1) points out that, in view of the fact that both the jury panel and the jury itself contained roughly the same proportion of Status Indians as were represented in the provincial population, it would be difficult to challenge the Court's decision on the question of representativeness. He submits, nevertheless, that there are grounds for challenging the Court's suggestion that only deliberate exclusion of persons of a particular race or origin from the jury would violate the Charter. Citing the Supreme Court decision in the Andrews case (to be discussed next), Gibson points out that it has now been confirmed that the Charter prohibits unintentional, systemic discrimination as well as deliberate discrimination. He contends, therefore, that if procedures for jury selection had the systemic effect of excluding or under-representing particular racial or ethnic groups from jury service, a Charter challenge could be put forward.

Andrews v. Law Society of British Columbia [1989] 1 S.C.R. 143, (1989), 56 D.L.R., (4th) 1, [1989] 2 W.W.R. 289.

In this case, the Supreme Court of Canada invalidated a provincial law requiring lawyers to be Canadian citizens because this law was held to violate the equality rights provision under s.15 of the Charter. The case was seen to have wide importance because it provided the first indication of the framework for analysis to be applied by the Supreme Court in interpreting the Charter's equality provision (Black and Smith 1989: 591).

The original petitioner, Mark Andrews, was a British subject who had become a permanent resident of Canada. He had obtained all of the requirements for admission to the practice of law in British Columbia except Canadian citizenship, for which he was not yet eligible. His petition alleged that the statutory requirement of citizenship violated s.15 of the Charter. By the time the case reached the Supreme Court, Andrews had become a citizen and had been admitted to practice, but another petitioner, Elizabeth Kinersly, had been added, to keep the case alive (Black and Smith 1989: 592).

The Supreme Court held that a challenge under s.15 must show, first, a denial of one of the four equality rights set out in the first part of the section (equality before and under the law and the equal protection and equal benefit of the law) and, second, that there has been discrimination.

As stated by Justice McIntyre, the concept of equality underlying s.15 'should be that a law expressed to bind all should not because of irrelevant personal differences have a more burdensome or less beneficial impact on one than another'. As indicated in an earlier discussion of this case (page 253), McIntyre J. criticized the narrow conception of equality underlying the 'similarly situated test', a test for violations of Charter provisions used by the lower courts in many Charter challenge cases. This test provided that similarly situated people should be similarly treated and that differently situated people should be treated differently. McIntyre J. reasoned that identical treatment, in some cases, can lead to inequality of results, and that differential treatment in some cases can lead to equality of results. In McIntyre J.'s view, the equality concept underlying s.15 must incorporate values of equal concern, respect, and consideration, and a large remedial component with regard to discrimination. The Court adopted Justice McIntyre's broad definition of discrimination as a distinction, intentional or not, based on grounds relating to the personal characteristics of an individual or group which has the effect of imposing disadvantages not imposed on others or of limiting advantages available to others. This definition was not intended to eliminate all distinctions; rather, the Court sanctioned an approach tied to the grounds of distinction covered by s.15, by limiting distinctions to those found in the enumerated grounds and in grounds analogous to them.

In assessing the facts in the Andrews case, McIntyre J. maintained that non-citizens are a minority group analogous to those enumerated under the grounds of s.15 and that they come within the protection of s.15. He held further that the citizenship requirement imposed a burden in the form of a delay on permanent residents who had acquired some or all of their legal training abroad and was therefore discriminatory. He concluded, therefore, that the law requiring citizenship was in violation of s.15.

The judgment of the Supreme Court in the Andrews case has profound implications for Canada's disadvantaged minorities. Most importantly, it affords clear support for minority group rights. The broad concept of equality endorsed by the Court protects groups as well as individuals, and extends protection beyond the enumerated grounds of s.15 to cover other grounds analogous to them. The Court's judgment in this case strongly orients s.15 in the direction of ensuring that the legal and governmental system does not exacerbate the disadvantage of persistently disadvantaged individuals and groups in society rather than in the direction of protecting against isolated incidents of discrimination against advantaged individuals (Black and Smith 1989: 605).

The Purposive Approach to Equality Rights: What does the concept of 'equality' mean?

Taking their lead from the judgment in the Andrews case, Black and Smith (1989) have adopted a purposive approach in their analysis of the equality rights provisions of the Charter. They argue that the concept of equality incorporated in s.15 must protect against the more common types of discrimination associated with each of the enumerated grounds (1989. 570). To ascertain the meaning of equality behind the section, account must be taken of the legislative history of the section and of its broader constitutional context. Further assistance may be provided by looking at the non-discriminatory provisions of Canadian human rights statutes and of international human rights instruments.

The authors begin with a consideration of 'the larger objects' of equality rights. In light of the provisions of s.15(2), they hold that a primary purpose of equality rights is to eliminate or reduce conditions of disadvantage (1989: 571). Further, when s.15 is read in the context of s.28 and of s.25 and s.35, Black and Smith conclude that another purpose of equality rights is to remedy conditions of social and cultural subordination (1989: 572). Related to the previous two points is the authors' assertion that a central objective of s.15 is to remedy inequality between groups as well as between individuals.

What meaning of equality, then, fulfils these three objectives? Black and Smith put forward the following features of a paradigm of equality rights.

First, they assert that the section takes account of long term as well as immediate results of discrimination. Second, they hold that it takes account of both intended and unintended consequences of discrimination. Both of these features of the paradigm, they point out, are consistent with the prevailing interpretation of discrimination in human rights statutes which takes into account not only individual discrimination but also institutional and systemic discrimination (1989: 574). Third, they contend that the section takes into account disadvantage related to the unique characteristics of protected groups (1989: 575). This, they hold, would ensure that the concept of equality enshrined in the section would not be interpreted to mean sameness of treatment when the unique characteristics of a group necessitate equivalence of treatment. Related to this assertion, a fourth feature of the paradigm is that the section incorporates a duty of reasonable accommodation. The authors point out that a duty to accommodate differences between groups has been incorporated into human rights statutes and is essential if section 15 is to afford a significant measure of equality to persons with disabilities (1989: 576).

The Purposive Approach to Multicultural Rights: What does the concept of 'multicultural heritage' mean?

Magnet maintains that a purposive approach to multicultural rights must take into account the historical origins of the concept of multiculturalism enshrined in s.27 of the Charter. Background policies, statutes, and statements can shed light on the meaning and purpose of s.27 within the context of the Charter as a whole. Magnet traces the concept of multiculturalism to its beginnings in the recommendations of Book 4 of the Bi and Bi Commission (1969) and to its enshrinement as federal policy in 1971. He reasons that the meaning of the concept can be derived from two central themes of the federal policy, freedom from discrimination and cultural group survival, which comprise important elements of the constitutional background leading to the entrenchment of s.27 (Magnet 1989: 743-4).

Magnet points out that there was no mention of the multiculturalism principle in the Draft Constitution of 1980. In response to this omission, representatives of ethnocultural communities made vigorous and extensive submissions on the multicultural issue before the Hayes-Joyal Committee, stressing such themes as non-discrimination, equality, cultural autonomy, cultural maintenance, pluralism, heritage language rights, and educational autonomy (1989: 745). The Government response, in January of 1981, took the form of a suggested amendment which was identical to the current text of s.27 of the Charter.

Magnet's review of the constitutional background to s.27, however, revealed a wide array of opinion as to the content of the multicultural principle. Moreover, his review of the jurisprudence developed by Canadian courts again revealed contradictory interpretations of the concept (1989: 751). In order to advance meaningful interpretation of s.27, Magnet examined international sources. The model for s.27, he asserts, was article 27 of the ICCPR (the minority rights provision) which was rat-ified by Canada in 1976 (1989: 746). Magnet suggests that recent interpretation of this provision treats it as imposing affirmative obligations on states to recognize and protect the special needs of minority ethnocultural communities. While this estab-lishes a valuable precedent for interpretation of s.27 of the Charter, international sources can be found to provide no intelligible content for the multicultural principle.

In light of the fact that there is no agreed upon meaning for the concept of mul-ticulturalism enshrined in s.27 of the Charter, Magnet suggests that there is a need to develop 'mediating principles' for interpretation of the text. Mediating principles appropriate to s.27, he suggests, must satisfy three minimum conditions. They must be 1) capable of reconciling the interests of majority and minority groups, 2) capa-ble of balancing the principles of minority autonomy and diversity with the goal of national unity, and 3) highly analytically intelligible, and amenable to easy applica-tion by legal and political practitioners (1989: 755-6).

Magnet proposes three mediating principles of interpretation which satisfy the three pre-conditions outlined: anti-discrimination, symbolic ethnicity, and structur-al ethnicity.

In support of the anti-discrimination principle, Magnet argues that discrimina-tion is the 'principal pain' associated with preservation of distinctive cultural attri-butes. If the cost of maintaining ethnocultural distinctiveness is too high, assimila-tion—the antithesis of 'preservation and enhancement'—is encouraged. In support of the principle of symbolic ethnicity—voluntary self-identification with the cultur-al heritage of one's ethnic group—Magnet endorses the social psychological view which holds that ethnic identification meets a fundamental human need for com-munal roots and belongingness. In support of the principle of structural ethnicity—an institutional infrastructure for the maintenance of ethnocultural distinctiveness—Magnet adopts the social scientific position that an enduring ethnic community infrastructure is necessary in order to ensure the viability of the ethnic group as an integrated entity.

Magnet contends (772) that s.27, as mediated by these three principles, could ori-ent Charter interpretation in the direction of obligating governments to undertake affirmative obligations to ensure the 'preservation and enhancement' of the collec-tive cultural rights of Canada's ethnic minorities. This would be consistent with the current direction of s.27's international law precursor, Article 27 of the ICCPR. The principle of structural ethnicity is particularly challenging for interpretation of s.27, Magnet holds, because it implies a degree of autonomy for ethnic communities in order to control the institutional infrastructure required to 'preserve and enhance' distinctive cultures and identities. Mediated by this principle, s.27 would serve to extend Canada's constitutional collective rights mandate which has created limited autonomy for certain historical minorities (official language minorities and aborigi-nal peoples) to all ethnic minorities (1989: 780).

Toward the Full Recognition and Protection for Ethnic Minority Rights in Canada: Strategies for Change

In the Introduction to this book, I pointed out that international human rights instruments are continually being amended and expanded in response to input from minority representatives, in order to provide stronger and more explicit protection for the individual, categorical, and collective rights of ethnic minorities. Nevertheless, the current provisions of international instruments do not fully endorse minority claims for explicit recognition and protection of their collective cultural rights and/or nationhood rights within states. At the international level, then, one important strategy for change is to bolster the lobbying efforts and consultative roles of non-government organizations (NGOS) at the United Nations, whose platforms support specified protections for collective minority rights.

Similarly, within Canada, support for the lobbying efforts of minority rights organizations seeking strong and explicit legal protections for collective minority rights at both the statutory and constitutional levels is of the utmost importance. One significant step in this direction would be for the Courts to adopt the purposive approach to Charter interpretation, as represented in the forward-looking models of Black and Smith (1989) for 'equality rights', and Magnet (1989) for 'multicultural rights'. Should this approach be adopted, recognition and protection for the individual, categorical, and collective rights of Canada's ethnic minorities would be greatly enhanced. Insofar as the Constitutional Charter provides the national standard for all human rights statutes, it should follow that existing human rights statutes would be augmented to reflect expanded and improved Charter-endorsed protections for ethnic minority rights. To achieve this goal, it is essential that minority rights groups and coalitions work together with human rights commissions to ensure that the Charter standard is reflected in the legal protection for ethnic minority rights at the statutory level.

In addition to legal human rights protection, it is important that social policy measures designed to ameliorate group-level disadvantage among racial and ethnic minorities be expanded and implemented at all levels of government. Minority rights organizations and coalitions can play an important role here by lobbying for improved policy measures directed toward equitable treatment of ethnic minorities. Affirmative action programs, currently limited almost exclusively to the educational and work spheres, could be extended beyond the economic domain to provide forms of redress against institutionalized political, social, and cultural inequality of minorities.

The typology of minority rights claims applied in the analysis throughout this book raises a number of serious questions for the reader and for future researchers in the area. For example: what kinds of new affirmative action programs could be implemented in order to ensure proportionate political representation of ethnic minorities in Canadian public life? Here, the question of ethnic representation through proportional quotas has been raised. Additionally, what kinds of affirmative action programs could be designed to ensure the continuing religious, linguistic, and cultural vitality of all of the multicultural tiles in the Canadian mosaic? And, finally, what (if any) kinds of affirmative action programs could serve to eradicate the dire poverty and marginalized status of Canada's aboriginal peoples? Here, the real limitations of affirmative action as a strategy designed to eliminate group-level disadvantage become all too evident. What needs to be considered by Canadian policymakers in this case is a redistribution of economic resources so as to ameliorate the situation of 'created dependency' which has resulted from paternalistic/colonialistic social policies and legislation towards aboriginal peoples.

Throughout this book, I have argued that human rights *legislation* is needed to combat and eradicate acts of ethnic discrimination. As a parallel strategy for change, I will argue that *education* is needed to counteract and eradicate the ethnic prejudices and stereotypes which serve as catalysts for discrimination. To truly reflect the multi-ethnic character of Canada, it is essential that all forms of public education, from the schools to the media, integrate multicultural and anti-racist mandates within their policy directives. It is equally important that public education include teaching about human rights which emphasizes the similarities and affinities among the peoples of Canada, as members of the same human family (species). Finally, the human rights mandate of public education could be extended so as to provide information on the structure of legal protection for human rights in Canada. With regard to the latter point, I would argue that unless Canadians are informed about human rights principles, legislation, and investigative and conciliation procedures, they may well be unaware of the help available to them in an instance of ethnic or other forms of discrimination. Hence, there is a need for much greater publicization of human rights materials, including codes, cases, and decisions, as well as the findings of research studies on human rights issues.

Probably the most glaring case of *omission* in this area lies in the neglect of formal instruction about human rights in the curricula of public education institutions in this country. It is essential that textbooks, at all educational levels, be reviewed regularly for errors of omission and commission to ensure that they accurately reflect the historical and contemporary cultures and social conditions of Canada's ethnic minorities. It is equally important that the teaching of human rights principles be emphasized at all educational levels. The latter point draws attention to the importance of teacher training in the area of human rights. At present, the omission of human rights principles as an integral aspect of teacher training represents a glaring lacuna in public education throughout Canada.

Table 6 schematizes the general areas in which the strategies for change outlined in the foregoing paragraphs can be implemented.

Glaser and Possony (1979: 236) contend that, in the last analysis, the problem of

Table 6 Protection for Ethnic Minority Rights in Canada

Law
Constitution/Charter
Human rights statutes

Specified and defined protection for the individual, categorical and collective rights of ethnic minorities including the right to self-determination of aboriginal First Nations

Public Policy
Implementation of multiculturalism and anti-racism mandates
Affirmative action programs designed to ameliorate group-level disadvantage in economic, political, social and cultural spheres
Public education about human rights principles and legislation
Equitable distribution of public resources across minorities

Public Practice
Support for NGOS at the international UN level
Support for minority rights organizations within Canada
Encouragement for the formation of human rights coalitions
Liaison between minority rights advocacy groups and human rights Commissions
Encouragement for the practice of human rights principles by Canadian citizens in everyday life

---

discrimination must be solved by people, rather than by governments. It is the people, in any society, who must work toward achieving the mosaic goal of mutual tolerance and respect, and, above all, it is the people who must develop the ability to accept group differences. In public policy, the need is for decentralization of authority to the people, enabling individuals to practise their fundamental freedoms without state interference, and allowing people of variant cultures to choose within differentiated resources the schools, curricula, and languages of instruction that best advance their development.

In support of this view are the sentiments quoted in the predecessor to this book and more fully developed here.

If our struggle towards full observance of human rights and fundamental freedoms throughout Canada is to be given more than lip service, we, as Canadian citizens, must insist upon and work for consistent enforcement of anti-racist legislation; and we must take upon ourselves the crucial responsibility for educating our children towards the spirit of human rights: we must demonstrate in our own public and private lives, that 'race' does not define 'place' in the truly just society. (Hughes and Kallen 1974: 214)

Notes

1 The analysis of the Charter's protection for minority rights in the section to follow has been adapted from Kallen: 'The Meech Lake Accord: Entrenching a Pecking Order of Minority Rights', *Canadian Public Policy:* The Meech Lake Accord, xiv Supplement (September 1988). For a broader analysis of the Constitutional issues relating to both ethnic and non-ethnic minorities, together with a full listing of sources drawn upon, see this work.

2 A research study which analysed the impact of the hate trials on a sample of Jewish-Canadian respondents was carried out by the author from 1985-1990. See Kallen, 1992 and Kallen and Lam, 1993. The discussion of the Zundel and Keegstra cases and the analysis of *Keegstra*, presented in the next section of this chapter, are drawn largely from Kallen, 1992: 'Never Again: Target Group Responses To The Debate Concerning Anti-Hate Propaganda Legislation', *Windsor Yearbook of Access to Justice* Vol. xi.

APPENDIX A

Universal Declaration of Human Rights

Adopted by United Nations General Assembly, December 10, 1948

WHEREAS recognition of the inherent dignity and of the equal and inalienable rights of all members of the human family is the foundation of freedom, justice and peace in the world,

WHEREAS disregard and contempt for human rights have resulted in barbarous acts which have outraged the conscience of mankind, and the advent of a world in which human beings shall enjoy freedom of speech and belief and freedom from fear and want has been proclaimed as the highest aspiration of the common people,

WHEREAS it is essential, if man is not to be compelled to have recourse, as a last resort, to rebellion against tyranny and oppression, that human rights should be protected by the rule of law,

WHEREAS it is essential to promote the development of friendly relations between nations.

WHEREAS the peoples of the United Nations have in the Charter reaffirmed their faith in fundamental human rights in the dignity and worth of the human person and in the equal rights of men and women and have determined to promote social progress and better standards of life in larger freedom,

WHEREAS Member States have pledged themselves to achieve, in co-operation with the United Nations, the promotion of universal respect for and observance of human rights and fundamental freedoms,

WHEREAS a common understanding of these rights and freedoms is of the greatest importance for the full realization of this pledge,

NOW THEREFORE, THE GENERAL ASSEMBLY PROCLAIMS

THIS UNIVERSAL DECLARATION OF HUMAN RIGHTS as a common standard of achievement for all peoples and all nations to the end that every individual and every organ of society, keeping this Declaration constantly in mind, shall strive by teaching and education to promote respect for these rights and freedoms and by progressive measures, national and international, to secure their universal and effective recognition and observance, both among the peoples of Member States themselves and among the peoples of territories under their jurisdiction.

Article 1
All human beings are born free and equal in dignity and rights. They are endowed with reason and conscience and should act towards one another in a spirit of brotherhood.

Article 2
Everyone is entitled to all the rights and freedoms set forth in this Declaration, without distinction of any kind, such as race, colour, sex, language, religion, political or other opinion, national or social origin, property, birth or other status. Furthermore, no distinction shall be made on the basis of the political, jurisdictional or international status of the country or territory to which a person belongs, whether it be independent, trust, non-selfgoverning or under any other limitation of sovereignty.

Article 3
Everyone has the right to life, liberty and security of person.

Article 4
No one shall be held in slavery or servitude; slavery and the slave trade shall be prohibited in all their forms.

Article 5
No one shall be subjected to torture or to cruel, inhuman or degrading treatment or punishment.

Article 6
Everyone has the right to recognition everywhere as a person before the law.

Article 7
All are equal before the law and are entitled without any discrimination to equal protection of the law. All are entitled to equal protection against any discrimination in violation of this Declaration and against any incitement to such discrimination.

Article 8
Everyone has the right to an effective remedy by the competent national tribunals for acts violating the fundamental rights granted him by the constitution or by law.

Article 9
No one shall be subjected to arbitrary arrest, detention or exile.

Article 10

Everyone is entitled in full equality to a fair and public hearing by an independent and impartial tribunal, in the determination of his rights and obligations and of any criminal charge against him.

Article 11

(1) Everyone charged with a penal offence has the right to be presumed innocent until proved guilty according to law in a public trial at which he has had all the guarantees necessary for his defence.

(2) No one shall be held guilty of any penal offence on account of any act or omission which did not constitute a penal offence, under national or international law, at the time when it was committed. Nor shall a heavier penalty be imposed than the one that was applicable at the time the penal offence was committed.

Article 12

No one shall be subjected to arbitrary interference with his privacy, family, home or correspondence, nor to attacks upon his honour and reputation. Everyone has the right to the protection of the law against such interference or attacks.

Article 13

(1) Everyone has the right to freedom of movement and residence within the borders of each state.

(2) Everyone has the right to leave any country, including his own, and to return to his country.

Article 14

(1) Everyone has the right to seek and to enjoy in other countries asylum from persecution.

(2) This right may not be invoked in the case of prosecutions genuinely arising from non-political crimes or from acts contrary to the purposes and principles of the United Nations.

Article 15

(1) Everyone has the right to a nationality.

(2) No one shall be arbitrarily deprived of his nationality nor denied the right to change his nationality.

Article 16

(1) Men and women of full age, without any limitation due to race, nationality or religion, have the right to marry and to found a family. The are entitled to equal rights as to marriage, during marriage and at its dissolution.

(2) Marriage shall be entered into only with the free and full consent of the intending spouses.

(3) The family is the natural and fundamental group unit of society and is entitled to protection by society and the State.

Article 17
(1) Everyone has the right to own property alone as well as in association with others.
(2) No one shall be arbitrarily deprived of his property.

Article 18
Everyone has the right to freedom of thought, conscience and religion; this right includes freedom to change his religion or belief, and freedom, either alone or in community with others and in public or private, to manifest his religion or belief in teaching, practice, worship and observance.

Article 19
Everyone has the right to freedom of opinion and expression; this right includes freedom to hold opinions without interference and to seek, receive and impart information and ideas through any media and regardless of frontiers.

Article 20
(1) Everyone has the right to freedom of peaceful assembly and association.
(2) No one may be compelled to belong to an association.

Article 21
(1) Everyone has the right to take part in the government of his country, directly or through freely chosen representatives.
(2) Everyone has the right of equal access to public service in his country.
(3) The will of the people shall be the basis of the authority of government; this will shall be expressed in periodic and genuine elections which shall be by universal and equal suffrage and shall be held by secret vote or by equivalent free voting procedures.

Article 22
Everyone, as a member of society, has the right to social security and is entitled to realization, through national effort and international co-operation and in accordance with the organization and resources of each State, of the economic, social and cultural rights indispensable for his dignity and the free development of his personality.

Article 23
(1) Everyone has the right to work, to free choice of employment, to just and favorable conditions of work and to protection against unemployment.

(2) Everyone, without any discrimination, has the right to equal pay for equal work.
(3) Everyone who works has the right to just and favorable remuneration insuring for himself and his family an existence worthy of human dignity, and supplemented, if necessary, by other means of social protection.
(4) Everyone has the right to form and to join trade unions for the protection of his interests.

Article 24
Everyone has the right to rest and leisure, including reasonable limitation of working hours and periodic holidays with pay.

Article 25
(1) Everyone has the right to a standard of living adequate for the health and well-being of himself and of his family, including food, clothing, housing and medical care and necessary social services, and the right to security in the event of unemployment, sickness, disability, widowhood, old age or other lack of livelihood in circumstances beyond his control.
(2) Motherhood and childhood are entitled to special care and assistance. All children, whether born in or out of wedlock, shall enjoy the same social protection.

Article 26
(1) Everyone has the right to education. Education shall be free, at least in the elementary and fundamental stages. Elementary education shall be compulsory. Technical and professional education shall be made generally available and higher education shall be equally accessible to all on the basis of merit.
(2) Education shall be directed to the full development of the human personality and to the strengthening of respect for human rights and fundamental freedoms. It shall promote understanding, tolerance and friendship among all nations, racial or religious groups, and shall further the activities of the United Nations for the maintenance of peace.
(3) Parents have a prior right to choose the kind of education that shall be given to their children.

Article 27
(1) Everyone has the right freely to participate in the cultural life of the community, to enjoy the arts and to share in scientific advancement and its benefits.
(2) Everyone has the right to the protection of the moral and material interests resulting from any scientific, literary or artistic production of which he is the author.

Article 28
Everyone is entitled to a social and international order in which the rights and freedoms set forth in this Declaration can be fully realized.

Article 29

(1) Everyone has duties to the community in which alone the free and full development of his personality is possible.

(2) In the exercise of his rights and freedoms, everyone shall be subject only to such limitations as are determined by law solely for the purpose of securing due recognition and respect for the rights and freedoms of others and of meeting the just requirements of morality, public order and the general welfare in a democratic society.

(3) These rights and freedoms may in no case be exercised contrary to the purposes and principles of the United Nations.

Article 30

Nothing in this Declaration may be interpreted as implying for any State, group or person any right to engage in any activity or to perform any act aimed at the destruction of any of the rights and freedoms set forth herein.

(Constitution Act, 1982, Part I)
Canadian Charter of Rights and Freedoms

WHEREAS Canada is founded upon principles that recognize the supremacy of God and the rule of law:

Guarantee of Rights and Freedoms

1. The Canadian Charter of Rights and Freedoms guarantees the rights and freedoms set out in it subject only to such reasonable limits prescribed by law as can be demonstrably justified in a free and democratic society.

Fundamental Freedoms

2. Everyone has the following fundamental freedoms:
   (a) freedom of conscience and religion;
   (b) freedom of thought, belief, opinion and expression, including freedom of the press and other media of communication;
   (c) freedom of peaceful assembly; and
   (d) freedom of association.

Democratic Rights

3. Every citizen of Canada has the right to vote in an election of members of the House of Commons or of a legislative assembly and to be qualified for membership therein.
4. (1) No House of Commons and no legislative assembly shall continue for longer than five years from the date fixed for the return of the writs at a general election of its members.
(2) In time of real or apprehended war, invasion or insurrection, a House of Commons may be continued by Parliament and a legislative assembly may be continued by the legislature beyond five years if such continuation is not opposed by

the votes of more than one-third of the members of the House of Commons or the legislative assembly, as the case may be.

5. There shall be a sitting of Parliament and of each legislature at least once every twelve months.

Mobility Rights

6. (1) Every citizen of Canada has the right to enter, remain in and leave Canada.
(2) Every citizen of Canada and every person who has the status of a permanent resident of Canada has the right
    (a) to move to and take up residence in any province; and
    (b) to pursue the gaining of a livelihood in any province.
(3) The rights specified in subsection (2) are subject to
    (a) any laws or practices of general application in force in a province other than those that discriminate among persons primarily on the basis of province of present or previous residence; and
    (b) any laws providing for reasonable residency requirements as a qualification for the receipt of publicly provided social services.

Legal Rights

7. Everyone has the right to life, liberty and security of the person and the right not to be deprived thereof except in accordance with the principles of fundamental justice.

8. Everyone has the right to be secure against unreasonable search or seizure.

9. Everyone has the right not to be arbitrarily detained or imprisoned.

10. Everyone has the right on arrest or detention
    (a) to be informed promptly of the reasons therefor;
    (b) to retain and instruct counsel without delay and to be informed of that right; and
    (c) to have the validity of the detention determined by way of *habeas corpus* and to be released if the detention is not lawful.

11. Any person charged with an offence has the right
    (a) to be informed without unreasonable delay of the specific offence;
    (b) to be tried within a reasonable time;
    (c) not to be compelled to be a witness in proceedings against that person in respect of the offence;
    (d) to be presumed innocent until proven guilty according to law in a fair and public hearing by an independent and impartial tribunal;

(e) not to be denied reasonable bail without just cause;

(f) except in the case of an offence under military law tried before a military tribunal, to the benefit of trial by jury where the maximum punishment for the offence is imprisonment for five years or a more severe punishment;

(g) not to be found guilty on account of any act or omission unless, at the time of the act or omission, it constituted an offence under Canadian or international law or was criminal according to the general principles of law recognized by the community of nations;

(h) if finally acquitted of the offence, not to be tried for it again and, if finally found guilty and punished for the offence, not to be tried or punished for it again; and

(i) if found guilty of the offence and if the punishment for the offence has been varied between the time of commission and the time of sentencing, to the benefit of the lesser punishment.

12. Everyone has the right not to be subjected to any cruel and unusual treatment or punishment.

13. A witness who testifies in any proceedings has the right not to have any incriminating evidence so given used to incriminate that witness in any other proceedings, except in a prosecution for perjury or for the giving of contradictory evidence.

14. A party or witness in any proceedings who does not understand or speak the language in which the proceedings are conducted or who is deaf has the right to the assistance of an interpreter.

Equality Rights

15. (1) Every individual is equal before and under the law and has the right to the equal protection and equal benefit of the law without discrimination and, in particular, without discrimination based on race, national or ethnic origin, colour, religion, sex, age or mental or physical disability.

(2) Subsection (1) does not preclude any law, program or activity that has as its object the amelioration of conditions of disadvantaged individuals or groups including those that are disadvantaged because of race, national or ethnic origin, colour, religion, sex. age or mental or physical disability.

Official Languages of Canada

16. (1) English and French are the official languages of Canada and have equality of status and equal rights and privileges as to their use in all institutions of the Parliament and government of Canada.

(2) English and French are the official languages of New Brunswick and have equality of status and equal rights and privileges as to their use in all institutions of the legislative and government of New Brunswick.

(3) Nothing in this Charter limits the authority of Parliament or a legislature to advance the equality of status or use of English and French.

17. (1) Everyone has the right to use English or French in any debates and other proceedings of Parliament.

(2) Everyone has the right to use English or French in any debates and other proceedings of the legislature of New Brunswick.

18. (1) The statutes, records and journals of Parliament shall be printed and published in English and French and both language versions are equally authoritative.

(2) The statues, records and journals of the legislature of New Brunswick shall be printed and published in English and French and both language versions are equally authoritative.

19. (1) Either English or French may be used by any person in, or in any pleading in or process issuing from, any court established by Parliament.

(2) Either English or French may be used by any person in, or in any pleading in or process issuing from, any court of New Brunswick.

20. (1) Any member of the public in Canada has the right to communicate with, and to receive available services from, any head or central office of an institution of the Parliament or government of Canada in English or French, and has the same right with respect to any other office of any such institution where

(a) there is a significant demand for communications with and services from that office in such language; or

(b) due to the nature of the office, it is reasonable that communications with and services from that office be available in both English and French.

(2) Any member of the public in New Brunswick has the right to communicate with, and to receive available services from, any office of an institution of the legislature or government of New Brunswick in English and French.

21. Nothing in sections 16 to 20 abrogates or derogates from any right, privilege or obligation with respect to the English and French languages, or either of them, that exists or is continued by virtue of any other provision of the Constitution of Canada.

22. Nothing in sections 16 to 20 abrogates or derogates from any legal or customary right or privilege acquired or enjoyed either before or after the coming into force of this Charter with respect to any language that is not English or French.

Minority Language Educational Rights

23. (1) Citizens of Canada
(a) whose first language learned and still understood is that of the English or French linguistic minority population of the province in which they reside, or
(b) who have received their primary school instruction in Canada in English or French and reside in a province where the language in which they received that instruction is the language of the English or French linguistic minority population of the province,
have the right to have their children receive primary and secondary school instruction in that language in that province.
(2) Citizens of Canada of whom any child has received or is receiving primary or secondary school instruction in English or French in Canada, have the right to have all their children receive primary or secondary school instruction in the same language.
(3) The right of citizens of Canada under subsections (1) and (2) to have their children receive primary and secondary school instruction in the language of the English or French linguistic minority population of a province
(a) applies wherever in the province the number of children of citizens who have such a right is sufficient to warrant the provision to them out of public funds of minority language instruction; and
(b) includes, where the number of those children so warrants, the right to have them receive that instruction in minority language educational facilities provided out of public funds.

Enforcement

24. (1) Anyone whose rights or freedoms, as guaranteed by this Charter, have been infringed or denied may apply to a court of competent jurisdiction to obtain such remedy as the court considers appropriate and just in the circumstances.
(2) Where, in proceedings under subsection (1), a court concludes that evidence was obtained in a manner that infringed or denied any rights or freedoms guaranteed by this Charter, the evidence shall be excluded if it is established that, having regard to all the circumstances, the admission of it in the proceedings would bring the administration of justice into disrepute.

25. The guarantee in this Charter of certain rights and freedoms shall not be construed so as to abrogate or derogate from any aboriginal, treaty or other rights or freedoms that pertain to the aboriginal peoples of Canada including
(a) any rights or freedoms that have been recognized by the Royal Proclamation of October 7, 1763; and
(b) any rights or freedoms that may be acquired by the aboriginal peoples of Canada by way of land claims settlement.

26. The guarantee in this Charter of certain rights and freedoms shall not be construed as denying the existence of any other rights or freedoms that exist in Canada.

27. This Charter shall be interpreted in a manner consistent with the preservation and enhancement of the multicultural heritage of Canadians.

28. Notwithstanding anything in this Charter, the rights and freedoms referred to in it are guaranteed equally to male and female persons.

29. Nothing in this Charter abrogates or derogates from any rights or privileges guaranteed by or under the Constitution of Canada in respect of denominational, separate or dissentient schools.

30. A reference in this Charter to a province or to the legislative assembly or legislature of a province shall be deemed to include a reference to the Yukon Territory and the Northwest Territories, or to the appropriate legislative authority thereof, as the case may be.

31. Nothing in this Charter extends the legislative powers of any body or authority.

Application of Charter

32. (1) This Charter applies
    (a) to the Parliament and government of Canada in respect of all matters within the authority of Parliament including all matters relating to the Yukon Territory and Northwest Territories; and
    (b) to the legislature and government of each province in respect of all matters within the authority of the legislature of each province.
(2) Notwithstanding subsection (1), section 15 shall not have effect until three years after this section comes into force.

33. (1) Parliament or the legislature of a province may expressly declare in an Act of Parliament or of the legislature, as the case may be, that the Act or a provision thereof shall operate notwithstanding a provision included in section 2 or sections 7 to 15 of this Charter.
(2) An Act or a provision of an Act in respect of which a declaration made under this section is in effect shall have such operation as it would have but for the provision of this Charter referred to in the declaration.
(3) A declaration made under subsection (1) shall cease to have effect five years after it comes into force or on such earlier date as may be specified in the declaration.
(4) Parliament or a legislature of a province may re-enact a declaration made under subsection (1).

(5) Subsection (3) applies in respect of a re-enactment made under subsection (4).

Citation

34. This Part may be cited as the Canadian Charter of Rights and Freedoms.

(Constitution Act, 1982, Part II)
Rights of the Aboriginal People of Canada

35. (1) The existing aboriginal and treaty rights of the aboriginal peoples of Canada are hereby recognized and affirmed.

(2) In this Act, 'aboriginal peoples of Canada' includes the Indian, Inuit and Métis peoples of Canada.

(3) For greater certainty, in subsection (1) 'treaty rights' includes rights that now exist by way of land claims agreements or may be so acquired.

(4) Notwithstanding any other provision of this Act, the aboriginal and treaty rights referred to in subsection (1) are guaranteed equally to male and female persons.

Declaration on the Rights of Persons Belonging to National or Ethnic, Religious and Linguistic Minorities

Adopted by United Nations General Assembly, in plenary, December 18, 1992

Article 1

1. States shall protect the existence and the national or ethnic, cultural, religious or linguistic identity of minorities within their respective territories, and shall encourage conditions for the promotion of that identity.

2. States shall adopt appropriate legislative and other measures to achieve these ends.

Article 2

1. Persons belonging to national or ethnic, religious and linguistic minorities (hereinafter referred to as persons belonging to minorities) have the right to enjoy their own culture, to profess and practise their own religion, and to use their own language, in private or in public, freely and without interference, or any form of discrimination.

2. Persons belonging to minorities have the right to participate effectively in cultural, religious, social, economic and public life.

3. Persons belonging to minorities have the right to participate effectively in decisions on the national and, where appropriate, regional level concerning the minority to which they belong or the regions in which they live, in a manner not incompatible with national legislation.

4. Persons belonging to minorities have the right to establish and maintain their own associations.

5. Persons belonging to minorities have the right to establish and maintain, without any discrimination, free and peaceful contacts with other members of their group, and with persons belonging to other minorities, as well as contacts across frontiers with citizens of other States to whom they are related by national or ethnic, religious or linguistic ties.

Article 3

1. Persons belonging to minorities may exercise their rights, including those set forth in this Declaration, individually as well as in community with other members of their group, without any discrimination.

2. No disadvantage shall result for any person belonging to a minority as the consequence of the exercise or non-exercise of the rights set forth in this Declaration.

Article 4

1. States shall take measures where required to ensure that persons belonging to minorities may exercise fully and effectively all their human rights and fundamental freedoms without any discrimination and in full equality before the law.

2. States shall take measures to create favourable conditions to enable persons belonging to minorities to express their characteristics and to develop their culture, language, religion, traditions and customs, except where specific practices are in violation of national law and contrary to international standards.

3. States should take appropriate measures so that, wherever possible, persons belonging to minorities have adequate opportunities to learn their mother tongue or to have instruction in their mother tongue.

4. States should, where appropriate, take measures in the field of education, in order to encourage knowledge of the history, traditions, language and culture of the minorities existing within their territory. Persons belonging to minorities should have adequate opportunities to gain knowledge of the society as a whole.

5. States should consider appropriate measures so that persons belonging to minorities may participate fully in the economic progress and development in their country.

Article 5

1. National policies and programmes shall be planned and implemented with

due regard for the legitimate interests of persons belonging to minorities.

2. Programmes of cooperation and assistance among States should be planned and implemented with due regard for the legitimate interests of persons belonging to minorities.

Article 6

States should cooperate on questions relating to persons belonging to minorities, including exchange of information and experiences, in order to promote mutual understanding and confidence.

Article 7

States should cooperate in order to promote respect for the rights set forth in this Declaration.

Article 8

1. Nothing in this Declaration shall prevent the fulfilment of international obligations of States in relation to persons belonging to minorities. In particular, States shall fulfil in good faith the obligations and commitments they have assumed under international treaties and agreements to which they are parties.

2. The exercise of the rights set forth in this Declaration shall not prejudice the enjoyment by all persons of universally recognized human rights and fundamental freedoms.

3. Measures taken by States to ensure the effective enjoyment of the rights set forth in this Declaration shall not *prima facie* be considered contrary to the principle of equality contained in the Universal Declaration of Human Rights.

4. Nothing in this Declaration may be construed as permitting any activity contrary to the purposes and principles of the United Nations, including sovereign equality, territorial integrity and political independence of States.

Article 9

The specialized agencies and other organizations of the United Nations system shall contribute to the full realization of the rights and principles set forth in this Declaration, within their respective fields of competence.

REFERENCES

Abella, Judge R.
1984   *Equality in Employment:* A Royal Commission Report. (Ottawa: Supply and
        Services Canada).
Abella, R.S., and M.L. Rothman, eds
1985   *Justice Beyond Orwell.* (Canadian Institute For the Administration of Justice).
Adachi, K.
1976   *The Enemy That Never Was.* (Toronto: McClelland & Stewart).
Albrecht, G.L., ed.
1976   *The Sociology of Physical Disability and Rehabilitation.* (Pittsburgh: University of
        Pittsburgh Press).
Anderson, A.B.
1967   'Anti-Semitism and Jewish Identity in Montreal.' Unpublished M.A. thesis in
        Sociology, Graduate Faculty of Political and Social Science. (New York: New
        School for Social Research)
———— and L. Driedger
1980   'The Mennonite Family: Culture and Kin in Rural Saskatchewan' in Ishwaran,
        ed., pp. 161-80.
———— and J.S. Frideres
1980   'Multiculturalism and Education: Update'. *Canadian Ethnic Studies Association
        Bulletin* VII, 3.
1981   *Ethnicity in Canada: Theoretical Perspectives.* (Toronto: Butterworths).
Anderson, G.M.
1979   'Spanish and Portuguese-speaking Immigrants in Canada' in Elliott, ed., pp. 206-
        19.
Anderson, W., and R. Grant
1975   *The Newcomers.* Report in typescript.
Asch, M.
1984   *Home and Native Land: Aboriginal Rights and the Canadian Constitution.*
        (Toronto: Methuen).

Ashworth, M.
1979   *The Forces Which Shaped Them*. (Vancouver: New Star Books).
Bagehot, W.
1873   *Physics and Politics, or Thoughts on the Application of Principles of 'Natural Selection' and 'Inheritance' to Political Society*.
Baker, Martin
1981   *The New Racism: Conservatives and the Ideology of the Tribe*. (London: Junction Books).
Banton, M.
1967   *Race Relations*. (London: Tavistock).
Barrie, M., *et al.*
1982   *Images of Women*. Report of the Task Force on Sex-Role Stereotyping in the Broadcast Media. (Hull: Quebec Minister of Supply & Services Canada).
Barrett, S.R.
1987   *Is God a Racist? The Right Wing in Canada*. (Toronto: University of Toronto Press).
Barth, F.
1969   *Ethnic Groups and Boundaries*. (Boston: Little Brown).
Bear, S.
1987   Quoted in Chapter One of *Enough is Enough: Aboriginal Women Speak Out*. (Toronto: The Women's Press).
Beaudoin, G., and F. Ratushny, eds
1989   *The Canadian Charter of Rights and Freedoms*. (Toronto: Carswell).
Beckton, C.F.
1987   'Section 27 and Section 15 of the Charter' in *Multiculturalism and the Charter* in CHRF, pp. 1-14.
Behiels, M.D., ed.
1989   *The Meech Lake Primer: Conflicting Views of the 1987 Constitutional Accord*. (Ottawa: University of Ottawa Press).
Bendix, R., and S.N. Lipset, eds
1953   *Class, Status and Power*. (Glencoe: Free Press).
Bennett, J.W.
1969   *Plains People: Adaptive Strategy and Agrarian Life on the Great Plains*. (Illinois: Adline).
————, ed.
1975   *The New Ethnicity: Perspectives From Ethnology*. (New York: West).
Bennett, R.B.
1928   *House of Commons Debates*. June 7, pp. 3925-7.
Berger, Mr Justice T.R.
1977   *Northern Frontier, Northern Homeland* . A Report of the MacKenzie Valley Pipeline Inquiry. Vol. One. (Ottawa: Minister of Supply and Services Canada).
Berkeley, H., C. Gaffield, and W.G. West, eds
1978   *Children's Rights: Legal and Educational Issues*. (Toronto: Ontario Institute For

Studies in Education. Symposium Series 9).

Bernier, B.
1981   'Construction d'un espace national et identité ethnique: le cas du Quebec 1930-
        1970', *Culture* 1, 1.

Berry, J.W., R. Kalin, and D.M. Taylor
1977   *Multiculturalism and Ethnic Attitudes in Canada.* (Ottawa: Minister of Supply and
        Services Canada).

Betcherman, L.R.
1975   *The Swastika and the Maple Leaf.* (Toronto: Fitzhenry & Whiteside).

Binavince, E.S.
1987   'The Juridical Aspects of Race Relations'. Paper presented for *Canada 2000*, a
        conference held at Carleton University, Ottawa. November 1.

Black, W., and L. Smith
1989   'The Equality Rights' in Beaudoin and Ratushny, eds, Chapter 14.

Blauner, R.
1972   *Racial Oppression in America.* (New York: Harper & Row).

Block, E., and M.A. Walker, eds
1981   *Discrimination, Affirmative Action and Equal Opportunity.* (Vancouver: The Fraser
        Institute).

Bogardus, E.
1925   'Measuring Social Distance', *Sociology and Social Research* 9, pp. 299-308.

Boldt, E.D., and L.W. Roberts
1980   'The Decline of Hutterite Population Growth'. Comment. *Canadian Ethnic
        Studies* XII, 3, pp. 111-17.

Boldt, M , and J.A. Long, eds
1985   *The Quest For Justice: Aboriginal Peoples and Aboriginal Rights.* (Toronto:
        University of Toronto Press).

Bourassa, R.
1971   'Objections to Multiculturalism'. Open letter to Prime Minister Trudeau, in *Le
        Devoir*, 17 November.

Boyd, M.
1987   *Migrant Women in Canada. Profiles and Policies.* (Ottawa: Employment and
        Immigration Canada).
1993   'Gender Concealed, Gender Revealed: The Demography of Canada's Refugee
        Flows'. Paper presented at the Conference on Gender Issues and Refugees:
        Development Implications, held at York University. 9-11 May.

Breton, R.
1964   'Institutional Completeness of Ethnic Communities and the Personal Relations of
        Immigrants', *The American Journal of Sociology* LXX, 2, pp. 193-205.
1978   'The Structure of Relationships Between Ethnic Collectivities' in Driedger, ed.,
        pp. 55-73.

Broadfoot, B.
1977   *Years of Sorrow, Years of Shame.* (Toronto: Doubleday).

Brody, H.
1975   *The People's Land: Eskimos and Whites in the Eastern Arctic.* (Middlesex: Penguin Books).
Brotz, H.
1980   'Multiculturalism in Canada: A Muddle', *Canadian Public Policy* VI, 1, pp. 41-6.
Brym, R.J., W. Shaffir, and M. Weinfeld, eds
1993   *The Jews in Canada.* (Toronto: Oxford University Press).
Bryne, N. and J. Quarter, eds
1972   *Must Schools Fail?* (Toronto: McClelland & Stewart).
Buchignani, N.L.
1977   'A Review of the Historical and Sociological Literature on East Indians in Canada', *Canadian Ethnic Studies* IX, 1, pp. 86-108.
Bullivant, B.M.
1979   *Pluralism, Teacher Education and Ideology.* Report presented to the Education Research and Development Committee. Canberra. June.
Burnet, J.
1975   'Multiculturalism, Immigration and Racism', *Canadian Ethnic Studies* 7, pp. 35-9.
1976   'Ethnicity: Canadian Experience and Policy', *Sociological Focus* 9, 2, pp. 199-207.
1978   'The Policy of Multiculturalism Within A Bilingual Framework: A Stock-taking', *Canadian Ethnic Studies* X, 2, pp. 107-13.
1981   'The Social and Historical Context of Ethnic Relations' in Gardner and Kalin, eds, pp. 17-35.
Caibaiosai, L.R.
1970   'The Politics of Patience' in Waubageshig, ed.
Cairns, A., and C. Williams, eds
1986   *The Politics of Gender, Ethnicity and Language in Canada.* (Toronto: University of Toronto Press).
Campbell, M.
1973   *Halfbreed.* (Toronto: McClelland & Stewart).
Canada
1966   Report to the Minister of Justice of the Special Committee on Hate Propaganda in Canada. M. Cohen, Chair. (Ottawa: Queen's Printer).
1970   Report of The Royal Commission on Bilingualism and Biculturalism. *Book IV: The Cultural Contribution of the Other Ethnic Groups.* (Ottawa: Information Canada).
1971   *House of Commons Debates.* Statement of Prime Minister P.E. Trudeau. 8 October.
1984   INAC Response of the Government to the Report of the Special Committee on Indian Self-Government. (Ottawa: Minister of Indian Affairs and Northern Development) 5 March.
1984   *Multiculturalism: Building the Canadian Mosaic.* Report of the Standing Committee on Multiculturalism. G. Mitges, Chair. June.
1984   *Equality Now!* Report of the Special Committee on Visible Minorities in

Canadian Society. B. Daudlin, Chair. (Ottawa: House of Commons).

1985   *House of Commons*. Bill C-31: An Act to Amend the Indian Act.

1987   *House of Commons*. Bill C-[93]: An Act for the preservation and enhancement of multiculturalism in Canada. The Secretary of State of Canada, 22427-27-11-87. (Enacted 1988).

1987   Meech Lake Accord. Constitutional Amendment, 1987. (Defeated 23 June 1990).

1992   Charlottetown Accord. Consensus Report on the Constitution. (Defeated 26 October 1992).

Canadian Bar Association

1988   *Aboriginal Rights in Canada: An Agenda For Action*. Committee Report. Ottawa.

Canadian Bill of Rights

1960   An Act passed by the Parliament of Canada and assented to on 10 August.

Canadian Council on Children and Youth

1978   *Admittance Restricted: The Child as Citizen in Canada*.

Canadian Ethnocultural Council

1989   'A Dream Deferred: Collective Equality For Canada's Ethnocultural Communities' in Behiels, 1989, pp. 335-48.

Canadian Human Rights Commission

1979   *Discrimination in Canada*. Ottawa. September.

Canadian Human Rights Foundation (CHRF)

1987   *Multiculturalism and the Charter: A Legal Perspective*. (Toronto: Carswell).

Canadian Jewish Congress

1990   INTERCOM 9, 2, Summer.

Canadian Review of Sociology and Anthropology

1978   Special Issue: The National Question; 15, 2.

Cardinal, H.

1969   *The Unjust Society*. (Edmonton: Hurtig).

1977   *The Rebirth of Canada's Indians*. (Edmonton: Hurtig).

Carmichael, S., and C. Hamilton

1967   *Black Power: The Politics of Liberation in America*. (New York: Random House).

Carstens, P.

1981   'Coercion and Change' in R. Ossenberg, ed.

Case, F.I.

1977   *Racism and National Consciousness*. (Toronto: Plowshare Press).

Chamberlain, H.S.

1899   *Foundations of the Nineteenth Century*.

Cholewinski, R.I., ed.

1990   *Human Rights in Canada: Into the 1990's and Beyond*. (Ottawa: Human Rights Research and Education Centre, University of Ottawa).

Clark, S.D., J.P. Grayson, and L.M. Grayson

1975   *Prophecy and Protest: Social Movements in Twentieth-Century Canada*. (Toronto: Gage).

Clement, W.
1975   'Access to the Canadian Corporate Elite', *Canadian Review of Sociology and Anthropology* 12, 1, pp. 33-52.

Collins, D.
1979   *Immigration: The Destruction of English Canada.* (Richmond Hill: BMG Publishing).

Condon, R.G.
1987   *Inuit Youth: Growth and Change in the Canadian Arctic.* (London: Rutgers University Press).

Coon, C.S.
1962   *The Origin of Races.* (New York: Knopf).
1965   *The Living Races of Man.* (New York: Knopf).

Corpus.
1979   *The Canadian Family Tree: Canada's Peoples.* (Ottawa: Minister of Supply and Services).

Costa, E., and E. Di Santo
1972   'The Italian-Canadian Child, His Family, and the Canadian School System' in Bryne and Quarter, eds.

Cotler, I.
1985   'Hate Literature' in Abella and Rothman, eds.

Cowan, S., ed.
1976   *We Don't Live in Snowhouses Now: Reflections of Arctic Bay.* (Ottawa: Canadian Arctic Producers).

Criminal Reports (Third Series)
1987   *R. v. Zundel* (1987), 31 C.C.C. (3d) 97, 35 D.L.R. (4th) 338, 58 O.R. (2d) 129, 56 C.R. (3d) 1 (C.A.).

Curtis, J.E., and W.G. Scott, eds
1979   *Social Stratification: Canada,* 2nd ed.(Toronto: Prentice Hall).

Curtis, J., E. Grabb, N. Guppy, and S. Gilbert, eds
1988   *Social Inequality in Canada: Patterns, Problems, Policies.* (Scarborough: Prentice-Hall Canada).

Dahlie, J., and T. Fernando, eds
1981   *Ethnicity, Power and Politics in Canada.* (Toronto: Methuen).

Dailey, R. C., and L.A. Dailey
1961   *The Eskimo of Rankin Inlet: A Preliminary Report.* (Ottawa: Northern Coordination and Research Centre, Department of Northern Affairs and Research Resources).

Daniels, H.W.
1979   *We Are the New Nation: The Métis and National Native Policy.* (Ottawa: Native Council of Canada). March.
1979   *The Forgotten People: Métis and Non-Status Indian Land Claims.* (Ottawa: Native Council of Canada). April.

Darroch, A.G.

1979   'Another Look at Ethnicity, Stratification and Social Mobility in Canada', *Canadian Journal of Sociology* 4, 1, pp. 1-25.

Darwin, C.

1859   *On the Origin of Species By Means of Natural Selection or The Preservation of Favoured Races in the Struggle For Life.*

Das Gupta, Tania

1986   *Learning from Our History: Community Development by Immigrant Women in Ontario 1958-1986. A tool for action.* (Toronto: Cross Cultural Communication Centre).

Day, S.

1990   'The Process of Achieving Equality' in Cholewinski, ed., pp. 17-30.

Despres, L.A.

1975   'Ethnicity and Ethnic Group Relations in Guyana' in Bennett, ed., pp. 127-47.

DIAND

1980   *Indian Conditions: A Survey.* (Ottawa: Indian and Northern Affairs).

Dion, L.

1976   *Quebec: The Unfinished Revolution.* (Montreal: McGill- Queen's University Press).

Douglas, R.A.A.

1979   Cited in Leavy, pp. 11-14.

D'Oyley, V.R.

1978   'Schooling and Ethnic Rights' in Berkeley *et al.*, eds, pp. 137-44.

———, ed.

1978   *Black Presence in Multi-Ethnic Canada.* (Toronto: Ontario Institute for Studies in Education).

Driedger, L., ed.

1978   *The Canadian Ethnic Mosaic.* (Toronto: McClelland & Stewart).

1988   *Mennonite Identity in Conflict.* (Lewiston, New York: The Edwin Mellen Press).

Driedger, L., and N. Chappell

1987   *Aging and Ethnicity: Toward an Interface.* (Toronto: Butterworths).

Dwivedi, O.P., R.D. D'Costa, C.L. Stanford, and E. Tepper, eds

1989   *Canada 2000: Race Relations and Public Policy.* (Guelph: University of Guelph, Department of Political Studies).

Dyck, N.

1981   'The Politics of Special Status: Indian Associations and the Administration of Indian Affairs' in Dahlie and Fernando, eds, pp. 279-91.

Eaton, J.

1970   'Controlled Acculturation: A Survival Technique of the Hutterites' in M. Kurokawa, ed.

Elliott, J.L., ed.

1971   *Minority Canadians 1: Native Peoples, and 2: Immigrant Groups.* (Scarborough: Prentice-Hall).

1979   *Two Nations, Many Cultures.* (Scarborough: Prentice- Hall).

————, and A. Fleras
1990   'Immigration and the Canadian Ethnic Mosaic' in Li, pp. 51-76.
Enloe, C.H.
 1973   *Ethnic Conflict and Political Development.* (Boston: Little Brown).
Epp, F.H.
1974   *Mennonites in Canada 1786-1920: The History of a Separate People.* (Toronto: Macmillan).
Evans, S.
1985   'Some Developments in the Diffusion Patterns of Hutterite Colonies', *Canadian Geographer* 29,4.
Evans-Pritchard, E.E.
1940   *The Nuer.* (Clarendon: Oxford University Press).
Fanon, F.
1967   *Black Skins, White Masks.* (New York: Grove).
Flint, D.
1975   *The Hutterites: A Study in Prejudice.* (Toronto: Oxford University Press).
Foucher, P.
1990   'Language Rights in the 1990's' in Cholewinski, pp. 117-38.
Fretz, J.W.
1974   *The Mennonites in Ontario.* (Waterloo: The Mennonite Historical Society of Ontario).
Frideres, J.S.
1988   *Native Peoples in Canada: Contemporary Conflicts,* 3rd ed. (Scarborough: Prentice Hall Canada).
1990   'INTRODUCTION' in *Canadian Ethnic Studies*, Special Issue: *First Nations: The Politics of Change and Survivial* XXII, 3.
1993   *Native Peoples in Canada: Contemporary Conflicts,* 4th ed. (Scarborough: Prentice Hall Canada).
Gardner, R.C., and R. Kalin, eds
1981   *A Canadian Social Psychology of Ethnic Relations.* (Toronto: Methuen).
Gee, E.M., and M.M. Kimball
1987   *Women and Aging.* (Toronto: Butterworths).
Gibbins, R., and J.R. Ponting
1986   'An Assessment of the Probable Impact of Aboriginal Self-Government in Canada' in Cairns and Williams, eds, pp. 171-239.
Gibbon, J.M.
1938   *The Canadian Mosaic.* (Toronto: McClelland & Stewart).
Gibson, D.
1990   *The Law of the Charter: Equality Rights.* (Toronto: Carswell).
Gilroy, Paul
1991   *There Ain't No Black in the Union Jack: The Cultural Politics of Race and Nation.* (Chicago: University of Chicago Press).

Glaser, K., and S.T. Possony
1979   *Victims of Politics: The State of Human Rights.* (New York: Columbia University Press).

Glazer, N., and D. Moynihan, eds
1975   *Ethnicity: Theory and Experience.* (Cambridge: Harvard University Press).

Glickman, Y.
1976   'Organizational Indicators and Social Correlates of Collective Jewish Identity.' Unpublished Ph.D. dissertation. Department of Sociology, University of Toronto.

Gobineau, J.A. de
1854   *Essai sur L'Inégalité des Races Humaines.* (Paris).

Goffman, E.
1963   *Stigma: Notes on the Management of Spoiled Identity.* (Englewood Cliffs, N.J.: Spectrum Books).

Gordon, M.
1964   *Assimilation in American Life.* (New York: Oxford University Press).

Gove, W.R.
1976   'Societal Reaction Theory and Disability' in G.L. Albrecht, ed.

Graburn, N.H.
1969   *Eskimos Without Igloos: Social and Economic Development in Sugluk.* (Boston: Little Brown).
1981   '1,2,3,4 . . . Anthropology and the Fourth World', *Culture* I, 1, pp. 66-70.

Gregorovich, A.
1972   *Canadian Ethnic Groups Bibliography.* (Toronto: Department of the Provincial Secretary and Citizenship of Ontario).

Harper, A.G.
1945   'Canada's Indian Administration: Basic Concepts and Objectives', *America Indigena* 4, 2, pp. 119-32.

Hawthorn, H., ed.
1955   *The Doukhobors Of British Columbia.* (Vancouver: Dent and University of British Columbia).
1967   *A Survey of the Contemporary Indians of Canada,* 2. (Ottawa: Queen's Printer).

Head, W.A.
1975   *The Black Presence in the Canadian Mosaic.* A Study of the Perception and the Practice of Discrimination Against Blacks in Metropolitan Toronto. Report submitted to the Ontario Human Rights Commission, September.

Heagerty, J.L.
1928   *Four Centuries of Medical History in Canada,* I. (Toronto: Macmillan).

Hendrickson, Robert.
1987   *The Facts On File Encyclopedia of Word and Phrase Origins.* (New York: Facts on File Publications).

Henry, F.
1977   *The Dynamics of Racism in Toronto: A Preliminary Report.* (Toronto: York

University).

1993 'Democratic Racism and the Perpetuation of Inequality in Canada'. Plenary Address for the Twelfth Biennial Conference of the Canadian Ethnic Studies Association. (Vancouver: November 27-30).

———, and E. Ginsberg

1988 'Racial Discrimination in Employment' in Curtis *et al.*, pp. 214-20.

Herberg, E.N.

1989 *Ethnic Groups in Canada: Adaptations and Transitions.* (Scarborough: Nelson Canada).

Herman, S.N.

1977 *Jewish Identity: A Social Psychological Perspective.* (London: Sage).

Hill, D.G.

1977 *Human Rights in Canada: A Focus on Racism.* (Canadian Labour Congress).

———, and M. Schiff

1988 *Human Rights in Canada: A Focus on Racism,* 3rd ed. (Ottawa: Human Rights Research and Education Centre, University of Ottawa).

Hill, L.B.

1974 'Institutionalization, the Ombudsman and Bureaucracy', *American Political Science Review* 68, pp. 1075-85.

Hostetler, J.A.

1971 *Children in Amish Society: Socialization and Community Education.* (New York: Holt, Rinehart and Winston).

———, and G.E. Huntington

1967 *The Hutterites in North America.* (New York: Holt, Rinehart and Winston).

House of Commons Debates

1971 Statement of Prime Minister Trudeau, 8 October.

Hudson, M.R.

1987 'Multiculturalism, Government Policy and Constitutional Enshrinement—A Comparative Study' in CHRF, pp. 59-122.

Hughes, C.C.

1965 'Under Four Flags: Recent Culture Change Among the Eskimos', *Current Anthropology* 6, 1, pp. 3-73.

Hughes, D.R., and E. Kallen

1974 *The Anatomy of Racism: Canadian Dimensions.* (Montreal: Harvest House).

Hughes, K.

1920 *Father Lacombe: The Black-Robe Voyageur.* (Toronto: McClelland & Stewart).

Hussain, A.

1981 'Have Power, Have Rights?' Paper presented for the International Peace Research Association, Ninth General Conference. Geneva Park, Ontario, 21-26 June.

Inuit Tapirisat of Canada (ITC)

1979 *Political Development in Nunavut.*

Isaacs, H.R.

1977 *Idols of the Tribe: Group Identity and Political Change.* (New York: Harper & Row).

Isajiw, W.W.

1970   'Definitions of Ethnicity', *Ethnicity* 1: 1.

1977   'Olga in Wonderland: Ethnicity in a Technological Society', *Canadian Ethnic Studies* 9, 1, pp. 77-85.

1977   *Identities: The Impact of Ethnicity on Canadian Society.* (Toronto: Peter Martin Associates).

1980   Cited in Report of a Conference on Minority Rights. Sponsored by the Canadian Human Rights Foundation, York University, 29 February.

Ishwaran, K., ed.

1980   *Canadian Families: Ethnic Variations.* (Toronto: McGraw-Hill Ryerson).

Ittinuar, P.

1985   'The Inuit Perspective on Aboriginal Rights' in Boldt and Long, eds.

Jack, H.

1970   'Native Alliance for Red Power' in Waubageshig, ed.

Jackson, M.

1979   'The Rights of the Native People' in Macdonald and Humphrey, eds, pp. 267-88.

Jaenen, C.J.

1972   'Cultural Diversity and Education' in Byrne and Quarter, eds.

Jain, H.C.

1989   'Affirmative Action/Employment Equity Programs and Visible Minorities in Canada' in Dwivedi, D'Costa, Stanford, and Tepper, eds.

Jansen, C.J.

1978   'Community Organization of Italians in Toronto' in Driedger, ed.

Jenness, D.

1964   *Eskimo Administration 11.* Canada Arctic Institute of North America. Technical Paper No. 14. May.

Joy, R.J.

1972   *Languages in Conflict.* (Toronto. McClelland & Stewart).

Kallen, E.

1977   'Legacy of Tutelage: Divided Inuit' in Paine, ed., pp. 129-43.

1977   *Spanning the Generations: A Study in Jewish Identity.* (Toronto: Longman Canada/Academic Press).

1982a   *Ethnicity and Human Rights in Canada.* (Agincourt: Gage).

1982b   'Multiculturalism: Ideology, Policy and Reality', *Journal of Canadian Studies* 17, 1, pp. 58-63. Reprinted in Curtis *et al.*, eds, 1988, pp. 235-47.

1987   'Multiculturalism, Minorities and Motherhood: A Social Scientific Critique of Section 27' in CHRF, pp. 123-38.

1988   'The Meech Lake Accord: Entrenching a Pecking Order of Minority Rights'. *Canadian Public Policy.* Special Issue: *The Meech Lake Accord.* Supplement to Vol. XIV, pp. 107-120. Reprinted in *The Meech Lake Primer.* Behiels, ed. 1989, pp. 349-71.

1990   'Multiculturalism: The Not-So-Impossible Dream' in Cholewinski, ed., pp. 165-82.

1992   'Never Again: Target Group Responses To The Debate Concerning Anti-Hate Propaganda Legislation', *Windsor Yearbook of Access to Justice*. Vol. XI. (Windsor: Faculty of Law, University of Windsor).

————, and L. Lam

1993   'Target For Hate: The Impact of the Zundel and Keegstra Trials on a Jewish-Canadian Audience', *Canadian Ethnic Studies* XXV, 1.

Kallen, H.

1915   'Democracy Versus the Melting Pot', *The Nation*, 18 and 25 February.

Kelner, M.

1969   'The Elite Structure of Toronto: Ethnic Composition and Patterns of Recruitment'. Unpublished Ph.D. dissertation. Department of Sociology, University of Toronto.

Kelner, M., and E. Kallen

1974   'The Multicultural Policy: Canada's Response to Ethnic Diversity', *Journal of Comparative Sociology* 2, pp. 21-4.

Kemar-D'Souza, C.

1981   Political Economy and Human Rights. Paper presented for the International Peace Research Association, Ninth General Conference. Geneva Park, Ontario. 21-26 June.

Kennedy, J.R.

1944   'Single or Triple Melting Pot? Intermarriage Trends in New Haven, 1870-1940', *American Journal of Sociology* XLIX, pp. 331-9.

Kidd, B.

1894   *Social Evolution.*

Killiam, L.M.

1968   *The Impossible Revolution?* (New York: Random House).

Kilson, M.

1975   'Blacks and Neo-Ethnicity in American Political Life' in Glazer and Moynihan, pp. 236-66.

Knox, R.

1850   *The Races of Man: A Fragment.* (London: Renshaw).

Krauter, J.F., and M. Davis

1978   *Minority Canadians: Ethnic Groups.* (Toronto: Methuen).

Kurokawa, M., ed.

1970   *Minority Responses.* (New York: Random House).

Lai, V.

1971   'The New Chinese Immigrants in Toronto' in Elliott, ed., 2, pp. 120-40.

Lam, L., and A.H. Richmond

1987   'A Decade in Canada: Immigration, Human Rights and Racism, 1978-1987', *New Community* XIV, 1-2, (Fall).

Latimer, B.A.

1979   Cited in Leavy, p.18.

Lautard, H., and N. Guppy

1990   'The Vertical Mosaic Revisited: Occupational Differentials Among Canadian Ethnic Groups' in Li, ed., pp. 189-208.

La Violette, F.

1948   *The Canadian Japanese and World War II.* (Toronto: University of Toronto Press).

Leavy, J.

1979   Working paper for a series of regional conferences on minority rights, sponsored by the Canadian Human Rights Foundation. October.

Lee, D.J.

1979   'The Evolution of Nationalism in Quebec' in Elliott, ed., pp. 60-74.

Lévesque, R.

1968   *An Option For Quebec.* (Toronto: McClelland & Stewart).

Levy, J.

1979   'In Search of Isolation: The Holdeman Mennonites of Linden, Alberta and their School', *Canadian Ethnic Studies* XII, I, pp. 115-30.

Lewin, K.

1948   *Resolving Social Conflicts.* (New York: Harper Bros).

Li, P.S.

1980   'Immigration Laws and Family Patterns: Some Demographic Changes Among Chinese Families in Canada 1885-1971', *Canadian Ethnic Studies* XII, I, pp. 58-73.

————, ed.

1990   *Race and Ethnic Relations in Canada.* (Toronto: Oxford University Press).

Lieberson, S.

1961   'A Societal Theory of Race and Ethnic Relations', *American Sociological Review* 26, pp. 902-10.

Lincoln, C.E.

1961   *The Black Muslims in America.* (Boston: Beacon).

Loehlin, J.C., G. Lindsey, and J.N. Spuhler

1975   *Race Differences in Intelligence.* (San Francisco: W.H. Freeman).

Lupul, M.

1982   'Political Implementation of Multiculturalism', *Journal Of Canadian Studies* 17, 1 (Spring).

Lyons, J.

1976   'The (Almost) Quiet Revolution: Doukhobor Schooling in Saskatchewan', *Canadian Ethnic Studies* VIII, I, pp. 23-37.

McDiarmid, G., and D. Pratt

1971   *Teaching Prejudice: A Content Analysis of Social Studies Textbooks Authorized for Use in Ontario.* (Toronto: Ontario Institute for Studies in Education).

Macdonald, R.J.

1976   'Hutterite Education in Alberta: A Test Case in Assimilation 1920-1970', *Canadian Ethnic Studies* VIII, I, pp. 9-21.

Macdonald, R. St J., and J.P. Humphrey
1979   *The Practice of Freedom.* (Toronto: Butterworths).
Mckie, C., and K. Thompson, eds
1990   *Canadian Social Trends.* (Toronto: Thompson Educational Publishing).
Maclean, J.
1896   *Canadian Savage Folk: The Native Tribes of Canada.* (Toronto: Briggs).
McRoberts, K.H., and D. Posgate
1976   *Quebec: Social Change and Political Crisis.* (Toronto: McClelland & Stewart).
Magnet, J.E.
1987   'Interpreting Multiculturalism' in CHRF, pp. 145-54.
1989   'Multiculturalism and Collective Rights' in Beaudoin and Ratushny, eds, pp. 740-80.
Magsino, R.M.
1978   'Student Rights in Canada: Nonsense Upon Stilts?' in Berkeley *et al.*, eds, pp. 89-107.
Makabe, T.
1976   'Ethnic Group Identity: Canadian-born Japanese in Metropolitan Toronto'. Unpublished Ph.D. dissertation. University of Toronto.
Malcolm X.
1966   *The Autobiography of Malcolm X.* (New York: Grove).
Manuel, G., and Poslums
1974   *The Fourth World: An Indian Reality.* (New York: Free Press).
Marshall, I.
1981   'Disease as a Factor in the Demise of the Beothuck Indians', *Culture* 1, I, pp. 71-8.
Matejko, A.
1979   'Multiculturalism: The Polish-Canadian Case' in Elliott, ed., pp. 237-49.
Maxwell, T.R.
1979   'The Invisible French: The French in Metropolitan Toronto' in Elliott, ed., pp. 114-22.
Mealing, F.M.
1980   'The Doukhobors: Family and Rites of Passage' in Ishwaran, ed., pp. 181-97.
Mede, M.P.
1979   Cited in Leavy, pp. 3-4.
Miles, R.
1989   *Racism.* (London: Routledge).
Millett, D.
1971   'Religion as a Source of Perpetuation of Ethnic Identity' in *Social Space: Canadian Perspectives.* D.I. Davies and K. Herman, eds (Toronto: New Press), pp. 174-6.
1979   'Religious Identity: The Non-Official Languages and the Minority Churches' in Elliott, ed., pp. 182-94.

Milner, H., and S.H. Milner

1973 *The Decolonization of Quebec: An Analysis of Left-Wing Nationalism.* (Toronto: McClelland & Stewart).

Montero, G.

1977 *The Immigrants.* (Toronto: James Lorimer).

Morris, R.N., and C.M. Lanphier

1977 *Three Scales of Inequality: Perspectives on French- English Relations.* (Toronto: Longman Canada/Academic Press).

Morse, B.W., ed.

1985 *Aboriginal Peoples and the Law: Indian, Métis and Inuit Rights in Canada.* (Ottawa: Carleton University Press).

Nichols, P.

1971 'Since the Days of Barter' in *People of Light and Dark.* M. Van. Steensel, ed. (Ottawa: Information Canada), pp. 20-4.

Noel, D.L.

1968 'A Theory of the Origin of Ethnic Stratification', *Social Problems* 16, pp. 157-72.

Ossenberg, R., ed.

1971 *Canadian Society: Pluralism, Change and Conflict.* (Toronto: Prentice-Hall).

Paine, R., ed.

1977 *The White Arctic: Anthropological Essays on Tutelage and Ethnicity.* (St John's: Memorial University of Newfoundland).

Palmer, H.

1976 'Mosaic vs Melting Pot? Immigration and Ethnicity in Canada and the United States', *International Journal* xxxi: 3.

Parsons, T.

1953 'A Revised Analytic Approach to the Theory of Social Stratification' in Bendix and Lipset, eds, pp. 92-128.

Patterson, E.P.

1972 *The Canadian Indian: A History Since 1500.* (Toronto: Collier-Macmillan Canada).

Pelletier, W.

1974 'For Every North American Indian That Begins to Disappear I Also Begin to Disappear' in Frideres, ed., pp. 101-9.

Pentney, W.F.

1989 'Interpreting the Charter: General Principles' in Beaudoin and Ratushny, eds, Chapter Two.

Peter, K.

1978 'Multi-cultural Politics, Money and the Conduct of Canadian Ethnic Studies', *Canadian Ethnic Studies Association Bulletin* 5, pp. 2-3.

1980a 'Problems in the Family, Community and Culture of Hutterites' in Ishwaran, ed., pp. 221-35.

1980b 'The Decline of Hutterite Population Growth', *Canadian Ethnic Studies* xii, 3, pp. 97-110.

1981 'The Myth of Multiculturalism and Other Political Fables' in Dahlie and

Fernando, eds, pp. 56-67.

1987   *The Dynamics of Hutterite Society: An Analytic Approach.* (Edmonton: The University of Alberta Press).

Pie, B.

Undated 'Affirmative Action: Can the Voluntary Approach Work?' *Viewpoint.* (Toronto: Ontario Ministry of Labour, Women's Bureau).

Ponting, J.R.

1990   'Public Opinion On Aboriginal Peoples' Issues' in Mckie and Thompson, eds, pp. 19-27.

———, and R. Gibbins

1980   *Out of Irrelevance: A Socio-Political Introduction to Indian Affairs in Canada.* (Toronto: Butterworths).

Porter, J.

1965   *The Vertical Mosaic.* (Toronto: University of Toronto Press).

1975   'Ethnic Pluralism in Canadian Perspective' in Glazer and Moynihan, eds, pp. 267-304.

———, ed.

1979   *The Measure of Canadian Society: Education, Equality and Opportunity.* (Agincourt: Gage).

———, ed.

1979   'Melting Pot or Mosaic: Revolution or Reversion?' in Porter, ed., pp. 139-62.

Price, A.G.

1950   *White Settlers and Native People.* (Melbourne: Georgian House).

Putnam, C.

1961   *Race and Reason.* (Washington: Public Affairs Press)

Radecki, H., and B. Heydenkorn

1976   *A Member of a Distinguished Family: The Polish Group in Canada.* (Toronto: McClelland & Stewart).

Ramcharan, S.

1976   'The Economic Adaptation of West Indians in Toronto, Canada', *Canadian Review of Sociology and Anthropology* 13: 3.

Redi, H., and C. Young

1939   *The Japanese Canadians.* (Toronto: University of Toronto Press).

Red Paper

1970   *Citizens Plus.* Response of the Indian Chiefs of Alberta to the White Paper (1969), presented to Prime Minister Trudeau. June.

Reference re: An Act To Amend The Education Act. 25 D.L.R. (4th) 1, 53 O.R. (2nd) 513, 13 O.A.C. 241 (Ont. C.A.).

Remillard, G.

1989   'Quebec's Quest for Survival and Equality via the Meech Lake Accord' in Behiels, ed., pp. 28-42.

Repo, M.

1971 'The Fallacy of Community Control', *Transformation: Theory and Practice of Social Change* I, I.

Richard, M.

1991 *Ethnic Groups and Marital Choices: Ethnic History and Marital Assimilation, Canada 1871 and 1971.* (Vancouver: University of British Columbia Press).

Richmond, A.H.

1972 *Ethnic Segregation in Metropolitan Toronto.* (Toronto: York University, Institute for Behavioural Research).

1974 'Language, Ethnicity and the Problem of Identity in a Canadian Metropolis', *Ethnicity* 1, pp. 175-206.

1975 'The Green Paper: Reflections on the Canadian Immigration and Population Study', *Canadian Ethnic Studies* VII, I, pp. 5-21.

1975-76 'Black and Asian Immigrants in Britain and Canada: Some Comparisons', *Journal of the Community Relations Commission* IV: 4.

Rioux, M.

1971 *Quebec In Question.* (Toronto: James Lewis & Samuel).

Rocher, G.

1976 'Multiculturalism: Doubts of a Francophone' in *Report of the Second Canadian Conference on Multiculturalism.* (Ottawa: Canadian Consultative Council on Multiculturalism).

Rose, P.I.

1968 *The Subject Is Race.* (London: Oxford University Press).

Rosenstock, J., and D. Adair

1976 'Multiracialism in the Classroom: A Survey of Interracial Attitudes in Ontario Schools.' Report prepared for the Multicultural Directorate, Department of Secretary of State, Ottawa. September.

Rosenthal, P.

1990 'The Criminality of Racial Harassment' in *Canadian Human Rights Yearbook (1989-90).* (Human Rights Research and Education Centre University of Ottawa) pp. 113-66.

Roy, N.

1979 Cited in Leavy, pp. 14-17.

Sanders, D.

1964 'The Hutterites: A Case Study in Minority Rights.' *Canadian Bar Review* XLII, pp. 225-42.

1987 'Article 27 and the Aboriginal Peoples of Canada' in CHRF, pp. 155-66.

1989 'The UN Working Group on Indigenous Populations' in *Human Rights Quarterly* 11. (John's Hopkins University Press).

1990 'The Supreme Court of Canada and the "Legal and Political Struggle" Over Indigenous Rights', *Canadian Ethnic Studies* XXII, 3, pp. 122-9.

Saskatchewan Human Rights Commission

1974 *Prejudice in Social Studies Textbooks: A Content Analysis Of Social Studies Textbooks Used in Saskatchewan Schools.* Saskatoon.

Sawchuck, J.

1978   *The Métis of Manitoba*. (Toronto: Peter Martin).

Schermerhorn, R.A.

1970   *Comparative Ethnic Relations: A Framework For Theory and Research*. (New York: Random House).

Sealey, D.B., and A.S. Lussier

1975   *The Métis: Canada's Forgotten People*. (Winnipeg: Manitoba Métis Federation).

Shaffir, W.

1976   'The Organization of Secular Education in a Chassidic Jewish Community', *Canadian Ethnic Studies* VIII, I, pp. 38-51.

Shibutani, T., and K.M. Kwan

1965   *Ethnic Stratification: A Comparative Approach*. (New York: Macmillan).

Simpson, G.E., and J.M. Yinger

1972   *Racial and Cultural Minorities: An Analysis of Prejudice and Discrimination*, 4th ed. (New York: Harper and Row).

Slobodin, R.

1971   'Métis of the Far North' in Elliott, ed., Vol. 1, pp. 150-68.

Stasiulis, D.K.

1990   'Theorizing Connections: Gender, Race Ethnicity and Class' in Li, ed., pp. 269-305.

Steensel, M. van, ed.

1966   *People of Light and Dark*. (Ottawa: Information Canada).

Stewart, W.

1970   'Red Power' in Kurokawa, ed., pp. 364-72.

Stonequist, E.V.

1937   *The Marginal Man*. (New York: Scribner's).

Sunahara, A.G.

1981   *The Politics of Racism*. (Toronto: James Lorimer).

Sunahara, M.A.

1979   'Federal Policy and the Japanese Canadians: The Decision to Evacuate, 1942' in Ujimoto and Hirabayashi, eds, pp. 93-120.

Supreme Court of Canada

1990   *R. v Keegstra* (13 Dec. 1990, S.C.C. file no. 21118)

Surtees, R.J.

1971   *The Original People*. (Toronto: Holt, Rinehart and Winston).

Taieb-Carlen, S.

1992   'Monocultural Education in a Pluralist Environment: Ashkenazi Curricula in Toronto Jewish Educational Institutions', *Canadian Ethnic Studies* XXIV, 3, pp. 75-86.

Taras, D., and M. Weinfeld

1993   'Continuity and Criticism: North American Jews and Israel' in Brym, Shaffir, and Weinfeld, eds, pp. 293-310.

Tarnopolsky, W.S.

1975   *The Canadian Bill of Rights*, 2nd ed. (Toronto: McClelland & Stewart).

1979   'The Control of Racial Discrimination' in Macdonald and Humphrey, eds, pp. 289-307.

1982   'The Equality Rights' in Tarnopolsky and Beaudoin, eds.

————, and G.A. Beaudoin, eds

1982   *The Canadian Charter of Rights and Freedoms: Commentary.* (Toronto: Carswell).

Tepper, Elliot.

1993   'Multiculturalism in Canada: Twenty Years On—And Under?' Paper presented for the Twelfth Biennial Conference of the Canadian Ethnic Studies Association. Vancouver November 27-30.

Thériault, Y.

1971   *Agaguk.* (Montreal: l'Actuelle).

Thompson, W.P.

1984   'Hutterite Community: Its Reflex in Architectural and Settlement Patterns', *Canadian Ethnic Studies* XVI, 3, pp. 53-72.

Troper, Harold

1993   'As Canadian as Multiculturalism: An Historian's Perspective on Multicultural Policy' Plenary Address for the Twelfth Biennial Conference of the Canadian Ethnic Studies Association. Vancouver. 27-30 November.

Ujimoto, K.V., and G. Hirabayashi, eds

1979   *Visible Minorities and Multiculturalism: Asians in Canada.* (Toronto: Butterworths).

United Nations

1978   *International Bill of Human Rights.* New York.

Urban Alliance for Race Relations

1977   'Affirmative Action: What Is It.' *Newsletter . . .* October, p. 4.

Vallières, P.

1971   *White Niggers of America.* (Toronto: McClelland & Stewart).

Van den Berghe, P.I.

1967   *Race and Racism: A Comparative Approach.* (New York: Wiley and Sons).

1978   'Race and Ethnicity: A Sociobiological Perspective', *Ethnic and Racial Studies* 1, 4.

Vanstone, J.W.

1971   'Influence of European Man on the Eskimos' in M. van Steensel, ed., pp. 10-13

Wade, M.

1970   *The French-Canadian Outlook.* (Toronto: McClelland & Stewart).

Wallace, A.F.C.

1956   'Revitalization Movements', *American Anthropologist* 58, April.

Waubageshig

1970   *The Only Good Indian.* (Toronto: New Press).

Weaver, S.M.

1977   'Segregation and the Indian Act: The Dialogue of Equality vs. Special Status' in Isajiw, ed., pp. 154-61.

1981   *Making Canadian Indian Policy: The Hidden Agenda 1968-70.* (Toronto:

University of Toronto Press).

Weinfeld, M.

1981   'The Development of Affirmative Action in Canada', *Canadian Ethnic Studies* XIII, 2, pp. 23-39.

Weizmann, F., N.I. Wiener, D.L. Wiesenthal, and M. Ziegler

1990   *Eggs, Eggplants and Eggheads: A Rejoinder to Rushton.* (North York: York University). Report # 40: The LaMarsh Research Programme Reports. October.

Wilson, J.

1978   'Come, Let Us Reason Together' in D'Oyley, ed.

Winks, R.W.

1971   *The Blacks in Canada: A History.* (Montreal: McGill-Queen's University Press).

Wirth, L.

1951   Quoted by H.M. Hacker in 'Women as a Minority Group' in *Social Forces*, 30: 60-9.

Woodcock, G., and I. Avakumovic

1968   *The Doukhobors.* (Toronto: Oxford University Press).

Woodsworth, J.S.

1972   *Strangers Within Our Gates.* (Toronto: University of Toronto Press).

Wuttanee, W.I.C.

1971   *Ruffled Feathers.* (Calgary: Bell Books).

Yalden, M.F.

1979   'The Office of Commissioner of Official Languages' in Macdonald and Humphrey, eds, pp. 375-82.

Yetman, N.R., and C.H. Steele

1975   *Majority and Minority*, 2nd ed. (Boston: Allyn and Bacon).

Yinger, J.M.

1970   *The Scientific Study of Religion.* (New York: Macmillan).

Yusyk, P.

1964   Senatorial Address. 3 May.

1967   *Ukrainian Canadians: Their Place and Role in Canadian Life.* (Toronto: Ukrainian Canadian Business and Professional Federation).

Ziegler, S., and A.H. Richmond

1972   *Characteristics of Italian Householders in Metropolitan Toronto.* (Toronto: York University, Institute for Behavioural Research).

INDEX